A YANKEE REGIMENT IN
CONFEDERATE LOUISIANA

A YANKEE REGIMENT IN CONFEDERATE LOUISIANA

The 31st Massachusetts Volunteer Infantry
in the Gulf South

LARRY LOWENTHAL

LOUISIANA STATE UNIVERSITY PRESS
Baton Rouge

Published by Louisiana State University Press
Copyright © 2019 by Louisiana State University Press
All rights reserved
Manufactured in the United States of America
FIRST PRINTING

DESIGNER: Mandy McDonald Scallan
TYPEFACE: Whitman
PRINTER AND BINDER: Sheridan Books

Maps 1, 3, and 4 created by Mary Lee Eggart

Library of Congress Cataloging-in-Publication Data
Names: Lowenthal, Larry, author.
Title: A Yankee regiment in Confederate Louisiana : the 31st Massachusetts
    Volunteer Infantry in the Gulf South / Larry Lowenthal.
Description: Baton Rouge : Louisiana State University Press, [2019] |
    Includes bibliographical references and index.
Identifiers: LCCN 2019029915 (print) | LCCN 2019029916 (ebook) | ISBN
    978-0-8071-7190-5 (cloth) | ISBN 978-0-8071-7249-0 (ebook) | ISBN 978-0-8071-7247-6
    (Adobe PDF)
Subjects: LCSH: United States. Army. Massachusetts Infantry Regiment, 31st
    (1861–1865) | United States—History—Civil War, 1861–1865—Regimental
    histories. | Louisiana—History—Civil War, 1861–1865.
Classification: LCC E513.5 31st .L69 2019 (print) | LCC E513.5 31st
    (ebook) | DDC 973.7/444—dc23
LC record available at https://lccn.loc.gov/2019029915
LC ebook record available at https://lccn.loc.gov/2019029916

To Isaac and Eleanor:

thanks for being successful and caring people

CONTENTS

PREFACE / ix

ACKNOWLEDGMENTS / xv

1. BORN IN CONTROVERSY: 1861–February 1862 / 1

2. A PERILOUS JOURNEY: February–April 1862 / 30

3. ON THE MISSISSIPPI: April–May 1862 / 45

4. THE OCCUPATION OF NEW ORLEANS: May–August 1862 / 56

5. A REGIMENT DIVIDED: August–December 1862 / 81

6. A DEVIOUS ROUTE TO PORT HUDSON: January–May 1863 / 108

7. THE ATTACK ON PORT HUDSON: May–July 1863 / 135

8. MOUNTED WARRIORS: July 1863–February 1864 / 153

9. THE RED RIVER CAMPAIGN: February–June 1864 / 182

10. THE RED RIVER BLAME GAME: December 1864–March 1865 / 218

11. GUERILLA WARFARE: June 1864–February 1865 / 234

12. MOBILE AND HOME: March–October 1865 / 261

NOTES / 285

BIBLIOGRAPHY / 323

INDEX / 329

PREFACE

In an ideal world, an historian would locate a topic that intrigued him and pursue it to completion—the effortless publication of a book—unless some unforeseen development derailed him. In the world we actually inhabit, a project often arrives unexpectedly, like a surprise package at the front door, that is so compelling and deserving that it becomes impossible to refuse. It is the latter route that led to the writing of this history of the 31st Massachusetts Volunteer Infantry Regiment in the American Civil War.

In late 2013 a random inquiry from a military researcher in Louisiana arrived at the Museum of Springfield History (officially the Lyman & Merrie Wood Museum of Springfield History). That person, in the course of pursuing possible leads, asked if the museum had any information about the 31st Massachusetts. The archivist, Cliff McCarthy, soon discovered that the collection contained several boxes of material on that regiment that had been donated to a predecessor museum many decades before and had never been fully processed. Even a cursory glance showed that the collection had extraordinary research value. The boxes could no longer be ignored, especially while the nation was commemorating the 150th anniversary of the Civil War (and finding that many of the same controversies of that period persisted). Cliff applied for a grant to scan a selection of the material and place it on a website sponsored by the museum. The Massachusetts Sesquicentennial Commission of the American Civil War must have been impressed by the collection and approved the grant. Knowing of my interest in the Civil War, Cliff asked me to write a summary to make the information more intelligible to site visitors. This began my association with the 31st Massachusetts.

At that point I had no prior direct acquaintance with the unit. Since I knew that Massachusetts Civil War regiments were numbered as high as sixty, I assumed that there must be a thirty-first in its proper place; but I never gave it any particular thought. I was aware of the illustrious record of regiments such as the 10th Infantry and the 27th Infantry, recruited largely in western Massachusetts, where I lived; and I had written an article about the 27th. During my career I also edited a diary kept by a soldier in the 22nd Massachusetts and reviewed a book about the 57th Regiment; also, my wife and I edited a collection of correspondence between an officer in the 46th Massachusetts and his wife. No matter how many times I had visited the Boston Public Library, I was always awed by the marble lions honoring the 2nd and 12th Regiments. So, although I had many points of contact with Massachusetts regiments over the years, the 31st never rose to the surface. And added to that, I was only dimly aware that Massachusetts regiments had served in the Gulf region. Like the men who went off to Louisiana under General Butler in February 1862, I now embarked on a new adventure, though one much less dangerous.

The story of how collections of Civil War documents were assembled and preserved often approaches (but should never equal) the level of interest contained in the documents themselves. That is certainly true of the 31st Massachusetts collection, which embodies a story both extraordinary and nearly tragic. Countless books and movies have established that the average Civil War soldier was young and impressionable. Many came from isolated places with limited opportunity for human interaction. Virtually everything they encountered in military life, even its monumental boredom, had no parallel in their previous existence. For three or four years, these young men developed experiential and emotional bonds that were more intense than anything they had known in civilian life, with the possible exception of their relationship to their mothers and perhaps other members of their immediate family. In the background loomed always the specter of death, whether in combat or from insidious disease. Yet at the same time, they hoped to prove their courage in battle when that moment came. No matter how hard they tried, it was difficult to convey to outsiders feelings and references that were innate and unspoken among fellow soldiers.

For those soldiers who survived the war in reasonably good condition, as much as they were happy to be home again, it was difficult to suddenly break off relationships forged under conditions of great stress. After the war there arose an irresistible impulse to gather in veterans' organizations, either at the regimental level or as part of national organizations such as the Grand Army of the Republic. Beyond promoting sociability, which always took precedence, these organizations had several functions. They exercised political influence to ensure that veterans were treated well in terms of pensions and other benefits, erected memorials to their service, and sought to immortalize the record of their accomplishments and sacrifices by publishing regimental histories.

Somewhat surprisingly, the 31st Massachusetts apparently waited until 1871 to launch a veterans' association. (The year is uncertain because the man who held the early regimental records refused to return them; they are now lost.) Beginning in 1888, there is an unbroken run of records that extends to the disbanding of the group more than forty years later. By 1888 L. Frederick Rice, who attained the rank of major during the war, had established himself as the regimental historian and put forth an annual plea for members to give him historical material. Especially around the twenty-fifth anniversary of the war's end, Rice encouraged members to record their reminiscences and present them to him. He continued to gather material and conduct interviews as late as 1905, but if he began a draft of a regimental history, it has not been found. Rice died on April 14, 1909, and no one assumed his role as historian. Regardless, the task would have become increasingly futile, as the melancholy attrition that had begun among the soldiers during the war now rapidly advanced among the veterans. The records indicate that by 1916 only 190 "comrades" were still living.[1]

At every annual gathering for many years, Rice gave a report on the history and explained why the project had not been completed. (Unfortunately, the minutes record only that he gave a report and do not elaborate on the contents.) It is unlikely that money was the reason, as these publications were almost guaranteed to at least recover their costs because of the captive market of members, families, and local institutions. Moreover, in 1893 Rice reported that he had obtained state legislation to purchase five hundred copies at two dollars each.[2] Rice ran a business in Boston, and as time passed he may have found the task of compiling a regimental history in his spare time to be overwhelming. In addition to the information he collected, each year brought forth new histories and autobiographies for him to absorb, soon joined by the federal government and its colossal effort of publishing the official records of the war. There is no indication in the association records that Rice had help in his historical efforts. Because he lived in Brookline and worked in Boston, it might have been difficult for anyone to collaborate with him, as most of the members who remained in Massachusetts lived farther west in the state.

While the overload aspect should not be dismissed, I suspect that another factor was responsible for blocking Rice's progress on the book. The information he collected only reinforced what he knew from harsh personal experience about controversies that had surrounded the regiment. These conflicts were intensely personal and were fresh in the minds of the protagonists, most of whom were still alive in the 1880s. Perhaps to his dismay, Rice found that many of the letters and diaries submitted to him included disparaging comments about various officers, observations reflected in his own writings. It would be inappropriate for him to take sides, yet it would be irresponsible to ignore the controversies and produce a bland account of the regiment's movements. Rice simply may not have been able to find a way out of this dilemma.

The optimum period for producing conventional regimental histories was the 1880s and 1890s. By the time Rice died in 1909, that window had closed. The remaining veterans were too old, and their numbers were diminishing steadily. By 1929 only two or three members were showing up at the annual reunions, and in that year the association donated its historical collection to the Connecticut Valley Historical Society. That organization and its successors preserved the documents in the hope that there would someday be sufficient staff to process them, but that glorious day never arrived.

Few of the documents Rice accumulated are truly originals. It seems that most of the actual diaries and letters were loaned to him to be transcribed by typists in his office. If there were typing errors, it is now impossible to compare with an original. It appears, however, that there are very few instances in which a possible typo makes the meaning unclear. With the generous support of his comrades, Rice succeeded in amassing an exceptional collection of documents from one regiment. Several items could probably be published as standalone annotated books. Thousands of collections of Civil War manuscripts have been published over the decades, but usually they are presented individually, with little reference to other writings from the same regiment or a larger unit.

As I became acquainted with the 31st Massachusetts collection, I realized that I had stumbled into an extraordinary opportunity to revive a genre out of its time by producing a modern Civil War regimental history, taking advantage of the more balanced perspective we hope has been achieved in the 150 years since the war ended. That distance would remove the danger of personal offense that might have impeded Rice, for the political controversies of yester-year would no longer be fresh in anyone's mind. In addition, I could benefit from the immense body of scholarly work on the war that has appeared in the last hundred years.

Once the 31st Massachusetts website became available, several individuals brought to our attention additional source materials of which Rice had no knowledge; further research discovered still more. This resulted in an aston-ishingly rich, perhaps unrivaled, body of original material on a single regi-ment. Yet all of this material, despite its immense value, still fell short of being a book itself. To round out the story, it was necessary to consult other pri-mary sources, notably the massive *Official Records,* as well as various secondary works. In reality, references to the 31st Massachusetts in secondary sources re-main scanty, and any history of the regiment that relied on published sources, if feasible at all, would be flat and uninteresting. It is the unpublished mate-rial, which we are fortunate to possess in abundance, that gives the story of the 31st Massachusetts its vividness and vitality—in short, its humanity.[3]

Whether penned in the moment or copied retrospectively at Rice's request, the documents express the individuality of the writers. It is important to de-scribe campaigns and battles, as did the traditional regimental histories, but it is the men's depictions of army life and their impressions of Louisiana that are now of greatest interest. It reminds us that the Civil War, for all the political abstractions that were employed, was in the end a human story. In writing this book I felt grateful that I had been given an unexpected opportunity to preserve the memory of the men who fought in the 31st Massachusetts and to honor their service and their sacrifice under perpetually trying conditions.

ACKNOWLEDGMENTS

I am grateful for the assistance of archivist Cliff McCarthy of the Wood Museum of Springfield History, who was generous with his help throughout this project. My thanks also extend to Stan Prager for technical assistance; Carolyn Jones, Margaret "Mimi" Dakin of Amherst College Archives and Special Collections; Elizabeth Dunn of the David M. Rubenstein Rare Book and Manuscript Library at Duke University; Madeline Snipes for valuable research assistance; and staff members of the American Antiquarian Society. The excellent modern maps were prepared by Mary Lee Eggart. It was not feasible for my wife, Koren, to assist as much as she would have wished in the production of this book, but, like the support services of Civil War armies, she helped keep me going.

A YANKEE REGIMENT IN
CONFEDERATE LOUISIANA

1

BORN IN CONTROVERSY

1861–FEBRUARY 1862

In the fall of 1861, Benjamin Franklin Butler, having not yet acquired his unforgettable and indelible nickname "The Beast," was busy recruiting New England men to serve in the Union army. This was the gestation period of the 31st Regiment of Massachusetts Volunteer Infantry, a time of troubles and portents that shaped the unit throughout its service. True, numerical inevitability dictated that there would be a thirty-first regiment, if only to fill the space between thirty and thirty-two, but the character the 31st displayed during its existence was largely determined by Butler. He was its sire, and although his direct involvement with it lasted not much more than a year, its history cannot be understood without examining this remarkable man.

We often find that the controversies that surround a person during his lifetime are carried forward by historians—one hopes in a more thoughtful form. Butler attracted controversy as a warm body draws mosquitoes, so it is not surprising that scholarly disputes about his career continue to rage. In an age of outsized, wildly individualistic personalities for whom pride was by no means a sin, Butler still stands out. He was born in the rustic New Hampshire village of Deerfield on November 5, 1818, of distant Irish ancestry, presumably a descendant of the powerful Norman-Irish Butler family.[1] His father, John, was obviously a hero worshipper. When his first son, Andrew Jackson Butler, was born in 1815, the child's namesake was famous primarily for his victory at the Battle of New Orleans in that year; his terms as a president who profoundly remade the American political system could hardly be predicted. But it was John's next son who, like Jackson, turned out to be both a democrat in his public philosophy and a partisan Democrat in his political career, craving too the military glory Jackson had obtained.

Like his own distinguished namesake, Benjamin Franklin Butler had to climb a steep uphill path in order to advance in life. His deficiencies in wealth and family background were not compensated by a commanding physical presence, eventually standing only five feet, four inches tall (though his shortness was mostly in the legs). In addition, he had unusual red hair, a squeaky voice, and a lazy eye, which made it difficult to tell where he was looking or what he was seeing. His father had served courageously in the War of 1812, which is why he considered General Jackson a model, but he perished under obscure circumstances as captain of a privateer in the West Indies when Ben was only a few months old. Probably with some assistance from relatives, Ben's mother supported the family. Her struggle undoubtedly gave her son a lasting appreciation of the difficulties confronting women in nineteenth-century society.

Pitted against massive disadvantages, Ben Butler arrayed a powerful intellect driven by irrepressible ambition. Whether or not his mother's intention, when she moved the family to Lowell, Massachusetts, to operate a boarding house, it opened up limitless opportunities for her younger son. Lowell, on the Merrimack River, had been created as a planned city only a few years before by some of the wealthiest men in Massachusetts, who proposed to manufacture cloth using advanced concepts of technology, management, and capitalization. Sending Ben off to school, his mother hoped that he would become a minister, but it soon became apparent that he was unsuited by intellect and temperament for that profession. His dearest goal was to enter the U.S. Military Academy at West Point, New York, but his family lacked the necessary influence, so he was not nominated, a rejection that left enduring resentment.[2] Upon observing lawyers at work, however, he instantly recognized the calling that would make the fullest use of his wide-ranging abilities.

After passing his bar exam in 1840, Butler rapidly built up one of the most successful practices in Massachusetts, specializing in the combative field of criminal law. This newfound prosperity enabled him to court and, after some delays and setbacks, to marry Sarah Hildreth. Based on their extensive correspondence, the two were a devoted, caring couple. Sarah was a well-traveled actress, intelligent, and self-confident; she did not hesitate to express her opinions. It was an intensely emotional relationship, and their complaints about missing each other when they were apart seem to reach beyond conventional courtesy. The marriage sustained Ben through his incessant struggles, and, although he was accused of many failings, infidelity was never one of them.

It was expected that a lawyer as conspicuous as Butler would enter politics. In his political orientation, true to his working-class, Jacksonian origins, he gravitated naturally to the Democrats, although the party was generally a minority in his home state. He appears as a delegate to the Democratic national convention in 1844, the year of his marriage. It was probably the last fluid period in the American party structure, after which the deepening sectional discord created an overwrought atmosphere, inflamed by fiery stump speeches. It was not a setting that was designed to restrain Butler's passionate nature.

At the same time, Butler was actively pursuing his military ambitions, which his failure to enter West Point had only strengthened. Once the Civil War began, he was classified as a "political" general, indeed, almost a prototype of that disdained species. But this is a misreading of his history. While still studying for the bar exam, Butler had already marched the first steps on a military career, enlisting in a militia company formed in Lowell in 1839. He joined as a private, hoping to learn the profession from the ground up. In the years that followed, Butler worked his way up the ranks, "never attempting to pass a grade without filling a position in due order of promotion," until finally elected colonel of his regiment.[3]

Butler's unfailing common touch earned him the loyalty of the men he commanded. On one memorable occasion this brought him into sharp conflict with a newly elected governor. A member of the anti-immigrant Know-Nothing Party that briefly dominated Massachusetts politics, the governor ordered him to disband a company made up of Irish Catholic Democrats; Butler refused. The governor seemingly won this confrontation by reorganizing the entire state militia to deprive him of command, but Butler, in a characteristically adroit flanking maneuver, positioned himself to be elected by the officers to fill a vacant brigadier-general position.[4] As a result of skill and persistence over twenty years, Butler was one of the highest-ranking officers in the Massachusetts militia when the crisis of 1860 exploded. His probing intellect had probably led him to read at least as much military theory as officers in the regular army, and he was thoroughly familiar with military organization. Because the U.S. Army was small and scattered, most of its officers had not had the opportunity to command large bodies of men in maneuver. As Butler later wrote, by encamping with his brigade in the years 1857 through 1860, he "had commanded a larger body of troops, duly uniformed and equipped, than any general of the United States army then living except General [Winfield] Scott."[5]

Yet since the state militias were voluntary, largely social organizations, their drills and training were often farcical. The important advantage that regular officers had over men like Butler, and which they never tired of flaunting, was that most had experienced combat during the Mexican War (1846–48), even if only at the company or regimental level.

As the country spun down the vortex of disintegration in 1860, Butler was swept along. Outside of the formal but increasingly shaky structure of the federal government, the Democratic Party was nearly the last institution holding the country together. Even religious denominations had divided. Butler went to the national convention in Charleston, South Carolina, in April as a delegate pledged to support Sen. Stephen A. Douglas of Illinois for the presidency. As it became apparent that Douglas could not prevail, Butler switched his vote to former Secretary of War Jefferson Davis of Mississippi on the grounds that the Southerner was a moderate who could hold the sections together. As the voting dragged on without resolution, Butler cast fifty-seven futile ballots for the Mississippian.[6] Afterward, in the general election that followed, he ran for Massachusetts governor as a Democrat on a ticket backing Kentucky aristocrat John C. Breckinridge, the sitting vice president. Having antagonized most segments of his party, Butler received less than 4 percent of the vote. In normal times such a humiliating repudiation might have spelled the end of any political aspirations, but by then his attention was focused elsewhere. According to one of his modern biographers, Butler foresaw that the Republican candidate, Abraham Lincoln, would win against divided opposition, after which some Southern states would try to secede from the Union. This would inevitably create the opportunity for the military glory he craved.[7]

Early in 1861, as the country faced its greatest crisis, Butler stood on the threshold of fame. Previously little known outside his home state, he was about to become a national figure, which meant that the controversy that always seemed to surround him would expand greatly in scope. Butler was one of those people who are best defined by examining the enemies he accumulated—in his case a diverse aggregation. What accounted for this assembly of animosity? Among his law colleagues there was the usual resentment of success, but beyond that many felt that Butler used sharp and unscrupulous tactics to win release for defendants who seemed obviously guilty. Moreover, he often did nothing to preserve the dignity of those he had outwitted. Having achieved financial success, he purchased a mill in Lowell, but his continued public expressions of support for the workers offended his wealthy fellows. Nativists, still numerous despite the fading of the Know-Nothings, objected to his ties to Irish Catholics. His opportunistic shifts at the 1860 convention had alienated most of the state's Democrats, while the rising Republicans had no use for him. Once the war began, Butler created a whole new legion of enemies among regular-army officers, who despised him for pretending to know the secrets of their esoteric profession and for his scorn for the forms and regulations that governed their existence. In battle, where the first response of someone like Ulysses Grant or Braxton Bragg was usually a frontal assault, Butler was always looking for a clever flanking approach, much as he had done in his law practice. He also displayed his emotions like a badge, was often immoderate in his opinions, did not try to conceal his intelligence, and wore out associates with his abundant energy. Everything about Butler made it difficult for others to view him dispassionately. At the start of 1861, probably no one imagined that Massachusetts would ever have need for volunteer regiments numbered as high as thirty-one. But when that eventuality came to pass, those volunteers, often unsuspecting, picked up the long baggage train that Benjamin Butler had accumulated in his lifetime.

Butler's experience at the national conventions had probably given him a clearer sense of where the country was heading than his more provincial colleagues. The Massachusetts militia had a reputation of being better prepared than its counterparts in other Northern states, but they were essentially parade-ground soldiers, by no means ready for battle. Butler understood the urgency of weeding out those who were physically or politically unfit for service and equipping the remainder for serious duty. In the first days of 1861, he called on newly elected Republican governor John Albion Andrew to advocate his case. The tortured relationship of these two men colored the wartime history of Massachusetts and left an indelible imprint on the 31st Massachusetts.

Superficially, Andrew and Butler had much in common. They were the same age and had both been admitted to the bar in 1840. Both came from the periphery: Butler from rural New Hampshire and Andrew from a small town in Maine (still part of Massachusetts when he was born). With the exception of John Butler's military reputation, neither family was distinguished or prosperous. As members of the relatively small legal fraternity, the two men were acquainted, but, with their oversize egos and opposing political viewpoints, the outlook for harmony was unpromising. Andrew was not only a Republican but also a "radical," the most dedicated abolitionist of any of the war-time Northern governors. Andrew accepted the need to prepare the militia for sterner duties; he was less sure about how much of this effort to entrust to his former gubernatorial rival. Meanwhile, Butler secured a contract for his mill to manufacture overcoats for the soldiers. He maintained that troops on active duty would require sturdier uniforms than those used for militia drills, but his critics saw this as exploiting the crisis for his own financial gain.[8] Probably both statements were correct, but it furnished another example of the discord that swirled around Butler's every move and aroused strong reactions whenever his name was mentioned.

The foresight displayed by Andrew and Butler and their temporary willingness to patch over innate feelings of distrust paid dividends in a grave hour. After joyous Confederate forces, in one of the most unwise decisions ever recorded, fired on Fort Sumter in Charleston harbor, the Lincoln administration called for troops to defend Washington, D.C., surrounded as it was by slave states. Secretary of War Simon Cameron contacted Governor Andrew for troops, knowing that the Massachusetts militia had a reputation for being in an advanced state of readiness and that the railroad system could bring them to the capital fairly promptly. Andrew called first on the 6th Massachusetts Regiment, which Butler had purged of unreliable elements. Meanwhile, Butler had pulled strings in Washington to persuade the administration that a brigadier general was needed to command the soldiers coming to defend the city; he also obtained a personal financial commitment from a friendly bank to cover the immediate expenses of the expedition. Despite looming misgivings, Andrew apparently concluded that he had no choice but to name Butler to the general's post.[9] He thereby risked placing his political rival in a position to proclaim himself the savior of the Union, setting in motion an enduring animosity that soured Massachusetts and national politics and hindered the war effort.

On the way to Washington, the 6th Massachusetts had to pass through the streets of Baltimore between railroad stations. There it was attacked by a secessionist mob, with men on both sides killed in the resulting battle. This was the first bloodshed of the Civil War, though actual soldiers were engaged on only one side. At this time Butler was moving toward the capital at the head of the 8th Massachusetts. Unsure whether rail links around Baltimore were intact and unwilling to risk another bloody passage through the city, he cunningly diverted his forces to Annapolis. There he suppressed Maryland's inclination to secede, protected the U.S. Naval Academy, rescued the revered ship USS *Constitution*, and, more importantly, secured a rail line to Washington. In May, with Washington reasonably safe, Butler secured the rail line to Baltimore and then, in a surprise maneuver, occupied the city in a bloodless stroke. In less than two months, he had achieved brilliant successes of the sort that appealed to journalists, especially in those innocent days when they still believed that the war would be won by individual deeds of valor and could not imagine what a grinding, debilitating struggle it would become. Unfortunately, in the process Butler antagonized two men who could derail his march to destiny. In promising to help the governor of Maryland suppress any slave uprising that might occur, he angered his own state's governor, an abolitionist, or at least gave him justification for the hostility he had always felt. Butler might have thought his slick capture of Baltimore would win praise, but instead it brought criticism from the ancient, imperious army commander Winfield Scott (1786–1866). What irritated the venerable warrior was probably that Butler had accomplished by cleverness what Scott had planned to achieve by means of a multipronged land-and-naval assault, as prescribed in the textbooks.

Perplexed by the tempestuous but now-idolized Butler, the Lincoln administration responded by promoting him to major general. Scott remained unimpressed. After reprimanding Butler for his conduct in seizing Baltimore, he sent him off to take command of Fortress Monroe, a strategic post at the lower end of Chesapeake Bay; Butler, on request, had already dispatched two of the Massachusetts volunteer regiments to that place. Earlier in his career, Scott had reorganized the army, creating a small but professional force officered almost entirely by West Point graduates, who were generally acquainted with one another in what resembled a large but contentious family. The thought of amateurs being elevated to ranks to which few regular officers could aspire in the peacetime army must have caused severe dyspepsia in the old warrior. True, the volunteer generals were not yet commanding regular troops, but, with the vast disruption taking place, anything was possible. Scott may have thus drawn perverse satisfaction from a military fiasco in Butler's department in June, when the upstart general sent a force inland against Confederate defenses at Big Bethel. The attack was botched in almost every respect by the inexperienced soldiers, tarnishing Butler's reputation even though he was not personally in command (for which he was also criticized). In those days the small action seemed like a major engagement, and Southern newspapers played it into a great victory.

One of Butler's rather offhanded decisions at Fortress Monroe was to have far-reaching implications. Apparently to the surprise of both sides, once Yankee soldiers appeared on the scene, slaves in the vicinity fled into their lines and asked for protection. This was a profound shock to Southerners, who in justifying slavery had persuaded themselves that the slaves were content with their lot. (They seemed to overlook the inconsistency in holding to that view while demanding enforcement of the Fugitive Slave Law of 1850.) It was the first of many upheavals in the complacent worldview that plantation owners had cultivated. The Lincoln administration, seemingly caught by surprise as well, offered no guidance. Desperate to avoid antagonizing the four border slave states that had not seceded, and perhaps hoping that some seceding states might yet reconsider, the administration had no interest at that time in promoting abolition. The sensitive situation was left to commanders on the scene to resolve, and Butler came up with an ingenious solution. In his political career he had never been outspoken on the subject of slavery—remarkable in view of his temperament and the passion with which the issue was debated. He seemed more interested in preserving the unity of the Democratic Party than in dealing with slavery. Nevertheless, he argued that, if Virginia and the other Confederate states had by seceding declared themselves independent, the Fugitive Slave Law no longer applied and thus did not oblige him to return any who escaped to his lines. Instead, using the mental processes that had prevailed in many courtrooms, he coined the term "contraband of war" to describe the self-liberated slaves.[10] This was a brilliant stroke, as it turned Southern arguments on their head: if slaves were merely property, there was no more reason to return them to their owners than there was for crops, livestock, munitions, buildings, or any other form of property with military value.

Butler's improvised policy had consequences far beyond anything he anticipated in the small-scale combat of that period. In the early years of the war, the Confederacy was able to mobilize a higher proportion of its white males because slaves were left behind to continue agricultural work. As Northern forces gained footholds in various parts of the South and slaves flocked into their lines, it chipped away at one of the few material advantages the Confederacy enjoyed. Of course, the situation was a mixed blessing for commanders like Butler. There was not enough room inside Fortress Monroe to house the men under his command, much less the thousands of contrabands who came into the Union lines. Male former slaves could work on fortifications and other construction, while women could serve as laundresses and similar tasks, but that left large numbers of children and old people who had little value as workers but had to be cared for. This developed into a major headache for the administration and its field commanders. Butler himself, while basking in his creative solution to the problem, called the influx of escaped slaves a "disaster."[11]

The first major clash of the war, at Manassas, or Bull Run, Virginia, on a steamy July 21, 1861, provided a foretaste of what lay ahead. It reinforced the unrealistic expectations of the South and panicked the North. With Washington seemingly threatened, General Scott had an excuse to take away most of the regiments Butler commanded, then compounded the insult by pulling a happily retired regular general back into service to take charge of the department. This left Butler as a highly visible major general with almost no troops to command, hardly a satisfactory position for a man with his limitless ambition. After trying to make the best of the situation at Fort Monroe and capturing a Confederate fort in North Carolina, he again exerted his potent political influence in Washington.

As Butler understood completely, he wielded enormous leverage on the Lincoln administration merely by existing. The president, aware that a purely partisan war would have little chance of ultimate success, desperately needed to retain the support of Northern Democrats who, however indifferent to slavery, were willing to fight for the Union. Butler was a prime specimen of this genus, but officials nevertheless dithered for several months before figuring out how to use his services. There was no hope of giving him an active command as long as Scott remained commanding officer, and the administration was not sure enough of itself to push the aged, corpulent general into well-deserved retirement. Moreover, despite his numerous infirmities, Scott still had probably the clearest strategic mind in the army.

In the end, accepting his proposition that he would have "four-fifths of every regiment good, true Democrats, who believe in sustaining the country and in loyalty to the flag of the Union, and who will fight for the country under command of officers I shall choose," Lincoln in early August authorized Butler to recruit up to six regiments for the Union army.[12] This would give the general scope for his abundant energy, though it would not satisfy his craving for military glory. For the administration, it represented an awkward compromise between the conflicting impulses to hold Butler's goodwill while keeping him away from a field command, despite the initiative and imagination he had displayed. No one could guess at that time what a rare commodity initiative would prove to be among Northern generals, while imagination was always suspect to the military establishment. By this action, Washington officials planted the seeds of what became the 31st Massachusetts. What they did not realize was that these seeds were sown on cold ground. Although five of the six New England governors were responsive and helpful to the general's efforts, Governor Andrew opposed Butler with every tactic he could employ.

Butler's pressure had won a commitment from Lincoln that would authorize him to recruit in New England, but until this was put in writing and the respective governors notified, he could do little. For approximately a month he fretted at Fortress Monroe, pleading with his contacts in Washington to expedite his case. It is easy to suspect that the delay reflected the conflicting attitudes within the administration. Finally, on September 10, 1861, the critical documentation appeared:

> Major General B. F. Butler is hereby authorized to raise, organize, arm, uniform, and equip a volunteer force for the War in the New England States, not exceeding six (6) Regiments of the Maximum Standard, of such arms and in such proportions, and in such manner as he may judge expedient; and for this purpose his order and requisitions on the Quartermaster, Ordnance and other staff Departments of the Army are to be obeyed and answered, provided the cost of such recruitment, armament, and equipment does not exceed in the aggregate that of like troops now, or hereafter raised for the service of the United States.[13]

At the same time, Lincoln sent a message to the New England governors "respectfully" requesting them to aid Butler.[14] This was all he could realistically do, as he knew better than to thrust the federal government into recruiting for the state volunteer regiments. This placed Butler into the unpleasant situation of having to depend on the goodwill of the various state leaders. He certainly understood this and felt qualms about accepting the commission, but it seemed that he had little choice: the administration had made it clear that it was not offering him an active command, whereas if he recruited troops he would be able to command them in the field.[15]

Lincoln and Butler were undoubtedly correct in assuming that there were several thousand men in New England who would respond to the general's call but might be reluctant to serve under an abolitionist Republican. The problem lay in getting these men on the rolls and organized. Butler decided not to recruit in Rhode Island, where he would be competing with a well-regarded favorite son, Brig. Gen. Ambrose Burnside. Four of the other New England governors proved helpful. New Hampshire was tardy, but that was mainly because it wanted to complete its own quota, not due to any fundamental opposition to him. As for Andrew, he initially seemed accommodating. In a telegram to Lincoln, the governor promised "to help General Butler to the utmost," though he added a phrase that proved to be ominous: that he had to fulfill other obligations first.[16] From there things went rapidly downhill.

On October 1 the War Department carved the temporary Department of New England out of the existing Department of the East. This was done not because there was any danger of secession or Confederate invasion, but to give Butler a command "while engaged in recruiting his division."[17] Yet two weeks earlier the War Department had issued an order stating that "all persons having received authority from the war Department to raise volunteer regiments, batteries, or companies in the loyal states, are . . . placed under the orders of the Governors of those States."[18] Seizing on this, the Andrew administration issued General Order 23, stating that no recruiting "is authorized or can be encouraged" except to fill the two Massachusetts regiments then being formed, the 28th and 29th.[19] To compound the clear contradiction, Cameron had assured Andrew that "it was the intention of this Department to leave to your excellency all questions concerning the organization of the troops in your State, and the Orders to which you refer were designed to be subject to the approval and control of the Executive of Massachusetts."[20] Only a few days later, however, Cameron ordered his (Federal) paymasters to pay the men being recruited by Butler from the date they were mustered.[21]

In trying to appease all parties, the administration had created a conflict that could be resolved only by a copious application of goodwill—but that commodity was the first of the wartime shortages in Massachusetts. Insofar as there were genuine issues beyond rampant personal animosity, they involved what to do about partially formed volunteer regiments, whether they would apply toward the state quota, and, in particular, who had the right to name and commission officers for the regiments Butler assembled. Andrew's hostility was inflamed by two subordinates, Adj. Gen. William Schouler and Military Secretary A. G. Browne. Schouler, a former newspaper editor, had clashed with Butler early in his career and nurtured intense animosity.[22] It is impossible to sort out the individual contributions of each, but together they generated overpowering rancor toward Butler.

Andrew, relying on the order that put an end to individual recruiting and ignoring the orders that authorized Butler to recruit, contended that the general, "in disobedience to my orders," had proceeded to recruit an "irregular force," which retarded the completion of regiments he had promised Burnside and T. W. Sherman.[23] Andrew offered him the 26th Regiment, which was essentially complete; the 28th, which was still being filled; and possibly another regiment. If Butler was proposing to raise six regiments in New England, this was a fair share, if not more, for Massachusetts, even taking into account that it was the most populous of the six states. Yet Butler was not interested in simply commanding troops but wanted to recruit men who wished to serve under him, which he believed he had the right to do. Andrew's self-righteous rigidity, facing Butler's emotional, confrontational style, made negotiation nearly impossible.

Occasionally, the protagonists seemed to want to escape the current that was sweeping them toward a smash up. Fairly early in the controversy Andrew wrote, "I cannot conclude this note without an expression of keen regret that my plain and clearly-defined official duty has brought me into any collision with a gentleman whom in other spheres I have known so long, whose capacity and zeal for the public service is unquestioned by me, and between whom & myself there ought to be nothing inconsistent with cordial, patriotic and kindly cooperation in the support and defence of a cause grand as the proportions of the heritage of our fathers & blessed as their own immortality of fame."[24] In an odd but perceptive note to Andrew on December 29, Butler, perhaps mellow at the turn of the year, wrote to his adversary, "May I call your attention to the facts that the rules in regard to set-off used in the profession which we both practice, and which perhaps it had been better for both and the Country if we had never left, do not apply to the courtesies of life."[25]

Despite these flickers of apparent remorse, the conflict plunged ahead on its seemingly relentless course of intensification. Andrew appeared averse to meeting Butler face to face, and their frequent exchanges of messages did nothing to resolve the dispute. At a heated meeting with Schouler, Butler compared Andrew's emphasis on states' rights to that of the secessionist governor of Kentucky.[26] This was Butler's genuine feeling on the matter, as he wrote to a friend that Jeff Davis "seems to have a singular coincidence of opinion with some Massachusetts Governors upon the Doctrine of State Rights."[27] Andrew showed signs of becoming obsessed with the controversy, as a Butler ally in Washington informed him that the governor had sent Sen. Charles Sumner a package of sixty to eighty "copies of all his petulant and vindictive complaints and charges against you," with the request that the senator would read them to Lincoln.[28] Sumner, though no admirer of Butler, was a man of principle and refused to serve as an errand boy on such a demeaning assignment, so it is unclear whether this packet of vituperation was ever presented to the president. It is deplorable to think that, amid a terrible war, with men being asked to shed blood for a cause, the governor of an important state found no better use of his time than to assemble such a tawdry parcel.

Andrew also sent the packet to the other Bay State senator, Henry Wilson. In his cover letters for these packages, the governor seemed to be consumed by rage: "I am compelled to declare, with great reluctance and regret, that the whole course of proceeding under Major-General Butler in this Commonwealth seems to have been designed and adapted simply to afford means to persons of bad character to make money unscrupulously, and to encourage men whose unfitness had excluded them from any appointment by me to the volunteer military service."[29] One wonders what the men who had signed up with Butler, particularly those who had done the recruiting and become officers, many of whom belonged to leading families in their towns, would have thought had they known of Andrew's disparaging opinion.[30]

Nevertheless, recruiting went forward. While arguments continued over which Massachusetts regiments would be assigned to Butler, he was actively recruiting two entirely new units. He referred to these as the Eastern and Western Bay State Regiments and set up camps to accommodate them in Lowell (Camp Chase) and in Pittsfield (Camp Seward). Butler's sensitive political antennae had discerned the wisdom of naming the camps after two influential cabinet officials, Treasury Secretary Salmon Chase and Secretary of State William Seward.

Butler's home base was Lowell, and he traveled frequently around New England and to Washington. So, especially in western Massachusetts, he did not personally do the recruiting, entrusting it instead to associates in whom he had confidence. Probably the most important of these was Charles M. Whelden of Pittsfield.[31] Born in Boston in 1821, the son of Quakers, Whelden developed an early interest in becoming a druggist and at the age of thirty purchased a drugstore in Pittsfield, beginning his association with the Berkshire city. Whelden must have had a strong element of independence in his makeup, as he turned away not only from his family's metal-fabricating business but also from its Quaker pacifism. Like Butler, if to a lesser degree, he was fascinated by things military. When only twenty he joined the Washington Light Guard in Boston and in 1850 became a member of the Ancient and Honorable Artillery, a famed social, as much as military, organization. While the Wheldens were not among Boston's elite, Charles's acceptance in the artillery shows that they were respectable. Taking his avocation with him, Whelden later joined the Pittsfield Guard and by 1860 had risen to the rank of captain. He volunteered as a staff officer in the 8th Massachusetts when it was dispatched to Washington and in this way, if not earlier, came to Butler's attention.

The general was impressed by Whelden and, when recruiting for the Western Bay State Regiment began, named him lieutenant colonel, with the rank to become permanent when the regiment was mustered into Federal service. His importance in the process may explain why Camp Seward was located in the westernmost county of the state. Although Whelden was in overall charge, recruiting was still conducted on a town-by-town or even a man-by-man basis. Much depended on finding respected, articulate men to take the lead locally. An ambitious man might try to fill up a company of one hundred in the hope that he would be named captain. Recruiting often took place at a fair or rally to drum up enthusiasm.

The Hampshire County town of Ware presents a typical example. It was one of many southern New England towns that retained its same boundaries but shifted its center to waterpower sites and developed into a mill town. "War fever" had flared at a high level since the attack on Fort Sumter, culminating at an agricultural fair on October 10. Some of the leaders of the recruiting drive announced a "war meeting" for that evening. By then, Butler's authorization to recruit in New England was known, and it was assumed that the new unit would become part of his command. After several stirring speeches, an enlistment roll was placed out, and within two or three days, eager volunteers had filled the company roster. This became Company D of the 31st Massachusetts. The officers chosen were the leaders of the recruitment drive, with lawyer W. S. B. Hopkins elected captain.[32]

William Swinton Bennett Hopkins unintentionally straddled the widening chasm between North and South. His father, Erastus, a member of a distinguished Northampton, Massachusetts, family, had been educated as a minister. He fell in love with a young woman linked to some of the leading families in Charleston, South Carolina, who was vacationing in the Connecticut Valley, a common destination among upper-class Southerners. After they married, Reverend Hopkins took up his first parish in a small town in South Carolina. It would be interesting to know how that played out, since he already professed strong abolitionist ideas, but he was not happy there and seized an opportunity to lead a congregation in Troy, New York.[33] W. S. B., named for his mother's father, was born in 1836 while they were still living in South Carolina; out of the abundant name choices, his family generally called him Swint. His mother died, probably due to childbirth, when he was two years old. His father remarried about three years later and fathered seven children with his second wife, of which only two daughters survived to adulthood. Swint and his half-sisters all referred to the second wife as "Mother."

When Reverend Hopkins settled in Northampton, he gave up the ministry and turned his talents to business and politics. He became president of the Connecticut River Railroad, a successful line that extended from Springfield through Northampton to a junction near the Vermont border. At the same time, he became ever more active in the abolition movement. Erastus was an active participant in the figurative Underground Railroad while he also managed a physical rail line. Because he hired men who were sympathetic to his views, he was sometimes able to give seats to runaway slaves on the Connecticut River Railroad in open defiance of the detested Fugitive Slave Law.[34] Correspondence between him and his son survives, but it deals with mundane family matters and does not address the large issues of the day. As a result, there is no clear evidence as to whether W. S. B. shared his father's increasingly passionate advocacy of abolitionism.

Edward P. Nettleton, a twenty-five-year-old alumnus of Yale College who was then principal of the high school at Chicopee Falls, was eager to raise a company of "men of good habits and sound bodies, men determined not to suffer this ungodly rebellion to destroy the Union because of lack of patriotism in the Northern States."[35] Nettleton wrote to Whelden, informing him that he already had clearance to become an officer in the next regiment raised by the state but that he was unwilling to wait for that to happen, preferring to serve in the regiment being raised by Butler. He listed as references some of the leading men of Springfield and did not fail to mention that his father, Alpheus Nettleton, had been major general in the Massachusetts militia.[36] Whelden must have accepted, as Nettleton plunged ahead with recruiting.

Because of the individualistic way the companies were recruited, each one presented a distinctive character:

- Company A, originally organized by Capt. Edward P. Hollister, included many men from Berkshire County as well as from nearby communities in New York State, such as Stephentown. Most of them were enlisted October 20 and mustered into Federal service November 20.

- Company B comprised men largely from the western hill towns between the Connecticut Valley and the Berkshires. Most were mustered under Capt. Elisha A. Edwards on November 20.

- Company C was recruited under Capt. John W. Lee, mainly from the hill towns on both sides of the Connecticut River, and also mostly mustered on the twentieth.[37]

- Company D, as noted, included a large contingent from Ware and the neighboring towns of Belchertown and Hardwick, mostly mustered on November 20.

- Company E was drawn from scattered towns in western Massachusetts, especially the northern Berkshires, with a number from nearby Vermont towns like Pownal as well as a sizable contingent from Chicopee. Most of the men were mustered on December 10 under Captain Nettleton, who had led the recruiting.

- Company F included a number of men from Belchertown and some from the Berkshires, with others from locales scattered throughout western Massachusetts. The formal muster took place on the late date of February 19, 1862, under Capt. Eliot Bridgman.

• Company G was also diverse, though with many residents of Spring-field and its neighboring communities. It was mustered on February 20, 1862, under Capt. Cardinal H. Conant.

• Company H also contained not only many Springfield men but also quite a few from southern Berkshire towns, such as Sheffield and Great Barrington. It also included more men from Worcester County than any of the other companies, many of whom were employed in that county's thriving shoe industry. With Capt. Edward Page Jr. in charge, many were mustered on January 27, 1862.

• Company I was drawn from western Massachusetts, with a heavy representation from Berkshire County and quite a few from nearby New York towns, such as Berlin, a break with custom for men to enlist in the regiment of another state. But the presence of the New Yorkers supports the longstanding observation that Berkshire's ties to Boston were weaker than the other Massachusetts counties, while it had stronger social and economic links to adjacent portions of New York and Vermont. The muster date for the bulk of this company was January 28, 1862, under command of Capt. William W. Rockwell, who had done most of the recruiting. At least six men had prior military service in the short-term regiments organized in the first days of the war, notably the 8th Massachusetts.

• Company K was an anomaly, made up of men from the Boston area and added to fill out the total strength of the regiment. Butler cryptically remarked of this: "Company K stands upon different grounds. It was recruited at the expense of the United States wholly."[38] Initially under the command of Capt. William Fiske, the company was not mustered into service until February 14, 1862. As many as twenty of its members may have benefited from previous service in short-term regiments.[39] (There was no "J" company because of possible confusion with the letter "I.")

Company D included a handful of students from Amherst College, who mostly became officers and left a distinctive stamp on the unit. Hopkins was a graduate of Williams College, which provided many officers for the Union forces (but not particularly for the 31st Massachusetts). One of the Amherst men was Luther Clark Howell, who came from the Southern Tier of New York and signed up within a week of the attack on Fort Sumter in April 1861, one of seventy-five students pledged to be "ready to march at a moment's notice."[40] This pledge list, intentionally recalling the Revolutionary-era minutemen, was compiled by William Smith Clark (1826–86), a professor of chemistry at the college. Clark was an enthusiast for the war who initiated military drill at the college and later helped organize and eventually commanded the 21st Massachusetts Infantry Regiment. Apparently, authorities decided not to enlist the college volunteers until better preparations had been made, so in October Howell was still busy recruiting. He wrote to his sister from Ware, "Well, here I am hard at work trying to persuade men that it is their duty to be patriotic at such a time as this, but sometimes I am ashamed at my countrymen." Overall progress seemed encouraging, however, and he informed her, "Our Co. is prospering finely, have about 70 men on the list now & hope to fill it up during the coming weeks" (as they succeeded in doing).[41]

A local newspaper printed an informative list of occupations of the Company D recruits. It shows the diversity of jobs that would be expected in a textile mill town like Ware, yet farmers from outlying districts still made up the largest single category: one lawyer (Captain Hopkins), eight students, one printer, one bleacher, six clerks, three smiths, one wool sorter, thirty-four farmers, one artist, nine laborers, four carpenters, two saddlers, three sailors, five painters, one teamster, one landlord, one mason, one tailor, four hostlers, three mechanics, one weaver, one butcher, one baker, one cabinet maker, two shoemakers, and one scythe maker.[42]

Most of the men began arriving at the camp, located on the fairgrounds at Pittsfield, in early November, and reception and training began on the ninth. A full company was supposed to contain one hundred men, but on that first day only sixty enlistees from Company D showed up.[43] Some might have been delayed; otherwise, another recruiting drive would be needed. The recruits, housed in agricultural buildings, at first had no bunks or bedding, so they slept on the wooden floors. With no effort to soften the transition from civilian society, they endured a rough but predictive introduction to military life. Soon men like Luther Fairbank, who had been a carpenter in Ware, were put to work building bunks.[44] It is uncertain who paid for the materials and construction of bunks along with other necessary facilities: the dispute between Butler and Andrew made it unlikely that state funds would have been provided. Perhaps the general used his own money, though if he were responsible, he never took credit for it, which would have been uncharacteristic.

Whelden was pleased by the initial response at Camp Seward. "Everything is working finely," he informed Butler. "Men are coming in faster than I can provide for their comfort. I want overcoats very much, as it's getting somewhat cold in these mountains." In an obvious attempt to ingratiate himself, he observed, "The Governor's friends are trying their utmost to break up all your regiments, but give me the means and time, and this shall be the Banner Regt. of the State." Perhaps overoptimistically he reported, "The class of men are A No. 1,—but two cases of drunkenness in camp as yet."[45]

Days were short and cold by then, and the agricultural buildings had not been intended for year-round use. Recollections of Camp Seward describe cold, snow, and other forms of discomfort. One soldier remembered going down to the Housatonic River on his first morning in camp and finding it full of floating ice, which cut the men's hands when they washed.[46] At that moment it seemed inconceivable that they would spend most of their service in sultry Southern swamps. "The fellows can hardly keep warm in the barracks," complained James B. T. Tupper, "and you can see them lying around in their bunks with their overcoats and mittens on covering themselves with blankets when they are not on duty."[47] Some nights were so cold that guard duty was limited to one-hour shifts. In January 1862 there were frequent snowstorms, and the men had to keep their drill field cleared off for use. One soldier referred to "a real old fashioned storm" on January 20, proving that even in distant times the snows of yesteryear seemed more memorable.[48]

Recruits continued to be hauled in throughout the time the regiment was in Camp Seward. One man recorded the unusual circumstances of his enlistment: "I was out in the woods chopping with Charles Nowlton [sic, Knowlton] and was just thinking of going home for the night, when Lieut. Geo. S. Darling came out where we were to work, seeking for recruits, and as I had been wanting to enlist, this was just the opportunity, so I took his pencil and paper upon an oak stump and made myself a soldier for three years in Co. F, 31st Regiment." The following day this young man, Richard F. Underwood, traveled from Belchertown to Pittsfield by train. Although the railroad had been in service for twenty years, it was his first train ride, an illustration of the rapid broadening of experience the war brought. "I was homesick enough on my first night in Camp," Underwood admitted. "I had to sleep on a board and only one blanket for three of us. I caught a cold that night that never went off till I was far down in Dixie."[49]

There were several instances of brothers enlisting, but nothing to rival the record of the Frink family from Mount Washington in the extreme southwest corner of Massachusetts. The 1860 census gave the population of this town as 321. Five Frink brothers, ranging in age from eighteen to twenty-eight, enlisted together in Company F. They were the sons of Elias Smith Frink (1807–73) and Harriet Brazee Frink (1812–71). The family originated in adjacent Litchfield County, Connecticut, and lived in Mount Washington for only about ten years, from around 1855 to 1865. Two of the sons listed their occupations as farmer while the other three listed collier, an ancient and demanding craft of making charcoal for furnaces in the Salisbury iron district. The five men who joined the 31st Massachusetts were not the end of the Frink story, as two other brothers enlisted in the 8th Connecticut; the youngest brother was turned down when he tried to sign up. The Frinks also three had daughters, but each died in childhood.[50]

These men found themselves in the ranks of the 31st Massachusetts through the efforts of Joseph Hallett, one of the young men who had taken on the duty of recruitment, probably in hopes of being commissioned as an officer in the new regiment. Although Hallett was born on Cape Cod and was living in Springfield, he somehow made his way to the most isolated corner of Massachusetts, where he found likely prospects: "In the sparsely settled town of [Mount] Washington, in the Berkshire Hills far from railroads, I came across a band of charcoal burners, a sturdy set of men, six feet or more in height, of physical build, just the kind I was desirous to enlist in my Company and for Uncle Sam." Though an outsider, he quickly perceived that "watching the fires of the wood ovens was monotonous labor and it was not difficult to corral a dozen brawny fellows who were willing to enroll their names on the mustering list. Among the number were five brothers by the name of Frink, they all enlisted, made good soldiers and served through the war, excepting one who was killed in battle."[51] Hallett, who was nineteen years old, also journeyed to Agawam, closer to home, where he "found a party of men in a barn stripping tobacco. They were much older than myself, and it was embarrassing to address strangers of twice my age, and I shrank from approaching them. It was the 'cause' coupled with a sense of duty that gave me courage." By overcoming his natural diffidence, Hallett obtained several enlistments.[52]

One consequence of throwing together, under harsh conditions, a large number of men who were not acquainted and were not used to being part of a crowd was the rapid spread of disease. Tupper reported, "The Hospital is full and the rest [of the men] lie around in their bunks depending on the kindness of their comrades and officers for proper treatment." Captain Hopkins, newly elected, was among those afflicted. Soon after, forty-three recruits were sent to a house that had been rented as a hospital.[53] Though few probably realized it at the time, this provided an authentic introduction to army life. Beneath the flag waving and the noble abstractions of the recruiters festered the reality of dysentery, pneumonia, and a multitude of persistent digestive and lung complaints that often brought death or discharge after long, debilitating hospital stays; chronic poor health plagued many of those who survived.

The recruits spent most of their time drilling. These parade-ground maneuvers were not always useful on the battlefield, but they gave the men something to do, accustomed them to boredom, and suppressed individuality. In time they might think of themselves merely as cells in an invincible blue organism. It is not certain when muskets arrived or whether there was any live-fire training. One account relates that the officers went out shooting for the first time only on January 12.[54] Capt. John W. Cushing, who may have had prior military experience, had been giving Tupper individual rifle instruction.[55] Yet there were diversions from drudgery: the men were given furloughs to visit home and could go into town to hear lectures, to attend religious services, and to meet friends. Camp experience thus provided a valuable transition between the freedom of civilian life and the rigidity of the military. On his last visit home, Hallett, now a lieutenant, was surprised when friends presented him with a sword made by the Ames Company "encased in a gold mounted sharkskin scabbard."[56] Based in Chicopee, Ames produced the bulk of the swords carried by Union officers.

Sword presentations to new officers were a regular rite of passage, with multiple layers of meaning. In February Lieutenant Colonel Whelden received a sword in a ceremony conducted by his brother Masons. Also in Pittsfield, Captain Rockwell was presented with a sword at the residence of Thomas F. Plunkett. In a similar ceremony a sword was presented to Robert Bache of

Pittsfield, who had been serving as adjutant but had been named major.[57] The weapons were almost always described as "elegant."

With so many young men thrown together in unfamiliar circumstances, life at Camp Seward was not always sedate. After only a week there, one recruit with strong religious sensibilities wrote, "There is no evading the simple fact that the camp is a trying place for *christian character.*" He concluded that "the natural tendency of the heart is to evil and there are times here to everyone when feeling lonely, time hangs heavily on his hands. Then he is tempted to many ways of *killing time,* not among the least of which is playing cards and trifling talk."[58] It is evident that primeval Calvinism had not entirely lapsed in rural Massachusetts.

A shocking incident took place November 23, 1861, when a deranged "Irishman from Springfield" named Michael Sullivan stabbed Captain Lee. Initially it was feared the captain would not live, but he survived.[59] Probably the most direct explanation of the incident was provided by Howell: "The man guilty of a deed so dastardly was a hard drinking private, who being deprived of his accustomed dram was taken with the 'Horrors.'"[60] Sullivan was not after Lee personally; the captain had the ill fortune to be the first person to respond to the pounding on the door to the officers' room. At first Butler wanted to shoot the culprit, then reconsidered and decided to employ more regular procedures. Sullivan was put in irons and carried with the regiment until he was drummed out of the service on June 20, 1862.[61]

In contrast to Whelden's glowing report in the first days, Frank Knight described "a company from Pittsfield, of about 60 men, all Irish, poor, miserable, ragged vagabonds, who are continually getting into a row. We put 10 of them into the Guard House last night."[62] (There was no "Pittsfield company" as such, although men from that and nearby towns were heavily represented in Companies A and I.) Some of these recruits may have been dismissed before being formally mustered. Tupper reported on another row occurring when a group tried to release a companion who had been locked up for desertion.[63] Knight's opinion was confirmed by Howell, who similarly reported: "We have one company of real *roughs,* and I have heard that my life had been threatened. Guess I shall have to hurry up about getting my pistol." His overall assessment was positive, however: "Outside of this one company I think I never saw a lot of men better disposed. Every man of our company will stand by me until the last breath is drawn."[64]

At the beginning of December 1861, the men were issued their "Fatigue Suits consisting of cap, short sack coat, pants of blue also drawers, shirt, stockings, overcoat—the cloth is not of the finest texture but they keep us warm, though the buttons will come off."[65] Food at camp was plain but usually plentiful. Hash made frequent appearances on the menu, but the men complained that it was often sour. At that point they could still receive parcels from home, which had both gustatory and sentimental appeal, but those days were drawing to a close.

Heralded by cannon, General Butler came out to inspect the regiment on Tuesday, January 7, 1862. His years in the militia had taught him to conduct a thorough inspection. While the men were at dinner, "he passed around sticking his fingers into the meat pans and going out *munching a slice of bread.*"[66] That night all went into town to hear him give a speech. Butler evidently was pleased by what he saw, informing Lieutenant Colonel Whelden: "I have been much gratified with the appearance, discipline, and proficiency of your regiment, as evidenced by the inspection of to-day. Of the order, quiet, and soldierly conduct of the camp the commanding general cannot speak too much praise." He added pointedly, "Notwithstanding the difficulties of season, opposition, and misrepresentation the progress made would be creditable if no such obstacles had existed."[67]

Butler's reference to "obstacles" and "misrepresentation" acknowledged his continuing conflict with the governor, an admission that was necessary because it was intruding directly on the future of the regiment. As early as the beginning of December, a recruiter in the town of Montague had alerted Butler, "I find a great deal of inconvenience in recruiting here from the fact that the Country People do not *fully* know to their *satisfaction* that they will receive state aid for their families."[68] The state had passed legislation earlier in the year to give aid to soldiers with families since such men could not reasonably be expected to support them on the basic private's pay of thirteen dollars a month. At first the question was whether this payment was discretionary so that selectmen in each town would have the authority to determine who was eligible. Later the threat of losing the aid became real, as Governor Andrew seized on the law as another weapon in his conflict with Butler. He contended that the general's recruits, as "irregulars," were not eligible for state assistance.[69]

Andrew's campaign to undermine Butler culminated in early January, when the Eastern Bay State Regiment, whose development was always a little ahead of its Western counterpart, was already on a steamer preparing to head south. Its commander reported that surreptitious messages had been passed to the men claiming that they were an "irregular force" raised by Butler "against the lawful authority of the State, and the United States." As a result, according to a letter signed by an "Assistant Military Secretary," the men "may seem to have voluntarily deprived" their families "of the benefit of the soldier's family relief act." If these poisonous messages failed to incite mutiny, it was "only from a want of credence in the authenticity of the letters or the accuracy of the statements they contain."[70] There is little reason to doubt that these letters were legitimate—they employed the same language the governor had used in private correspondence—but it cannot be certain that he authorized their distribution. In any case, it was a shocking attempt to subvert military discipline. It is little wonder that, even after the passage of many years, Butler wrote that Andrew "had the good quality of cultivating malignity as a parlor plant."[71]

While the troops may not have understood the legal arguments or the depth of personal vituperation, they were well aware of the consequences. As the stay at Camp Seward lengthened, there were increasing rumbles of discontent. A delay in distributing pay contributed to the grumbling. Tupper warned, "The men are getting rather mutinous and there will be trouble if the promises which the officers have made to the men are not fulfilled in regard to State Aid."[72] Even the strongly religious J. W. Hawkes concurred: "Two things are settled in my mind that we do not leave here till *we are paid off* and the *state aid* is decided."[73] Many of his comrades probably shared these feelings, so the atmosphere at Camp Seward must have been strained.

Under pressure, Butler reassured Whelden, "I will personally, and from my private means, guarantee to the family of each soldier the aid which ought to be furnished to him by his town, to the same extent and amount that the State would be bound to afford to other enlisted men."[74] If nothing else, this confirms that the general was a man of considerable means before he left Massachusetts. But as he explained in his autobiography, he did not consider this really risky: "The towns paid the State aid, and as every town wanted every soldier in it to be credited to its quota, I knew they would, as they did, pay the State aid, and there was neither risk nor hazard about it."[75]

With two stubborn men butting heads, the conflict seemed irreconcilable. Andrew's proposed solution was to revoke Butler's command of the Department of New England and distribute the "irregulars" he had amassed among the incomplete 28th Regiment and two other regiments that had suffered heavy losses in the disastrous defeat at Balls Bluff.[76] Whelden was presumably aware of this plot when he informed Butler, *"The Governor's friends are trying their utmost to break up all your regiments."*[77] Butler and Andrew never met in person, nor was there any formal treaty or agreement between them. Possibly their aides met, but there seems to be no record of it. Left to themselves, the two adversaries might have gone on squabbling indefinitely.

It was a brief telegram from President Lincoln to Governor Andrew that began to break the impasse. Written in the president's usual polite style, it nevertheless left no doubt that his patience was running out: "I will be greatly obliged if you will arrange somehow with General Butler to officer his two unofficered regiments."[78] By then the antagonists may have become receptive to this outside pressure. For his part, Butler was committed to a campaign that promised great glory. As of February 9, he had two thousand men in camp on Ship Island off the Mississippi Gulf coast, including the 26th Massachusetts, which he had accepted for his command.[79] He could hardly afford to leave two or more additional Massachusetts regiments behind, which made him more agreeable to compromise. Back in Boston, Andrew perhaps was beginning to see that his obsessive pursuit of prerogatives that mattered only to him and to certain of his vengeful staff members threatened to put him in the position of preventing organized Massachusetts troops from going into action.

The controversy is much better documented than the solution, which apparently relied mainly on tacit understanding, verbal instructions, and informal communication. The War Department facilitated progress by giving Butler command of the newly created Department of the Gulf on February 23. At the same time, the temporary Department of New England was abolished, eliminating Butler's authority to recruit and removing the direct source of controversy. The governor, probably advised that these moves were forthcoming, agreed to accept the regiments Butler had formed. Andrew, who as recently as December 27, 1861, had declared that "nothing whatever has occurred to change my determination not to commission officers over these irregular troops," now agreed to give commissions to officers in these regiments.[80] The governor exercised his prerogative to issue commissions but accepted most of the officers who had already been chosen, with the exception of a few against whom he had some personal objection.

On January 17, 1862, Lieutenant Colonel Whelden ordered an end to furloughs and transfers, seemingly a signal that the regiment was about to enter a new phase; even then, more than four weeks remained in its sojourn at Camp Seward.[81] Finally, on February 12, after a hectic night of preparation, the regiment departed its unloved temporary camp and marched through the streets of Pittsfield to the railroad depot. A reporter noted that the men made "a very creditable display." They carried a regimental flag that had been presented by General Butler as well as a "silk Banner" presented by Mrs. Sarah Morewood, a leader in Berkshire social and cultural life, to Captain Hollister of Company A, regarded as a "Pittsfield Company." This banner bore the somewhat enigmatic gilt motto "By Courage, not by Craft."[82] By then the men had been paid and understood that the state-aid issue was being resolved. Although it was early morning, a large number of people had gathered at the depot, "and when that long train moved off many were the damp eyes and moist handkerchiefs. The air was full of white cambric and loud rang the voices until lost in the distance."[83] The regiment left behind a quantity of broken and intact bottles, confiscated during inspections after Company A stirred up a row on February 6.[84]

The Western Railroad provided a train of three locomotives and twenty-three passenger cars for the regiment, a surprising amount of spare equipment, unless some regular trains were annulled. "At every station on the route crowds were gathered so that our whole journey was a kind of *perpetual ovation*."[85] At Springfield the citizens treated the men to wheat bread and ham with coffee; later they were offered beer so that some of "the boys were pretty happy and tight." Many greeted friends for the last time.[86] It was a thrilling, rather joyous journey, but it almost ended in catastrophe when drawbars on the long train separated twice while coming downhill, probably on the steep grade into Chester. Trainmen had to climb up on the cars and set handbrakes to keep the detached cars from racing out of control, which could have resulted in a smashup that devastated the regiment.[87] No one suspected that this was the first of several disasters that threatened the survival of the 31st before it reached its destination in the Gulf. At Worcester the regiment transferred to the Worcester & Nashua Railroad and completed the trip to Camp Chase in Lowell around 7 P.M.

The men spent about a week at Camp Chase, occupied in inspections, equipment issues, and other preparations. An air of expectancy pervaded the troops as they were constantly reminded that the serious phase of their work was fast approaching. General Butler bustled around, busily examining and observing. The men noticed that accommodations were pleasanter here than at Camp Seward, which must have reawakened the resentment felt by those from the western part of the state felt toward the dominant eastern portion. The divergent Company K was here united with the other nine companies. Men in this company had been recruited in Boston, came overwhelmingly from the eastern part of the state, and had never been at Camp Seward.[88]

Camp Chase was surrounded by a tight fence, which presented a challenge to unruly young soldiers. One night a number of them climbed over the fence and proceeded into Lowell, where they conducted a major "jollification." Eventually, they were rounded up and thrown into the guardhouse, along with some of the men who had been sent to guard them. It happened that General Butler was coming out, and the next day, like naughty schoolboys, they were hauled into his presence. Here Butler demonstrated that his years in the militia had taught him how to deal with volunteer soldiers. More in sorrow than anger, he began by saying, "My young friends I am very sorry to meet you in this manner." He concluded by appealing to their higher sense of responsibility, reminding them that "when we leave the city of Boston behind us, we must leave behind us all our boyish tricks, and all the notions that we may have entertained that we are going south just to have some fun. Behave yourselves like Men and I believe you will find in me one who besides being your General will try to be your friend."[89] A West Point officer would never have adopted this approach, and it might not have succeeded with troops from another part of the country, but Butler knew his New Englanders.

The foray into town was probably a consequence of the soldiers having been paid after a long wait. An account by Tupper brings to mind the expression about money burning a hole in one's pocket: "Those that got paid have bought all the pies and cakes the sutler had, and he has nothing but crackers and cheese left, and they are howling around and stoning his shanty like a pack of hungry wolves."[90] Other men went into town to make impulse purchases or to have their picture taken. While there they got into a brawl with "some rowdies," and "[Constant E.] Southworth got knocked down with a club, and his face is quite swollen."[91]

The underlying history of Civil War regiments is the process of attrition.

A full regiment was supposed to have one thousand men, though most were somewhat short of that maximum. In one report from this period, Butler listed his infantry regiments as having a strength of nine hundred each.[92] The gradual and relentless decay began while the regiment was still in its home state. Official records show that twenty-two men were discharged for disability at Pittsfield and Lowell, while another thirty-three had made a rapid assessment of military life and deserted. Thus the regiment's nominal strength was already reduced by about 6 percent before it really got started. Apparently, not much was done about the deserters, though one wonders how they explained themselves at home. A few of these men later joined other units, perhaps after bounties began to be offered. It is a testimony to the dedication of the vast majority of the recruits that, despite ample evidence of inefficiency and after the demoralizing conflict over state aid, they remained true. One would have hoped that this was the last time the common soldiers would be disappointed by their leadership, but that was hardly the case.

On a raw February 20, 1862, the regiment was taken to Boston by train, "marched through the streets in *slosh* nearly knee deep," and at Long Wharf boarded the steamer *Mississippi*.[93] The bad luck that hung over the regiment in state persisted to the end, as the men had to stand in snow for two hours before leaving Lowell because the train's engine was stuck.[94] After passing a night crowded in the confined quarters of the vessel, the troops, including four companies of the 13th Maine, departed on the twenty-first. A pilot accompanied them to the limits of the harbor, after which the Bay State shore, itself an unfamiliar sight to most of the men from inland towns, fell away. Several weeks earlier a twenty-three-year-old soldier, returning from what he expected was his last furlough, wrote, "I took a last long look at all the old scenery of Charlemont, the impression of which will remain upon my mind as long as time shall with me last."[95] Now they were cut loose from their link to home, relentlessly pulled away on their grand and unknown adventure. Symbolizing their entry into a mature phase, the men departed as the 31st Massachusetts Volunteer Infantry, no longer the Western Bay State Regiment; the Eastern Bay State Regiment likewise transformed to become the 30th Massachusetts. Another result of the patched-up truce between Butler and Andrew was that subsequent commissions issued by the governor dated to February 20.

Captain Hopkins had been married for three years to the former Elizabeth "Lizzie" Sarah Peck, and they had a little daughter, Sarah (called Sadie). Lizzie did not know that her husband had left Boston until February 23, when she received a letter from him. The shock of that discovery released a rush of emotion that represented what thousands of women felt as they confronted the disruption to their lives caused by a catastrophic war: "Oh! how my heart sank when I found you had really left these shores. God grant you may soon return. But Oh! the anxiety I shall feel, and you are going so far that one can't hear from you often. . . . Oh Swint my heart is *so* full almost to bursting I can't bear to think of it or of anything. I feel so unsettled I can't read or work, in fact do anything."[96]

2

A PERILOUS JOURNEY

FEBRUARY–APRIL 1862

According to their writings, several men of the 31st Massachusetts knew that their destination was Ship Island, a sandbar off the Mississippi coast—and in the way of armies since the beginning of time, if one soldier knew, they all did.[1] James B. T. Tupper may have had greater access to information because he was serving as a clerk. If he had the further knowledge that their ultimate objective was to seize New Orleans, it is likely that many others knew it too.

Like everything else in the Civil War, the decision to attack New Orleans was tangled in politics and personal rivalry. True to Napoleon's maxim that victory has a thousand fathers, many later claimed credit for originating the idea. After the other major protagonists were dead, U.S. Navy commander David D. Porter (1813–91) grabbed an expanding amount of credit, including the claim of having selected the commanding officer for the operation. Horace Greeley attributed the plan to Butler, though the general himself apparently never made that assertion. In the view of one historian who studied this campaign, Asst. Secretary of the Navy Gustavus V. Fox deserves most of the honor.[2] Regardless from whose brain the plan sprung, Lincoln, needing a victory, quickly adopted it. After the capture of Port Royal, South Carolina, on November 7, 1861, and the Cape Hatteras forts in North Carolina early in 1862, taking New Orleans seemed to lie within Union capabilities. Butler indirectly figured in the decision because he had led the army portion of the joint attack on Hatteras. These offensives indicated that steam-powered vessels could run past fortified positions in a style that would have been unacceptably risky for sailing ships.

It is not entirely clear when Butler was selected to lead the army portion of the expedition. Probably it was in November 1861, when Capt. David Glasgow

Farragut (1801–70) was chosen to lead the naval force, though formal orders did not come through until later. Fox, an ally and informant of Butler's, may have made the suggestion for his command.[3] On October 11, in one of his strained communications with Governor Andrew, Butler had written that he was "most anxious to get his division organized so as to start upon an expedition already planned in the service of his country."[4] The War Department had issued an order that authorized the general "to fit out and prepare such troops in New England as he may judge fit for the purpose, to make an expedition along the eastern shore of Virginia, *via* the railroad from Wilmington, Delaware, to Salisbury and thence through a portion of Maryland, Accomac, and Northampton Counties of Virginia to Cape Charles."[5] This proposed operation, which would entail passing a long distance through two states that had not seceded in order to reach a detached fragment of Virginia, is so ridiculous that one cannot help thinking it was devised mainly to keep Butler out of circulation for a while. Whatever little strategic value Cape Charles offered could be gained by a quick seaborne raid. What would Butler do there with six regiments that would justify the constant flow of ships needed to supply them? This plan illustrates the muddled thinking that prevailed in Washington early in the war.

Although New Orleans was wisely substituted for Cape Charles as an objective, Butler would not have disclosed this information to Andrew. Once the expedition was approved, the general, possessing a sizable independent force, stood out as a logical candidate to command it. Not the least of the considerations in Washington circles was that the Gulf served better than Cape Charles to remove Butler to some remote place where he would be able to exert his overflowing energy and ambition and less likely to stir up controversy or capture the attention of newspapermen. The first of his units sent out of New England, the 26th Massachusetts and the 9th Connecticut, under Brig. Gen. John Phelps of Vermont, arrived at Ship Island on December 3. This was only a staging area, however, and did not guarantee that they would be sent against New Orleans.

Even with nineteen hundred of Butler's men on Ship Island and more on the way, there remained many obstacles on the path to New Orleans other than the Confederate forts that guarded its approach via the Mississippi River. The administration, looking for an American Napoleon, had named youthful Maj. Gen. George B. McClellan general in chief, replacing Winfield Scott.

McClellan at first seemed to favor the New Orleans campaign, but around the turn of the year he began having doubts. Fearful both that Butler would not have enough men to complete the task and that he could not afford to lose so many troops from the defenses of Washington (although Butler's recruits had never been assigned there), on January 1, 1862, he ordered Butler to "remain where you are," then ordered troops that were on their way to Ship Island to be diverted to Washington and Fortress Monroe.[6]

It is striking that, although he may never have met McClellan, Butler formed a quick assessment of his character, telling his wife, "Either McClellan has got to advance or he will be superseded."[7] At this point, McClellan was still widely seen as the savior of the Union. Although both men were Democrats, Butler had no illusions. McClellan would not move until he had amassed overpowering strength, but in what a later generation would call a "Catch-22," that was almost impossible because he extravagantly overestimated enemy numbers.

Butler was saved when Edwin Stanton replaced Cameron as secretary of war and vigorously supported the New Orleans expedition. McClellan had no choice but to comply, although he eventually did so with good will, adding three midwestern regiments to Butler's complement and holding out the prospect that other forces might be diverted to him. Adding the three regiments was surprisingly generous, as they were already in the Washington-Baltimore area. McClellan also contributed an officer who was to prove extremely valuable, the engineer Lt. Godfrey Weitzel. On February 23 McClellan formally established the Department of the Gulf, with Butler in command, and issued full orders.

"You are assigned to the command of the land forces destined to co-operate with the Navy in the attack upon New Orleans," began the instructions. "You will use every means to keep your destination a profound secret, even from your own staff officers, with the exception of your Chief of Staff and Lt. Weitzel." McClellan, emphasizing that "the object is one of vital importance," listed the force elements of all arms, which totaled eighteen thousand men. He expected that the navy could reduce the two forts guarding the city, but if not, they would have to be carried by assault. If New Orleans fell, Butler also was to occupy Algiers, across the river. He added, "It may be necessary to place some troops *in* the city to preserve order, though if there appears sufficient Union sentiment to control the city, it may be best for purposes of discipline to keep your men out of the city."

The commanding general then let his imagination roam. After obtaining possession of New Orleans, "Baton Rouge, Burwick [*sic,* Berwick] Bay, and Fort Livingston will next claim your attention. . . . A feint on Galveston may facilitate the objects we have in view." Beyond Baton Rouge, Butler was instructed to aim for Jackson, Mississippi, then consider combined-force attacks on Mobile, Pensacola, and Galveston. McClellan had to admit that "it is probable that by the time New Orleans is reduced, it will be in the power of the Government to reinforce the land forces sufficiently to accomplish all these objects."[8] He had laid out an agenda far more ambitious than anything he himself would be likely to attempt. Certainly, McClellan was not seeking to build up a rival, and since he had once asserted that it might take fifty thousand men to reduce the forts below New Orleans, perhaps he was trying to set Butler up for failure.[9]

The first day on board the *Mississippi,* February 21, was relatively quiet, but the sea grew rougher the following day, with predictable effects on the men. Most had never been at sea and soon, as one soldier phrased it, began "to cast up their accounts."[10] Another charmingly observed of his fellows that "some of them are looking at the bottom of their shoes to see if there is anything more they can throw up"[11] Thomas Norris, a sixteen-year-old who had signed up as a drummer boy, added his voice to the deep-throated chorus: "When we got out [of] sight of the land I began to feel dizzy and got sick, but I could not vomit, but that night when I drank some of the tea they had I let every thing up that I had ate for the last week."[12] Joseph Hallett added that the lad "was so sick that he piteously begged us to throw him overboard."[13] J. W. Hawkes surely delighted the folks at home by informing them, "I would like to picture to you a scene where we were all spewing over the rail."[14]

After delays due to fog and the lack of a pilot, the *Mississippi* docked at Fortress Monroe on February 24. Butler, who had arrived earlier at the familiar post, came on board with his wife. In his baggage, like invisible bacteria waiting to plague the regiment, was the old unresolved controversy about command. Butler continued to hope that his favorite, Charles Whelden, who had traveled overland with him and did not rejoin the regiment until it reached Fortress Monroe, would eventually take command of the 31st Massachusetts.

But when the regiment left Massachusetts, Whelden was still a lieutenant colonel, and he was now outranked by another officer. This was Col. Oliver P. Gooding of Indiana, who had been a first lieutenant in the regular army and had been elevated in rank sufficiently to command a volunteer regiment. A journal kept by an aide to Butler—and likely used by the general in preparing his memoirs—confirms that Gooding was officially the commanding officer of the regiment.[15] Probably, Gooding had been selected by the War Department, and it is unlikely that Governor Andrew knew him. Nevertheless, the fact that he was not a Butler appointee was in his favor, while the general was presumably unimpressed by the fact that the colonel was a graduate of the U.S. Military Academy.

The *Mississippi* departed Virginia on the evening of the twenty-fifth. Initially, the troops enjoyed "a beautiful sail, calm and warm." It had been cold when the New Englanders had arrived, but now the men "were all out on deck, smoking, talking and laughing and having a good time generally."[16] It was a deceptive interlude before catastrophe once more threatened the 31st Massachusetts. Off Cape Hatteras, the steamer encountered a terrific storm, which the people on board described in apocalyptic language: "only a plank between us and eternity."[17] Mrs. Butler, who had a talent for colorful prose, wrote, "The seas roaring, phosphorescent, gleaming as serpents' backs, struck the quivering ship like heavy artillery."[18] Mountainous waves smashed over the deck, and many times it seemed doubtful that the ship would rise out of the troughs. "Among it all it was amusing to hear the men; some were praying, others heaving up Jonah and a few were stealing sugar and others were bailing water that came down the hatches," though these were hard pressed to keep up with the water pouring in.[19] Writing with the calm perspective of many years' distance, Hallett summarized, "the lullaby was taken out of the song A life on the Ocean Wave, and a home on the Rolling Deep which had put us to sleep in the days of our infancy."[20] Despairing of meeting the storm head on, the captain finally swung the ship northward to ride before it, which may have helped save it but gave back much of the distance gained from Fortress Monroe.

The next day was utterly different, with the benign sun trying to banish memories of the dreadful night the passengers and crew had endured. As if rejoicing in its salvation, the *Mississippi* ran rapidly down the Carolina coast, making up time lost to the storm. Alas, this calm, bright phase proved to be only a lulling overture to another brush with disaster. In a sudden interruption to this reverie, while the people on board were having breakfast, "there came a surging, grating sound from the bottom of the vessel—a pause, a hush of dread throughout the ship—it worked again—the engine stopped—began again, another heavy lurching, and quivering of the ship—again the engine stopped."[21] Due to a gross navigational error by the captain, the vessel had run aground on Frying Pan Shoals, ten or so miles east of Point Lookout, North Carolina. The adjacent coast was in rebel hands, although they lacked a fleet. If the *Mississippi* began to break up, however, its crew would be forced into boats to make for the shore. There they, along with General and Mrs. Butler, would likely fall into enemy hands.

Efforts to free the ship with the engine failed, and lightening the vessel by throwing overboard provisions, baggage, and even valuable ammunition were to no avail. Another tactic, having the men run back and forth on deck to rock the ship free, was similarly unsuccessful. To compound the distress, the hull sprung a leak. Many were surprised to learn that this was caused by the captain casting over an anchor, although, as Mrs. Butler succinctly observed, "one would have thought we were fast [i.e., stuck] enough without the anchor."[22] She was unaware that the captain may have been trying to employ the technique of warping to work the vessel free. But as the wounded ship lurched about in this effort, it struck the anchor, which punched a hole in the hull. As in a melodrama, just as things seemed hopeless, another ship was spotted in the distance. Fortunately, it proved to be the Federal gunboat USS *Mount Vernon,* engaged in duty with the North Atlantic Blockading Squadron under Cmdr. Oliver S. Glisson (1809–90). With much struggle, the *Mount Vernon* sent a hawser to the *Mississippi* but could not pull the grounded vessel free. After that, the crewmen began the laborious process of transferring soldiers (and Mrs. Butler) to the *Mount Vernon* in small boats. While engaged in the chivalrous deed of assisting the general's wife, Whelden managed to drop into the ocean the sword his friends had presented to him in Pittsfield. Around 7 P.M., with perhaps three hundred men of the total complement of more than fourteen hundred having been moved, the *Mississippi*, due to its reduced load or an exceptionally high tide, suddenly came free.

On the following morning, those who had been transferred off came back to the *Mississippi*.[23] It was still down at the bow, where the anchor had punctured, so pumps had to be kept working constantly. That the ship survived at all was due to the fact that it was constructed with compartments: although the forward compartment was so flooded that the pumps could barely keep up, the other compartments remained dry and kept it afloat. At Butler's request the *Mount Vernon* escorted the damaged steamer, its pumps straining, to Port Royal, South Carolina, with a brief intermission to chase down a blockade runner. Federal forces had captured Port Royal less than four months earlier, otherwise the expedition might have had to turn back to Hatteras Inlet or risk another passage of Cape Hatteras to return to Fort Monroe. During this passage, Butler somehow located a sword, described as "highly tempered with gilt scabbard beautifully engraved," which he gave to Whelden to replace the one he had lost while performing a knightly deed for the general's wife.[24] So much of their provisions having been tossed overboard in the vain attempt to free the ship, the men now were reduced to a diet of "salt junk and hard bread" with a few boiled potatoes.[25]

On March 3, eleven eventful days out of Boston, the *Mississippi* landed at Hilton Head, just outside Port Royal. Even though the men did not find this land attractive, they felt enormous relief when they first set foot on it after the ordeals they had experienced: "Wasn't I glad to get off ship on to terra firma once more," declared Hawkes, "though my legs were so weak I could hardly stand."[26] Here, barely sixty direct miles from Charleston, the incubator of secession, most of them made their first contact with the South and its plantation system. Mrs. Butler was unimpressed: "Level fields, yellow pine trees, in the distance, a ditch or two, here and there a scattering palmetto, stunted looking things, with a few leaves clustered at the top, rattling away like sticks. How can one think them comely?"[27] Some of the men, however, enjoyed the warm days—like June in New England—and the orange and peach blossoms.

As far as the soldiers of the 31st knew, the entire island was one plantation, owned by James Seabrook. For this reason, the temporary post was called Camp Seabrook. The master, however, had gone off to serve as a Confederate officer, leaving the plantation and its slaves unmanaged, apparently another unforeseen consequence of launching the rebellion. The first Union troops to arrive had mistreated the slaves, so initially they were fearful, but afterward the "soldiers have always paid them for whatever they took so they are quite familiar now."[28] Almost as soon as they landed, the New Englanders went down to the slave huts to supplement their shipboard diet with hoecakes and oysters. Indeed, when not drilling or working the pumps on the *Mississippi*, the soldiers spent much of their idle time obtaining and consuming oysters and sweet potatoes. Hallett observed that the dwellings were "small cabins of two rooms each. Where the army of little tots that were running about like so many chickens were stored was past finding out."[29] Hawkes continued, "The negroes still live here with no one to make them work when they don't want to."[30] Without supervision, they worked to meet their needs, but many soldiers noted that they had begun plowing for the year's cotton crop. One can speculate that seeing this gave Butler the idea for the "free labor" plantations he later established in Louisiana.

In a significant portent, the slaves had begun liberating themselves without waiting for permission from higher authority. When asked if they wanted their master to come back, they said, "No, we want to be free." One of them informed Hallett that he had been part of a force of four hundred slaves. When the Yankees approached, "Massa made a sudden retreat by vessel, taking the negroes with him to the interior." This individual, apparently trusted, "was sent ashore and told to go back, kill the horses and live-stock, burn the cotton-gin, and houses that they might not come into the hands of 'you folks' and then to come to him, upcountry." Instead, he took a boat, rowed to a fort that had been captured by Northern forces, and revealed to the commanding officer where a large quantity of cotton was stored.[31] This incident confirms that many plantation owners genuinely had persuaded themselves that the slaves would remain loyal and resist the temptations that the war presented, a misperception that led to the greater miscalculation of firing on Fort Sumter.

In his autobiography Butler takes credit for devising a clever method of patching the hole in the *Mississippi*'s hull.[32] This seems like bragging, but it is quite likely that there was no one in the vicinity who had any better idea of how to proceed. The temporary patch held all the way to Ship Island, into the Mississippi River, and then back to Boston before a permanent repair could be made. Pumping out the water and repairing the *Mississippi* was a slow business, and Butler and his officers fretted that Farragut's armada had already entered the Mississippi River and was cursing the army for delaying their attack. Being held responsible for fouling navy plans was hardly an enticing prospect.

In the next century Hilton Head would flourish as a prestigious resort, but the men of the 31st remained largely immune to its charms. Although the days were generally pleasant, the nights were uncomfortably chilly, a couple actually producing frost. Most of the soldiers, while reluctant to reacquaint themselves with a ship they considered unlucky, were happy to leave the island. But even departure was no simple affair. On March 10, with some of the troops on board and others being brought out by tugs, the *Mississippi* ran aground on a dense oyster bed. It was necessary to tie hawsers from the mast to a tree on land to keep the ship from tipping over at low tide.[33] Men and cargo were loaded and unloaded in cold, rainy weather while tugs snapped several ropes trying to pull the vessel free. Four steamers working together failed in the attempt, and it was mainly a rising tide that finally floated the luckless ship.[34]

Fog further delayed departure until the thirteenth, by which time the *Mississippi*'s captain, A. H. Fulton, had been placed under arrest. Many of the men suspected that he was a rebel supporter and several times had deliberately placed the ship in a position where it could be destroyed or captured. Hallett actually maintained that a search of Fulton's papers revealed that he "was a native of South Carolina, a rebel sympathizer, and had done his best to deliver us into the hands of the Southern Confederacy." He added that Butler, despite "his well known severity in discipline," did not hang the suspect captain but put him in irons and sent him to Fort Warren, in Boston harbor, where he remained for the duration of the war; there is no confirmation for these assertions of disloyalty.[35] Of course, Fulton's supposed schemes would have entailed putting his own life at risk long before suicide bombing became fashionable. In his letter to the disgraced captain, Butler did not openly accuse him of trying to destroy the ship but confined himself to listing his mistakes, concluding "that through your neglect or incompetency the lives of fourteen hundred men had thrice been in peril, that the important interests of the Government in the speed of this voyage had been greatly injured, and its objects much delayed and perhaps thwarted."[36] When the *Mississippi* finally sailed on March 13, it was under a new captain, a U.S. Navy officer.

Compared to the earlier part of the voyage, the journey to Ship Island was relatively uneventful. With the water pumped out of the forward compartment, the ship rode normally and recovered its previous performance. Generally, the men were fortunate in not knowing any details of the emergency patch or fretting excessively about it. Pleasant days at sea were occasionally interrupted by showers and storms. On one warm night the men were sleeping on deck, "and everything was tranquil until about eleven o'clock when a shower came up which soon drove us to our Quarters, where it was so hot we almost suffocated."[37] After some men were suspected of breaking into the cargo, the entire regiment was assembled on deck for an inspection of knapsacks and equipment. "A madder set of men I never saw," noted William Shaf-toe.[38] This search confiscated assorted knives, pistols, and tobacco. There were interludes of enjoyment during the journey, unknowingly anticipating the pleasure cruises of the next century. Mrs. Butler observed the delights of one such balmy night: "The officers, a little apart, were singing. The swift moving ship, the dancing glittering waters, and the deep-toned music were in exquisite harmony." Yet she could not avoid reflecting "how free and careless they felt, with no spot for the sole of the foot but that they must win by the sword."[39]

During this relatively tranquil portion of the trip south, two soldiers who were probably already ill, and whose conditions had been worsened by being repeatedly soaked and chilled, died and were buried at sea. Men who had al-ready begun to think about their mortality were deeply moved by these simple, somber ceremonies. Luther Fairbank recorded his observations of one funeral, at the end of which the corpse of the novice soldier was slid down a raised plank on the deck and into the waters below: "One sudden plunge and the waves closed over his youthfull [sic] body forever."[40] The dead man's brother, serving in the same company, turned and walked away in silence.[41]

Even the end of the long journey confirmed the fears of those who consid-ered the Mississippi an unlucky ship. Reaching Ship Island on March 20, it had to go back out to sea because of a storm. Later attempts to land at the flimsy pier failed when the ship crashed into other vessels or became tangled in their rigging. Only half-jokingly, Mrs. Butler noted, "She might be said to have 'run amuck.'"[42] It was only on March 25 that most of the soldiers came ashore, ferried in on a tug while the larger vessel stayed offshore. Thirty-three adven-turous days had passed since the New Englanders had boarded the Mississippi in Boston and more than five months since Butler had received his authoriza-tion to raise troops. The men from western Massachusetts, few of whom were acquainted with the sea, underwent great stress and hardship before they ever saw combat. Low-level attrition continued; in addition to the two soldiers who died at sea, another was buried on Hilton Head, probably in a sandy grave now long forgotten. It was said of this unfortunate, a man from Rutland, Mas-sachusetts, that "his father came to see him at Camp Chase and told him that if he would not go to war that he would give him a deed of his property."[43]

On reaching land, Whelden's horse bolted and galloped a long way down the beach until either it ran out of steam or the lieutenant colonel regained control. If this was the animal's expression of joy at the end of the ocean voyage, it had good reason, as Tupper noted that of two hundred horses loaded at Boston, only one hundred survived the journey.[44] This was a portent of a wartime equine catastrophe of immense proportions. For the soldiers, after their trying and tiresome adventure at sea, Whelden's discomfiture provided a welcome source of amusement.

The Gulf beaches—another future tourist paradise—held little attraction to the men of Butler's division. Ship Island was a long barrier beach that could be almost entirely overflowed during a bad storm. On first seeing the island, one soldier expressed the opinion that it was "only a barren sand waste."[45] Another dismissed the future national seashore as "a dismal looking place; not a tree to be seen; not a spear of grass meets the eye; and as it appears to us now it is but a bed of white sand, over which the sun glistens as on a pane of glass."[46] Hallett summarized simply, "A more forlorn and desolate place for human habitation than Ship Island is unimaginable."[47] Mrs. Butler, always more poetic, perceived some beauty: "The island is attractive seen from the ship; a long curving line of smooth beach, where the surf rolls in and breaks gaily on the white sands. The tents, whitest of all, rise just beyond, and seem to cover half the Island, the center of which is not much higher than the beach, and you might easily think it was all floating."[48] The lady, however, did not have to work on the island, where loose sand made the ordinary operations of drilling and fetching wood an exhausting struggle. Picturesque at a distance, the insidious grains soon worked their way into every bite of food and every item of clothing and gear. Tupper summarized the men's feelings: "The sand is very troublesome. It is getting on our clothes when we sit down & you get your cup of coffee & sit down to drink it & somebody brushes along & about a pint of sand gets into your cup."[49]

In addition to the grit that infiltrated everything, the troops complained about the quality and quantity of their food. Because so much provision had been thrown overboard to lighten the *Mississippi* during its various ordeals, the regiment arrived with a severe shortage. Norris described the dismal fare on which the men had to sustain themselves: "We got the first week fresh Beef, but after that we had to live on salt junk, or horse as we call it, and Hard bread and coffee or chips and scraps, such stuf [sic] as you would not keep in the house."[50] Initially, neighboring regiments, such as the 6th Michigan and the 26th Indiana, displayed their sympathy by bringing ham and coffee to the New Englanders, but that was only a temporary expedient.[51] The simmering discontent came to a head when the men of Company K decided not to fall in for drill until their meals improved. Many were promptly placed under arrest. In the regular army such insubordination probably would have been considered mutiny resulting in court-martial and severe punishment, but once again the officers realized that they had to treat volunteer soldiers differently. After condemning their conduct, the colonel told the men that if they turned out immediately, he would forgive their behavior and look into their grievances. By then, the men were happy to reconsider their rash move, and so an incident that could have had disastrous repercussions passed harmlessly.[52]

Confederates had occupied Ship Island for a couple of months in 1861 but withdrew their small garrison in mid-September.[53] Probably it was a wise decision since, lacking a seagoing navy, they could not have protected the isolated troops; at most they might have fought a brief delaying action before being captured. Thus, when the first elements of Butler's force arrived there in early December, they faced no opposition. From a strategic viewpoint, the island was a good location, as it could be used as a base for an attack on Mobile or Pensacola as well as New Orleans. Even after the Crescent City had been selected as the objective, Butler tried to keep the enemy off balance by talking up Mobile.[54] It was only when navy ships entered the lower Mississippi River that New Orleans was confirmed irreversibly as the goal.

Entering the main channel of the river proved more trying than expected. Whereas Butler had feared delaying the navy, the opposite occurred. Naval authorities had failed to provide all the supplies Farragut needed, so Butler, ignoring regulations, gave him coal and other materials. Hauling the larger warships over the bar that blocked the main channel of the Mississippi consumed more time than anticipated. These delays freed days for drilling the troops, sometimes in larger units, and on one occasion Butler conducted a review of his entire command. In early April 1862 the 31st Massachusetts for the first time was given cartridges for firing practice, though these were only blanks.[55] Tupper observed that a neighboring Michigan regiment, probably the 6th, had exchanged their Springfield guns for Austrian rifles, which would hardly seem to be an improvement, and that "our men have been fixing up their guns, changing them, & getting ready."[56] Although it was due to necessity more than choice, this extended drilling in the resistant sand had the effect of working Butler's men into fine physical condition.

Two tragedies marred the regiment's sojourn on Ship Island beyond the routine discomfort of their situation. Dr. Eben K. Sanborn of Rutland, Vermont, the regimental surgeon, suddenly became deranged. A watch was kept to prevent suicide, but on April 4 he died.[57] There may be some organic cause to account for the sudden onset of his disorder, though if he wished to commit suicide, he had access to various compounds to accomplish that. Tupper, who seemed familiar with the situation, had a somewhat different slant, writing that Sanborn "has been insane since we came here. He came on board with our regiment, & they say his instruments, medicine, etc., were all thrown overboard while we were aground, & to come on here with no medicine, etc. worked on him so, that he lost his reason."[58] Tupper later added, "He refused to eat anything, & starved himself to death as much as anything."[59]

Mrs. Butler assumed that Sanborn would be buried alongside eight other recent graves, but instead the body was shipped home in a barrel of whiskey.[60] The eight burials were for enlisted men, three of whom had died of disease and five who had drowned while bathing. Two of the drowned men were from the 30th Massachusetts, but none were from the 31st.[61] Hallett observed that "a few scraggling shrubs and vines" at one end of the island provided the only sign of vegetation, "and this spot was so highly prized it was set apart for a cemetery." He also described the process of a military burial on Ship Island:

> One of the saddest scenes was the daily procession of a squad of soldiers with reversed arms and measured tread, bearing the uncoffined remains of a deceased comrade to burial; the roll of the muffled drums was doleful music, and brought sad reflections. Tramp, tramp, tramp, marched the little band, their feet sinking to their ankles in the sand as they wended their way to the cemetery. There a trench was easily prepared and the body was consigned to its final resting place, the last act was a volley of musketry fired over the lonely grave and the squad returned to their tents.[62]

Tupper added that "several graves have a pine board at the head with the name of the deceased, age, etc., painted on it, but many have no memorial & the sand heap only shows the resting place of a soldier."[63] This was an oppressive thought to have on one's mind as a landing in enemy territory approached.

Tupper felt considerable admiration for Dr. Sanborn, describing him as "a scholar & a man respected & esteemed by the Regt."[64] He was less impressed by the unfortunate physician's replacement, Asst. Surg. E. C. Bidwell: "I never have consulted him, & I hope I never shall have to. The boys complain of him, & I should think from the way he treats cases, he didn't know anything. If a man has the dysentery, he gives him a pill. For a cold, fever, or anything else, the remedy is the same. . . . He won't excuse anyone if he is able to stand."[65] Bidwell, a cultured man, went on to have a long history with the 31st Massachusetts; it is unknown whether Tupper's opinion of him changed over time. Other comments indicate that Tupper was a skeptic toward most medical practitioners and may have espoused a version of naturopathic treatment.[66]

A powerful thunderstorm passed over the island on the night of April 7–8, with torrential rain followed by a gale of wind, driving sand into every crevice and leveling tents. Most of the men had never experienced such a violent storm, but it was exceeded in fury by another only five days later. "The thunder peals reverberated from cloud to cloud, while streams of glaring lightning glittered amid the rain, which fell thick and fast, with a clamor more terrible than that of the approaching thunder gust."[67] Whether inside or out, everything and every man was thoroughly soaked. This was not a passing storm but continued with unabated ferocity for hours. At the height of the tempest, around 2 A.M., a bolt of lightning struck the 31st Massachusetts guard tent, instantly killing three men and knocking several others unconscious. A. P. Wheeler described how he gradually came back to life as his blood commenced to circulate again: "it seems as though ten thousand needles were sticking in me all at once."[68] George Young related that he had been asked to replace someone for guard duty, and although he was utterly drenched at his post, he returned to find that the man for whom he had substituted had been killed by lightning.[69] Some accounts from the 31st Massachusetts state that the dead men had been prisoners in the guard tent.[70] If that were the case, lightning bolt rendered their transgressions insignificant.

The next morning, as streams of rushing water threatened to subdivide the island into smaller parcels, soldiers milled around, gradually finding out what had happened overnight and trying to make sense of things. It was a somber experience for them to enter the blackened tent and see the twisted muskets and "all that was left of three young men who a few hours before were full of life and hope."[71] As Young's experience showed, a large element of fate was involved. Lacking other options, officers and preachers fell back on conventional statements to the effect that "it has pleased God to pick out from our great numbers these three young men to be offered up as a sacrifice to the honour of our common country."[72] That afternoon the entire regiment turned out for a military funeral. Two of the dead men were Roman Catholic, "and the Catholic chaplain sprinkled holy water and sand on the coffins three times."[73] This was the most memorable incident of the continuing attrition to this point, but the regiment saw another twenty-six men discharged while on Ship Island and three other deaths. One who was sent home was Horace Weeks, a farmer from Huntington serving in Company H. One imagines that he had tried to serve his country as a private, but his fifty-one-year-old body failed him. Another man was listed as deserting, though one wonders how anyone could be certain that he had deserted rather than being drowned and his body swept away, or even where he could desert to; at best he might have stowed away on a ship returning north.

Soon the men had other matters to occupy them. On April 7 Farragut had informed Butler that he had been able to bring his ships over the bar and that final preparations were being made for the attack on the forts defending the river to New Orleans. A new sense of urgency rippled over the assembled troops on Ship Island. On April 14 the men were issued forty ball cartridges and three days' cooked rations. Then on the following afternoon, smaller steamers brought them out to the familiar quarters of the *Mississippi*. True to form, the yard of the *Mississippi* knocked down both smokestacks of the other vessel. But the relief of the soldiers at leaving the "God forsaken Island" overcame some of the fear of what they were about to enter.[74]

3

ON THE MISSISSIPPI

APRIL–MAY 1862

New Orleans was vital to the South but presented a striking anomaly, a great city in a nation that defined itself by agrarian values. With an 1860 population of over 168,000 people, it was more than twice the size of the next two Southern cities, Charleston and Richmond, combined and included an astonishing diversity of foreigners and a significant number of free blacks. Its sophisticated international commerce and banking and its lively polyglot culture set the Crescent City apart from the rest of the Confederacy. Perhaps because of these differences, Confederate officials may not have fully appreciated the city's importance; or they may have convinced themselves that it was sufficiently protected. For its defense, New Orleans relied primarily on two forts, Jackson and St. Philip, located on a bend of the Mississippi some seventy-five river miles below the city. These had been part of the antebellum federal coastal-defense establishment, which in practice meant harbor defense; that they were far from both the sea and the city they were protecting was due to the peculiar geography of the region.

These forts formed part of what students of the subject term the Third, or Permanent, System of coastal defense—permanent because they were built of masonry and were expected to perform their function indefinitely. Beyond the interest they inspire as imposing physical structures, the forts represent fundamental American attitudes toward military matters in the nineteenth century—the need to protect a lightly populated but vast extent of coastline, distrust of a large standing army (since in wartime the forts could be garrisoned with militia), and a reliance on technological solutions. The fact that coastal defense was one of the few ongoing sources of federal construction contracts, spread over many districts, cannot be overlooked as a reason for

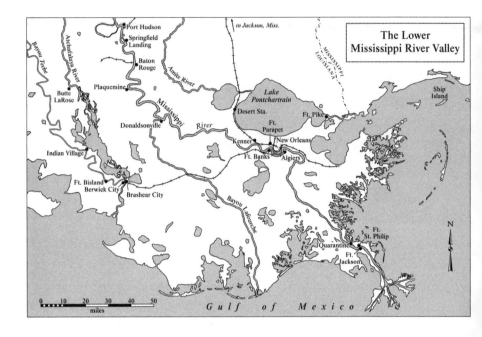

their appeal. Fort St. Philip, originally built by the Spanish, was taken over and upgraded by the Americans in 1808, just in time to hold off a British attack in 1815. Army engineers considered that the original structure was inadequate as a sole defense and erected Fort Jackson on the opposite side of the river between 1824 and 1832. A typical product of the Third System, Jackson had five corner bastions (giving it a shape that was often referred to as a "star fort"), and its brick walls were twenty-five feet high and twenty feet thick. Louisiana militia, on orders of pro-secession governor Thomas Overton Moore, walked in and occupied Forts Jackson and St. Philip without resistance in January 1861, even before the state voted to leave the Union.[1] There was nothing secret about their construction since numerous army engineers who remained loyal had circulated through them. In January 1862, during the planning for the attack on New Orleans, Brig. Gen. John G. Barnard, then chief engineer in the Army of the Potomac, submitted a detailed description of the two forts based on his personal experience at each.[2]

Despite the reliance they placed on them, the Confederates were haphazard in providing for the strongholds. They had increased their armament, but many of these guns were worn smoothbores and too light, limiting their effectiveness in opposing a modern fleet. There is a surprising diversity of figures for the artillery at the forts, a topic beyond the range of this history to reconcile. Probably, there was something on the order of seventy guns of assorted types at Fort Jackson, including what was called a "water battery," an emplacement directly on the river that could fire at the same elevation as any hostile ships.[3] In theory, armament was supposed to be determined by the specialized functions of various classes of guns, but in a practical sense it was decided by whatever the Confederates could lay their hands on.

The condition of the garrison looked even more unpromising. Most of its members were militiamen, and when ordered to move to Fort Jackson, many mutinied and had to be prodded onto transports at bayonet point—it was said that many were foreigners, Northern men, or Union sympathizers.[4] This ominous situation had been brought about partly by mismanagement, but it provided an early hint of the inadequacy of Southern manpower, transportation, and economic resources to conduct a war against a rising industrial power. The most strongly motivated troops, boasting the best training and equipment, had been sent out of Louisiana to fight in other theaters. They often performed splendidly, but their departure left a void at home. If the men who resisted being dispatched to Fort Jackson had been devoted to the Confederacy, they would not have been lingering at home to feel the sharp end of a bayonet on their backside. In addition to these deficiencies, the defense was hindered by divided counsel, as officials such as Navy Secretary Stephen Mallory professed to believe that the threat to New Orleans was at least as great from upstream as below, and divided forces. The various Confederate naval commands did not coordinate well with the army or with one another.[5]

Meanwhile, Commander Porter had persuaded Captain Farragut that he could reduce the defending forts with a fleet of twenty mortar ships he had assembled. (Mortars were tubby guns that could fire shells on a high trajectory to explode over the fort, bypassing its stout walls to damage or destroy armament and to kill or wound garrison troops.) Farragut appeared skeptical, but the plan had the support of General McClellan and others, so he had little choice but to try.

Preparations completed, Porter unleashed his bombardment on April 18, 1862, dispatching fourteen hundred 13-inch (diameter) projectiles, each weighing over two hundred pounds, against Fort Jackson. Many missed their target or failed to explode; but observers could see fires from wooden buildings set ablaze inside the fort. While Porter had promised to compel surrender in forty-eight hours, after nearly six days of battering, there was no sign that the forts were ready to submit.

Increasingly impatient, Farragut determined to make the dash past the forts that he had always preferred. He sent an advance detachment to break a chain and remove other obstructions the Confederates had placed in the river, obstacles that never met with as much success as they had intended. After midnight on April 24, Farragut began his epic run. Inside the forts, the men, a motley aggregation to begin with, had endured "almost unbearable" living conditions due to high ground water, yet the intense bombardment had not broken their ability to resist.[6] Forts Jackson and St. Philip, on opposite sides of the curving river, could produce overlapping fire against any vessel or fleet trying to force its way past them. Firing furiously at the approaching Federal warships, they presented a terrible gauntlet for Farragut's wooden ships to run. The confusion of smoke and flame, however, nullified much of the advantage of the forts' placement and the ranges its gunners had precalculated. Most of the fleet broke through, leaving the forts grumbling behind. Porter's mortar boats, with ammunition in short supply, did not attempt the passage, instead remaining below the forts under the protection of some of Farragut's ships left behind.

The men of the 31st Massachusetts were reluctant spectators for much of this action, partly because plans had never been fully coordinated with the navy. At the earlier combined actions at Cape Hatteras and Port Royal, the engagement by troops and ships had been nearly simultaneous. But at New Orleans, where Porter and Farragut had promised to compel the surrender of the forts with naval power alone, Butler's role was ambiguous. Two regiments, the 26th and 31st Massachusetts, plus an artillery battery spent the night of April 15–16 on board the *Mississippi*. Late on the night of the sixteenth, the ship weighed anchor, towing the sailing ship *North America*, loaded with more of Butler's troops, the 30th Massachusetts and 9th Connecticut. They passed over the bar into the main channel of the Mississippi on the seventeenth and after anchoring overnight proceeded up the river to within ten or fifteen miles of Fort Jackson.[7] From there, Butler sent word to Secretary Stanton that he was "ready to cooperate with the fleet, who move today, or so I believe, upon the Forts."[8]

Afloat on the turgid river but safely out of range of enemy guns, the regiment witnessed a spectacular display as Porter's mortars went into action: "No rockets could ever equal the brilliancy of the shells with their lighted fuse as the air was filled with them. Never, No Never will one of us aboard of the ship ever forget that sight."[9] One night the humid sky was luridly illuminated by fire rafts the Confederates sent down the current, hoping to ignite enemy vessels, but Union sailors grappled them aside with little damage. Writing when the awe he felt was still fresh, Capt. Edward P. Hollister gushed:

> The course of the shells could be distinctly traced by the burning fuse, and their revolving motion gave the exact appearance of twinkling stars—the constant flash of the guns and mortars was like continuous flashes of lightning, and on the whole the sight from two till four this morning was perfectly grand, excelling by far any fireworks; besides, the roar of the guns was terrific and constant.[10]

The breathless immediacy of Hollister's description reminds us that when these men signed their enlistment papers, they committed themselves to a multitude of experiences and impressions that were entirely alien to the quiet, secluded hill towns from which most of them came. Even a good-sized town like Pittsfield, except in the vicinity of the railroad, retained some of the settled stillness of the previous century. In the water-powered factories that proliferated in Massachusetts, belt-driven machinery could make conversation impossible, but that was in no way preparation for the noise of the bombardment the men witnessed on the Mississippi only two months after departing Boston.

Despite the unforgettable free show, discontent smoldered among the men of the 31st. In addition to anxiety about the unfolding battle, they suffered from overcrowding, sweltering heat, insomnia, and wretched food. "We lie here like dead heads and the men are getting discouraged, for we have hardly room to breathe, let alone to move," complained William Shaftoe.[11] Another described their subsistence in dismal terms: "All we have to eat now is a cup of coffee in the morning, and at night, and a piece of rotten magotty [sic] bacon and perhaps a rotten potatoe [sic] or two, and what sea bread we want."[12] Shaftoe reported that the men were "ragged and dirty," half of whom had dysentery.[13]

The erratic movements of the troopships seemed puzzling and may have reflected higher-level indecision. On April 21 the *Mississippi* retreated downstream only to return on the following day, when it anchored even closer to Forts Jackson and St. Philip. This suggests that Butler still expected the forts to fall to naval action alone; if they had to be taken by land assault, it would be foolhardy to begin from the river directly under their guns. Once he learned that Farragut had passed the forts but that they were still resisting, Butler went ahead with a contingency plan he and the captain had formed before the operation commenced and dropped back down the river on the twenty-fourth. The idea was to come in behind Fort St. Philip and cut off both forts by linking up with Farragut at Quarantine Station, a few miles upriver. Butler confirmed this arrangement by sending a trusted aide, Capt. C. H. Conant of the 31st Massachusetts, whom he described as "having made a reconnaissance in the rear of St. Philip night before last," to locate Farragut, adding that Conant "may be most implicitly relied upon and trusted."[14] Porter was consulted on this proposition and agreed; with ammunition short and concerned about the rebel warships remaining near the forts, especially the ironclad ram *Louisiana*, he had little choice but to stay out of range. Butler then issued orders to his various troopships. This seeming retreat in the face of the enemy had initially disheartened some of the men, but by evening of the twenty-fifth, they understood that the retrograde movement had been made so as to approach Fort St. Philip from the rear.

Delayed for a day when his navy escort, the USS *Miami*, grounded, Butler came into position on the twenty-sixth and placed the 26th Massachusetts, which he had previously praised as "one of the very best regiments that ever left Massachusetts," aboard the *Miami*.[15] This warship, which drew only seven and a half feet of water, came aground six miles from the fort. The advance force, which included a Massachusetts battery and portions of the 4th Wisconsin and 21st Indiana, then rowed four and a half miles until the water became too shallow even for rowboats. Butler described this as "a fatiguing and laborious" effort, but the exertion was exceeded in the final mile and a half, when the men, in water up to their waists, were forced to drag the boats against a strong current.[16] That this maneuver was possible at all was due in considerable measure to Lieutenant Weitzel, who was in the early stages of his rapid ascent in a brilliant military career. Like most army engineers, Weitzel had been assigned to coastal fortifications, and it happened that he had spent considerable time at those protecting New Orleans. While hunting waterfowl, he learned his way around the intricate web of swampy channels in the vicinity.

With the advance elements on terrain that passed for land, the 31st Massachusetts transferred to the steamer *Lewis*—whose smokestacks had been knocked over by the rampant *Mississippi* off Ship Island—on April 28, expecting to follow their route. Shaftoe described the *Lewis* with restrained affection as "an old rickety thing carrying one gun, made more like a flat boat."[17] Nevertheless, he professed to feeling good, as they were finally going ashore with the prospect of some action. At this point it would seem that Butler was in a precarious position. He had only one regiment of infantry and parts of two others on land, the 31st Massachusetts had not yet disembarked, and his other regiments were scattered on various transports. Based on the experience of the 26th Massachusetts, it would take a long time for them to wade into position, not to mention the problem of supplying them through the treacherous waterways afterward. The general had every intention of assaulting the stubborn forts, but whether he had sufficient strength or what he would do if the first attack was repulsed was uncertain.

In the event, these critical questions never had to be answered. During the night of the twenty-seventh, the garrison at Fort Jackson mutinied and spiked their guns. As Butler summarized, "they said they had been impressed and would fight no longer."[18] Troops at Fort St. Philip did not immediately participate, but with the command disintegrating, resistance was impossible. The defenders, reluctant warriors from the outset, heard rumors that Farragut's warships were before New Orleans and that their escape routes were blocked by Butler's soldiers and by ships that Porter had moved to the rear of Fort Jackson. They were aware that the forts had been designed to resist naval bombardment, not an attack by land, and probably did not know—or care— how few men or guns Butler had at his immediate disposal. The Confederate commander, Brig. Gen. Johnson K. Duncan, and some resolute units had been determined to fight and had rejected an initial demand to surrender, but they could not resist the tide of mutiny and desertion. Porter soon negotiated and accepted their surrender without reference to the army or Butler, who at the moment was probably upstream on Farragut's flagship. This action was fully in character for Porter, a notorious glory seeker, and offended Butler, who had his own ravenous thirst for fame, provoking hostility that lasted for the rest of their lives. Years later in his autobiography, Butler still fumed over "how untruthfully and villainously Capt. David D. Porter behaved through this whole transaction of the capture and surrender of the forts."[19]

When the general learned that Farragut had made it past the forts, he sent a message of effusive praise: "Allow me to congratulate you and your command upon the bold, daring, brilliant and successful passage of the Forts of your fleet this morning. A more gallant exploit it has never fallen to the lot of man to witness."[20] He took a different tone in writing to his wife two days later, by which time he knew that Farragut had continued upriver to New Orleans. This Butler deemed "wholly an unmilitary proceeding on his part, to run off and leave forts behind him unreduced, but such is the race for the glory of capturing New Orleans between him and Commodore [Andrew Hull] Foote that thus we go."[21] This was an uncharitable statement but not unjustified, but it probably represented the last time Butler and Porter (who also faulted Farragut) agreed on anything for the remainder of their careers. According to their plan, Butler expected Farragut to be waiting at Quarantine so that they could reduce the troublesome forts by joint effort. In dashing up to New Orleans, the flag officer left behind forts with most of their armament intact as well as several potentially dangerous Confederate warships. If six days of bombardment had failed to persuade the rebel defenders to submit, there was little likelihood that Porter's reduced force could accomplish the task. That left it up to Butler's infantry, supported only by a few field guns, to finish the job. Whatever else the Fort Jackson mutineers accomplished, they preserved several military reputations.

Meanwhile, Farragut had got himself into a bind at New Orleans. His guns overawed the city, already staggered by the sudden and unexpected appearance of Union warships, but he lacked the strength to compel its surrender. The few Confederate forces in the vicinity had departed northward, leaving no military authority to surrender, and the mayor found ways to procrastinate. As civil government broke down, the city fell into the hands of a mob of ruffians who screamed curses and threats against the Federal naval officers who entered the city for discussions. Displaying extraordinary courage, these officers passed through the rabble to the mayor's office. One rowdy tore down a U.S. flag that the sailors had raised over the mint and distributed torn pieces to participants in the mob. Running out of patience, Farragut sent a detachment of marines to seize several vital buildings, but he did not have the manpower to occupy New Orleans; the more men he sent into the streets, the fewer he would have to serve the guns of his ships if it became necessary. What Farragut would have done if the forts had delayed Butler for several days is unclear, but with resistance ended downriver, he asked Butler to bring his troops up promptly.

Instead of having to attack a fortified position, the 31st Massachusetts returned to the Mississippi River and sailed up the liberated waterway as conquerors. At sunrise on April 30, on board the ship *Mississippi* once again, the soldiers reached the forts that had been their goal but that they had never seen. It had been a day of celebration, with bands playing patriotic music and flags waving, but actually seeing the positions was a sobering experience: "It is a mystery to us all how under Heavens our Gun Boats ever got by those forts," wrote one soldier.[22] After counting thirty-six guns in Fort St. Philip and many more in its partner, Frank Knight was forced to agree: "'Tis a wonder to me we ever took those Forts."[23] The wonderment was shared to a more devastating degree by the stunned citizens of New Orleans, who in time fell back on conspiracy theories in the belief that only betrayal could explain how the defenses had failed. "The idea prevails here among some classes," James Tupper reported, "that the General in command at Fort Jackson betrayed the cause for a large sum of money—they can't see how it could have been taken any other way."[24]

The awe and relief the men of the 31st felt when they saw the forts close up was fully justified. During his bombardment, Union ships had hurled 16,800 mortar shells at the fortifications, yet they were still capable of stout defense.[25] Butler had a personal interest in demonstrating that Porter's boastful bombardment had been ineffective, and he found abundant evidence to support that conclusion. When Weitzel inspected the forts a few days later, he found surprisingly little damage. Fort St. Philip, he said, "with one or two slight exceptions, is to-day without a scratch." As for Jackson, despite the spectacular fires in the wooden buildings, "it is as strong to-day as when the first shell was fired at it." It could be that, as an engineer, Weitzel had a stake in showcasing their durability, but another officer affirmed that only four guns had been disabled and eleven carriages damaged at Fort Jackson during the mighty bombardment.[26] By the end of the war, the massive forts of the Third System had been rendered as obsolete as medieval castles, to the immense dismay of a generation of engineers who had labored to make them not only invincible but also esthetically pleasing—in 1862, however, they were still formidable.

Now, after so many months of preparation, hardship, and danger, all that remained for the troops was a leisurely cruise up the great river in absolute safety. The slight rebel resistance above the forts had been brushed aside, and so much dependence had been placed on the forts that proposals to strengthen defenses closer to New Orleans had never progressed. "All along the river on both sides are pleasant plantations with their niggers to work hoeing sugar cane, both men, women and children, the driver with his whip in his hand looking on," noted Shaftoe.[27] Although on board the same ship, another soldier offered quite a different perception, perhaps reflecting a different political orientation: "The negroes seem overjoyed as we pass the plantations. They leave their work and swing their hats and hoods and shout 'Hurrah for the Yankees.' . . . We went by some noble sugar plantations. A sugar house on each, and the negro quarters arranged so neat that there could be no fault found with them."[28] Hawkes wrote home, "Fields of sugar cane extending as far as the eye could reach, with the orange trees and the deep green of the tropical vegetation, was a scene ever to be remembered."[29] Somewhat ruefully, Fairbank observed that the slave huts, neatly arranged in rows, were "better houses than a great many live in there in Ware."[30]

In the early afternoon of May 1, the *Mississippi* came up to the New Orleans wharf alongside Farragut's triumphant warships. Various accounts give different times, partly because they were not recording the same stage of the process. Frederick Rice, who seems to offer the most reliable chronology, states that the ship anchored at New Orleans around 11:30 A.M., orders to disembark were issued around 3:30 P.M., and the soldiers commenced marching through the city between 4:30 and 5:00 that afternoon.[31] As they approached, the men could see and smell the remains of bonfires set by the Confederates to destroy valuable commodities like cotton as well as items of military use. Because the 31st Massachusetts had not actually landed during the attack on the forts, it was complete and organized on deck, a logical choice as the first Union regiment to enter the city. Having battled nothing more than the lice they had shared on the crowded vessel, the troops were supposedly in good condition, though they might have been a little unsteady on their feet. (Although they were supposed to be soldiers, not sailors, the men had spent forty-two of the seventy days since leaving Boston on ships, primarily the *Mississippi*.)

Much of the accumulated misery of those days was forgotten as the men prepared to land. "This has been one of the proudest days of my life!" wrote one soldier. "Secession is at a discount."[32] A sergeant in Company I exulted, "We shall all remember this day as long as we live."[33] In a major battle the consequences are usually evident almost immediately. With the loss of New Orleans, the Confederacy had received a probably mortal wound, but because the effects were largely economic and diplomatic, they took longer to be felt fully. Rather than cutting down a tree for quick removal, this was more like girdling it so that it died slowly.

4

THE OCCUPATION OF NEW ORLEANS

MAY–AUGUST 1862

Formed on deck in sight of the bitter, resentful New Orleans crowd, the soldiers of the 31st Massachusetts loaded their muskets, being sure to hold the balls up in full view before dropping them down the barrel "so that they can see we are loaded with balls and mean business."[1] Company by company they disembarked and confronted the seething mob, many in it wearing portions of Confederate uniforms and spitting curses and threats, punctuated by cheers for Jeff Davis or hometown favorite Gen. P. G. T. Beauregard. Accompanied by the regimental fifers and drummers playing "Yankee Doodle," with the 4th Wisconsin's regimental band playing other patriotic tunes, and under strict orders not to yield to provocation, the troops marched through the streets of the Crescent City. Although four field pieces were supposed to inspire awe, and "squads of mounted men on the flanks and in the rear did all in their power to keep the mob back, . . . [o]n our flanks especially were we hooted and jeered, some of the boys would get as close to us as they could and while keeping step with us would sing or whistle the Bonnie Blue flag, or I wish I was in Dixie."[2] In deep twilight they reached the Custom House, a massive five-story granite building originally planned by Beauregard but still lacking a roof. One soldier saw its incomplete state as "a proof of southern enterprise."[3] While some critics regarded these movements as dilatory, Butler asserted in his autobiography that it was intentional. He maintained that for various reasons, such as the fact that muzzle flashes would be easily visible, it was better to enter a hostile city after dark.[4] Here the 31st came to rest, using the second floor as quarters, except for one company that remained on the sidewalk posted as guards. Butler and his wife set up housekeeping in the Saint Charles Hotel, guarded by members of the 31st.

Many in the crowd strained to catch a glimpse of their conqueror, who had gained considerable notoriety even before he arrived. General Butler, inflamed by reports of a riotous mob and desecration of the flag, was prepared to rule the city harshly. Such activity would have reminded him of the situation in Baltimore almost exactly a year earlier. Moreover, most Northerners considered the South an inherently violent place. They noted incidents like the brutal attack on the defenseless Massachusetts senator Sumner on the floor of the Senate several years before, which was widely applauded in the South, as well as the Southern penchant for fighting duels and the intrinsic violence of the slave system, of which millions had recently read in *Uncle Tom's Cabin*. True, a Northerner, John Brown, had committed violent acts, but these could be dismissed as the work of a fanatic, not a central element of the culture. In this frame of mind, Butler launched his rule by issuing a stern proclamation setting out the conditions under which the turbulent city would be administered.

Members of the 31st were justifiably proud of being the first to march through the streets of New Orleans, even though they had not had to fight their way in. Therefore, they were shocked and enraged when they learned in early June 1862 of a May 24 column in the *Boston Journal*, a paper that circulated widely:

The first troops to come on shore was the 31st Massachusetts regiment. They landed from the steamship Mississippi soon after 5 o'clock. It was fully an hour after they landed before they took up the line of march. I had a good look at them and was much surprised to find a majority of the regiment were foreigners, and the balance looked like mere country boys. Some of the boys did not look to be over 14 years of age. They were very dirty. The officers were many of them fine looking men, but the privates looked feeble, dejected and woe-begon. I could not but pity them; many of the boys had tears in their eyes, and all expressed astonishment that there was not one person to receive them with a welcome. The people present looked upon them with as much indifference as they would have done at a ship load of cattle. There was disposition on the part of the people to treat them with unkindness, but every one was surprised to see such inferior looking troops, and find them so poorly drilled. They had the appearance of a lot of prisoners. One other regiment landed and the two marched downtown, headed by General Butler, as far as the Custom House, where they are quartered.

In their outrage, men in the 31st developed at least two theories to account for the devastating review, both of which were flawed. James Tupper's opinion was that "some miserable secessionist wrote that."[5] Yet the offensive piece came at the end of a string of periodic reports that seemed not at all pro-secession; later reports—assuming they were written by the same person—are quite favorable to Butler. It seems unlikely that a paper like the Boston Journal would solicit news from an avowed secessionist, and the tactic of one country trying to influence opinion in another by planting unfavorable news was not then widely practiced. Most likely, the report came from one of the many Northerners who had business in the Crescent City.

Luther Fairbank offered another explanation. "No citizen of New Orleans wrote it," he declared, attributing it instead to "disappointed rivals" in the 26th Massachusetts.[6] According to him, the two regiments fought constantly while together on the Mississippi, "each brag[ging] that their regt would be the first to land and their brass band be the one that would escort Butler through the streets." It is true that the 31st was later chosen to be the general's bodyguard, which would have galled jealous members of the 26th. This part of Fairbank's theory is believable, for the 26th Massachusetts was made up predominantly of men from urban eastern Massachusetts, mustered and trained in Lowell. Many had served previously in the short-term 6th Massachusetts, the regiment attacked earlier by the Baltimore mob. Expressing the longstanding animosity between the eastern and western sections of the state, they would have regarded the 31st as rubes. Governor Andrew, with unaccustomed generosity, had given the 26th to the expedition and did not attempt to take it back after he accepted for service the two regiments Butler had raised. The unit had been formed before the general began recruiting, and its members probably had a different political orientation than the Democrats Butler tried to enlist.

Fairbank's explanation is gratifying but presents a serious factual problem: the Journal column, though published on May 24, was dated May 1 by its source. At that time the 26th was still aboard ship, and it is questionable whether it could have witnessed the 31st disembarking and marching to the Custom House. Nor is it likely that anyone in that regiment would have been able to dispatch a timely report to Boston. Fairbank's theory would thus require misdating or later interference, either of which could be accomplished only with the connivance of the newspaper's editor, which seems unlikely.[7]

If the two comforting rationales become unsustainable, the *Journal* report remains troubling. By its members' own testimony, the 31st had been cooped up on the *Mississippi* for many days with poor food and water, no facilities for washing, and troubled by lice. Still, that would not entirely account for the state of wretchedness described in the article. Very few members of the regiment were in any sense foreigners, and how would an observer be able to discern that they were? Their age distribution was similar to all Union regiments at that time, if anything possibly older. The disparaging statements about the 31st stand out as virtually the only negative and vehement comment on any subject submitted by this New Orleans correspondent, nor do subsequent reports revisit the subject. A soldier in Company K, recruited in the Boston area, promised to send a rebuttal to the *Boston Herald*, but no such letter has been found.[8]

As soon as they settled into the Custom House, the Massachusetts troops, probably motivated more by curiosity than avarice, thoroughly ransacked the place. The building had been used as a post office, and the soldiers, with officers joining in, enjoyed perusing the undelivered mail. "We have great fun reading love letters that girls have written to their fellows in the army," chortled Fairbank, who reveled in the experience of writing with Confederate ink "on the desk of the paymasters of the Southern Confederacy Navy."[9] An abundance of Confederate currency, stamps, and letters seized at the Custom House found its way to Massachusetts as souvenirs.

The company that guarded General Butler at the Saint Charles occupied what was formerly the Bar Room, described colorfully by one of the soldiers: "It is large, of circular form, a marble counter runs around about one half— this is the bar. It was also [a] kind of general auction room. There are several stands and I have the testimony of a 'resident' that on two stated days every week there was an auction of 'niggers' held here, at which time liquor and blood flowed freely." He marveled at the prospect of "your boy as sleeping on the very spot where souls were formerly struck off to the highest bidder" but was pleased by the fact that "the room is lighted by gas, and with plenty of water in an adjoining room, it seems rather preferable to laying in the sand."[10]

So hasty was the Confederate evacuation of New Orleans that they left behind on a pier a diverse collection of more than four hundred bells. These items had sentimental as well as practical value, as they had been donated by schools, factories, churches, and private individuals throughout the state in the expectation that they would be melted down and cast into cannons and other implements of war for the Confederacy. Instead, probably with a wink from General Butler, they were auctioned off at a wharf in East Boston for their scrap value: thirteen cents a pound for brass, copper at twenty-one cents, and iron at seventeen dollars per ton. A few were preserved intact so that they might continue to ring in schools and churches, albeit in an unfamiliar atmosphere.[11]

In his general orders McClellan had expressed the hope that Butler could station his men across the river in Algiers and keep them out of New Orleans itself. Presumably, he was worried that they would succumb to the multitudinous temptations the city offered or the ever-present possibility of disease and that the sight of blue-coated soldiers could provoke riots. He also believed that without the soldiers on the streets, strong Union sentiment would come to the surface and make it possible to govern the city without overt military interference. It was true that in 1860 a considerable part of the Louisiana population had been Unionists or people who sought compromise short of secession. But the newly elected governor, Thomas O. Moore, had maneuvered the state into secession; once that faction took control, Union feelings were steadily suppressed.

Under these conditions, Butler decided to quarter most of his men in New Orleans, although he maintained outposts all around, including the captured forts. He attempted to work through the existing city administration, but it proved incapable or unwilling to cooperate. Thus, step by step, the general established a personal dictatorship in the captured city. In all of this, as he said in his memoirs, "I never received any direction or intimation from Washington or anywhere else how I should conduct the expedition or carry on the administration of the government."[12] In his early days in New Orleans, Butler did not attempt to occupy the entire city but stationed troops at several vital points, such as the Custom House, city hall, and the U.S. Mint, as well as the Saint Charles Hotel. Various companies of the 31st performed guard duty at one or another of these locations. Fairbank enjoyed his time at the mint, where "trees fill the large yard, and . . . makes it cool and shady," but Company D remained there only two days.[13]

As they settled in, the soldiers continued to be stunned by the persistent hostility they encountered. As one man wrote home in May: "At your distance it is hardly possible to conceive of the intense enmity of this people toward us. They will not recognize any of us upon the street, will not answer a civil question." More galling was that "ladies upon the streets insult our officers, their sex securing them from retaliation. This people are not susceptible to moral influence and fail altogether to appreciate the humanity that was exercised toward them in not burning their city, and the lenity General Butler is exercising toward them."[14]

Even Butler's numerous critics acknowledged his extraordinary capacity for work, and while his strategic sense might be debatable, no one questioned his organizational ability. In the absence of both guidance and organized opposition, he set about running the territory under his control according to his principles. After his first week in New Orleans, his attitude, an individualistic mixture of ire and astonishment, was expressed in a general order. (Many of his general orders, stamped by his distinct personality, are couched in more personal and emotional terms than was customary in the army): "The United States have sent land and naval forces here to fight and subdue rebellious armies in array against her authority. We find, substantially, only fugitive masses, runaway property burners, a whiskey-drinking mob, and starving citizens with their wives and children. It is our duty to call back the first, to punish the second, root out the third, [and] feed and protect the last."[15]

As Butler observed, economic disruption had left many of the poor inhabitants "in a starving condition."[16] Letters from men in the 31st are full of cost figures for common items, which struck them as excessive even by home standards. Some once-common commodities were simply not available: "Butter cannot be had at any price," wrote Frank Knight.[17] Many of those who depended on food handouts had been paid in Confederate money, which sellers now refused to accept. Among the thousands who swarmed around the Custom House waiting for food deliveries was one old man who Joshua Hawkes saw as symbolic. A veteran of the War of 1812, with a wooden leg as a reminder of that service, he had been refused aid by local authorities because he was a Unionist. When Butler's men gave him food, he exclaimed: "Thank God! Thank God! I've had nothing for three days. It's more than I expected."[18]

Butler found ways, some of them blunt, to feed the hungry population. Using supplies intended for Confederate forces and any other stores he could seize, he began massive distributions of food on May 12. Fairbank reported that the Federals distributed two hundred barrels of meat to "men, women and children of all nations."[19] "All nations" did not include African Americans, though, as Butler supplied them from other sources. The general was as yet no abolitionist, but by caring for the blacks he earned their gratitude, and they responded by telling him where their masters or employers had concealed valuables.[20] Consistent with policies he had espoused in Massachusetts, Butler made the rich, who he blamed for starting the war, pay for the support of the lower classes, which bore its consequences. The wealthy inhabitants—those who remained—were not likely to support him in any case.

Soldiers were surprised to learn that rations they disdained, such as hard-tack, were highly prized by the starving residents. One private swapped five crackers for a pint of blueberries, and others were able to sell portions of their meals.[21] Fairbank shared a similar experience: "if you don't like your dinner why only just step to the fence and you can trade for pies cakes or cigars or melons and such like."[22] Later, obviously amazed, he told the folks back home, "there is good respectable looking men and women will come in and give 20 cts for our dinner and sit down and eat it out of our dishes and are glad to get it."[23] Butler's efforts could not relieve hunger entirely, as Fairbank reported a few days later: "It would please you to see the crowd stand around the cooks stand when they deal out our hard tack (crackers). [E]ach one has his money in his hand." He sold his own crackers three for a picayune (five cents) and also "sold my dinner for two bits day before yesterday. [T]hey must be in a starving condition to be around so. [S]ome negro came and want to buy crackers for massa when we first got paid off."[24]

When the troops entered the city, a common taunt from the jeering crowd was "Yellow Jack will get you," referring to endemic yellow fever. Northern soldiers would have no resistance, so the snarled threats had a fearful basis. Soldiers in the Thirty-first developed their own effective non-medical response to the maledictions: "when any one begins to tell us about our dying with the yellow jack we tell them that we have the small pox that we can let out against Jack and it will lick him all out."[25] Butler had conducted a personal study of "Jack," and although its cause remained unknown, he concluded that its progress was related to filthy conditions. With minimal help from the local government, he made the city cleaner than it had been in decades. He used the occasion to land another jab at West Point, saying that "[sanitary] science is not taught" there, although "the want of its proper application to the troops in the field kills more men than are killed by bullets."[26]

Any men who objected to Butler's rule had the option of joining the Confederate army, or at least the secessionist home guard. One member of the 31st observed: "Especially were those fellows who wore the Confederate uniforms most insulting. Many of them had deserted their regiments while en route from the city, while others had belonged to the Home Guards, and had hid themselves away in their Homes during the surrender, and now came forth full of that bravado which is always to be found in cowards."[27] The high-born women were a different matter. They remained unrestrained in their vituperation, insulting or spitting on Union officers, throwing waste on them from their balconies, or making conspicuous gestures of contempt, such as ostentatiously getting off streetcars when Federal soldiers boarded. The situation was undoubtedly galling to Butler, who posted a sign on the door to his office that read, according to Lt. Joseph Hallett, "There is no difference between a he adder and a she adder."[28] The women's behavior became increasingly intolerable to the Northern officers, and after hearing their complaints, the general devised another of his imaginative solutions. As he said, it was hardly possible to pursue the women into their boudoirs or drag them through the streets; instead, he issued General Order 28, the famed "Woman Order," dated May 15, 1862:

> As the officers and soldiers of the United States have been subject to repeated insults from the women (calling themselves ladies) of New Orleans, in return for the most scrupulous non-interference and courtesy on our part, it is ordered that hereafter when any female shall, by word, gesture, or movement, insult or show contempt for any officer or soldier of the U.S., she shall be regarded and held liable to be treated as a woman of the town plying her avocation.[29]

This provoked instant outrage, some of it staged, throughout the South and among certain elements in England. It appeared that Butler was assaulting the central myth of Southern (white) womanhood by declaring that they were all prostitutes. Southern propaganda played up this interpretation to the fullest, trying to renew patriotism in the aftermath of several damaging defeats. In fact, as Butler explained, proper behavior toward prostitutes was to ignore them, and his proclamation indeed seemed to bring a rapid decline in offensive incidents. There was no reconciliation, but a chilly modus vivendi now prevailed. Butler's subtle approach to the problem earned him the indelible alliterative nickname "Beast." The seasoned attorney had a thick skin on some parts of his person and probably found this epithet amusing.

According to one account, another unflattering nickname came about through actions of the 31st Massachusetts. Some members of Company K were stationed at the Adams House Hotel and promptly "began to investigate the cupboards and closets to see if the former inmates had left anything behind that could be converted into cash."[30] They discovered some spoons with the hotel monogram, which they sold to a pawn shop and converted to "several canteens of whiskey." Later, the "old Jew" who ran the shop testified that Butler's soldiers had brought the spoons there, but he could hardly know to which regiment they belonged. This report somehow became transformed into an allegation that the general himself had stolen or confiscated the tableware. He probably found the nickname "Spoons" Butler less amusing, as it highlighted the persistent accusation that he and brother Andrew Jackson had enriched themselves through private transactions during their tenure in Louisiana.[31]

Northern soldiers were amazed at how peaceful the occupied city soon became. Shock at the sudden fall of New Orleans and Butler's severe rule had overawed the hostile part of the population so that soldiers could walk the streets without being annoyed physically or verbally. The general himself stirred up some excitement one night by ordering a "long roll" of drums and firing a rocket to call his troops to assemble. Many thought the rebels were attacking, but it was merely a test of how quickly the regiment could respond, and the 31st Massachusetts performed admirably. Only thirty-eight minutes elapsed for the men, most of whom had been sleeping, to dress, form up, and march to the Saint Charles. With the insults of the *Boston Journal* article still smoldering, Fairbank boasted, "Now I call that pretty quick time for a regt that has no officer, is owned by no bragade [sic], and made up of small boys and broken down men to get up out of a sound sleep, dress, fall into line, and march 1 ½ miles to the St Charles."[32]

The regiment had not been paid since leaving Lowell, but that drought came to an end on June 23, when the men received four months' pay. It is hard to know how they got by until then; perhaps they had been able to hold on to remnants of their previous pay or had received money from home. As noted, they were able to trade rations for money or more interesting food once in New Orleans. One correspondent reported that the troops sent home thirty thousand dollars by Adams Express, being two-thirds of the collective total the regiment received.[33] It is not known how he obtained these figures, but the ratio is believable and testifies to the ingrained sense of responsibility of these mostly rural New England volunteers. In their joy at being paid, the soldiers were probably unaware that it had been made possible by another of Butler's devious maneuvers. As described in his autobiography, there were few "greenbacks" available in New Orleans, not nearly enough to pay all the men. The general developed a scheme with Adams Express in which the company returned to Butler the money the soldiers were sending home in exchange for his voucher, which allowed him to recycle the same greenbacks.[34] This method would only work if the men sent the bulk of their pay home and thus helps confirm that they did.

Independence Day proved to be rather dull by New England standards. The 1st Maine Battery fired salutes at sunrise and noon.[35] Gunboats in the river fired several salutes, and the 31st marched through the streets to Butler's residence and fired a volley of ten blank rounds.[36] Tupper noted that an un-usually large number of U.S. flags were evident.[37] Rumors regularly circulated that General Beauregard or Maj. Gen. Earl Van Dorn was approaching with an enormous army to retake New Orleans, but as time passed these alarming stories lost their potency, residents finally concluding that the Federal army was there to stay. Butler did not use the occasion for a patriotic address; perhaps he was afraid to reveal how few troops he had available or did not want to risk having only a paltry civilian crowd show up.

In his initial report to Secretary of War Stanton after the fall of New Orleans, Butler asserted, "Mobile is ours whenever we choose, and can better wait."[38] But he and Flag Officer Farragut found that they lacked the strength both to hold the Crescent City and to capture another Gulf port. Farragut was eager to disentangle from the sticky situation he had got himself into at New Orleans and wanted to open up more of the Mississippi before his colleagues farther north could do so. He moved his fleet, accompanied by a force of fifteen hundred soldiers (including the 30th Massachusetts but not the 31st) under Brig. Gen. Thomas Williams, a regular-army officer, upriver and occupied the state capital of Baton Rouge. The combined force then came up before the Confederate stronghold of Vicksburg in late June, accompanied by Porter's mortar fleet. While the naval guns could not be elevated enough to batter Vicksburg, high on a bluff, neither were the mortars effective. Lacking either naval or ground forces sufficient to take the position, Farragut decided on June 28 to run past the defenses as he had done below New Orleans. Once again he succeeded, another dress rehearsal for his exploit at Mobile later in the war (one that would earn him lasting glory and a superb statue in New York City by the famed sculptor Augustus St. Gaudens).

Having accomplished that, with risk and loss, Farragut found that his overall position was scarcely improved. Butler, true to character, devised a scheme to dig a channel that would divert the Mississippi into a new course—the sort of thing it did regularly of its own accord—that would leave Vicksburg inland and impotent. Using slaves who had escaped or been taken from surrounding plantations, Williams began this project. It was not an inherently bad idea— General Grant later adopted it—but the river defeated the plan by dropping to an unusually low level. Williams commenced another canal, this time using his own troops as well as plantation labor. Described as a "martinet" with little concern for his men, he drove them brutally, amassing a casualty list that would have been considered severe if it had occurred in battle.[39] One of the suffering regiments was the 9th Connecticut, a largely Irish unit that Butler had taken in hand at Camp Chase when it appeared unmanageable to authorities in its home state. Having been molded into an effective organization, many of its members found final rest in unmarked graves hastily dug in the Mississippi mud.

Though they may not have been aware, the 31st Massachusetts nearly shared this miserable fate. Butler had some fifteen thousand men in his division, but he soon learned that, after garrisoning outlying posts, providing for administrative functions, and allowing for sickness, he had relatively few effectives to send on expeditions. On June 6 he informed Williams that he was about to send him the 31st Massachusetts, a Vermont regiment, and some cavalry and artillery units.[40] Fortunately for the 31st, outside events caused Butler to reconsider. On the tenth he advised Stanton: "By the news which has come . . . of the repulse of [Maj.] Gen. [Nathaniel] Banks [in the Shenandoah Valley] and the danger of the capital, now aided by exaggerated reports of the rout of the troops under General McClellan, the city is so much moved that weakening my force here too much might possibly provoke a demonstration. . . . I have scarcely 3500 men in the city fit for duty, and to take away a good regiment would be hazardous."[41] Tupper was aware that the only regiments in the city were his own, the 26th Massachusetts, the 13th Connecticut, and the 12th Maine, with the 1st Maine Battery as the only artillery.[42] If a private, even a well-informed one like Tupper, had this knowledge, it must have been known to the enemy as well. Butler had demonstrated that he did not hesitate to subject regiments he had personally organized to danger; indeed, he preferred and often requested New England soldiers for hazardous duties. Fortuitous circumstances thus spared dozens of men in the 31st Massachusetts from disease and death while digging a canal.

Increasingly worried about a threat to Baton Rouge, Butler ordered Williams to return there from Vicksburg on July 16. Farragut likewise saw the futility of persisting up the Mississippi and came back down the river a week later. Thus the first campaign against the Confederate citadel ended in abject failure, pushing the problem into another year and a much more costly struggle. The same was true of Mobile. On the Confederate side, Major General Van Dorn replaced Maj. Gen. Mansfield Lovell, who was being made the scapegoat for the loss of New Orleans. Van Dorn ordered former U.S. vice president and now Confederate major general John C. Breckinridge to retake the Louisiana capital. Ironically, Breckinridge was the man who Butler had, with some reluctance, supported for president in 1860. For all its immensity, the Civil War sometimes spun in a tight vortex. A substantial battle was fought at Baton Rouge on August 5 in which neither side covered itself with glory. The Confederates had counted on support from the ironclad ram CSS *Arkansas,* but its commander was not present, and the vessel needed major overhaul. It made a valiant effort to join the fray, but engine failure disabled it and forced its destruction, a severe blow to Confederate efforts to defend the waterways.[43] The Union garrison, supported by gunboats, barely held on, but Butler withdrew it from the capital city on August 21. In the battle the 30th Massachusetts was held in reserve, while the 31st was not present. General Williams was killed during the fighting.

Soon afterward, some 350 sick and wounded men arrived in New Orleans from Baton Rouge. Asa Wheeler wrote, "I was at the wharf when they were brought on shore,—some were able to walk,—others were conveyed on stretchers borne by 2 men to the different ambulances which were waiting for them."[44] Others were taken to the Marine Hospital, which Hawkes reported as "filled (some 700) with sick brought from up the river—one of our boys who is on guard there was up to camp this morning. He describes it as the saddest place he was ever in, the men being literally wasted away from exposure &c., many having what is called the swamp fever."[45]

Also downriver came rebel prisoners: "There were some fifty of them and a hardy looking set of fellows. They were mostly Kentuckians and Louisianians with some Albamians [sic]. There were two or three of the former as *rough* specimens of humanity as ever I saw." Hawkes may have been dismayed to see that "only a *very few* seemed glad to be captured, the rest had no hesitation in expressing their determination to *fight us* if they could get [the] chance." He further observed, "When first brought down their clothing was filthy in the extreme—it was of all sorts, few having anything like a uniform." Donations of clothing enabled some of the captives to look "quite respectable."[46] If the North succeeded in its war aims, these men would be Hawkes's fellow citizens, voting in the same elections and sending representatives to the same Congress.

Tupper, who was detached from the regiment as a brigade quartermaster clerk and had relatively free run of New Orleans, made similar observations on seeing the steamer *Diana* bring down a load of rebel prisoners from Baton Rouge: "There are all sorts of looking fellows among them, gray-headed old rebels and young guerillas. No one had a full uniform. Some have a uniform coat & some pants & cap & all varieties of shirts, calico, etc." Their behavior, according to Tupper, was different than what Hawkes witnessed: "They seem to enjoy themselves first-rate & our boys are on good terms with them. They brought them their supper of coffee & hard bread while I was there. One prisoner hallooed 'Fall in, rebels,' & they gathered around the rations laughing & joking." He recounted a story that one reason the Southerners lost at Baton Rouge was that they stopped to loot the Yankee camps they had overrun because they had not been fed before going into battle, that one dead rebel was even found clutching a loaf of pilfered bread.[47]

On May 15 and 16, after two weeks in the city, the 31st Massachusetts was replaced at the Custom House by the 13th Connecticut and took up quarters at Annunciation Square, then a suburb.[48] The site was "a Square enclosed with an iron fence, . . . laid out in squares and plots," as William Rich described, with drainage so poor that water stood on the surface after any substantial rain.[49] The camp was named Morewood, honoring the woman in Pittsfield, Sarah A. Morewood, who had donated a flag to the "Pittsfield Company."[50] At the square, as Lieutenant Hallett observed, "the spire of Bishop [Leonidas]

Polk's Episcopal Church cast a shadow over our tents. The good bishop had become militant when the state seceded, had been commissioned a general by Jefferson Davis and, deserting his parish, was then in the Confederate Army." Perhaps Hallett was employing irony when he added, "we were thereby deprived of the sermons of an eloquent preacher."[51]

Colonel Gooding and other officers of the 31st settled into comfortable, "finely furnished" homes around the square that had been abandoned by their owners.[52] At first the enlisted men suffered in their tents from the heat, but in mid-June they were moved to better quarters. Various companies took up residence in cotton presses, sometimes called cotton sheds, in the vicinity of the square. Enclosed within a high board fence were five of these buildings, each described as a "long roomy shed some 100 feet long by 60 wide, built of brick with a floor . . . [and] open on one side."[53] The brick construction would have moderated the temperature to some extent. As some of the soldiers noted, these buildings were empty because of the collapse of the regional economy. Two companies remained in tents as of June 15, according to Hawkes, and it is not certain when or if they moved into a cotton press.[54]

At the same time, the troops were issued mosquito bars—frames supporting fine gauze that were large enough to cover a man's body. At Annunciation Square the men were able to bathe daily, which put them in an extremely rare class of soldiery in that war. The surgeon (probably at the brigade or division level) wisely forbade drilling in the hottest part of the day so as not to wear out the men. Together, these measures provided as idyllic an existence as possible. With good reason, Fairbank summarized, "we live like fighting cocks without the fight that we see very little of;" as he noted, the only fighting took place within the regiment when some men got drunk.[55] Providing mosquito bars, which must have cost a considerable amount in that quantity, impressed the soldiers with Butler's concern for their welfare. In general, they supported his stern administration of the city, which made their lives much more tolerable. In a letter written as the netting was being handed out, Fairbank concluded, "Gen. Butler is doing everything for the comfort and health of the troops."[56] A private in Company K, Timothy Z. Smith, concurred, writing that Butler was "a 'perfect brick,' and it may be said of him that no man has more warm enthusiastic friends, or more bitter enemies."[57]

In an indication that the regiment was being prepared for an extended stay, Fairbank and others were set to work building bunks. Fairbank was not inclined to weary himself at this assignment, but even if he had wanted to labor on the project, progress was often hindered by the lack of materials. He drew lumber, when it was available, from another cotton press, called the Reading after its owner.[58] This quartermaster depot was another guarded by men from the 31st. Fairbank's prevailing attitude was that he was "too lazy to work hard, and besides, a soldier has no business to fret himself—at least that is my principle. O, what a merry life to lead, this being a soldier!"[59] He had apparently not overexerted himself doing similar work at the Otis factory back home in Ware and concluded, "it has not help[ed] me in the least going to work for Uncle Sam. [H]e is an easy task master, but I am afraid when he discharges his workmen he will turn out a good many lazy men into the world, again."[60]

In his spare time, of which he appeared to have an abundance, Fairbank wandered into "one of the tobacco buildings where they barrel it up for the manufacturers." Here he made a startling discovery: The tobacco "is pressed in large hogsheads instead of barrels and any body that chews would be sick to see the old segar stumps that are pressed in with it. [T]hese stumps are probably picked up in the streets and groceries. [O]ne hogshead that I see was nearly half filled with these stubs."[61] Since he smoked rather than chewed, he must have decided that he had nothing to fear hygienically.

General Butler was not one to undergo more discomfort than was necessary, and he improved his situation by taking over the residence of Confederate major general David E. Twiggs (1790–1862). President Lincoln on July 12 had signed the Confiscation Act of 1862, permitting such property seizures, but by then Butler had already taken the Twiggs mansion.[62] This was a calculated action, for Twiggs, who had been U.S. commander in Texas in 1861, surrendered that state to the Confederacy when it might not have been entirely necessary. Reviled in the North as a traitor, he accepted a Confederate commission that March, at which time he was probably the South's highest-ranking military officer. He was placed in command of the department that included Louisiana, but at seventy-one he was slowed by age, a shadow of the powerful figure he had once been. Unable to inspect the numerous posts under his command, he pleaded to be relieved and was replaced by General Lovell in October 1861.

Twiggs was aware of his reputation in the North, and as Union forces approached New Orleans in May 1862, he decided that his wisest course was to flee. As Tupper phrased it, "Gen. Twiggs, the old traitor, lived here in the city till we came, but when we got around the old man had fled with his daughter."[63] The retired general returned to his ancestral home in Georgia, where he died a few months later. Members of the 31st went through his house on fashionable Prytania Street soon afterward but found nothing of current military value. With Butler and some of his staff people now living there and using it as headquarters, it became yet another facility for the regiment to guard. In July Richard Underwood wrote that he was "on steady duty" there.[64]

Considering the misfortunes the regiment had endured early in its history, it was lucky to escape both the Vicksburg expedition and the Battle of Baton Rouge. Instead, it was occupied with guarding a number of posts in and around New Orleans, escorting and protecting Unionists, performing a variety of provost-marshal duties, and searching out those who were aiding the Confederacy. In conducting these diffuse activities, the men daily encountered complex social and economic situations that could hardly have been anticipated or taught in training. Probably accustomed to thinking of the South as a uniform bloc, they must have been astonished by the human diversity they observed. One of the most troublesome issues had to do with slaves. Despite Butler's direct request for instructions, the Lincoln administration resolutely refused to take a firm public stand on the subject.

In Louisiana the difficulty was compounded by the actions of one of Butler's favorite officers, Brigadier General Phelps. A passionate abolitionist and a regular-army officer, a combination of which the Vermonter was a rare representative, it is a wonder how he survived in that environment. Butler had never met Phelps until they were stationed at Fortress Monroe but came to respect him despite immense differences in temperament, appearance, and political attitude. He had acquired Phelps's services by strong direct appeal. In earlier requesting that the Vermonter be promoted to brigadier, he wrote, "although some of the regular officers will when applied to say that he is not in his right mind, the only evidence I have seen of it is a deep religious enthusiasm upon the subject of Slavery, which in my judgment does not unfit him to fight the battles of the North."[65]

Placed in command of Fort Parapet, a post on the Mississippi near Carrollton, approximately seven miles from downtown New Orleans, Phelps began to enact his abolitionist principles, encouraging slaves to desert and sometimes taking them from plantations. He treated them as free labor, supported their dependents at government expense, and began to train some of the men as soldiers, all without the authorization of Butler and certainly not the approval of the administration in Washington. This behavior irritated other officers, among them Capt. Edward Page Jr. of the 31st Massachusetts, who was responsible for repairing a levee, preventing crimes by soldiers and slaves, and protecting Union sympathizers who had safeguards from Butler. The captain informed Butler that it was impossible to carry out these duties "if the soldiers from Camp Parapet are allowed to range the country, insult the planters, and entice negroes away from their plantations." He added, "If on any of the Plantations here a negro is punished when he most deserves it, the fact becoming known at General Phelps' camp, a party of soldiers are sent immediately to liberate them, and with orders to bring them to Camp." Page gave several examples and concluded that while "such acts are permitted, it is utterly impossible to call upon the negroes for any labor, as they say that they have only to go to the fort to be free, and are therefore very insolent to their masters." The captain also complained that Phelps had sent down eighty contraband women and children in the expectation that Page would feed them.[66]

Butler displayed unusual patience as Phelps disregarded orders and suggestions. Eventually, the commanding general ordered him to use some former slaves on a construction project. Phelps angrily objected, saying that he was not going to become a slave driver, and submitted his resignation. Butler did not accept this and refused to grant a leave of absence to him "in the face of an enemy," but he did forward the request to Washington, where it was approved.[67] Phelps's stormy career ended back home in Brattleboro, Vermont.[68]

At the time of his quarrel with Phelps, Butler shared and expounded the general opinion of white officers that liberated slaves would make poor military material. The evolution of his thinking on that subject is a microcosm of the overall Northern attitude, brought about largely by necessity. Butler's first step in that direction occurred in September with his adoption into Federal service of the Native Guard, an organization of free blacks to help defend New Orleans (thus making it impossible for the South to argue that he was fomenting a slave uprising). Apparently trying to make this move appear less threatening, Butler noted of the men in this unit that "the darkest . . . will be about the complexion of the late Mr. [Daniel] Webster."[69] Federal officials accepted the word of guard recruits that they were freemen; there was no reliable means of confirming their status even had they wanted to.[70] Although conducted under special circumstances, this may represent the first recruitment of African Americans into the Union army. Years later, in a vastly different political climate, Butler asserted this in his autobiography, proclaiming the Native Guards as "the first regiment of colored troops ever mustered into the service of the United States during the War of the Rebellion."[71] It is probably coincidental that the Emancipation Proclamation followed soon afterward, though it did not take effect until January 1863. Butler continued his efforts by mustering two more African American regiments. All of the recruits affirmed that they were free, which was physically true at that moment—how they had attained that status was not investigated.

With customary activism, Butler pursued other kinds of recruitment. As early as May 16 he had advised Stanton, "I can enlist a Regiment or more here, if the Department think it desirable, of true and loyal men." When he added archly, "I do not think however that *Governor Moore would* commission the officers," he undoubtedly was reminding the secretary of his dispute with Andrew over that issue.[72] Granted permission, the general quickly signed up underemployed whites, many of them foreigners, as well as former Confederates, including paroled veterans of the Fort Jackson and Fort St. Philip garrisons. Standards were probably lowered for these volunteers, leading Tupper to write: "They will let anybody out of Prison if they will enlist. More recruits have been got for the Louisiana Regiment out of prisons than palaces."[73] In little more than three months, Butler recruited a full infantry regiment and three cavalry companies of avowedly loyal men. He also filled the depleted ranks of his existing regiments, the 31st Massachusetts among them, with twelve hundred newcomers.[74] Tupper had his concerns: "These recruits, many of them make good soldiers, a good many of them have been in the Confederate service, but no reliance can be placed on them. They will desert, steal, & had better be in prison than anywhere else."[75] Notable among the New Orleans volunteers were four men named Schill—aged eighteen, nineteen, twenty-one, and sixty—who all signed up on May 12, 1862, and joined Company A. It is not known whether the three youngest were brothers, but the oldest may have been the father of at least some of them. While the three youths served to the end of their term, the older man died of disease in October 1863. Many local Irishmen replenished the ranks of the 9th Connecticut, perhaps reuniting with neighbors who had taken a different ship out of Cobh.[76]

Colonel Gooding was determined to secure a band, and local recruiting helped achieve that goal. Tupper soon was pleased to report that "every night they play in the square popular national airs."[77] In one of his reports to the home folks, "C" observed that the addition of music marked "the beginning of a new era in the history of the regiment."[78] Gooding did not remain in New Orleans to enjoy the music for long, as on June 10 he was placed in command of Fort Jackson, where the 26th Massachusetts was stationed.[79]

It seems that there was a concerted push to improve the quality of regiments like the 31st Massachusetts. On May 25, in Butler's first month in New Orleans, he sent Secretary Stanton a revealing exposition of his thinking on recruitment and health: "I am further inclined to believe that the idea that our men here cannot stand the climate, and therefore the negroes must be freed and armed as an acclimated force, admits of serious debate." Butler supported this assertion: "My command has been either here or on the way from Ship Island since the first of May, some of them on shipboard in the river since the 17th of April. All the deaths in the General Hospital in this city since we have been here are only 13 from all causes; two of these being accidental." He concluded, "From diseases at all peculiar to the climate I do not believe we have lost in the last thirty days one-fifth of one percent in the whole command, taking into account also the infirm and debilitated who ought never to have passed the surgeon's examination and come here."[80]

At that point Butler was still arguing against the need to employ black troops, but the key phrases may be those at the end. He was undoubtedly correct in asserting that in the eagerness to recruit, which could bring officer status to those who succeeded, many men slipped through who should not have been enlisted. A letter published in the *Springfield Republican* during this period supports Butler's position: "But send us *men* and not *moribund* bodies. Better draft at once than send such recruits as were admitted into some of our late regiments." Taking issue with the editor, who had complained of the "unnecessary strictures in the examinations at Worcester" now that the number to draw from was reduced, the writer asserted, "I doubt if you will find a surgeon or officer who has served six months in the army to support you." He added that many conditions that led to discharge were preexisting: "No men with flat foot, hernias, stiff joints, or inclined to rheumatism should be received. They will not last six months." In a ringing conclusion, he declared, "We might as well have 300,000 babies as to have that number made up of men whose organs and functions are not perfect."[81]

Judging by the results, Butler made a determined effort to sort out defectives, much as he had done to winnow the Massachusetts militia before the war began. In the months of May, June, and July 1862, eighty-two men were discharged for disability from the 31st Massachusetts, the great majority in the period June 16–22. This total was by no means evenly distributed among the companies, with only two discharged from Company C but sixteen from Company I (all eighteen on June 20, in what amounted to a major purge). It is possible that around that time a ship was due to sail north, which could return the sickly men to healthier climes. Among those discharged was probably the only resident of Cape Cod in the 31st Massachusetts. Bearing a characteristic Cape Cod name, Ira Nickerson, this forty-four-year-old fisherman from Harwich served only four months in Company K before being sent home on June 16. It is revealing that he was able to endure the rigors of deep-sea fishing, but serving in the army broke his health. Somewhat contradicting Butler's assertions about overall good health, eighteen men in the regiment died during those three months. Altogether, the regiment lost something in the range of 10 percent of its strength in that period, so it is not surprising that local recruitment was an appealing prospect.

Another three men were removed from the ranks after being convicted by a judge of the provost court. This was made into an instructive ceremony on June 20 when two were drummed out of camp at dress parade. "One of them was Old Sullivan, put and kept in irons for stabbing Capt. Lee at Pittsfield," noted Underwood. A great crowd watched as the disgraced men, surrounded by four guards in the first file; two in the next, one on each side of the prisoners; and two more behind them at charge bayonets, advanced in procession to the accompaniment of the Rogues March.[82] This was repeated for the third offender on June 22. The two other than Sullivan were privates in Company I, one of whom was dismissed "for disobedience and recklessness."[83] Sullivan had been tried on April 1, while the regiment was still on Ship Island, and apparently had been hauled in chains through all the regiment's travels from Camp Seward to this public square in New Orleans.[84] Underwood reported a fourth undesirable drummed out on July 3.[85]

Earlier, some members of the 31st had been present for another, and more consequential, public spectacle. Butler had been infuriated on learning that the U.S. flag at the mint had been torn down and desecrated in the interval between Farragut's arrival and his own and vowed to punish the offender. Almost immediately after arriving in the city, his troops arrested William B. Mumford for the deed. After trial by a military tribunal on May 30, Mumford was sentenced to be hanged in the courtyard of the mint on June 7. In unmistakable symbolism Fairbank noted (although not confirmed by other sources) that "the scaffold was made of the flag staff that he pulled the flag from."[86] Despite pleas from Mumford's family and others, Butler, in an act of calculated vengeance, carried out the sentence. He thus demonstrated that he meant business but at the same time created a Southern martyr. Tupper, with his strain of independent thinking, was unimpressed: "For my part, although I like to see the course of action which indicates the power & strength of our government, I don't think Mumford ought to have been hung more than 10,000 others in the City. . . .This poor fellow who, in the excitement of the hour & urged on by a mob, tears down the flag when our army was not yet in the City, hung. I can't see the justice of the thing."[87] Illustrating the complexity of his character, Butler took care of Mrs. Mumford after the war, aiding her when she was in danger of losing her house and her employment.[88]

Nettleton's sharp comment about "300,000 babies" was prompted by a subject much on the soldiers' minds at that moment: recruitment. McClellan's Peninsular Campaign (March–July 1862) and western battles like Shiloh (April 6–7, 1862) showed that the demands of war were insatiable beyond what anyone could have imagined in the bonnie spring of 1861. To feed this human furnace, the Lincoln administration obtained legislation in July 1862 to call up 300,000 militiamen for up to nine months. At the same time, under an earlier authorization, the government was recruiting another 300,000 troops to serve for three years. The overall effect was mitigated somewhat by a formula that counted one three-year man as four nine-months' men so that the total called up was considerably less than 600,000. By then the prewar militia had lost whatever structure it possessed as the individuals or entire units most capable of active service had volunteered. Each state was assigned a quota based on population; in Massachusetts, at least, that number was distributed among the counties and towns, also by population.

The subject was intensely interesting to the men of the 31st Massachusetts, who would be serving alongside the new recruits and might be acquainted personally with them, if any of the new Massachusetts regiments were assigned to the Department of the Gulf. There was also a current of envy and resentment because the new men were being offered bounties of varying amounts, which had not generally been the practice for the earlier volunteer regiments. Veteran troops, as the 31st Massachusetts now were, held conflicting feelings toward the newcomers—gratitude for the relief they would provide mixed with a taint of anger that it had taken a combination of threats (conscription) and bribes (bounties) to propel them forward. While William Rich and Thomas Norris took a certain pride in observing that Massachusetts, and the North in general, had not found it necessary to resort to conscription, Frederick Rice, characteristically, emphasized the opposite point. In early 1863 he wrote: "The best news I've heard lately is the passage of the Conscription Act. I hope it'll catch all those fellows that have been trying so hard to stay at home."[89] Norris displayed the internal clash of opinions, as he often referred to the nine-month recruits as "$200 men."[90]

Returning to the subject of conscription later in the year, Norris sounded almost as bellicose as Rice, with whom he was probably acquainted only slightly, if at all. By then, conscription was fully in force, while Norris had attained his eighteenth birthday. From this platform of greater maturity, he wrote:

> You say that they are going to commence the draft again next Jan. and I hope they will, and I hope this time that they will take every able bodied man and put them right in the field, for now is the time when they are wanted the most. I don't see what in time is the matter with the men of the North. Are they "*cowards*," or what is it. I should think when they heard that there were men wanted that they would rise in one body and show some of the blood of their "*Fore Fathers*" and make one *desperate strike,* and I'll *wager* this thing would be settled up in "short order," but no they had rather stay at home and hear the news of their countrymen being shot down.[91]

Private Tupper entered the discussion of recruitment with an astonishingly caustic remark: "To fool 100,000 more young, green patriots to take up arms to fight for slavery, Brigade Sutlers, & contractors for Army shoes is tough."[92] Subsequently, he used the occasion to express his immense disdain for his hometown of Hardwick, sardonically advising men from there to enlist: "I can't imagine one single reason why they should want to stay in Hardwick. If I was out of the army I should want more than $100 bounty to keep me at Hardwick."[93] His father, Rev. Martyn Tupper, had been the first pastor of the breakaway First Calvinistic Society of Hardwick when it was formed in 1828. He remained in that post until 1835 but then returned to be reinstalled in 1852.[94] Though not born in Hardwick, James Tupper had spent nearly half his life there, a familiarity that left him singularly unimpressed—he apparently was one of those whose main incentive for enlisting was to get away from home. Conversely, military life made Thomas Norris appreciate his own hometown all the more: "I have got it into my head that *Somerville* is my home and I do not know how it will seem to live anywhere else, and I do not think that I shall ever have such a good home again as that one afforded me."[95]

In his frequent wandering around the ever-fascinating Louisiana metropolis, Tupper developed an ability to discern subtle changes of mood. Like everyone, military or civilian, his antennae were constantly twitching to detect signs of how the struggle was progressing. At times he found indications that gave cause for hope, as when he wrote that "New Orleans is getting to be quite a respectable city. The people consider Yankees just as good as anybody else, & as I walk along the street folks bow politely as though I was an old resident."[96] In a similar vein he noted that "no man is afraid now to speak Union sentiments or raise the Union flag."[97] He was heartened by the number of U.S. flags he saw on July 4 and thought there would have been more if fabric had been available. Observing an enthusiastic Union meeting boosted his spirits, but watching the demonstration that occurred when three hundred Confederates were exchanged had the opposite effect: "There was a large crowd on the levee & the ladies waved their handkerchiefs to the deluded rebels who go out to battle against their country."[98] In the absence of public-opinion surveys, all these accounts were impressionistic and probably influenced by each man's most recent experience. A reasonable summation was provided by the correspondent of the *Pittsfield Sun:* "While we meet on every hand a courtesy and politeness that is studied, we are never relieved of the impression that it is cold and studied."[99] This represented a degree of improvement, however, over the "intense enmity" he had observed early in the occupation.[100] He seemed surprised to note a change in spirit, which he attributed to the fact that Butler by then required inhabitants to take an oath of allegiance before being allowed to conduct regular business.

Sickness of varying severity seemed widespread, though Butler may have been correct in claiming that it was not "at all peculiar to the climate" like the dread yellow fever. Much of the illness was probably due to unfamiliar water and food, which were even less clean than what the men were accustomed to.

Within the first month in New Orleans, one soldier in the 31st observed: "The hot weather and bad water begin to have a bad effect on the troops. Quite a number are sick and complaining."[101] The army had confiscated the Saint Charles Hotel for use as a hospital. Its physical elegance remained, but after a few weeks the atmosphere became greatly altered: "The surroundings of the hospital were not conducive to a rapid building up. In every ward and room lay strong men reduced to skeletons, with not a vestige of color in their faces, and wild cries of those in delirium rang through the corridors." Every day the dead were carried out, preceded by a corporal's guard as escort. "There was an indescribable sadness in their measured tread and the dull roll of the muffled drums as they passed down the street to the lone burial ground." In hindsight Hallett noted drily, "these scenes and the doleful music was not the best medicine to the invalid, nor was it conducive to an early recovery."[102]

Brightening this mournful picture to some degree was the presence of "two angels in mortal form and habiliments" who made daily visits to the hospital, as Lieutenant Hallett recalled, "dispensing without favor, wine, jellies, fruit and other delicacies." These were Mrs. Augusta M. Richards and her daughter Carol, ladies from Massachusetts, long residents of the South, and among the few who welcomed Union forces to New Orleans. The two women "sat by the dying [soldier], bathed his brow, read and spoke words of cheer, took the last message of love and affection to wife, mother, sister or friend, and finally closed the eyes of the patriot dead." They wrote hundreds of "last messages," for which they received grateful answers. "One day, they appeared with unusually bright and smiling faces bearing a large sized bundle containing handkerchiefs, knit stockings and other useful articles donated by fair ladies at the north, for distribution among the soldiers." Cheerful notes were attached, "signed by the loyal souls who wished they could fight with sword and gun instead of thread and needle." Further conversation with the lieutenant disclosed that Augusta Richards was from Cape Cod and was well acquainted with his family there. The extra attention she bestowed on him thereafter may have helped him survive his bout with malaria. Less consolingly, Hallett was present when Sgt. William Patch of Company G, "in a moment of delirium, jumped from the fourth-story to the court below and was instantly killed. Patch was a bright fellow and his unnatural death a great affliction to his parents, who are honored residents of the City of Homes [Springfield, Massachusetts]."[103]

Butler had his reasons for arguing that his men could tolerate the Louisiana climate. Some of it may have been wishful thinking: although it is true that most of the men in the 31st Massachusetts survived, there is no doubt that it was a difficult adjustment. Corporal Hawkes testified to this: "It is not the extreme intensity of the heat that is so prostrating, but 'tis so continuous. Clad in woolen coats buttoned up to the chin and burdened furthermore with belt and cartridge box containing 'forty rounds' I wonder not that we *sweat*, but that we have not *entirely dissolved*."[104] This was despite the fact that drilling was done only after sundown. In another letter he became almost poetic when he summarized, "The weather is so hot here that I live in a kind of listless, torpid state."[105] Hawkes, who came from the hill town of Charlemont, was then about twenty-four years old. His father had died, and he had a close relationship with his mother (to whom most of his letters were addressed). He made no effort to conceal his desire to be with her again. Although two shiploads of ice had arrived for the soldiers in late June, on a steamy day in August, Hawkes found spiritual refreshment by remembering home: "Upon such a sweltering day as this I think 'with longing heart and strong desire' Oh! for a draught of water from the spring on the old homestead, then let me spread my blanket under that large maple out near Mr. Taylor's and after a good nap I would call over and see mother a little while."[106]

When James Sullivan Fisherdick of Ware died on June 9, Tupper commented: "He was a large, fine looking man—6 feet, 2 or 3 inches—good figure. All who have died of our company have been from the head of the company." He added, "His constitution [was] impaired by a severe attack of measles at Camp Seward, weakened by continued diarrhea, [and so he] couldn't stand the Mississippi water, the heat & the damp, unhealthy nights."[107] This seems to confirm the belief that strong, healthy farmers fared poorly in the army. Contrary to what one might expect, city men, who had acquired greater immunity from their wider range of human contacts, had a better chance of survival in camp. Fairbank provided anecdotal confirmation of this notion: "Three of the most robust men in the company have been the first to be taken from the ranks. They are the last I should have thought to be the first but so it is. Those that were the most feeble at the north are the ones that the weather agrees best with here. At least it has proved so thus far."[108]

5

A REGIMENT DIVIDED

AUGUST–DECEMBER 1862

A critical point in the history of the 31st Massachusetts arrived in late August 1862, when the regiment was divided. Five companies (A through E) were sent to occupy Fort Jackson; three (F, G, and I) went to Fort Pike, a small prewar work that guarded an entrance to Lake Pontchartrain, to relieve part of the 13th Maine; and the remaining two marched to Kennerville (now Kenner), just west of New Orleans. Dividing a regiment in this way had been common in the prewar army, scattering its companies among a multitude of frontier outposts, but was more unusual in the enormous volunteer armies of the Civil War. There was a military need to station troops at these places, none of which truly required a full regiment, yet it is likely that other considerations were present in General Butler's mind. The smoldering controversy with Governor Andrew, never completely resolved, had flared up anew, though far removed from its source.

After leaving Fortress Monroe, both Col. Oliver Gooding and Lt. Col. Charles Whelden were on the *Mississippi* during its southward journey, but since Butler was conspicuously in charge, neither had much chance to exercise authority. Gooding was officially in command of the 31st Massachusetts, but the general probably still entertained hopes of replacing him with Whelden, his favorite. Even though he was department commander, it would have been difficult politically and institutionally for Butler to accomplish that. Still, the possibility that his devious mind would find a way to achieve this objective could never be dismissed.

Under the virtual truce that Butler and Andrew forged and that allowed the Western Bay State Regiment to depart Massachusetts, the general had conceded that the governor would commission its officers. Because this was decided at the last moment, many men who had been appointed at Butler's request left without having received a state commission or even being sure that they would. Whelden himself fell into this category, having been mustered as lieutenant colonel on November 25, 1861, by an army mustering officer.[1] After the regiment departed, its convoluted travels meant that mail service was irregular, and some commissions were not delivered until weeks later. More troublesome, those who had not received the document could not be certain whether their commission was simply delayed or whether Andrew was refusing to issue one. Well into the summer of 1862, men who had performed as officers since Camp Seward were still learning that they did not hold valid commissions, leaving them with the choice of resigning, finding a staff position, or accepting a commission in a new regiment (such as the 1st Louisiana); it does not appear that any chose to drop into the enlisted ranks. Even the original surgeon, Frank A. Cady of Pittsfield, failed to receive a commission and had resigned when the regiment left Massachusetts. Those who were forced to leave the 31st created vacancies that had to be filled by reshuffling officers or promoting sergeants. This prolonged instability impaired the regiment's efficiency and added another burden on enlisted men who were trying to become soldiers under already difficult circumstances—but that was not the governor's primary consideration.

The full account remained hidden for thirty years and emerged only through a series of accidents and the intervention of regimental historian L. Frederick Rice. His investigations revealed a story that, while sordid in many respects, is essential to understanding the singular history of the 31st Massachusetts. It turned out that Andrew had indeed issued a commission to Whelden and sent it forward to Colonel Gooding, thus reinforcing Gooding's position as commander. The colonel had previously approved Whelden's commission as well, but in the interval between that and the receipt of the document, he decided that he had "made a great mistake."[2] According to Gooding, Whelden, as soon as he learned that his commission was being forwarded, began to agitate to issue commissions to all the other officers Butler had appointed. Moreover, he stirred up this discord in the face of the enemy, that is, while the regiment was preparing to assault Fort St. Philip. Actions that Gooding regarded as insubordination continued: "*He has neither qualified himself nor supported me as he agreed to. He has always induced Gen. Butler to detach him from the Reg't whilst I was in command, and finally induced him to detach me* that *he* might *command.*" Whelden, thirteen years older than Gooding, demonstrably did not like to be in the same place as the colonel and resisted taking orders from him. Gooding further asserted: "The L't Col's *moral character* is perfectly *black.* If you wish *particulars* and *proof* of the same, they shall be forthcoming."[3]

Several officers in the 31st were so appalled by Whelden's conduct that they took the extraordinary step of sending a petition to Governor Andrew, in which they asserted:

> 1st. That we are satisfied, after full trial, that L't Col. C. M. Whelden is an unsuitable man to command the Reg't.
>
> 2nd. That Col. O. P. Gooding is thoroughly qualified for command, and is an acceptable and brave officer.
>
> 3rd. That we firmly believe that the interests of the Reg't and of the service would be greatly advanced by the removal of L't Col. Whelden from the Reg't.
>
> 4th. That under no circumstances would we *willingly* enter the field under command of L't Col. Whelden.
>
> 5th. That L't Col. Whelden has endeavored to create and foster among the officers a feeling of enmity toward Col. Gooding, to force him (Col. G.) into resignation; and in the rear of Fort St. Philip, when a land attack on the fort seemed imminent, he raised the question of Commissions among the Officers, to create trouble in the face of the enemy.[4]

This letter was signed by officers commanding six of the ten companies (one first lieutenant, the others captains) and even by the regimental surgeon, adjutant, and chaplain. Most of these men had either been appointed by Butler or had voluntarily recruited for his regiment, yet they addressed Butler's bitter enemy rather than the general, their overall commanding officer. It was an astonishing act, even by the standards of the volunteer regiments, and testifies to the extreme strain they were feeling. One officer who did not sign was Capt. Cardinal Conant, who had been on Butler's staff since Ship Island and had been trusted with several special assignments. Gooding referred to the captain as one of Butler's "favorites" and refused to recommend him for a commission. Conant remained, however, and did not resign until late 1863.

Since the earlier communication had not produced discernible results, in October several officers at Fort Jackson prepared another statement.[5] This document has no addressee, and it is not clear what the authors meant to do with it. Perhaps the intent was to use it to support Gooding in any hearings he might have. The statement repeated previous accusations against Whelden and added a few new ones. It depicted the lieutenant colonel as spending most of his time around headquarters ingratiating himself with Butler rather than drilling his troops. They charged that the various splits of the regiment, both in New Orleans and later at the three separate posts, were Butler's method of preventing Gooding from commanding a complete regiment. In support, they recounted a heated confrontation with several officers in which Whelden essentially declared that the regiment could be reunited only by putting him in command and "throwing Col. Gooding overboard." The statement also brought out new information that Butler had met with Gooding at an unspecified date and promised to try to persuade Whelden to work with the colonel. If this intervention took place, there is no sign that it had any effect.

Politics was undoubtedly a factor in the controversy. The statement was signed by Capts. Edward Hollister, William Hopkins, and Edward Nettleton as well as Surg. E. C. Bidwell and Adj. Elbert Fordham. Hopkins and Nettleton were certainly Republicans, and Hollister must have been since he later resigned to become an officer in a black regiment. The general's stated intention of forming regiments made up largely of Democrats may have succeeded with respect to enlisted men, but it appears that some potential officers whose political orientation was Republican went ahead and recruited companies, apparently without knowing or caring that they would be led by Butler.[6]

As the Whelden controversy heated up, an unexpected intervention threw more fuel onto the fire. Captain Hopkins's father, Erastus, was a dedicated abolitionist and prominent in Massachusetts Republican counsels. As such, he knew Governor Andrew well enough to send him personal letters. In this correspondence he passed along disparaging information about the lieutenant colonel that had been provided by his son, with particular stress on Whelden's abuse of alcohol.[7] This information undoubtedly reinforced the governor's opposition to him.

Maj. Robert Bache did not sign the letter from the officers, but he may not have been present when it was drafted. Since he and Whelden both came from Pittsfield and had been appointed by Butler, one might expect that they were in accord, but Erastus Hopkins assured Andrew that this assumption was incorrect. As reported in a letter from his son, the two Pittsfield officers had gotten into an argument, after which Bache declared: "Col. W., consider me hereafter your sworn enemy, let there be no misunderstanding."[8] Assuming that Whelden would soon be removed and replaced by Bache, Erastus Hopkins laid the groundwork to ensure that his son would be appointed major. He went to considerable length to establish that his son was regarded by all as the "senior captain" of the regiment and concluded with the blunt assertion that, if he were passed over, "it will be a great disappointment to him and to me. In this matter I cannot doubt your favorable *disposition,* and may I not hope that on the ground of personal regard to me . . . that you will strain a point in his favor to the utmost which is consistent with a controlling sense of fitness and of duty."[9] One wonders if the elder Hopkins, a religious man, would have used the same tone if he had known that the governor, in the height of his rage, had written that Butler's Bay State regiments had been set up "to afford means to persons of bad character to make money unscrupulously and to encourage men whose unfitness had excluded them from any appointment by me."[10]

Gooding had received Whelden's commission, but since the two men were in separate locations, as usual, he never forwarded it. Instead, he returned the vital document to the governor, saying that Andrew could issue it on his own account but not with Gooding's recommendation. Andrew neither issued it nor destroyed it, so it remained in his papers. It was only in the 1890s, after Butler and Andrew had departed the scene, that Whelden learned that his commission had actually been issued. Another curious feature of this tawdry episode is that Butler seems to have tried on more than one occasion to arrest Gooding or remove him from the 31st by other means but, when confronted by the colonel, hesitated to take the final step. Since the general rarely appeared reluctant to exert his authority in other situations, his caution in this case is noteworthy. It may provide a revealing example in the larger story of relations between civilian "political" officers and regulars. Volunteer generals did not, as Winfield Scott had feared, command regular troops, who were few in number anyway, but they did end up commanding regular officers who had been assigned to volunteer units, usually accompanied by a dramatic leap in rank. Butler seemed hesitant to remove or punish such men, and this became a factor when he commanded the Army of the James in Virginia late in the war and suffered failure that destroyed much of whatever military reputation he had built for himself.

In New Orleans in the summer of 1862, the best Butler could do under the circumstances was to separate Gooding and Whelden, placing them respectively in charge of Fort Jackson and Fort Pike, and hope that some opportunity would present itself to unify the regiment under Whelden. It may be argued, however, that Butler hesitated to entrust the regiment to the lieutenant colonel, who lacked field experience. Whelden was capable of drilling troops and marching them through the streets of New Orleans, but those were not sufficient qualifications for field command, as had been amply demonstrated elsewhere. Another striking aspect of this controversy is that almost no written record survives other than the documents that surfaced in the 1890s. Gooding at the time reported conferring with Butler, and since the two men were often not in the same locale, one would expect that there was correspondence. Yet the officers' names do not appear in this context in the published collection of Butler's Civil War correspondence.[11]

What had inspired Frederick Rice to launch a time-consuming investigation of events that occurred more than thirty years earlier? The backstory is even more bizarre than the papers he uncovered. According to one account, Colonel Gooding "created quite a sensation" in Pittsfield in 1893 "by his unwelcome attentions to a well-known society woman for whom he had conceived an insane love."[12] The name of the woman, of course, is not given, nor was it explained how he had become acquainted with her, if indeed he had. While spending many hours hanging around the park in the center of Pittsfield, Gooding encountered veterans of the 31st Massachusetts, among them Whelden. As Gooding explained the events of the distant past, he affirmed that he had held Whelden's commission out of fear that Whelden might replace him. This was partially true but ignores the fact that he had returned the commission to Andrew and assumes further that his powerful accusations against Whelden would remain buried in the archives. Based on these heavily redacted assurances, Whelden generously and mistakenly forgave both Andrew and Gooding, took Gooding to dinner, and escorted him around town.[13]

Gooding, who had spent most of his postwar years in Saint Louis, had never been in Pittsfield before his 1893 visit. At that time he was dressed respectably, but his odd behavior attracted the attention of the police. His condition must have worsened, for a marshal's jury in Washington pronounced him insane two years later and had him institutionalized.[14] Later in 1895, Rice's persistent digging finally located Whelden's signed but undelivered commission, which he transferred to Whelden in person with the compliments of

Gov. Frederic T. Greenhalge.[15] It is not known if Rice also informed Whelden of the violent assaults on his character expressed by Gooding and some of the officers in the regiment in 1862, having not been one of those who signed the petitions. He may not have signed because he was then stationed at Fort Pike, but other officers at that location and at Kennerville did sign. (Another who did not sign was Capt. William Rockwell, a member of a respected Berkshire family.)

While the officers' bold petition made their attitude readily apparent, the feelings of the enlisted men in this affair remain more difficult to discern. Many officers sought to remain aloof from their men, but so many points of contact existed that secrets were almost impossible to hold. Considering that wild rumors of every sort flourished like hothouse plants, the chances of concealing genuine information were almost nil. Cpl. Joshua Hawkes was sometimes a clerk and probably had occasion to overhear officer conversations. That he was aware of something amiss is shown in a letter from September 1862: "Col. Gooding has not been with the Regiment since our company went to Annunciation Square—some *trouble* somewhere. I do not know what though Col. & Lt. Col. never agreed very well."[16] By the end of the year, Hawkes was fully acquainted with the situation, writing after Whelden was mustered out of the service, "Cols. O. P. Gooding and Whelden have always been at logger-heads." He understood fully that "Col. Gooding was commissioned by Gov. Andrew and is an Andrew man, while Whelden is a Butler man and a fellow-mason." Hawkes was aware that the two "had a flare-up at the City and Whelden swore he would never act under Col. Gooding, so to humor Whelden the Regiment has been divided."[17]

In writing that "Col. Gooding is not a man of peculiarly attractive manners—though the ladies say he is—but a man of much military ability," Hawkes probably reflected the mixed feelings the men had toward their competing colonels. When Gooding departed for Fort Jackson, Hawkes wrote, "so the Regiment is now in command of Lt. Col. Whelden, whom we like much better than the Col."[18] Whelden was less demanding and shared the background of most of the men. By contrast, Gooding, "being a *thorough military* man things have to be about up to *square* now. There is I assure you a vast difference in officers between those bred in the military life and those taken from the walks of civil life." Since the colonel was a graduate of West Point and belonged to the regular army, Hawkes found that "he wishes to make us equal in discipline and drill to Regulars. He has the kind of stern, severe way with him, so that his reprimand is by no means a gentle one, nor do you desire its repetition."[19]

One officer who had felt the sharp edge of Gooding's wrath was the young, serious-minded Captain Rockwell. On at least one occasion, Gooding berated the officer "in such a way that the Captain turned white with suppressed indignation."[20] It might have been cause for a challenge in the prewar army or in European armies. As noted, Rockwell did not sign the complaints against Whelden, probably reluctant to take sides against another prominent resident of Pittsfield. Lt. Luther Howell, however, had developed a grudging respect for Gooding: "[He] has again sworn off on drinking and we are well satisfied with him. We know him to be brave and every man would follow him to the cannons mouth without a word."[21] Another officer, Lt. Joseph Hallett, may have been indirectly confirming Gooding's lack of polish when he described him as "not anything fancy." His overall appraisal was positive, however, as he said that the colonel "is a fine looking man . . . not a showy man but plain in dress, determined as he is fair in all his dealings."[22]

Probably the most balanced summation is provided by Rice, especially interesting in view of his persistent efforts three decades later to do belated justice to Whelden: "Col. Gooding has faults; serious ones. He is passionate, and quick tempered; will swear at the men and officers when excited, and has drank more than was good for him. At the same time, he knows his duty as an Officer, and to him the Regiment is indebted for all it is." Reviewing the origins of the Gooding-Whelden conflict, Rice conceded that the two officers had a "falling out" even before reaching Ship Island. The underlying cause was that "Col. Whelden's sole aim appears to be to ingratiate himself with Gen. Butler. He is ignorant of some of the simplest parts of a soldier's duty and almost totally so of Batallion [sic] movements, but at the same time one of the most conceited beings I ever knew." This influence was sufficient to have Gooding detached and sent to Fort Jackson, "where he had a falling out with Lieut. Col. [Alpha B.] Farr of the 26th Mass. (much such another man as Col. Whelden) and had charges of drunkeness [sic] and misconduct preferred against him by Col. Farr, whom he had placed under arrest." According to Rice these charges "were triumphantly refuted," but Gooding was still kept away from the regiment. With Whelden in charge, the officers had an opportunity to contrast him with Gooding, "and the result has been that Col. Gooding's faults have in comparison dwindled into insignificance, while his good traits have magnified themselves." He opined "that if the privates were to be asked tomorrow whether they would prefer to continue under Col. Whelden or have Col. Gooding back, they would 9 out of every 10, unhesitatingly call for Col. Gooding, although at the time he was detached, there was a very hard feeling against him on account of his severity." To illustrate how the officers felt, Rice noted the petition that had been sent to General Butler, "praying that Col. Gooding might be returned to the Reg. This was signed by *every officer but two* in the Reg." He added that Gooding, "different from Col. Whelden, can be taught something and can see where he has made a mistake. He has *entirely* stopped drinking. Will not even taste wine in lemonade." Rice understood that at first the colonel may have felt defensive, due to "a feeling that as Massachusetts men, the officers did not feel cordial toward him, an Indiannian [*sic*], but the petition before referred to has shown him to the contrary. If we ever get him back, he will be a very different man, and unless we are very much mistaken will if he has an opportunity, gain for the Regiment an enviable reputation."[23]

Not for the first time, the men in the ranks had been disappointed in their supposed superiors. By and large, they deserve credit for remaining devoted amid dissension, which was an avoidable hardship added to those of climate, sickness, poor food, and the constant need for caution in dealing with the local population inherent in the regiment's situation. Nor can the junior officers be faulted for having to grapple with the consequences of a dispute they had not created. Although the immediate protagonists might have adjusted their differences, they too were victims of the furious conflict between Andrew and Butler. Both of those men share blame, but the main fault seems to lie with Andrew for insisting on prerogatives that may have been legally justifiable but that interfered with military operations. He could have overlooked pride and accepted Butler's appointments, as did the governors of four other New England states. At a still higher level, the underlying cause of the controversy can be attributed to the Lincoln administration, which characteristically sought to please everyone and therefore issued conflicting orders and shied away from making difficult choices.

It is instructive to review Gooding's chronology with respect to what the 31st Massachusetts was doing in the closing months of 1862. Dispatched from New Orleans to take command of Forts Jackson and St. Philip, where the 26th Massachusetts was stationed, on June 10, he remained at that post until July

20. During that time, the 31st remained in New Orleans, presumably under Lieutenant Colonel Whelden. On July 21 Gooding was named chief mustering officer of the Department of the Gulf. As perceived by the officers who wrote the statement of October 15, both of these assignments were intended to get Gooding out of Whelden's way. This was especially true of his mustering duties, which Gooding said, with good reason, that he could fulfill in a couple of hours a week. The colonel thus was not present at Fort Jackson when part of the 31st was transferred there on August 25, with Major Bache in command. Gooding resumed command of the forts on September 20. It was during this interlude that the officers of the 31st sent their extraordinary petition to Governor Andrew. When Gooding returned to the regiment, it is quite likely that he was assigned to command of the forts, not specifically of the 31st Massachusetts. Since only part of one regiment was considered sufficient to garrison the forts, it is unlikely that any other units were stationed there, and with at least half the regiment located elsewhere, it could be justified not to place Gooding in command of the entire regiment. Butler may have hoped to use this interim to dispose of the colonel, but his own decapitation intervened. Finally, in late January 1863, with Maj. Gen. Nathaniel Banks now in charge, the 31st Massachusetts and Colonel Gooding were reunited in New Orleans.[24]

Lieutenant Howell expressed the rage that those officers who hungered for action and were eager to make a name for themselves felt at the dispersion and isolation of the regiment. In unsparing terms he referred to the Fort Jackson assignment as a "penance for sin against Gen. Butler simply because we as a regt. would not repudiate Col. Gooding whom the Gen. dislikes and curry to Whelden whom we all despise. Gen. Butler used his almighty power to tear us all in pieces and send us off in fragments never again to form a complete Regt. to be put in the field unless the War Dept. interferes."[25]

And then there was the Dudley situation. While he was forming his regiments in 1861, Butler had sought to place Nathan A. M. Dudley (1825–1910), a Massachusetts native then a captain in the 10th U.S. Infantry, in command of the Western Bay State Regiment.[26] Instead, undoubtedly through Andrew's intervention, he was given command of the sister Eastern Bay State Regiment, replacing Jonas French, a Butler favorite whom the governor detested. In the kind of comment that survives in the general's wartime correspondence, a friend wrote: "I see that French was obliged to give up his position at last. What a thick hide Governor Andrew's bullock must have."[27] Butler later was able to retain French's services by making him provost marshal in Louisiana. (Similarly, although Whelden returned home for a time, the general was able to bring him back as provost marshal in later commands he held.) Dudley was promoted to temporary ranks as high as brigadier general and commanded a brigade and later a subdistrict, though with mixed success. After the war he reverted to his permanent rank in the regular army and served on the frontier, where he was involved in many controversies before regaining the rank of colonel and retiring.

Other officers in the regiment also seemed to fall short of the soldiers' expectations. Corporal Hawkes was a keen observer of character, although his perceptions were slanted by his religious sensibility. He found that the captain of his company (C), John W. Lee, associated with his men more than some of the other officers, particularly those with a military background, and even wondered whether Lee might be "too lenient."[28] The captain had obviously recovered from being stabbed at Camp Seward, as Hawkes noted that he was now "as fat as a pig and as good natured a captain as any in the Regiment."[29] Nevertheless, though he "like[d] him as a Captain very well," Hawkes fretted that Lee, who had been a clergyman in civilian life, "never speaks to his men of any hereafter. I do not wish to judge any man but Rev. J. W. Lee, M. E. Minister and Capt. J. W. Lee in New Orleans are two different men."[30] Lee had been a minister in the neighboring town of Buckland, so Hawkes may have been acquainted with him before the war. Along similar religious lines, the corporal was unimpressed with the regimental chaplain, twenty-six-year-old Francis E. R. Chubbuck of Pittsfield, commenting acidly that he was "at the City *running around with the women*."[31]

Howell had likewise become disillusioned with Chubbuck while the regiment was stationed in New Orleans: "Our chaplain thinks his preaching does no good (an opinion which is well founded I think) and therefore does not preach to us any more. None of the men like to hear him so he simply stays at the hospital, comforts the sick and buries the dead." This was a deep personal disappointment to the lieutenant in view of ambitions he had once professed: "When I see a man as intelligent as he is doing so little for his country, not as much as the poorest private for he is utterly worthless to our Regt. I tell you Bell it sets my old ministerial dreams all askew."[32] Dr. Bidwell confirmed that Chubbuck stayed at the hospital and spent much of his time conducting funerals; James Tupper made a similar observation.[33]

It would be an overreaction to assume that Butler garrisoned and rehabilitated Fort Jackson primarily to separate Gooding and Whelden. That may have been a consideration, but there is little doubt that he genuinely feared a French attack.[34] Confederate forces were not a realistic threat to Jackson and St. Philip, which were now of little value to them; if they went on the offensive, it would likely take the form of a direct assault on New Orleans. It is hard to imagine that Butler would reduce the forces available to defend the city itself, and also reduce his potential to take offensive action, because of a personality clash in one regiment. His frequent and generally irritating interactions with foreigners, however, had convinced him of their hostile intentions. He felt a strong dislike for the British but considered the French a more immediate menace to his position in Louisiana.

In preparation for garrisoning Fort Jackson, Lt. Col. Frank S. Hesseltine of the 13th Maine inspected the post, and his report was transmitted by his superior, Brig. Gen. Neal Dow (1804–97). A Maine resident, Dow was an officer with a strongly delineated personality like General Phelps and went the Vermonter one better by being both an abolitionist and a prohibitionist. Hesseltine, though not an artillery officer, determined that "the burning of the citadel and the demolition of its walls, which are at present in progress, give the fort an appearance of confusion and ruin that does not really exist. I am surprised to notice the small amount of actual damage that the works have sustained by the severe bombardment to which it has been exposed." Filling in details, he noted that the ramparts were encumbered in many places with rubbish, the parapets were somewhat injured by neglect and abrasion, and the scarp walls were slightly harmed in a few places by shot and shell but, in sum, "no material damage has been sustained by them." He added that only five guns were dismounted during the bombardment, and with those only the carriages were affected. "In a word," he concluded, "the principal difficulty with the fort is slovenliness, as at Fort Saint Philip, apparently of long standing, and this I am endeavoring to correct as speedily as possible."[35] Considering that the forts were hardly in a superb state of maintenance before the attack, Hesseltine's report provides further evidence that Porter's mortars by no means impaired them, much less pounded them to rubble. Sgt. Francis A. Clary confirmed that the outer walls had suffered little from Porter's bombardment, though interior buildings such as the officers' barracks had been damaged severely.[36]

The companies that arrived at Fort Jackson thus found that "everything wore a desolate, forsaken, dusty look, and soon men were detailed to go to cleaning up the rubbish, removing broken bricks, painting and repainting gun carriages, as well as the piles of shells and cannon balls that were piled in heaps around each gun."[37] Since Colonel Gooding was detached, Major Bache was in charge of this work and, by one account, won "almost unbounded praise."[38] Under his supervision, former slaves removed weeds that had nearly concealed the guns, reopened drains, and leveled the ground; Captain Hopkins reported that the fort held a "family" of about 150 such contrabands, providing about eighty-five working men.[39] Improved drainage reduced the mosquito problem, which one soldier had described as "worse than in the city."[40] These descriptions may be somewhat exaggerated in favor of the 31st, for the 26th Massachusetts and Gooding had been present since June, and it is hard to believe that those troops did nothing to remedy the squalor that had been left when the forts surrendered.

Asa Wheeler noted that there were eighty-five guns of various descriptions in Fort Jackson.[41] For Hawkes, another feature captured his attention: "The moat is literally filled with alligators who reign supreme, it being a penal offense to molest them as they consume the refuse, &c."[42] Howell, angry at being there at all, summarized: "This Fort which cost us so much powder and shell is situated in the most pestiferous swamp one can imagine. Alligators, Bull-frogs and all sorts of *varmints* abound fever & ague is equaled in abundance only by the musquetoes [sic]."[43]

Although not its primary function, the fort held a considerable number of prisoners, leading secessionists as well as what Fairbank called "some of the robbers and cut throats" of New Orleans. Among them were two editors of the *Commercial Bulletin* whom Butler had arrested for treason.[44] Captain Hopkins, however, found that many of the prisoners were "gentlemen of high respectability and gentlemanly behaviour."[45] Luther Fairbank assumed that the alligators would protect the post from being stormed, so it must have been quite a surprise when three of the prisoners managed to slip past this toothy picket guard and escape by swimming across the moat. Once their absence was noted, search parties went out to scour the countryside, and the prisoners were recaptured about sixteen miles away.[46]

If alligators were the apex predators at Fort Jackson, at Fort Pike they were the mosquitoes. Richard Underwood reached that stronghold during the day on August 20 and at first rejoiced at the cool sea breeze. Night brought a different impression, though, as he reported the following morning:

> I feel most dead this morning. The mosquitoes bit so I fixed my bar, and as soon as I had got laid down, the mosquitoes came by the millions, and some of the small ones worked through, and then the large ones would put their bills through, and those already in would pull them through. It was like sleeping in a bee hive. I could not sleep, so I spread my blanket over my face, but that made me so warm that I could not sleep. In the morning, I found towards a peck of mosquitoes in my bar.[47]

Smoke and the bars had no effect on the pests, which were capable of biting through woolen uniform pants. After some nine months of service, the regiment had not yet encountered an enemy soldier but had waged an interminable guerilla war against mosquitoes.

Writing years later and influenced by the style of popular humorists like Mark Twain and Artemus Ward, another soldier gave humorous treatment to an experience that probably seemed less funny at the time: "We lost our best blood at the Fort. The mosquito reigned supreme there. Our first night there made a deep impression on us, and in fact we were all covered with impressions the next morning." The grass had been mowed that day, and the men, thinking it would make nice beds, filled their ticks with it. Soon, however, "slumbers were much disturbed, and curses loud, and as deep as the articles of war allowed, broke the stillness of the night air,—our soft beds were one mass of skeeters and they were hungry." By morning, "some had faces swelled so badly as to nearly close their eyes. We were all a cheeky looking lot."[48]

In his report Lieutenant Colonel Hesseltine had observed, "I think of nothing further which 'remains to be done' for the defense of Fort Jackson but the thorough drill in artillery of the infantry force now there."[49] Because no artillery unit had been assigned to the post, an infantry company was detailed to learn how to manage its big guns. Company D was chosen for this service, its men probably found it to their liking not only because of the novelty but also because it relieved them from guard duty. During their training, they lived in barracks on the parapet, a position that would have been untenable if the fort had come under attack.[50] Captains Hollister and Hopkins lived on the parapet in a "close little house," built of a house frame with shingled roof and canvas sides.[51] Who conducted the artillery instruction remains unknown; presumably, once he returned to take command of the post, Colonel Gooding, who would have acquired training in that art at West Point, performed that duty. Daily existence for the troops at Fort Jackson thus came to resemble that of the men who garrisoned the coastal defenses before the war, with the significant exception that most of those forts were closer to the cities they defended. New Orleans was too far away for day trips without passes, so Fort Jackson, constructed mostly on "made" land, was a lonely, dreary place; but it was possible to make shorter outings in the vicinity to acquire oranges or shoot alligators. These excursions came to a sudden end when yellow fever made its appearance, after which no one was permitted to go beyond the quarantine station. "'Good bye' to the orange groves and the pleasant sails up the Mississippi," lamented Francis Knight.[52]

One diversion was the presentation of colors to the 31st Massachusetts one Sunday in September.[53] Governor Andrew had only just sent these out, a noteworthy delay since stories of men dying as they held battle flags aloft already figured prominently in the heroic folklore of the war. Prior to this, the regiment had not had a state flag. General Butler, if he even knew of the arrival of new colors, was probably not eager to publicize a gift sent by the man who had done everything possible to obstruct him. If the flags had passed through New Orleans at all, he forwarded them to Fort Jackson, reasoning that that was where the bulk of the regiment was stationed. There Colonel Gooding took the opportunity to strengthen his credentials with the men, giving "a neat little speech," in the words of Corporal Hawkes.[54]

The other major post for companies from the 31st was Fort Pike, a brick structure belonging to the Third System. Louisiana militia had occupied it a few days after taking the larger forts on the Mississippi, and Union gunboats had arrived before it three days after Butler entered New Orleans. Access to Pike was difficult: "There is no solid ground near the Fort, nothing but Swamp. The only chance that we have to walk outside the Fort is on a shell road, built across the swamp to the other side of the point on which the Fort is situated."[55] According to Sergeant Rich, the fort was capable of mounting fifty guns, but only twelve were in service when they arrived, the Confederates

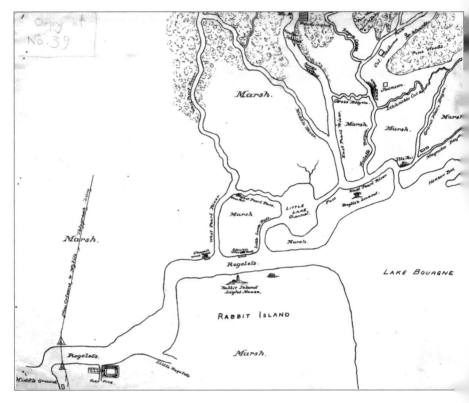

Fort Pike and vicinity. This map was probably drawn by 1st Lt. L. Frederick Rice, who had been trained as a civil engineer and later became historian of the regiment. Courtesy Lyman and Merrie Wood Museum of Springfield History.

having disabled the others.[56] During their stay, the companies of the 31st remounted some of the guns with new or repaired carriages and generally made them serviceable. In the early months of 1863, the men began practice firing and ranging the guns. Lacking the endless pageant of river traffic that enlivened life at Fort Jackson, the troops at Fort Pike must have felt even more isolated. One diversion took place when Butler came out in his yacht on October 6 to show that he had not forgotten the post, though perhaps also to conduct personal business.

Forays into the countryside from Fort Pike were not primarily recreational.

A company moved up the Pearl River to Pearlington, on the Mississippi side, to take machinery and lumber from a steam mill. Later, another detachment set off to capture cattle from a man on Bayou Bonfouca, north of Lake Pontchartrain, who had been supplying the rebels, and loaded 150 cattle onto the steamer *J. M. Brown*. On other occasions troops went out to seize cattle, wood, and slaves, and they raised schooners at Bonfouca that had been sunk to keep them from falling into Federal hands. Eventually, these incursions attracted the attention of guerillas, and there were several exchanges of fire, including artillery, but no serious injuries to the 31st.[57] During one of these raids early in 1863, Capt. George S. Darling was wounded in an attack on the *J. M. Brown*. Lieutenant Rice was notably unimpressed by this calamity: "Capt. Darling's wound don't amount to anything, though it probably itches somewhat and he makes more fuss over it than if he had lost his head. It was a mere scratch about three inches above the knee, and just an inch and quarter long, as he himself ascertained by carefull measurement."[58]

The men at Fort Pike became involved with the enigmatic personage of John F. H. Claiborne, the wealthy and intellectual owner of a nearby plantation. He professed to be a Unionist, though he had been a colonel in the Mississippi militia and had a son who was a Confederate officer. Claiborne provided valuable information, as well as cattle and other goods, to the Union forces and in return was allowed to sell cotton in New Orleans, undoubtedly at a large profit. (Around this time Tupper, who was in a position to know, reported that cotton was selling at one hundred dollars a bale.)[59]

On some of these ventures, the men loaded their haversacks with oranges and sweet potatoes. This fell within the bounds of acceptable foraging. Although both sides issued stern pronouncements about plundering and on occasion made a conspicuous example of some culprit, the practice was overlooked more often than not. Thus pillaging on both sides of an indefinite front line gradually impoverished the rural population in what had been a region of abundance. It is true that the North might have been marginally capable of feeding its troops by local purchases or shipments from outside, but the men obviously would prefer fresh pork or chicken, however clumsily butchered and prepared, to dried beans and canned meat. The number of men the North sent to Louisiana was perhaps no greater than those Louisianans who left to serve elsewhere in the Confederacy so that there was not a huge net population increase; but war is a destructive business, and repeated disruptions of the growing cycle and the supply chain reduced the quantity of food available in many locations. Butler established "free labor" plantations that mitigated such shortages to some degree, but these operations required soldiers to protect them and were subject to various abuses.

One of the major duties of the two companies stationed at Kennerville was patrolling the railroad line to Jackson, Mississippi. This need to roam about the countryside brought the New Englanders into revealing contact with a variety of inhabitants, both black and white. George Young of Company K told of a chance encounter that affected him deeply, leaving an impression that was still potent when he wrote his recollections more than twenty years later.[60] One day (he does not provide a date, though from the description it must have been during late summer, not long after his company arrived in August), he and a companion set off on a typical foraging expedition, "as we had nothing in the way of rations left but hardtack and coffee and a little Salt Hoss." They came upon a cornfield cultivated by what Young labeled "white trash," a term already in routine usage. "These families," he explained, "generally had a log house and a small patch of land away back in the rear of the Plantations, and as their place was always hard to get at from the River and consequently of very little value financially, they were allowed by common consent to stay there as long as they didn't interfere with the Niggers." Such people were in essence tolerated squatters or proto-sharecroppers.

Alerted by one of the "yaller dogs" that were ubiquitous on the homesteads of poor whites and blacks alike, a girl who had been cultivating a garden ran into the house screaming "Ma—the Yanks have arriv!" Young and his unnamed companion found a family consisting of a woman of about forty-five and children—two girls and three or four boys—ranging in age from sixteen to about three. No man was in evidence, but the woman was wearing a pastel dress—not mourning—so Young deduced that her husband was off serving the Confederacy. All were in terror until Young was able to persuade them that he and his comrade were only interested in purchasing some food. Relieved and amazed that the enemy soldiers could "talk so easy to poor folks," the housewife sent children off to collect edibles and began to prepare a meal for the two soldiers. "The woman's kindness, although there was no polish about it, touched me in a tender spot," Young conceded. "I could hardly keep the tears of gratitude back, for there was a frankness and sincerity about her invitation such as I never expected to get and such also, as it seemed to me, that was far above the circumstances in life in which she was placed."

When Young insisted that the family join them, the woman exclaimed, "Wa'al if you don't beat all," but she feared that the Northerners would "think we don't know how to behave at table for the boys never would behave at table when their Pa was to home." But the children nearly embarrassed the guests by bowing their heads for grace, which the "Yanks" had not thought to do. One would not have expected a woman in these circumstances to be literate, but she promised to exchange letters with Young; he apparently received at least one letter from her, although he could not produce it at the time he was writing his recollections. This unanticipated meeting, its intensity heightened by the fact that Young had not seen anything resembling normal family life for many months, led him to question the whole point of the war: "I thought to myself if all the Rebels are as kind and as good as this gentle hearted woman, how can we justify ourselves in their sight. What excuse can we make to them for robbing them of their husbands, sons and brothers, and for taking away their only means of making a living[?]" He might have concluded at the time that the war was launched by men who cared about abstractions more than people.

A later expedition out of Kennerville led to serious combat, followed by a desperate struggle to escape. On December 10 a detachment under 1st Lt. Nelson F. Bond of Ware was ordered to relieve part of a Maine company at Desert (often written as and apparently pronounced "Des Sair") Station on the Jackson railroad. According to Tupper, who was familiar with the rail line due to his quartermaster work, this station was located near Frenier, on the neck of land west of Lake Pontchartrain and only five to ten miles from the Mississippi. Bond had been transferred and promoted to Company K from Company D only days earlier, and it was said that his old company were "all down-hearted at the change."[61] Failing to find a boat, the twenty-four-man detachment slogged overland through swamps and bayous so that they were exhausted by the time they arrived at the station late in the afternoon. Bond overlooked regulations and allowed his troops to settle in and start preparing dinner before setting out pickets. In addition to their physical exhaustion and the gathering dusk, the lieutenant was probably concerned with the impression he was making on unfamiliar men in the one company with a background divergent from the others in the 31st.

Bond's lapse was quickly punished as a much larger Confederate force appeared before the cooking fires were even blazing. Part of the detachment took cover and fired at the rebels, but only half had serviceable guns, as the others had been soaked when a canoe overturned on the outward journey. After some of the New Englanders were wounded, it became apparent that the situation was hopeless, and Bond ordered the rest to scatter and try to make their way back to safety. This began an extraordinary ordeal as these men, with no food or camp equipment, tried to evade capture through woods and swamps in persistently cold weather. Bond and a private were the last to get back to Kennerville, arriving after seventy-two hours in the swamps and eighty hours with no food other than sucking on sugar cane. The lieutenant wore slippers during his escape, as his feet were severely swollen when he arrived at Desert Station and had immediately taken off his boots. Five of the party were captured, including John E. McCarthy, who was seriously wounded. Sgt. Lewis T. Wade, left to die by the Confederates but rescued by local residents, later succumbed to his wounds at the Marine Hospital, and Emil Drach was instantly killed, the first member of the 31st to die in combat. Three quite-detailed narratives of this action survive, and each gives a different account of how Drach died.[62] News of the encounter was initially disbelieved. Although Capt. W. I. Allen went out with a rescue party, it was too late to recover the missing men.[63]

Although only one of innumerable Civil War skirmishes, this fight made a deep impression, at least on Companies H and K, as it was the first time the regiment had lost men in action. Jeremiah McGraith placed much of the blame on the Maine soldiers they were sent to relieve, who had left their post early and begun walking back on the tracks, where they met the men of the 31st six miles from the station. He felt that if they had waited until Bond's detachment arrived, the Confederates would not have been able to lay an ambush. In a larger sense the incident illustrates the risks in sending small parties to guard inaccessible posts, thereby placing them "in harm's way" (a phrase much overused in our time) since the enemy could readily assemble a sufficient force to overwhelm them.

Because of his detail to quartermaster duties, Tupper held a responsible position for a private as conductor on the railroad, run by the government, on which the Desert Station incident occurred. He offered some interesting details on an otherwise obscure chapter of the history of Civil War military railroads. The government had contracted with a private company to run one train a day to carry military stores and troops over the so-called New Orleans & Carrollton & Jefferson & Lake Pontchartrain Railroad. Tupper described this route, with which he was intimately familiar from his daily travels: "Leaving the city, the road runs through Jefferson City, containing many fine residences of New Orleans merchants, by Camp Lewis where the 'Reserve Brigade' under acting Brig. Gen. [Halbert E.] Payne [sic, Paine] is stationed, to Carrollton about 6 miles." From there it struck through the swamps, "where the tall cypress trees grow & alligators thrive, to the lake 6 miles further." At that point there was a wharf where boats came from Ship Island to unload and take on stores. About halfway from Carrollton to the lake was Metairie Ridge, where there was a race course with its large amphitheater "now occupied by the 3 companies of regulars which for a while were encamped in Annunciation Square. Camp Williams, where acting Brig. Gen. Dudley's brigade consisting of the 1st Louisiana, the 30th Mass., 7th Vt., & 6th Mich. regiments, Reads Cavalry Co., the 6th Mass. battery & the 1st Maine battery, is about a mile from Metairie Ridge." A force of contrabands were engaged in building a rail line from the ridge to Camp Williams and Camp Parapet on the Mississippi. Tupper said his railroad made one run a day, starting from Camp Williams or Metairie Ridge in the morning and reaching New Orleans about 10 A.M. The return train left the city at 3:30 P.M. and typically ran to the lake, though sometimes only to the ridge. Tupper went back to New Orleans every night on the trains that ran every hour between there and Carrollton. He was thus able to spend the night in the city, though he had to get up at 6 o'clock in the morning to leave on the 7 A.M. train, and it was eight in the evening by the time he ate supper. When not on the road, Tupper told his family, he was receiving freight, "so you see I am kept pretty busy."[64]

On December 20, 1862, Lieutenant Colonel Whelden assembled the companies at Fort Pike for a farewell address. One soldier noted that the officer was "very much affected at parting."[65] As the men knew by then, he had resigned because his patron, General Butler, had been replaced in command of the department, removing any lingering hope that Whelden might someday head the 31st Massachusetts. Butler was removed not because of military failings, the "woman order," any measures he had taken with regard to slavery, or his complex personal and official financial dealings. His primary offense lay in the almost constant clashes with foreign consuls at New Orleans. To him (and he uncovered substantial evidence in support of his position), these men were local profiteers who wrapped themselves in foreign flags in order to support the Confederacy. The aggrieved consuls complained to their foreign governments, most of whom were to some degree sympathetic to the South, which then registered objections in Washington. Secretary of State Seward lived in mortal terror of becoming involved in a foreign war while fighting the South, especially with Great Britain, and thus "Beast" Butler was sacrificed. It was an ironic twist, as Butler had hoped to stay in Seward's good graces by having earlier named the reception camp at Pittsfield in his honor, but in the end the general attributed his downfall mainly to him.[66]

The whole affair was another bungled operation by the administration, as Butler's replacement, Nathaniel P. Banks, was sent out partly to get him away from the East (and possibly further away from a campaign for the presidency). In their eagerness to make these changes, government officials had not thought through the consequences on Butler and not prepared a new position for him, making it appear that he and his policies were discredited. Butler had discounted rumors that Banks would replace him, a notable failure of his intelligence apparatus in Washington, and it was only when Banks arrived that Butler learned definitely that he had been removed. The administration had succeeded in making the "Beast" a sympathetic figure—no easy task. Like Butler's troops, a large segment of the Northern populace admired the firm policy he had pursued in New Orleans and were not happy to see the government seeming to cave in to Southerners and their foreign sympathizers.

Before departing, Butler issued a farewell message to his men, which they must have found affecting, considering all they had been through together.[67] In the following days he composed and published a similar address to the citizens of New Orleans, a revealing and highly personal document that has not received the attention it merits, either at the time or subsequently from historians.[68] The general began by reminding his audience to be grateful that he had not ruled as harshly as other conquerors throughout history and landed a jab at the British by noting examples where they had treated subject populations brutally. Butler had arrived in New Orleans with the firm conviction that ordinary working people were victims of nefarious policies pursued by wealthy aristocrats, and he administered his realm on that basis. Nothing he saw in New Orleans caused him to alter his policies in that regard; in contrast, his attitude toward slavery underwent a revolution.

As he acknowledged in his address, "I came among you, by teaching, by habit of mind, by political position, by social affinity, inclined to sustain your domestic laws, if by possibility they might be with safety to the Union." This was the standard Democratic Party platform. But after several months observing the workings and consequences of slavery, he declared that the institution "cursed of God," and in language reminiscent of John Brown, vowed that it "will be rooted out as the tares from the wheat, although the wheat be torn up with it." He concluded that "it is incompatible with the safety either of yourselves or of the Union." The general exhorted, "Look around you and say whether this saddening, deadening influence has not all but destroyed the very framework of your society." This was not much different than something Lincoln might have expressed—if anything, it was farther out on the abolitionist spectrum. Even Governor Andrew might have approved. There was no requirement for Butler to release a statement of this kind. The fact that he went ahead to use inflammatory language to a populace that hated him, or at best felt grudging respect for his stern administration, shows how important the subject had become to him. He had in New Orleans undergone something resembling the conversion experience most New England Congregationalist churches required for full membership.

Their commander's stunning change of heart was probably not widely known to the men of the 31st, none of whom were in New Orleans itself, and none of their writings comment on his remarkable address. The portion of the regiment at Fort Jackson saluted the seven steamers bringing Banks's entourage as it passed on December 16. The general was aboard the *North Star,* first in line, and accompanied by a sizable contingent of "nine month" troops, many from Massachusetts. These men, with the additional incentive of bounties, had responded to Lincoln's call for 300,000 relatively short-term volunteers to maintain Union strength while the new conscription law was bringing in others to serve for a longer term. Hawkes described his feelings to his mother:

It made me feel good all over to see these big steamers running up the Mississippi freighted with some more of the hardy sons of New England. It was exhilerating [*sic*]—the boys literally lined the parapet and the band played "Hail Columbia" and the other national airs as the steamers steamed by, which were greeted with cheers from the boys on ship.[69]

As they watched the troop ships pass, observers in the 31st Massachusetts would have been surprised to learn that several former members of their regiment were on board, men who had been discharged for health reasons but had recovered enough to rejoin the army. Eight who had previously served in the 31st enlisted in nine-month regiments, primarily the 46th and 49th Massachusetts. The former was sent to North Carolina, but the 49th, which had been organized at Pittsfield and drew from some of the same territory as the 31st, was assigned to the Department of the Gulf, creating the possibility of encounters with old comrades.

Six more steamers passed by over the following two days. The well-remembered *Mississippi* was part of this parade, and Hawkes remarked with heavy-handed humor, "The old craft looked natural as life, wonder if she has forgotten her old habit of running on to sand bars."[70] Thus Banks would start out his command of the Department of the Gulf with many more men than Butler had ever had. After the recall of the Vicksburg expedition, Butler had never had sufficient strength to launch a major campaign. The largest action he had authorized was an expedition under Weitzel into the "Lafourche country" west of New Orleans in October 1862. With Butler's backing, Weitzel had been jumped from lieutenant to brigadier general, one of the most rapid advances in American military history, but his advances on the ground were more measured. So many of Butler's troops were scattered at outposts or on sick call that he would not have been able to muster a large offensive even had he wished to. Even at the Battle of Baton Rouge, a large portion of the Union defenders had crawled out of their sick beds to repulse the Confederate attacks.

Butler and Banks felt no mutual affection, despite the fact that both had risen from humble origins in the same region of the United States. Banks had started out as a bobbin boy in a textile factory and was still sometimes referred to in those terms, whether admiringly or not. (The South, with its caste system, would not have been impressed.) As "political generals" from the same state, they were bound to be rivals; moreover, they held opposing political affiliations. Considering his ample grounds for resentment, Butler made a genuine effort to inform his replacement about the situation he was inheriting.

From a perch in the Custom House, Lieutenant Hallett observed Butler's departure: "The levee or wharf was thronged with citizens and soldiers and cheer after cheer was raised as the steamer . . . moved out into the stream." He had a clear view of the general as he "stood alone near the wheel house, a large military cloak thrown over his shoulders, and as he was cheered took off his cap and waved his hands to the crowd on the ships and levee."[71] In a final testimonial to Butler's rule, Jefferson Davis published a proclamation declaring him a felon and an outlaw.

While they surely paid close attention to the change of command, the attention of the enlisted men at Fort Jackson was focused on a surprisingly lavish Christmas festival. By then the original Puritan hostility to Christmas was fading, and even the pious Hawkes was not offended: "We had a holiday Christmas and a first rate dinner." This consisted of baked pork—a pig weighing ninety-five pounds—baked beef, plenty of potatoes, bread, butter, and apple sauce. The men put together a table the whole length of the casemates that could accommodate the full company. Somewhat surprisingly, Hawkes did not condemn the fact that "Lieut. Andrews sent down two gallons of whiskey to the boys and the Captain bought two more so all that wished had a drink before dinner. . . . After roll call they had two pails of hot flip." There was plenty of liquor in camp that day and plenty of men who were more than "half tight," yet by order of the colonel, no man was to be put into the guardhouse for anything he might do that day.[72]

Hawkes added that Captain Lee "does not find much time to drill his company now that his wife is here." The captain's "mulatto girl," Maggie, told him that "they are as loving as a couple just married." Hawkes, who had known the Lees at home, had a more charitable opinion than Lieutenant Howell, who did not have this acquaintance: "Two ministers in our Regt viz Capt Lee & Lieut [Horace F.] Morse, both left a Methodist pulpit to enter the army, can now drink whiskey and swear to perfection to say nothing of their visits to disreputable houses. Their hypocrasy [sic] disgusts me. The Capts wife is here now and he is old 'Peaches & Cream' to her ministerial."[73] In a confidential letter home, Lieutenant Rice echoed Howell's sentiments: "Lieut. Morse is a minister by profession, and if he isn't a better preacher than soldier, I don't want to have to hear him. You know my ideas of what is proper for a minister to do are pretty liberal; some would call them loose, and yet I have seen some things in him that I cannot reconcile my mind to believe consistent with his former sacred calling.[74]

Despite any misgivings Hawkes may have had about his captain, he acknowledged that "it really seems good to see a woman from the North and I almost imagine myself there again."[75] He held a low opinion of Southern womanhood in general: "I venture to say that there are *very* few *virtuous women* above the age of 15. Every man has as many *white mistresses* as he can afford and if a slave owner *plenty that are not as white*. The wife finds out the husband's unfaithfulness, so she is bound to have revenge in the same coin." His observation led him to believe: "There are very few federal officers that did not find a 'Cousin' while at the city last summer. I could tell some rather scandalous stories about some officers in this Reg't but you might not credit them, and they *might leak* out in some way. These 'Southern Cousins' are some how very enticing!"[76]

Hawkes went on to describe how the men found it demeaning to spend time guarding plantations where a pretty wife or daughter resided. His sentiments are not surprising from one with such a puritanical strain, but they must have been based largely on hearsay. It is unlikely that a person of his temperament had much interaction with the opposite sex during his few weeks in New Orleans or at isolated Fort Jackson. Rice, with a more worldly perspective, reported: "I have made a few and very few friends with the N.O. ladies, one or two secesh ones, too. The sex at large, however, though far from friendly, are very careful since the publication of the famous 'No. 28' how they insult the Federal soldiers in the streets." He added that "if the men of N.O. had the pluck of the women and their sentiments, we shouldn't stay there 48 hours."[77]

The year ended on a distinctly gloomy note, as news of the disastrous defeat at Fredericksburg (on December 14) arrived. Tupper was forced to concede that "the South have demonstrated their ability to maintain their independence, but we've got to keep on fighting, I suppose, till Old Abe gets out of office."[78] The resigned, ambiguous tone of the concluding sentence is capable of various interpretations, none seemingly flattering to the administration.

In a New Year's Day letter to his sister Clara, with whom he had a close relationship, Lieutenant Howell expressed a somber view of the war: "God grant that this year may not desolate as many homes and cause as many heartaches as the last. But the prospect is not at all flattering. Darker bodes the future at every move our cause grows more desperate."[79] This attitude may reflect the young officer's personality more than the reality of the situation. It certainly ignored signal Union successes, such as the capture of New Orleans, the re-pulse of Lee's invasion of Maryland, the outcome of the dreadful Battle of Shi-loh, and the seizure of the North Carolina coast, among others. In the South generally, other than the successful defense of Richmond against McClellan, 1862 was perceived as a year of disasters. Howell's dismal assessment may stem from the fact that events had confirmed that the war would not be short or glorious as well as his concern that, at the close of Butler's administration, which coincided closely with the end of the year, the 31st Massachusetts had not yet seen major combat. Its only losses in action had been the two men killed at Desert Station, while other regiments in the same brigade had par-ticipated in battles like Baton Rouge. This situation was galling to officers like Nettleton and Rice, who blamed it on the Butler-Andrew feud as it played out in the conflict between Whelden and Gooding. Butler had attributed holding back the 31st to military considerations but knew better than to commit the other influence to writing, even if he had it in mind. Once the general sailed northward to an urgent but fruitless meeting with Lincoln, none of this mat-tered any longer in Louisiana. At the end of 1862, the 31st was still divided among three posts, but there were signs that the new year would bring a uni-fying change.

6

A DEVIOUS ROUTE TO PORT HUDSON

JANUARY–MAY 1863

Nathaniel P. Banks was a much handsomer fellow than Butler and a better orator as well. To a large extent, his unexpected talent for public speaking had propelled the former bobbin boy up the political ladder. Like any executive succeeding a controversial and strongly defined predecessor, Banks sought to establish a separate identity by stressing points of difference in style and policy. By temperament, he was milder and smoother than Butler, and his initial impulse was to rule less harshly. In time, however, he was compelled to restore some of Butler's practices. Banks had hoped not to enlist any more black troops, but in this too he had to adjust his policy. He also retained and even expanded the "free labor" plantations his predecessor had inaugurated.

Many of the soldiers missed Butler. Joshua Hawkes, for example, wrote: "I wish Gen. Butler would come back, for Banks does not seem to know *how to run New Orleans*. He is disposed to make friends with the rich, while Butler was no respecter of persons."[1] Thomas Norris, who expressed mature opinions for one his age, agreed: "all of the soldiers who came out with Butler much regret his removal, and besides the soldiers the citizens think it is rough, for they do find no such man in *Banks* as they did in *Butler,* and there is a great deal more secesh shown in the city now than there has been for a long time."[2] James Tupper voiced similar feelings, though with his usual individualistic slant: "I've nothing against Banks, but this policy of changing officers, Quartermaster's, Commissaries, etc. is a bad thing. I suppose Butler has made money & been guilty of extortion, but no Union man has anything to complain of. I approve of taking property from Rebels & if they get off with losing nothing but their property they ought to be glad."[3]

Lt. Joseph Hallett confirmed these sentiments: "The troops don't like the change in Generals at all. Banks is a smart man but Butler has done the work and is doing as well as could be desired. Give him the troops that Banks has and he would do a great work this winter." From a personal perspective he opined: "I don't see the point myself in removing Butler and if it's a political move, cursed be the man that done it. Politics is rotten, a political man is the meanest kind of a man nowadays. They had better leave their politics and go to studying tactics."[4] Hallett did not mention Lincoln by name, but he must have known that no change at that level of command could be made without the president's approval. After further reflection, he observed that "Gen Banks is a little busy with the secessionists. They are exhulting [sic] mightily over the changes in generals, and sing the Bonny Blue Flag and talk secession to their hearts content." In his opinion "Gen Butler knew no pardon to violators of the Stars & Stripes, those who hauled it down from the U.S. Mint were numbered with the murderers and swung at the ropes end. Traitors when known were severely punished, and Banks will have to put his foot down as Butler did or lose what Butler in his eight months gained."[5] With Butler gone, New Orleans seemed not to have the air of a city occupied by a hated enemy: "The citizens are celebrating Christmas Eve by a display of fireworks, i.e. rockets and roman candles while the little ones are firing crackers. The air, the music and all but the people make me think of our Fourth of July evenings at the North."[6]

Having brought a large contingent with him, Banks found himself in command of more than 42,000 troops, nearly three times as many as Butler had amassed on any occasion. Of the fifty-six infantry regiments in his department, twenty-two were nine-month men who had been recruited locally in the Northern states (much like calling up the National Guard in later conflicts). By the time they disembarked in Louisiana, these men had used up nearly two months of their term in processing, transit, and rudimentary training, so there was unmistakable pressure to put them to use in some operation that could be concluded before their discharge date. Since the Federals had established a firm base in Louisiana, there was a persistent temptation to gain a foothold in Texas, opening that vast area to Northern settlers who would, in theory, form a free-state government. But competing political considerations, primarily discontent in the Midwest that threatened Republican control, made it imperative to open fully the Mississippi instead.[7] The last two Confederate strongholds on the river were Vicksburg, Mississippi, and Port Hudson, Louisiana. Maj. Gen. Ulysses Grant was experimenting with various methods to subdue Vicksburg, leaving it to Banks to remove the obstacle at Port Hudson, 110 miles downriver.

In sharp contrast to Butler, Banks had no prewar military experience and had never displayed much interest in the subject. Propelling him instantaneously into a position of high command was an inexcusable mistake by the Lincoln administration, one that caused the unnecessary death and maiming of hundreds of young men. If he had been made a colonel, in charge of a single regiment, or even a brigadier general, Banks might have had a chance to absorb the profession gradually. As an early appointed major general, though, he was immediately thrust into the command of armies. With his shiny new commission, he outranked all but three men in the entire Union army and was thereby placed above officers who in peacetime had stagnated for years as lieutenants and captains in the regular service before creeping up the ladder of promotion. His appointment was certain to have a corrosive effect on an officer corps that was simultaneously close knit and jealous—these men had little incentive to do anything that would advance the career of such a flagrantly political officer. Banks's senior rank made it difficult for subordinates to offer advice even if they had wanted to, while a major general could hardly request instruction in routine matters. The most regrettable aspect of the situation is that there is every reason to believe that Banks would have made an excellent cabinet member, one who would have been at least as effective as the others. Moreover, it would seem that whichever faction Lincoln was trying to appease by elevating Banks to a lofty position would have been satisfied to see him in the cabinet. By all accounts, Banks made a fine appearance in uniform, but placing him in a military role was indefensible.

General in Chief Henry W. Halleck, nicknamed "Old Brains," was regular army all the way, and he expressed himself on the subject of political generals with greater decisiveness than he employed in issuing orders: "It seems but little better than murder, to give important commands to such men as Banks, Butler, [John] McClernand, [Franz] Sigel and Lew. Wallace, and yet it seems impossible to prevent it."[8] Of course, Halleck was as far from an impartial observer as one could find, and his scathing remark conveniently overlooked countless examples of lives squandered by professional officers, of which it suffices to mention Grant at Cold Harbor, Maj. Gen. Ambrose Burnside (reluctantly) at Fredericksburg, Maj. Gen. John Pope on several occasions, Confederate general Braxton Bragg customarily, and even Gen. Robert E. Lee with

"Pickett's Charge" on the third day at Gettysburg, among other occasions. But-ler was actually a contrary example since he sometimes overcompensated by using his fertile imagination to do everything possible to avoid ruinous frontal assaults.

Butler had not fretted excessively over military organization, perhaps his way of showing contempt for military hierarchy as well as keeping everything under tighter personal control. With his larger and more diverse force, how-ever, Banks could not afford a casual approach and formed a regular military structure, with brigades and divisions. Collectively, his troops were organized as the Nineteenth Corps. Under his organizational table, the 31st Massachu-setts formed part of the Third Brigade of the Third Division, commanded by Brig. Gen. William H. Emory (1811–87). Because of his detached duty, Pri-vate Tupper was probably one of the few men in the 31st Massachusetts who had occasion to see their division commander in person, and his description makes it evident that affection was not one of the feelings the Maryland gen-eral inspired: "[Emory] is a stern, soldierly looking man. It don't do for any soldier to speak to him. If they have a message to communicate, they must do it through the General's orderly, who is always outside of the room, or when the General is out, rides behind him on horseback."[9] On another occasion he described Emory as "a fierce looking fellow—has a red mustache & gray eyes & looked savage enough."[10]

Colonel Gooding was given command of the brigade. Organizational ar-rangements were frequently adjusted, and as best as can be determined, in January 1863 he was in charge of the 31st Massachusetts and three other reg-iments: the 38th Massachusetts and the 116th and 156th New York.[11] Good-ing was thus in command of the 31st Massachusetts but was not solely its commander. Considering how much strife had accompanied the position, it is ironic that Gooding spent very little time in exclusive command of the reg-iment.

Capt. William S. B. Hopkins was jumped to lieutenant colonel (after Whel-den's resignation), skipping the rank of major and placing him in command of the 31st. Tupper, although detached as a quartermaster clerk still followed the affairs of the regiment, knew Hopkins well and called it "a surprise to everybody, though he was rather expected to get the Majorship."[12] Hopkins had been elected captain by the men of his company, many of whom he had recruited and were his townspeople from Ware. His advance to command the regiment had been decided by his superiors, in which Gooding must have had a voice; but the intervention of his father (as described in chapter 5) was decisive. Governor Andrew would have little reason to choose Major Bache, an unknown Democrat, over Hopkins, the son of a fellow abolitionist and important Republican politician. This could not avoid the appearance of an affront to Bache, who had held the rank of major since Camp Seward. It seemed just that to Hawkes, who was becoming increasingly disillusioned and outspoken (in his letters): "We were rather 'taken down' on learning that Capt. Hopkins had been commissioned a Lt. Col., for Maj. Bache is a good fellow and we had supposed he was sure of the place."[13] Luther Fairbank agreed that Bache was a "good fellow," while Captain Hopkins himself described him as a "mild" man.[14] Though not as stormy as before, a cloud of discord persisted over the regiment.

Hopkins and even his female family members were aware of the tension, as Lt. Horace F. Morse, on a visit to Sarah Hopkins, spoke of her brother's "delicate position" but added that the new lieutenant colonel had "acted most honorably."[15] Erastus Hopkins had pushed to be sure that his son was selected to fill the vacancy that would be created if Bache moved up and was apparently surprised when Andrew jumped young Hopkins out of the regular progression. On learning of this startling move, the elder Hopkins sent the governor a heartfelt and revealing letter: "In making this appointment it is to be hoped and presumed that you were guided by motives higher than those of any personal friendship; uniting, possibly, with some conviction of personal merit. But no cold philosophy like the above, can repress the gratitude which I now express, for the honor and esteem which you have manifested toward, and conferred upon my son." Erastus was careful to note for the record "that so great [a] promotion should be assigned him was surely not at my suggestion, and it is the more gratifying & flattering because implying that he has a meritorious reputation in other and higher quarters." He then added a curious statement that seems to suggest, as openly as was possible, some internal doubt: "I *know* that he will be solemnly impressed with the responsibility of his new position, which impression, combining with the resources which I hope may be within him, afford the best augury that occurs to me, that the trust will prove itself not unworthily bestowed." He concluded with an exclamation that reinforces this hint of doubt about his son's fitness to bear the heavy responsibility: "I both rejoice and tremble."[16] If Erastus Hopkins actually harbored such misgivings, he dared not confess them to himself, much less to his son or to the governor of Massachusetts.

On January 22, 1863, the five companies of the 31st Massachusetts at Fort Jackson were recalled, joining the two companies from Kennerville; the three detached at Fort Pike remained there. At that time Company D reported only thirty-two men for duty, likely the least of any company, though some of the shrinkage was due to transfers to other units.[17] The Fort Jackson contingent arrived in New Orleans the next day and at Carrollton on the twenty-fourth.[18] They were replaced at Fort Jackson by three companies of the 2nd Louisiana Native Guards, a black regiment. The fact that military strategists were willing to trust the safety of the fort to a smaller number of presumably less reliable soldiers shows that they no longer perceived a serious threat to it. At the same time, the assembling of first-line units confirmed that serious campaigning was in store.

Black troops were still a novelty, and white soldiers were curious about their behavior, but in this instance they did not overlap long enough to allow much observation. Contact was further limited because the Native Guards camped in tents outside the walls rather than inside the fort itself. Especially in Louisiana, where the subject had been brought to the fore, it seems that every Northerner in uniform had an opinion about the suitability of African Americans to become soldiers. Often these feelings were mixed or contradictory. With time on their hands in July 1862, the New Englanders, Fairbank noted, held lengthy discussions of "the negro question." At that time, with manpower pressure not yet severe, his personal feeling was, "if we can't whip them without arming the negroes we had better give under."[19] On seeing the 2nd Louisiana, Hawkes termed them "a good looking set of men. Several of the Capts. are colored and nearly all of the Lieuts. Chaplain Barnes [formerly of Company F, 31st Massachusetts] says there are not more than forty men in the whole Reg't but that can read and write." He then added, "I confess to some feelings akin to those of contempt that the occupation of a soldier should be filled by negroes, yet I know that is not a right spirit."[20]

Lt. Luther Howell voiced similar contradictions. At Fort Jackson in August 1862, he was in charge of 180 contrabands and informed his sister, "I believe it will take years of independence to make them soldiers who will not cower like a whipped spaniel at sight of a white mans [sic] eye." But while concluding, "I don't believe that they are brave enough to fight," he added, "yet as soldiers we can't afford to throw away any arms."[21] As an educated man, the issue clearly weighed on his mind, as he had written earlier in the month, "Never a peace shall we have until the nigger question by some means is disposed of."[22] Lt. Frederick Rice disagreed with Howell's assessment, saying simply, "I am not one of those who think the darks won't fight."[23] Rice was able to keep an open mind on the subject, and on another occasion he observed of the black troops at Fort Pike: "Of their qualifications as soldiers, I can't give a very strong opinion, as they have never been tried, and I have never seen them except at one or two Parades and Inspections. I will say however they execute the Manual of Arms very creditably and march better than the majority of white troops that I have seen."[24]

Writing soon after the publication of the Emancipation Proclamation, Private Tupper, another collegiate soldier, adopted a more individualistic approach. Based on his interactions while with the Quartermaster Department, he brought out aspects of their situation that were usually overlooked: "About Emancipating the niggers. I think it is a good thing as it takes the property away from the Rebels & will ruin the South for this generation, but as far as its benefitting the blacks, I don't think it will unless they are taken away from the Army & sent off together somewhere where someone can look out for them." Drawing on personal experience rather than abstraction, he wrote: "I see how it is here when only a few, comparatively speaking, are with the Army. It is worse than slavery. Instead of having one master, every soldier thinks he has an interest in a government nigger & they abuse them out of pure malice. I never hear a soldier speak a good word for a nigger. If there is any work to be done, they are worked night and day." Tupper described an incident in which "a lot of them worked unloading a steamboat all day & didn't have anything to eat from 6 in the morning till after dark," concluding that "somehow the soldiers hate the negroes." He witnessed another occasion when "the 21st Indiana Regiment went off on board a boat, several darkies who had been living with the Regiment went aboard to go, too. The soldiers drove them off & one had a cane which he would beat over the poor negro enough to shock any one. So I don't think their condition will be much improved & I guess many a negro wishes he was with his master." The army paid the black workers ten dollars a month for their labor, deducting from these wages their clothing costs, and "if anything is lost they say the nigger stole it & take it out of their pay, so they don't get much. Two of the Quartermaster's niggers got 50 cents for last month's work." As a final abuse, Tupper described how their health suffered while with the army: "When they are sick nobody cares whether they live or not & sometimes they are kept to work till they are taken to the Hospital & then their bodies are almost cold in death. One negro was taken around in an ambulance to all the Hospitals . . . and had to be taken back to where they started because, as I said, the hospitals were for white folks."[25]

Tupper, as a quartermaster clerk, might have been in a position to employ ex-slaves but adopted a fixed policy against it: "I won't have anything to do with contrabands. It is more bother to watch them and keep them to work than they are worth."[26] While Tucker, Rice, and the others happened to be neutral or unenthusiastic about the subject of black soldiers, other members of the regiment who did not leave written accounts must have been more supportive since they later left the 31st Massachusetts to accept commissions in "colored" regiments.

When the Emancipation Proclamation was first published in New Orleans, Tupper was enthusiastic, though in a subtly shaded way, and his lack of reverence for the Constitution is startling in an age that has come to venerate it: "There is something to fight for now. The idea of restoring the union as it was under the Old Constitution was not worth fighting for. In the first place, I considered it impossible & even if it could be done, what object would be gained if they should come together to wrangle & fight over the inconsistencies of the Constitution. That document," he concluded bluntly, "is a dead letter—adapted to the exigencies of 75 years ago, but utterly powerless to save the country now."[27]

While supportive of emancipation in principle, Tupper thought the process would be more prolonged and tortured than many expected: "You'll see from the Plaquemine paper, Banks' order returning slaves to their plantations—good thing. Some think the slaveholders are running over Banks, but he knows what his business is." He added, "Slavery is doomed, but it is so connected with the civilization of this country, so deep-rooted, that it will take the rest of this century to obliterate it." Meanwhile, "any disposition of the poor miserable blacks so they can have any kind of care till their status is clearly defined is preferable to their flocking around the camps, impeding military operations, demoralizing the Army, and suffering as much & more than in a state of servitude." Chastened by his experiences in the South, Tupper finished by conceding, "I am still an abolitionist, but a little reflection will show that 3 million blacks cannot be emancipated at once without producing a great calamity to the class it intends to benefit."[28]

General Butler had occupied Baton Rouge largely at the behest of Captain Farragut, and when he abandoned the town he asserted that it was "of no possible military importance."[29] Whether or not that was true at the time is debatable, but when Port Hudson became the objective, Baton Rouge regained the value it had lost. One of Banks's first acts on taking over the department was to reoccupy the Louisiana capital, though much of it lay in ruins. In a straight line Baton Rouge was only about fifteen miles from Port Hudson, but there was no direct land route and no clear military path of approach. Banks decided to pursue an indirect strategy, cutting off the post from support, especially supplies from Texas. In January 1863 he sent a force under General Weitzel to clear Bayou Teche. Coming up from the Gulf, Weitzel pushed back the Confederates and accomplished the destruction of an enemy gunboat, though the effect on Port Hudson was questionable.

This provided the background for the first offensive move involving the 31st Massachusetts, an obscure foray mentioned in two summaries of the regiment's service and several personal accounts. According to these sources, seven companies of the 31st set off with the rest of Emory's division on February 12 to follow a water route and seize a place called Butte à la Rose (now Butte La Rose), where the Confederates had a fortified outpost along the Atchafalaya River near Grand Lake. (If Weitzel had pressed farther eastward, he would have come to the same point.) Banks's strategy, as he tried to explain later, was grounded in the fact that garrisoning the widespread posts for which he was responsible would leave him only twelve to fourteen thousand troops for an offensive against Port Hudson. According to the precepts of military science, that was far too few to invest or assault the stronghold, whose garrison at that time outnumbered the forces Banks considered he had available. Since an attacking army would have to occupy a longer line to invest the compact works, it would be vulnerable to penetration at any point. Banks therefore turned his attention to opening an interior route of approach and communication via the Atchafalaya River, which split off from the Mississippi between Port Hudson and the Red River. In theory this would enable him to establish contact with

Farragut and Grant and block the supply line down the Red River to Port Hudson.[30] The inspiration for this strategy may have been suggested by Weitzel, given his familiarity with the region. In Banks's estimation Butte à la Rose, which barely kept its head above the flooded country around it, was a place "of considerable strength, and is intended to defend the country above, including the capital of the State [then at Shreveport] and the Red River. . . . This post reduced, the way to the Red River is believed to be substantially clear."[31]

The expedition set off on board the steamer *Kepper,* which Fairbank described as "one of the slowest old coaches on the river."[32] It brought them from their base in Carrollton to the town of Plaquemine, some fifteen miles from Baton Rouge, though only after the pilots struck for higher wages, some of the crew refused to venture into dangerous territory, and their replacements ran the vessel aground in dense fog.[33] When the larger steamer *Iberville* attempted to pull the *Kepper* free, it damaged the stern and almost knocked over the boiler, which could have set off a ruinous fire; once again the 31st Massachusetts had narrowly escaped disaster on the water.[34] From Plaquemine, at least according to the maps, Bayou Plaquemine would connect through a series of shallow waterways to the Atchafalaya. Since this venture was meant to be a quick surprise raid, baggage and tents were left behind, and even the officers were not informed of the objective. A puzzled Lieutenant Howell observed, "How far and for what purpose are questions that you can answer quite as well as I can, for it is a profound secret."[35] Tupper, who observed the expedition as it departed, made a shrewd assessment of its purpose: "as the boats are of the lightest draft, it is expected they will ascend some of the bayous this side of Port Hudson & make a dash on the rear of the enemy or cut off some important line of communication." Such was the haste that ten or eleven men were absent when the regiment left and were arrested when they were able to report back.[36]

Companies D and E were detached southward and marched nine miles through knee-deep mud to a place called Indian Village, which consisted of a sugar mill and three houses on Grand Lake.[37] In the end, the entire expedition returned after a week without accomplishing anything. No enemy troops were encountered; the geography itself proved sufficient to thwart Banks. As he explained afterward, "This attempt failed on account of the complete stoppage of Bayou Plaquemine by three years' accumulation of drift logs and snags, filling the bayou from the bed of the stream to the surface, rendering it impenetrable to our boats, and requiring the labor of months to open it to navigation."[38] One might question why Banks could not have determined this without risking the lives and health of an entire division. Throughout his military career, one of the consequences of his inexperience was his inability to gather and employ intelligence.

Two men of the 31st fell overboard and drowned in the Mississippi on the first night of this fruitless venture. One was a man with a German surname who had signed up in New Orleans. (Other accounts confirm that a number of the Louisiana locals who filled out the ranks of the 31st were of foreign origin, especially Germans.) One of the victims was drunk, but the other was knocked over by a rope and sank from the weight of his uniform and equipment.[39]

The confusion inherent in following Civil War movements is compounded in the case of Port Hudson, where Banks launched two separate drives. His first was not intended to seize the fortified town but to create a diversion that would help Farragut run past the place with his fleet. The soldiers were not informed of this and so were baffled and resentful at the way the maneuver was conducted. Loosely coordinated with Farragut, Banks marched out of Baton Rouge on March 13 with 12,000 men, leaving 5,000 behind to guard the town. Five companies of the 31st Massachusetts had departed Carrollton on March 6 on the steamer *Algerine,* while Companies B and C were aboard the *Sallie Robinson,* described by Hawkes as "one of the fastest of the river steamers."[40] They arrived the following evening and set up at what they called Camp Magnolia, or Magnolia Grove, near Baton Rouge. A few days later they moved off with the rest of Banks's expedition as part of Gooding's brigade, which included the 38th and 53rd Massachusetts and the 156th and 175th New York.

At first the troops were in a festive mood, as recalled by Joseph Hallett: "How the blood tingled, how excited the brain, how elastic the step when the bugle's clear and sharp notes sounded the advance. The 31st was there with seven days' rations in knapsack, equipment bright as silver dollars and all eager to meet the enemy."[41] Thrilled to be released from the deadening routine of camp life and with the prospect of going into battle at last, the men burst out with songs and cheers. In addition to enthusiasm, they were encumbered by an excessive burden of equipment and personal gear, supplemented in some cases by domestic fowl killed along the road. As the day wore on, oppressive heat built up. There was no thought of singing, and even breathing became difficult for the profusely sweating men. Soon the road was littered with discarded equipment and clothing as well as dead birds. Even as shrewd a soldier as Fairbank confessed to throwing away his overcoat, drawers, and socks; only two days before he had observed that the morning was "cold as Greenland."[42] Banks and his subordinates were culpable for not having prepared their men with practice marches. The nine-month regiments had probably never experienced a forced march with full equipment, and even a relatively veteran regiment like the 31st Massachusetts had spent many months in stationary duty at Fort Jackson and Kennerville. Mounted on glossy, well-rested horses, the officers apparently had not thought about such training and soon lost control of the straggling army.

Banks bivouacked several miles below Port Hudson, ready to feign an attack. Becoming impatient, as he had before Fort Jackson, Farragut began his run on March 14, earlier than he had led Banks to expect; consequently, the army was not in position to create a significant diversion.[43] The general noted this in his report: "Up to this moment it had been understood that the passage of the fleet was to be made in the gray of the morning and not at night, but at 5 o'clock I received a dispatch from the admiral stating that he should commence his movement at 8 o'clock in the evening."[44] The reply from Banks to Farragut was carried at great hazard by Lieutenant Hallett, then detached to the Signal Corps. During the night, most of the Union troops were treated to a terrific display as Farragut launched his epic but agonizingly slow run upstream past the defenses. The 31st Massachusetts, however, had been detached to guard the eastern flank of the army and thus saw only distant flashes and heard the roar of big guns.[45]

Only two of Farragut's warships, their decks splattered with gore and body parts, made it past the rebel guns. (If his other employments of this tactic had produced similar results, he probably would not have been honored with a magnificent statue.) His last ship, the old side-wheeler USS *Mississippi* (different from the privately owned ship that had brought the 31st to Ship Island) was disabled by Confederate fire and exploded in the river with an enormous fiery blast. It was an inglorious end for a vessel that had been Commodore Matthew C. Perry's flagship when he "opened" Japan in 1853 by steaming into Tokyo harbor. Yet just the two warships that made it above Port Hudson were sufficient to disrupt traffic on the Red River and block supplies to the Confederate stronghold.

Once he learned that the vessels had succeeded in passing Port Hudson, Banks began to withdraw his forces. There was no reason for him to remain, and he was justified in fearing that the Confederates might turn on him. Some of the forward units, having witnessed the explosion of the *Mississippi*, thought the Confederates were attacking and began to panic, but their flight was contained. At a place called Cypress Bayou, protected only by shelter tents that Captain Hopkins declared "are good for nothing in hard rains," the soldiers "slept in the edge of the woods in water from 3 to 6 inches deep, through a succession of severe thunder showers."[46] Especially for men weakened by illness, this kind of exposure could lead to prolonged and irreversible decline. A New Hampshire officer wrote, "There is no doubt that scores of our regiment never after that mud march knew a well day."[47]

When they returned to Camp Magnolia on the twentieth, many of the men had lost confidence in Banks, and he never regained their full trust. On the outward march the soldiers had cheered when he rode past; on the return, he passed through silent ranks. These clues apparently passed unnoticed, and in his report at the end of the expedition, the general informed Halleck, "My troops are in good health and in the best spirit and condition."[48] In a general order Banks asserted that the expedition had been a success. But he had been trapped in a situation in which he could not explain to the men beforehand that they were only conducting a diversion without simultaneously alerting the enemy, so it seemed to many that he had retreated without having attempted a battle. Fairbank, always a realist, declared, "Here we shall rest until Gen. Banks wants another grand move on Port Hudson." Lt. Nelson F. Bond, who usually adhered to the official line, acknowledged that they had returned to their old camp "a disheartened lot."[49] Captain Hopkins was similarly unimpressed: "We have made a great show, marching & countermarching with no further result than the seizure of quite a quantity of cotton for the Government."[50] Hawkes asserted: "I forbear criticism. Though by a bold dash I think the place might have been taken."[51] This last is doubtful, since the same guns with which the Confederates had caused so much damage to the Union fleet could have been directed with effect against the Union army. In addition, at that time the Port Hudson garrison had approximately the same strength as Banks's force. The time to seize the Louisiana bastion might have been the previous year, when the Confederates were in disarray along the Mississippi after the fall of New Orleans, but it did not figure in anyone's strategic calculation.

Corporal Hawkes was becoming increasingly disenchanted with the whole enterprise. After noting how unhealthy the water supply was in the camp at

Baton Rouge and observing that seventeen men had died in hospital there on a single day, he admitted: "I will say I wish the *show was out.* Our being here seems simply to amount to getting us into unhealthy places, feeding us no meat but pork and drinking stagnant water then wondering *why* so many have the diarrhoea and mad because you are sick." His resentment took on a personal tone against the officers, many of whom he said "have no more regard for a *man* than a *mule.* This is particularly the case with some of these petty lieutenants. There are several that the boys say there is a question as to whether God made *them* or *they God.*"[52] By then, the corporal was ready to admit that he "was never made for a soldier" and expressed unrestrained longing to be home, asking on one occasion if there had "been much of a sugar season," referring to maple sugar. Hawkes was in an area famous for sugar-cane plantations, but it was very different from what he had known in New England. His growing discouragement may have affected his health, as he developed chronic digestive ailments that never abated until he was discharged in a gravely weakened condition.

Hawkes's feeling toward some officers was by no means an isolated case. It is striking that even in a regiment like the 31st Massachusetts, in which the officers and men came from similar backgrounds and often knew each other in civilian life, many enlisted men felt resentment toward officers. Fairbank, a carpenter by trade, was asked to do many small projects for officers and became well acquainted with them. On one occasion he built a partition in the guard house "so that the Off'rs w'd not be obligd to mingle with the Privates. What a pity! I suppose we are not good enough for retired lawyers, shoemakers and teamsters."[53]

In marked contrast to such expressed contempt, Fairbank was devoted to Lieutenant Bond. When that officer was transferred in December 1862, Fairbank wrote: "Our loved and honored Second Lieut., N. F. Bond, has been taken from us and promoted to First Lieut, Co. K. He took leave of us tonight, and bid us farewell at roll call." One might think that Bond's replacement, Sgt. Milton Sagendorph, would be pleasing to Fairbank, as they were both "mechanics" as the term was then used (Sagendorph a painter and Fairbank a carpenter); both were from Ware and almost the exact same age (twenty-one). Nevertheless, Fairbank reported, "The company are all downhearted at the change."[54]

In his purposeful wanderings around New Orleans, Private Tupper was constantly sniffing out clues as to the outlook for the war. He understood the importance of morale and was sensitive to shifts in public opinion, but in early

1863 the signs remained disconcertingly mixed. Attending a lively Unionist meeting was so heartening that "it almost shakes the faith which for the last few months has been growing stronger & stronger in my mind that a separation would be the ultimate result of the struggle."[55] A few weeks later this hopeful impression was counterbalanced when Tupper watched Confederate prisoners being exchanged: "I went down to the levee to see the rebel prisoners off. The steamer *Empire Parish* was waiting with the white flag raised above the Stars & Stripes. I haven't seen so much Secesh feeling exhibited since the first day or two of our coming into the city." The prisoners "were walking freely among the crowd, dressed very handsomely in the gray uniform of the Confederates. Some were very handsome fellows & no doubt belong to the first families of the state. The women were perfectly wild, waving their handkerchiefs & saying 'God bless you.'" Tupper heard one say: "'How good it does me to see this gray. I am perfectly sick of the Yankee Blue.'"[56] The continued resistance of Port Hudson and Vicksburg was bound to encourage such sentiments.

Conversely, another 31st Massachusetts officer, Lieutenant Hallett, professed to be altogether unimpressed by the men over whom the women were swooning: "I have seen a great many rebel prisoners but as with Southerners generally they have a great gift of gab, can talk and brag but can't do the work when it comes to soldiering that Yankees can." With rich sarcasm he noted: "My eye has watched rebel officers on parole in N.O. their uniforms covered with gold. They walk as though they were Kings or Generals when in fact they are poor subjects of Gen Butler. Prisoners of War. In their own domain, Lieutenants." By contrast, he observed: "how different they appear from the Federal officers with their plain neat uniforms, unassuming manners. The place where the Federal soldiers show their dignity and worth is on the battle field, the Confederates in the city where all is quiet and fire arms of little value."[57] In writing this Hallett was setting forth his perception of a core cultural difference between the two nations.

By April 1863 the 31st Massachusetts (what remained of the original contingent) had been in service nearly a year and a half, roughly one-half of its total commitment. In that span the men had seen only minor combat and few wearying marches, but that was about to change. Over the next four months, they grew hardened by long marches through unfamiliar country, punctuated by frequent skirmishing and several major battles before they settled back into camp routine in the final months of the year. First-person accounts by members of the regiment are thin for this period, which is understandable: only seven companies participated, and these probably retained only about half of their original complement. It does not appear that the Louisiana replacements left personal documentation—or at least it was not solicited at the time Rice and others were compiling the regimental history. (Andrew Hanselmann, a Swiss immigrant who joined the 31st Massachusetts in May 1862, left an account many years later, probably around the turn of the twentieth century, but it is so confused and garbled that it cannot be considered reliable.)[58] The men were constantly on the move, often under arduous conditions, which did not encourage writing. Fortunately, the main source available for this period is the diary of Luther Fairbank, a bluntly honest observer who did not hesitate to express trenchant opinions. It would be simplistic to describe him as disillusioned, but he was encumbered by few illusions from the start and did not resort to the cloying religiosity or other sentimentalism that offered a common refuge. His concerns were the typical ones of a soldier, primarily relating to food, sleeping conditions, and weather. Yet his carpentry work gave him opportunities to mingle with officers and men in other companies as well. The tasks he was given were simple construction jobs like laying a floor in a tent, not fine carpentry, which suggests that the impression of rural Yankees as being competent jacks-of-all trades may be somewhat overdrawn. While it remains unknown exactly what Fairbank used for tools, it is unlikely that he had brought his tool chest from home.

On paper at least, Banks mounted one of the more impressive formations in the Union army, with most of its members relatively fresh and well equipped. It is surprising, therefore, that he was given so little in the way of guidance by Secretary of War Stanton or Major General Halleck as to how to employ his formidable forces. Halleck, born in central New York State in 1815, had earned the nickname "Old Brains" because of his scholarly habits. He was appointed general in chief in July 1862 in the hope that his knowledge and intelligence could formulate a winning strategy, but the nickname had a double edge, making it just as likely that the "old brains" resided within a body too feeble to move decisively. Basically, there were three possibilities open to Banks: march into interior Louisiana to try to destroy the small Confederate army defending that region; reduce Port Hudson; or assist Grant at Vicksburg either in person or by dispatching troops. Each of these presented opportunities and risks: if Banks pursued the rebels deeper into Louisiana, it would have only an indirect effect on opening the Mississippi; if he concentrated on Port Hudson or Vicksburg, it would free the small rebel army to cause mischief in Louisiana; if he did not invest Port Hudson, it would give the Confederates there time to strengthen its defenses.

Banks was not as hopeless a strategist as is sometimes depicted. Some politicians in high office have the ability to assess the totality of a problem, even if they cannot always devise a means of solving it. His failings as a commander lay not so much in analyzing objectives and consequences as in the mechanics of moving troops—determining how much space they occupied, calculating how much supply they required, and deploying them effectively on a battle-field or a line of march. When he decided to move into central Louisiana, Banks was not necessarily misguided in believing that it would contribute to subduing Port Hudson. By pushing the Confederates there back, he would prevent them from reinforcing the Mississippi stronghold with men or supplies. At the same time, it would protect the scattered garrisons he had left at New Orleans, Baton Rouge, and lesser points, which might be vulnerable if the Confederates were able to concentrate against any one of them.

If Banks's ultimate objective was Port Hudson, his push into central Louisiana approached it in a roundabout way. Portions of his Nineteenth Corps began moving out in the last days of March 1863. On the thirty-first, Colonel Gooding conducted a full review and inspection of his brigade, which left camp the next day on various transport vessels and arrived at Algiers, where it set up camp early the following morning. Orders came down to be ready to depart, but the brigade did not leave until the ninth. In an odd incident on April 8, a cavalryman in the 1st Louisiana (U.S.) attempted to shoot Gooding and another officer but either missed or did not get the shots off. He was promptly arrested.[59]

Finally, on the morning of April 9, the men boarded railroad cars and traveled to Brashear City (now Morgan City), where they arrived about 5 P.M. Fairbank, who observed that "the first Port Hudson march taught me to go light," reported that the rail journey passed through swamps "lined with snakes and alligators" for roughly eighty miles.[60] It is surprising that the rail line was still in good enough condition and had enough equipment to transport so many men and their gear efficiently. Private Tupper was not with the 31st on this journey but later spent time at Brashear City after the quartermasters set up a temporary headquarters there. Probably, he resented being hauled away from his cozy nest in New Orleans, and this feeling soured his perception of the town: "Brashear City is the worst place I've been in since I left Hardwick & I don't know but I should prefer to live in Hardwick, even. Ship Island is much preferable. A little village of half a dozen houses, hot, full of mosquitoes, bay water to drink, no women or children to amuse yourself with, the situation of a fellow is rough indeed."[61]

For a long while after they left Algiers, every day took the Union forces farther from Port Hudson and the river it guarded. On the first night the 31st crossed the Atchafalaya River to Berwick City. Fairbank resorted to sarcasm when he wrote that Brashear and Berwick were "large cities about the size of Ware centre."[62] From there on the troops encountered rebel skirmishers and heard occasional gunfire almost every day as they ventured deeper into the country. Supported by naval gunboats, they reached Pattersonville on April 11. They were now approaching a Confederate earthwork defense known as Fort Bisland, which might have to be taken by assault.

Most accounts imply that the name "Fort Bisland" was more impressive than the actual position. The earthwork stretched across a narrow neck of land and to the high ground on both sides across the Bayou Teche, a quiet waterway that Banks could easily shift men across on a pontoon bridge as the situation demanded. On either side of this strip of land lay swamps that were considered impassable. The site not only presented some defensive advantages but also held the possibility of becoming a trap for its defenders. Banks had perceived this potential, sending Brig. Gen. Cuvier Grover's division on a flanking movement up the Atchafalaya River toward Franklin to block any Confederate escape. But Grover's advance was so dilatory that even Banks, no dynamo himself, became impatient and began probing the defenses before the division was in place.

At this point the Union commander still held hopes of eliminating the entire Army of Western Louisiana, which opposed him in this region. That little force was commanded by Maj. Gen. Richard Taylor (1826–79), a favorite son of Louisiana and also a son of former president Zachary Taylor. As commander of a Louisiana brigade in Virginia the previous year, he had fought against Banks in the Shenandoah Valley, an encounter that had not generated any overwhelming respect for the New Englander's military ability. A brilliant intellectual, Taylor was at the same time a bold and active commander. He had never attended a military academy but had educated himself by exhaustive study of military history and by serving as his father's aide during the Mexican War. As a Democrat, he had attended the disastrous Charleston convention and, like Butler (with whom he probably was acquainted), had sought to prevent the party from splitting. Taylor was also closely associated with President Davis, whose first wife was one of Taylor's sisters.

Official reports by General Emory, Colonel Gooding, and Lieutenant Colonel Hopkins together present a reasonably coherent account of the battle at Fort Bisland, which extended over three days. Gooding's brigade, including the 31st Massachusetts, engaged Confederate cavalry skirmishers on April 12, before sending the 31st across the bayou in the afternoon to aid the 175th New York on the east side. That night the entire Union force pulled back out of artillery range and bivouacked along the bayou.

On the next day Lieutenant Bond, who was then attached to brigade headquarters, recorded that "the first salutation this morning early was a few shots from the rebel artillery." Bond carried orders from Banks to Emory to bring the remainder of Gooding's brigade, consisting of the 38th Massachusetts, the 53rd Massachusetts, the 156th New York, and a section of a Maine battery, to support the 31st Massachusetts and the 175th New York on the east side of the Teche. By noon, skirmishing on both sides of the bayou was "very lively" in Bond's words. Gooding ordered Hopkins to detach two companies of the 31st as skirmishers on the extreme right flank. He selected Companies A and K, and after a "sharp skirmish along the woods," these were joined by the rest of the regiment. Emory ordered Gooding to knock out a field battery that was supposedly firing into a Union brigade across the bayou. The 31st was one of the elements leading this advance, and as Gooding reported, the attack was "hotly contested." After about three hours, the 31st's men had used up their ammunition and were replaced in the line by the 38th Massachusetts. By then, it had become apparent that the supposed enemy battery did not exist. During the final stage of that day's fighting, in which the Northerners pushed the rebels back into prepared positions, the 31st Massachusetts supported the 156th New York. A charge by the New Yorkers captured an outlying breastwork, and the 31st was close enough behind "to receive some of the last shots of the retreating enemy," as Hopkins put it. Scattered firing continued until dark. That night the brigade once again slept on the ground in proximity to the enemy, with tents and campfires prohibited.[63]

Taylor now faced a difficult decision. By nature an aggressive fighter, his normal tendency would be to attack and try to maul the Union army sufficiently to stop its further advance. In fact, he had ordered an attack on the morning of the thirteenth, but Brig. Gen. Henry H. Sibley had failed to carry it out. But Taylor was greatly outnumbered, and the reports brought in by his cavalry kept him informed of Grover's threat to cut off an escape route. On the morning of the fourteenth, with Grover finally in position, Banks was prepared to assault the Confederate lines. The 31st Massachusetts expected to be heavily engaged; by then the men had seen enough fighting to understand that even incomplete earthworks like Fort Bisland gave the defenders an enormous advantage.

As they were nerving themselves for the attack, word came back from advance parties that the Confederates had abandoned the position—"done skedaddled" in the night, as a soldier then might say. On the extreme left of the enemy position, Capt. W. I. Allen of Company D "entered a redoubt, palisaded in rear, capable of mounting three guns, with a ditch of five feet of water in front, and from which some of the best sharpshooting against us had been done on the previous day." But this time the redoubt was abandoned, and Allen found only "25 bodies of the enemy's dead and 1 wounded, some 20 dead horses, and 40 pieces of small arms."[64] Hopkins reported that he had captured thirty-three men during the engagement, presumably included in the total of 130 prisoners listed by Gooding. Taylor had decided that it was more important to preserve his army, the only organized mobile force the Confederates had in Louisiana (since the larger body of troops at Port Hudson was committed to holding a static position), than to further contest the position. As the 31st entered the abandoned works, Fairbank observed, "Everything showed marks of the late action, and dead men and horses lay all around."[65] In all the action around Fort Bisland, the regiment had lost only one man killed—William Hickey, a farmer from Easthampton, who was forty-two years old when he enlisted in late 1861—and five wounded. It was another fortunate escape.

During the battle, the Confederates had been actively supported by the captured gunboat CSS *Diana*. The vessel was under the command of Capt. Oliver J. Semmes, son of the Confederate naval officer Raphael Semmes, captain of the famed commerce raider CSS *Alabama* (and regarded by many Union men as a pirate). The younger Semmes, however, was an artillery officer, a West Point graduate, and had no particular acquaintance with naval matters. Regardless, little seamanship was required in the narrow waters of the Teche, where the *Diana* served essentially as a floating battery. The vessel performed admirably while suffering heavy damage and loss of life among its crew. After covering the retreat of Taylor's forces, Semmes followed orders blew up his gunboat at Franklin. With the surviving crewmen, he was among the last to depart the area and was soon captured by Federal cavalry.[66] Captain Semmes was put in prison in New Orleans, where his days were brightened by visits from a stream of "high-toned" rebel ladies. As he was departing the prison—sources differ as to whether he was released or managed to escape—he apparently left behind some diary pages, which were picked up by Pvt. James M. Allen of Company C, a resident of Rowe.[67]

The fiery General Taylor was infuriated by the conduct of the battle at Fort Bisland. He arrested and brought charges against General Sibley, blaming him both for failing to attack on the morning of the thirteenth and for the loss of the *Diana*. A court-martial held in September 1863 agreed that Sibley had performed poorly but determined that he had not deliberately disobeyed orders, and he was released.[68]

Meanwhile, still hoping to capture the entire Army of Western Louisiana, part of which had engaged Grover in a fairly substantial fight, generally known as the Battle of Irish Bend, near Franklin, Banks set off in pursuit on the morning of the fourteenth. With a smaller and less encumbered command, Taylor had some advantage of speed and was able to slow the Union pursuit by burning bridges and creating other obstacles. Still, the pace told, and the rebels experienced a steady trickle of desertions and stragglers, who fell into Federal hands. Many of the Louisianans seized the opportunity to take unauthorized leave at home, creating some danger that the retreating army would melt away.

As they pursued Taylor, generally following the course of Bayou Teche, the men of the 31st Massachusetts encountered a previously unfamiliar and not altogether unpleasant portion of Louisiana. Moving steadily after the fall of Fort Bisland, they passed through Centerville, which Lieutenant Bond described as "a thrifty looking town for La.," and Franklin, which he called "a very beautiful town." Bond's experience as a staff officer on horseback was much different than foot soldier Fairbank. As the troops got ready to move out on the fifteenth, the infantryman reported that they were given two days' rations of raw salt pork, "(pretty stuff to give a man) and no time to cook it." After marching all day, the men slept in the mud with nothing to eat but the "western pork," which when cooked on a stick "would all melt away." Nevertheless, they were up early the next morning for another day's hard marching that brought them to New Iberia. Just as they were settling in for supper and a supply of rum, orders came to move on, and the soldiers marched another mile and a half to camp outside the town. The next day's effort took them beyond Saint Martinsville.[69]

Although the Confederates burned bridges to slow the Union advance, their pursuers maintained contact with them, and the Federals often caught sight of rebel cavalrymen. On one occasion this brought about an artillery exchange. Taylor seemed intent on preserving opportunities to harass Banks's army even at the risk of losing more stragglers. On April 16 the Federals came upon the smoldering remains of the unfinished Confederate gunboat *E. R. Hart,* which the rebels had been forced to destroy to avoid its capture. The inability of the South to complete advanced warships that might have radically altered the course of the river battles was a recurring theme of warfare in Louisiana, going back to the passage of the New Orleans forts. Whether this ruinous failure was due to poor management, the inadequate capacity of Confederate industry, or both remains debatable.

After passing through Vermilionville (modern Lafayette) and rebuilding burned bridges, Banks's army reached Opelousas on April 20. This town had surrendered and welcomed the Union forces, to their enormous relief and delight. A band played "Yankee Doodle" as the soldiers marched up the main street of the town, which Fairbank described as "the first place where they seemed glad to see us." That same day Union forces finally captured Butte à la Rose, taking with it sixty men and two large guns. Banks boasted that "these works constituted the *key* of the Atchafalaya, and being in our possession, opened the way to Red river."[70] In a triumphant mood he staged a dress parade and used the anniversary of Lexington and Concord, which was also the second anniversary of the attack on Federal troops in Baltimore, to issue a proclamation praising the bravery of his men, though the ever practical Fairbank observed, "if he had sent up something to eat we would have appreciated it better."[71]

Not only was Banks unable to offer special treats but also the overstretched regular supply system was no longer able to meet the soldiers' needs. This deficiency was soon remedied by irregular means, as Fairbank described: "This A.M. there being no signs of rations, the Capt. went and got permission for us to go out and kill some beef. We soon had a nice cow picked out, but must catch it with our hands. We got her cornered up, when she darted." At this critical moment, though, "Freeman, our cook, caught her tail, and away she went, with the nigger froze to her tail, dragging him until she got tired of going, when we caught up, and Geo. Marsh knocked her in the head with a small hatchet."[72]

The army now rested and regrouped for several days, implying that Banks's main objective was no longer the active pursuit of Taylor, though he seemed uncertain what direction to take. From April 25 to May 1, he traveled to New Orleans to deal with administrative matters. Like Butler, Banks was responsible for the civil administration of the captured territory, but he placed higher priority on commanding troops in the field. Of course, Butler had never had a sufficient mobile force to justify the presence of the commanding general outside the city. Unexpectedly idle in Opelousas on May 1, Fairbank meditated: "How different the day has seemed from some of the May Days I have seen in my home in New England, when I have strolled off to the fields to gather the first flowers of Spring."[73] Howell used the unaccustomed free time to describe the recent campaign to his sister: "The worst & most pitiable sight was the unburied dead of the enemy," one of which was looking up "with the most serene expression I ever saw on a human countenance."[74] His letter shows that, after a year and a half in service, the consequences of warfare were still startling to men of the 31st Massachusetts—that would soon change.

While the soldiers might have been happy to extend their period of recuperation in Opelousas, it made no sense strategically to remain there. By Lieutenant Bond's calculation, they had marched 104 miles from Berwick City, but all that distance had brought Banks no closer to resolving his basic dilemma. At Opelousas he faced the same choices he had when he began the campaign. When the general visited New Orleans, he may have hoped that some message waiting there would give him guidance, but apparently none appeared. Regular mail came to his corps at intervals so that the men were informed belatedly of events in the war. Because of intervening Confederate territory, it was difficult for Banks to communicate with Grant, then actively operating against Vicksburg. By the time messages arrived they were outdated, and ambiguous phrasing left each commander uncertain as to how they should proceed. Each seemed to hope, or expect, that the other would come to their assistance. The question remained: Should they combine against Vicksburg or deal with it and Port Hudson separately and simultaneously?

Banks sent one brigade on to seize Washington, Louisiana, but this did nothing to clarify matters. Other units went out into the countryside from Opelousas to capture cotton and other valuables as well as to supplement their food supply. Howell recorded that the army was transporting wagon loads of cotton to New Orleans.[75] Although orders were given to be ready to march on May 1, Emory's division did not actually set off until the fifth. On that day they passed through Washington in the morning and covered twenty miles before halting at 5:30 P.M. Fairbank described the following day as a hard march, "as my feet were all blistered," so that he had to cut the tops off his shoes.[76] Worse was to come. On May 7 the 31st brought up the rear, behind the wagon trains and artillery, which meant that the men absorbed great clouds of dust raised by the soldiers and horses ahead of them. By day's end, their uniforms and facial hair were the color of the terrain around them. Fairbank declared that "it was the hardest days march we have had yet," adding that "if we stopped to rest, which we seldom did, our legs were more like a couple of sticks than a travelling concern for man."[77] Even Lieutenant Bond, on horseback, affirmed that "the dust has been almost intolerable."[78] Nevertheless, they covered twenty more miles after moving twenty-two the previous day. By then, they were only a few miles from Alexandria, which they reached on the eighth. They paused at the fine plantation from which Governor Moore had been forced to flee precipitously, yet another example of how the men who promoted secession somehow believed that the resultant war would be conducted without threatening their property.

Independent of its military results, Banks's campaign severely disrupted the plantation economy of the areas he invaded. Many of the owners fled, and large numbers of slaves deserted their plantations and entrusted themselves to the protection of the Federal army. For weary Union soldiers, there was pleasant relief in having these contrabands, who sought to justify their presence by bearing the men's loads like the personal servants officers often confiscated. But these individually appealing benefits came at the collective price of taking on the responsibility for thousands of dependents. The troops also went about destroying cash crops that otherwise might have supported the region. Army doctrine maintained that the needs of the men would be furnished by the regular supply chain, but in the field this ideal was seldom achieved. Technically forbidden, foraging was accepted in practice as a necessity. Caring for escaped slaves on the march added an unsupportable burden on an already stressed system so that these camp followers themselves expanded the ranks of the foragers; the resultant ravages thus were spread over a wider area and conducted more thoroughly.

The self-liberation of slaves had emerged as an issue during Butler's command at Fortress Monroe, and in Louisiana it overtook him and his successor on a vastly larger scale. While the administration in Washington displayed a propensity for debating interminably the great questions of slavery and emancipation, the slaves themselves often resolved the matter on the ground. Once they fled their masters, it would have been difficult to restore them to the previous state of bondage. Although many returned to their plantations for the greater security and familiarity they offered, the conditions of labor were permanently altered, and they usually did not revert to their former submissiveness.[79] A handful of Northern officers like Phelps abetted the self-liberation, but few members of the officer corps shared such attitudes. For most, the contrabands, while sometimes useful, were considered an annoyance.

One of the strongest expressions of this was provided by Weitzel, a man who was probably not sympathetic to slavery as an institution. During his incursion into the Lafourche country in October 1862, the first substantial Union offensive since the seizure of New Orleans, he vented his feelings to Butler:

> What shall I do about the negroes? . . .My train was larger than an army train for 25,000 men. Every soldier had a negro marching in the flanks, carrying his knapsack. Plantation carts, filled with negro women and children, with their effects; and of course compelled to pillage for their subsistence, as I have no rations to issue to them. I have a great many more negroes in my camp now than I have whites. . . .These negroes are a perfect nuisance.[80]

Weitzel sent a similar letter a few days later after capturing Berwick Bay. The enemy left "in such a hurry," he wrote, "that they left over 400 wagon loads of negroes behind at Brashear City. To substantiate this report the negroes are already returning. Now, what shall I do with them? I have already twice as many negroes in and around my camp as I have soldiers within. I cannot feed them; as a consequence they must feed themselves."[81]

The cavalrymen who entered Alexandria were surprised to find Commander Porter's fleet already there, having ascended the Red River. Porter disliked Banks almost as much as he did Butler, which is not surprising since he had little regard for anyone but himself. After Banks settled in, Porter took his vessels back down the Red and then ascended the Mississippi toward Vicksburg. At Alexandria on May 12, Banks finally received a recent message from Grant, who, having moved to the west side of the Mississippi, now asked him to unite with him in the campaign against Vicksburg, effectively withdrawing Grant's earlier offer to reinforce Banks. The Gulf commander responded with a long explanation of why he could not comply, citing his lack of boats and the risk to undefended portions of Louisiana. General in Chief Halleck was thoroughly unimpressed by what he called Banks's "eccentric movements" and stressed the importance of opening the Mississippi.[82] Perhaps it revealed a characteristic lack of imagination, but Halleck failed to see any connection between what Banks had been doing and the reduction of Port Hudson. After further dithering, Banks resolved to focus on Port Hudson. Yet even then he could not completely abandon his hopes of overtaking Taylor and sent a brigade under Brig. Gen. William Dwight Jr. (1831–88), after him in the direction of Shreveport.[83]

Lieutenant Bond calculated that, through May 8, the soldiers had performed "the very best of marching," covering eighty-five miles in four days but halting at 3:30 each afternoon.[84] From the different perspective of those who had worn out shoe leather, Fairbank would have welcomed a long period of rest. At Alexandria he wrote, "We are in the best place that we have been in since we left Algiers, and I hope that we can stay here awhile."[85] The duration of their stay was determined by plans bubbling and bursting in the brain of General Banks. When he at last decided on May 14 to begin the move against Port Hudson, he planned to send part of his force by river and the larger portion overland. The 31st Massachusetts was in the overland segment and set off on the road again before dawn on the fifteenth. The men were reversing the route they had taken to Alexandria, and on the first night camped in the same location they had used on May 7. General Emory had taken ill and returned to New Orleans, leaving Brig. Gen. Halbert E. Paine (1826–1905), an abolitionist lawyer from Wisconsin, in command of the division. Dwight's brigade, which had pursued Taylor more than forty miles beyond Alexandria, had to retrace its steps to catch up with the rest of the corps. On May 16, several miles south of Cheneyville, Paine's division swung off the road it had been using and turned eastward toward Simmesport. As most of the men must have realized, they were now irrevocably committed to Port Hudson.

The march of May 17 brought the division within nine miles of Simmesport. This tour of duty had elements of a tour in the other sense, as Lieutenant Bond remarked that their course on the seventeenth had been "mostly through a new country, where clearing the land by girdling the trees and burning them is the method pursued." Moreauville was the only village they encountered during the entire day's march.[86] Observations like this remind us that the Union troops were constantly encountering unfamiliar parts of Louisiana, which was still a young state, with large portions of the interior only recently settled. After crossing the Atchafalaya on the ferry *Laurel Hill* on the nineteenth, the 31st followed generally the "Old River" (a former channel of the Mississippi) to Morganza. There they boarded ships that brought them several miles downriver to Bayou Sara, a formerly thriving little river port on the eastern bank that had been destroyed by naval gunnery in retaliation for irregulars sniping at navy vessels.

On May 18 Bond had acquired a horse from among those that had been confiscated in the countryside ("spoils of war" was the accepted euphemism). Later in the day an order showed up at headquarters relieving him of staff duty and returning him to the 31st Massachusetts "in accordance with the request of the commander of my regiment on account of the scarcity of officers to command the Companies."[87] He was reassigned to Company K and immediately occupied himself issuing clothing to the men, "of which they were sadly in need." He also tried to arrange care for his ill brother, 2nd Lt. Sylvester Bond of Company G. Nelson Bond had to return his horse after only a day. It was clear that a fight for Port Hudson was approaching, and he would have no need for it. He must have been heartened by the return on parole of the five men who had been captured under his command at Desert Station.[88] They arrived just in time to participate in the regiment's most severe test. On the night of May 23, the 31st Massachusetts was sent out to protect Union batteries that were being emplaced to bombard the Port Hudson defenses. Heavy gunfire could be heard nearby.

7

THE ATTACK ON PORT HUDSON

MAY–JULY 1863

A great irony of the battle for Port Hudson is that it was almost not necessary. Earlier, President Davis had ordered the commander at that post, Maj. Gen. Franklin Gardner (1823–73), a Confederate born in New York City, to "hold it to the last." Thinking within the Southern high command subsequently shifted to concentrate on saving Vicksburg, and on May 19, 1863, the departmental commander, Gen. Joseph Johnston, ordered Gardner to evacuate Port Hudson "forthwith." This message did not arrive until the twenty-first, and by then it was too late; General Banks had begun moving his army into position, making it impossible for Gardner to evacuate his entire garrison, not to mention his artillery and supplies.[1] It is ironic that, having gone off on his diversion along Bayou Teche for nearly two months, with only indirect effect on Port Hudson, and then dithering several more days before resolving to focus directly on the rebel stronghold, Banks now moved with such alacrity that the Confederates were forced to defend their post. Gardner's troops might have made a difference in the contest for Vicksburg, although given that Banks would likely have joined General Grant or detached part of his corps to help him, the balance might not have changed much. Moreover, General in Chief Halleck was apparently contemplating placing Banks in overall command, above Grant, which could have had incalculable consequences on the conduct of the war.[2]

During the preliminary maneuvers, as Banks closed the circle around Port Hudson, two regiments of Massachusetts nine-month troops panicked and fled to the rear. This must have been unsettling to the longer-term volunteers who might have to depend on their steadiness in battle and highlighted the complex relationship between the two classes of soldiers. The nine-month men were drawn from the same population, and when they arrived, men in the older regiments, such as the 30th and 31st Massachusetts, often took great trouble to look up hometown friends. Lt. Nelson Bond, for example, found time to visit acquaintances in the 52nd Massachusetts and caught up on Amherst news.[3] Yet a fundamental difference in character remained, and the short-term men, who could count off the days to a foreseeable end of their service, always seemed like civilians in uniform rather than real soldiers (much as regulars disdained all volunteers). Back in February, before any in the 31st had seen combat, Thomas Norris had noted that the nine-month men "are all complaining here so quick and they are glad that they have not [a] very long time to serve. This shows that there is not much patriotism in them, but I guess they will see a great deal harder times before they get home."[4]

Cpl. Joshua Hawkes observed, "In going into any of the 'nine months' Regt's I am struck with the familiarity with which the officers associate with the men, as a natural consequence the men *respect* them." With surprising asperity he added, "The officers of our Reg't are seemingly a *superior race of beings* from the men, rarely speaking to them except to *command*." Hawkes excepted his own captain, John W. Lee, noting that other officers "have remarked that [he] is altogether too intimate with his men," but concluded with the shocking assertion, "I know several men who declare they will shoot certain officers [at] the first favourable opportunity—and they are men who will remember their word too."[5] In both the three-year and nine-month regiments, most of the company-grade officers had been elected by their men, but in the 31st Massachusetts some of those officers had been replaced due to the Andrew-Butler controversy. Furthermore, the nine-month regiments were usually not commanded by regular officers who might employ harsh discipline and social separation.

By the close of May 22, Banks had largely completed his investment of Port Hudson, marking the commencement of the siege. In the course of the war, the Confederates fared poorly when trying to hold strongpoints through a siege (although Charleston repelled several combined-force attacks, that city was never actually besieged). The Confederacy seemed to lack the manpower to relieve a sustained siege and also lacked the economic resources to prepare a garrison to hold out for an extended period. Such troops might have done better maneuvering in the field, as Taylor's army did after Fort Bisland, but that would have prevented them from deploying the heavy guns needed to contest

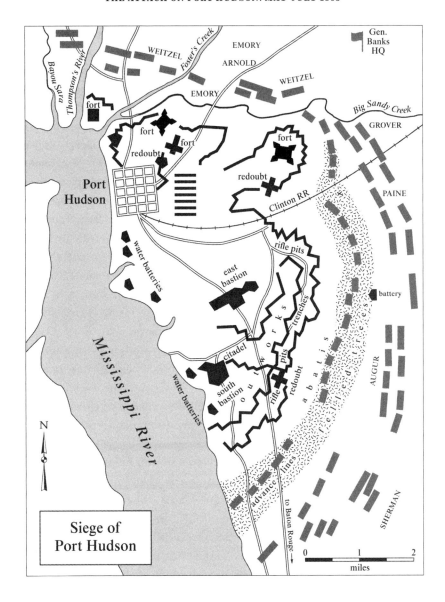

Siege of
Port Hudson

the passage of Union naval vessels on the waterways. It was the Confederacy's insoluble dilemma in trying to defend the Mississippi and other river systems.

Part of the 31st Massachusetts was engaged in a minor action in advance of the main fighting. General Paine on May 25 ordered Col. Edward Prince of the 7th Illinois Cavalry, which had participated in Col. Benjamin Grierson's daring raid through Mississippi in late 1862, to Thompson's Creek to destroy Confederate boats. Prince's force comprised two hundred men of his own regiment, two guns of a Maine battery, and Companies D and H of the 31st Massachusetts, the only infantrymen in the detachment. After a march of eight miles, the little expedition captured two rebel steamboats, the *Starlight* and the *Red Chief*, along with their crews. With acceptable impudence, Prince wrote, "I took the liberty of disobeying the instructions of the department commander as to the destruction of the boats, as I found I could place them where a light guard would be sufficient."[6] Company D went on the boats and guarded the crews while Company H remained on shore as pickets. Though a minor engagement, this action further disabled the already shaky Confederate transportation system. No casualties were reported among the 31st. On the contrary, the participants were well rewarded for their successful foray. Fairbank reported, "We got plenty of tobacco and whiskey, and some of the boys got leave and went out and got some sheep and baked them, and had plenty of hoe cake."[7] While Fairbank and the others were savoring the fruits of their victory, heavy fighting had broken out around Port Hudson. As a result the companies of the 31st quickly received orders to rejoin their regiment. Leaving the captured boats to the cavalry, they marched overland, "thereby missing an order telling us to stay," according to Fairbank. "After much tramping thro' the woods, running over reg'ts that were lying down," the companies found their way back to their regiment just in time for the great battle of May 27.[8]

While the two companies were detached on the expedition to Thompson's Creek, Company A was assigned to guard an important ravine. The Union forces engaged in wide-ranging combat on May 25 as Banks tested and tried to push back the Confederate lines. In this fighting the remaining four companies of the 31st participated in continuous skirmishing until dark. The regimental loss in this action was three killed and sixteen wounded.[9] At the end of the day, the defenders were generally forced back into their prepared positions so that siege warfare was truly underway. One historian of the battle believed that, "if Banks had attacked the garrison in full force" on the twenty-sixth, he probably "would have won a victory."[10] Although the Confederates had had many weeks to prepare their defenses while Banks was chasing Taylor and contemplating strategy, Gardner had detected weaknesses in their position. His garrison troops now used the twenty-sixth to patch up these defects. Mean-

while, Banks conferred with his officers. He issued attack orders that seem
not to have been entirely clear, though none of the high-ranking officers asked
for clarification, perhaps believing that they could do better on their own.

The Union line extended from its two anchors on the Mississippi some six
miles through rough country, hemming in the Confederate garrison. Banks
had taken pains to place his forces in position for a siege, yet he refused to
allow siege tactics to play out against the defenders, who would gradually consume their supply of food and ammunition with no means of replenishment.
Perhaps worried that Grant would take Vicksburg and win an excessive share
of the glory, Banks decided to launch a direct assault on the works. Back in
February, before beginning his roundabout move up Bayou Teche, he had advised Halleck that the defenses at Port Hudson were "too strong for a direct
attack by men who have never fired a gun. Such an attempt would result as
at Fredericksburg and Vicksburg [in 1862]."[11] In May, after the Confederates
had used three additional months strengthening their defenses, Banks had
changed his mind about them. True, some of his men had "fired a gun" in the
interim, but Fort Bisland was hardly comparable to what they now faced.

Port Hudson was selected to be a stronghold on the Mississippi with good
reason. It sits on a bluff overlooking a sharp bend of the river. The area is cut
by numerous ravines, many filled with dense undergrowth. To these natural
advantages, the defenders had added felled trees and other obstructions as
well as carefully planned gun and rifle emplacements. All in all, it was poor
country for an infantry attack, despite the great Union advantage in numbers and weaponry. Banks's army numbered some 25,000–27,000 effectives.[12]
After sending infantry reinforcements to Vicksburg, Gardner could muster
only about 7,000 men, although experts had calculated that it would require
more than twice as many to properly defend his lines.[13] Moreover, the rebel
commander was outgunned something on the order of ten to one, including
the Union naval guns, and many of his pieces were light or obsolete. Despite
the usual tendency of Banks to overestimate enemy strength, the Federals had
reason for optimism as they readied their attack.

Banks had planned a coordinated assault on the Confederate perimeter,
and if that had occurred, it might have overwhelmed the defenders with sheer
numbers and firepower. In actuality, the Union divisions were sent in piece-
meal, either through misunderstanding or faulty communications, allowing
the Southerners to shift their beleaguered forces to the most directly threat-

ened portion of their line. Deadly small-arms fire pinned down the Federals, forcing them to seek whatever meagre cover was offered by trees or irregularities of terrain. Initially organized charges by massed regiments quickly degenerated into a stalemate of continuous skirmishing and sniper fire.

Generally speaking, that was the experience of the 31st Massachusetts, except that it did not actually charge an enemy position. Early in the morning of the twenty-seventh, Weitzel and Paine sent their divisions forward without being sure what the other was doing. After hard fighting, Weitzel succeeded in driving back the enemy skirmishers facing him, but his men were stopped well short of their objective by murderous massed fire. Once these attacks stalled, Paine sent Gooding's brigade forward in two waves; the 31st was held in reserve and did not advance. Later uncoordinated Union attacks, including one by two black regiments, said to be the first major combat between black and white troops, were snuffed out with considerable loss. By late afternoon, the Federal assaults were spent, and an informal truce allowed both sides to collect their wounded; many Northerners took the opportunity to crawl away from exposed positions.

The 31st Massachusetts could neither advance nor retreat, and as with many of the other Union regiments, its men found scanty cover behind trees and logs. Occasionally, the soldiers might try to get off a shot, but raising one's head to aim was a risky affair, the air above filled with a deadly storm of projectiles. Lacking sufficient conventional artillery ammunition, the Confederates fired loads of scrap iron and, as Lieutenant Bond reported, "pieces of railroad track iron 18 inches in length," the screeching of which "as it went through the tree tops over our heads was more to be dreaded from the noise it made than from the execution that resulted."[14]

One historian of the battle, Lawrence Lee Hewitt, notes that seven of nineteen Federal regiments "did not actively participate in the assault," adding that "virtually none of the casualties occurred in the 31st Massachusetts." He concludes that the "failure to breach the Confederate defenses, coupled with a loss of only 8 percent of the attacking force, strongly indicates that the Federals who entered 'the valley of the shadow of death' clearly lacked the determination needed to achieve victory." This seems to be a grossly unfair judgment since many Northern soldiers advanced bravely into ruinous fire. If there is fault to be found, it is more readily placed on the overall management of the attack. In speaking of "widespread Yankee shirking" immediately after noting that the 31st Massachusetts did not advance, Hewitt implies that this regiment was conspicuous among the shirkers, although there is no evidence that it was ever ordered to advance. Hewitt then makes the remarkable conclusion, "One can only speculate about the consequences if that regiment had participated in the final advance."[15] The seven companies of the 31st present at Port Hudson amassed a total strength of about three hundred men. After thousands of well-equipped Union infantrymen had failed to penetrate the Confederate defenses, it is hard to imagine that this last three hundred would have been decisive. The "8 percent" Hewitt refers to amounted in numbers to more than two thousand casualties, a devastating price to pay for a few yards of tangled woods that left the Federal army still outside the Confederate entrenchments.

For more than two weeks after the violent repulse of May 27, Banks did not attempt another major assault. There was a ghastly interval of quiet on the day after the battle, when a truce extending eleven hours allowed both sides to bring in their dead and wounded. At 7 P.M., as Fairbank put it, "the ball opened again." He added that this seemed "pretty spiteful," but by then the war had its own logic.[16] Almost constant sniping and probing kept the soldiers on edge. Banks had requested the navy to fire its mortars at night to disrupt the Confederates' rest; but even if they were perfectly aimed, it is hard to see how the Union troops would be shielded from the noise. Vastly outgunned, the rebels fired their artillery sparingly so as not to give away their positions. Units were rotated in and out of the front lines, a wise practice, though in many locations standing up in daylight was a dangerous act.

With each passing day, Confederate provisions diminished until eventually the men in local units, who might have been accustomed to the rich cuisine of prewar New Orleans, learned to savor mule meat. Though the besiegers talked about starving out the enemy, their own situation seemed hardly better. On June 9 Fairbank complained, "The fresh meat, as they called it, was all maggots and stunk like carrion." Anger over this miserable fare quickly spilled over into resentment of the supposedly pampered treatment of the nine-month units. "Talk of starving the rebs out of Port Hudson!" Fairbank sputtered. "We shall get starved out first at this rate . . . but the nine months men are having their potatoes, beans, &c. They are of more concern than the 3 year-men. Yes, the babies should have something to eat,—so they should!" Finally, after "the boys began to make so much fuss about our rations," the officers went to General Paine, who "gave the Commissaries fits" and brought at least temporary improvement.[17] All this took place against a background of ever-thickening stench from thousands of soldiers confined in a small space using shallow "sinks," with added seasoning provided by unburied dead men and horses, all mingled in a broth of the country's excessive heat and humidity. Older units like the 31st had had a year to adapt to the climate (or be thinned by death or discharge of those unable to tolerate it), but the nine-month troops would never have time for that process to take effect.

Confederate cavalry harassed the eastern fringes of Banks's corps, capturing supplies and prisoners and generally embarrassing the Federals. During an interval of relative quiet, Banks resolved to eliminate this nuisance by destroying the horsemen's base at Clinton, in his mind something like clearing out a nest of pirates. Grierson's cavalry was already in the vicinity, and on June 5 Banks dispatched six infantry regiments (the 31st, 38th, 52nd, and 53rd Massachusetts; 8th New Hampshire; and 91st New York), aided by a battery of regular artillery. This formidable force numbered some four thousand men, but one can question how well suited it was to pursue tough, hard-riding cavalry units.

Clinton lay about twenty miles away at the terminus of a railroad line from Port Hudson. Even after the rigorous marching in the Teche country, this expedition became memorable in the annals of the 31st Massachusetts due to sweltering temperatures that were extreme even by Louisiana standards. The men were ready to set off in the cool of an early June morning, at 4 A.M., but after the usual delays did not begin marching until eight.[18] Adelbert Bailey recalled that they passed a running stream early in the march ("the only one I think we ever saw in Louisiana," a poignant contrast with the multitude of fresh brooks that sparkle through the New England woods). The soldiers were told to take as much water there as they could carry because they might not come upon another source.[19] The march halted for about an hour around midday, but when it resumed in even more oppressive heat, men began to drop out by the dozens; several cases of sunstroke were reported. Finally, the brigade surgeon recommended a halt, an extraordinary intervention that confirmed the severity of the conditions.[20]

When the expedition had been announced, the men were probably thrilled at the prospect of escaping the monotony and danger of the rifle pits, but any joy was quickly smothered by the stifling heat. It seemed to confirm that military service offered only a choice between different forms of misery, no doubt requiring great efforts of imagination to recall whatever feelings of patriotism or adventure had motivated the men while in faraway Massachusetts. On June 6 the weather was no more tolerable, and though the detachment started off at 6 A.M., the exhausted men dragged along at a slow pace and halted at ten. At that point they were on the Comite River, still eight miles from Clinton. Banks's admonition to Paine that it was "essential that the object shall be accomplished as speedily and as thoroughly as possible" now had curdled into a joke.[21] One consolation was that the troops were camped in an area with a great abundance of blackberries, ripe weeks earlier than they would have been in New England. "We ate them all day & I cannot see as we have thinned them out any," Fairbank declared in amazement.[22] The Northerners seemed at last to have found a resource that could withstand their plundering, though one has to wonder about the effect on their already fragile digestive apparatus.[23]

On June 7 the temperature still had not abated. The soldiers started out not long after midnight, but even a forced march during the relatively cool hours left them two miles short of Clinton. While the column trudged along, scouts from Grierson's cavalry informed Paine that the rebels had departed, leaving Clinton to be burned by the Federal horsemen, which must have been like throwing coal on the fires of hell. The expedition halted for breakfast and then turned back toward Port Hudson. At 9 A.M. the men reached the previous night's camp, where they remained through the heat of the afternoon. In the evening they marched to the first night's camp near Redwood Bayou, some five miles from their starting point. Lieutenant Bond described it as "another terribly hot day" in which "the men suffered very much."[24] They started out at 4 A.M. the next day, taking a different and shorter route, but even so the intense heat kept them from finishing the march until 6:30 P.M., leaving them utterly exhausted. Their commanders allowed the men to rest in the shade through the next day; as Bond noted, "hardly a man has gone out of the woods."[25] So ended the Clinton march, an ordeal that scorched the memory of all who participated. The expedition had little to show for the agony that accompanied it, returning with only a few sick Confederates who had been left behind.[26] The rebel cavalry lost some supplies but remained free to annoy Banks.

By then the besieging troops were in wretched condition, indescribably filthy. Clad in the remains of their heavy wool uniforms, the soldiers had had no opportunity to wash, shave, change clothes, or launder their clothing since arriving at Port Hudson, and probably not during the hard marching that preceded it. The only slight relief was provided by occasional rain showers. Luther Howell summarized by writing: "I am perfectly well but ragged dirty & Lousy. I presume three long weeks in the trench when one can hardly stir without getting a bullet fired at him is quite sufficient to make one feel that he is of the earth."[27] The only small consolation was that, although they were disturbed by snakes and lizards, the mosquitoes were less troublesome than they had been around New Orleans.

Understandably, memories like this remained vivid when George Young composed his recollections more than twenty years later. "[A]side from the hard work of using picks and shovels, which to many of us was bad enough, the condition of the place was something terrible. Day after day and week after week," he wrote, "gangs of men had been going there working, eating sleeping and in other ways complying with the just demands of nature until now everything and everybody seemed to be covered with filth and alive with vermin. At all hours of the day officers and men alike would be seen with their shirts or drawers or perhaps both off ridding themselves of those most troublesome pests." He finally conceded, "(I may as well say it, it was lice)." The men threw the insects into the sand, "where they would be taken up by the man who should come next, he in his turn would in like manner pass them along with their increased numbers, and so on and on, until I believe about every man in the camp was literally alive." Added to the scarcity of proper food and the miserable water, Young declared that it was no wonder that there were so many taken to the rear sick.[28]

Meanwhile, Banks was relying on time-tested siege tactics to push his line laboriously forward. It was work that required immense mental and physical concentration, and he may not have been temperamentally suited to this painstaking process. Union intelligence was bringing him mixed signals from Confederate captives and deserters about conditions within the post. There was no doubt that the rebels were facing increasing hardship as their food, medical supplies, and ammunition dwindled. A couple of Southern regiments had come close to mutiny, yet morale remained high among most of the defenders. Despite their privations, they were heartened by their success in beating back the vastly more numerous enemy on the twenty-seventh. Matters apparently were not moving to a conclusion quickly enough to suit Banks, so he decided on another assault. It seemed not to have occurred to him that he might have already largely achieved the supposed strategic goal of the campaign. With many guns disabled, ammunition in short supply, and a reluctance to fire the remaining guns for fear of the enormously superior Union response it would provoke, the Confederates' ability to interfere with traffic on the Mississippi must have been seriously degraded. There still would have been risk in trying to pass Port Hudson, but it would have been greatly reduced since Farragut's initial run. Communication between the Union army and navy was something short of intensive, and such strategic analysis appears never to have taken place.

This time Banks conceived of a more elaborate plan than he had for the May 27 attack, when he had tried to simply overpower the outnumbered defenders. He now perceived something of the difficulty of cracking fixed defensive positions, however inadequately manned. A poorly managed and inconsequential reconnaissance in force on June 11 did not discourage the Union commander, and he proceeded with plans for a major assault on June 14. This attack would be conducted in waves, each with a specific function, and if all went according to plan, the final waves would breach the defenses. For a couple of days before the attack, units and individuals were assigned specific tasks and given an opportunity to practice. This was particularly true of the 31st Massachusetts, which was given the unaccustomed task of carrying bags of cotton to help scale the outside of the earthworks.

On the day before the attack, Union artillery, including naval guns, opened a prolonged bombardment of the Confederate enclave. During a pause, Banks formally requested Gardner to surrender, to which the rebel commander responded with a formal refusal. Before dawn on the fourteenth, Banks's plan began to unfold. After a heavy bombardment, parties of pioneers went forward, carrying tools that would be used first to remove obstacles and then to open up Confederate earthworks to the guns. They were followed by the storming party, each man carrying a bag of cotton that would enable him to climb over the outer wall. Behind them came skirmishers, followed by the 4th Massachusetts, armed with improvised hand grenades that were supposed to cause the defenders to take shelter while the other units did their work. Then came the 31st Massachusetts, carrying bags of cotton that they were supposed to lay down to provide a surface so the artillery could cross over a ravine (which was shallow enough for men to cross, but too steep for the guns). Finally came the main force, consisting of two full brigades and part of Gooding's. General Grover held overall command of this operation, and he selected General Paine to lead the assault. Young of the 31st recalled that, in place of coffee, each man in the storming party was issued a half-pint cup half-filled with whiskey—the portions of those who refused the ration were gladly consumed by others.[29]

Paine, who had previously commanded the 4th Wisconsin, believed in leading from the front. Standing at the head of his men, he roared the order to advance over the crash of artillery. Despite the careful preparations, the plan of attack quickly disintegrated. The regiment carrying the grenades, not known for aggressiveness, had cut the fuses too long or threw them too soon, allowing the Confederates to toss them back at the Federals with at least equal effect. Neither the artillery barrage nor any other Union tactic sufficiently suppressed the defenders, who rose up from behind their parapets and fired searing volleys at the attackers, often using rifles captured on May 27. Subsequent charges by the other Union divisions were not well coordinated, allowing the Confederates could deal with them in detail. A scattering of Northerners reached and attempted to scale the earthworks, but they were shot down or taken prisoner. The rest were pinned down until nightfall, when they were able to trickle back into their original positions, having suffered another eighteen hundred casualties.

At that point in their service, the soldiers of the 31st Massachusetts had seen men slain or horribly wounded in battle and worn down by miserable diseases. They had endured a stunning variety of hardships and discomforts, and they had observed entirely too much of the waste, destruction, and mismanagement of war. Yet until June 14, 1863, they had never had occasion to charge an enemy position against resolute defenders (and it is well to remember that even this experience was shared by only the remnant of seven companies at hand). They had not previously "seen the elephant," to use the slang of the rustic soldiers of that time. On June 14, in addition to the usual weight of uniform and equipment, the troops were burdened by bags of cotton that weighed thirty pounds or more; whether or not they succeeded in depositing these bags in the intended location is uncertain. As they advanced into increasingly heavy fire, the men were driven to ground, taking shelter behind what little protection the sacks of cotton or ripples in the terrain provided. Having crossed over an unwooded part of the battlefield, they lay all day in the scorching sun, unable to fire back or even to reach for a canteen. Rebel sharpshooters fired at any target that presented itself, and the prone men were liable to be struck at any instant by a random chunk of flying metal. When the

soldiers dragged back from the front lines in the evening, they were dealt another ration of whiskey; Fairbank said drily, "I was willing to drink mine."[30]

"The death missiles have flown thick and fast all day," wrote Fairbank.[31]
Many found their mark, and losses among the officers were especially heavy.
Rallying his men for a second charge, General Paine went down with a leg
wound, after which the Union drive deflated. The severely wounded briga-
dier lay on the open field, slightly sheltered by cotton bales. Several Union
soldiers lost their lives attempting to aid him, among them Sgt. Edward P.
Woods of Company E, 31st Massachusetts, a twenty-five-year-old resident of
Chicopee Falls who had listed his occupation as gunsmith. Eventually, Pvt.
Patrick Cohen of the 131st New York was able to throw a canteen of water to
Paine, which may have saved his life.[32] He was taken off the field after dark,
survived the amputation of his leg, and returned to the army and later went
into Wisconsin politics. Lt. Joseph Hallett, serving with the Signal Corps, happened to see Paine being carried off "in great agony and . . . hollering like a
lunatic from suffering."[33] This was not the sort of thing that was emphasized
in heroic paintings or fictional narratives of the war.

Earlier during the Teche campaign, Lieutenant Bond noted that "several
of the prisoners recognize the writer as the man on the gray horse in the fight
at Bisland last Monday, and relate how hard they tried to bring both rider and
horse to the ground." This may indicate that Bond was one of those officers
who tried to make a conspicuous show of bravery on the battlefield. On June
14 he was not mounted but may have been in an exposed position when he was
shot through the right breast, the bullet passing through his lung and almost
coming out his back. To anyone familiar with wounds, it appeared mortal.
Bond turned over his money, watch, and other valuables to the quartermaster,
but fortunately he was in a position from which he could be carried quickly to
the rear, where Dr. Bidwell picked out the ball and showed it to him. The surgeon's personal intervention was probably critical to the lieutenant's recovery,
as he decided not to send Bond to the hospital at Baton Rouge, fearing, with
good reason, that the journey by wagon to Springfield Landing, "some twelve
miles over a road by no means of the best . . . , might deprive him of his last
slender chance of recovery."[34]

After consulting with the wounded lieutenant's brother, Sylvester, who had
recently discharged himself from the hospital and offered to serve as a nurse,
Bidwell decided to keep Bond "in camp under my own observation. Accord-

ingly, a bunk or cot was constructed of such materials as we could command, a tent made of a few shelter tents, and the ordeal inaugurated with but a trembling hope of ultimate success."[35] Unable to breathe normally, Bond wrote that he "could only pant in breathing like a dog," which further drained his strength. Yet under the care of Dr. Bidwell, brother Sylvester, and Lts. Luther Howell and Charles Rust, he gradually recovered. Bond's informative diary comes to an end when he was sent to a hospital at New Orleans on July 1, as he "shall know nothing of the doings of the regiment for a while at least."[36]

Bond's loss was deeply felt throughout the regiment, as he seems to have been highly regarded and was familiar to most of the men due to recent details in command of different companies. At almost the same time, Capt. W. I. Allen was wounded in the shoulder blade by a stray piece of shrapnel from a Union gun; he too eventually recovered. Pvt. John Williams in the ambulance corps was killed, and George Marsh of Ware "had a musket ball hit him in the upper jaw while looking to see some of our men go over the breast works, prisoners. 'My God,' he said, 'I guess I'm a goner,' and ran to the rear."[37] Marsh survived but never returned to service; he was discharged in December.

A grievous loss to the regiment was the death of Color Sgt. Francis A. Clary of Conway, a classmate of Lieutenants Howell and Bond at Amherst College. Back at Camp Seward, Howell had written: "Clary is a grand fellow, six feet tall, good looking, intelligent and brave as a lion. He has been chosen Color Sergeant—a very responsible [position] and one full of danger, but he'll 'bear the stars and stripes aloft and bear them till he dies' without a single flinch."[38] This proved to be startlingly prophetic, though it is hard to see how Clary could have given evidence of bravery at that time. He was deeply, almost ostentatiously, religious and before the war broke out had planned to labor as a missionary in China. Like Howell and several other classmates, he signed up immediately after Fort Sumter, but the authorities decided not to organize a unit at that time. His reputation as the ideal soldier may be slightly tarnished by the fact that he was placed under arrest in New Orleans in May 1862 for "not doing his duty."[39] But this blemish may be mitigated by the fact that the arrest had been made by Colonel Gooding, who made a practice of arresting people for minor infractions.

Clary had an element of fatalism in his makeup. In letters to his family, he observed that his position as color sergeant placed him in exceptional danger and told friends that he expected to perish in the first severe engagement.[40]

There are divergent reports of how Clary died. Probably the most accurate was provided by Lt. Col. William Hopkins, who said that he died clutching the colors, though not aloft. Clary was taking cover on the ground with the rest of the regiment and, while in that prone position, was shot in the neck and died within minutes.[41] His body was recovered after dark and buried with Williams.[42] Clary's life was regarded as so exemplary that an inspirational biography was published by the American Tract Society.[43]

As the odors of decomposition became unbearable, a truce was agreed on June 17 so that search parties could recover the dead. Two men of the 31st were found alive, and Sergeant Wood's body was brought back.[44]

One man who perished almost anonymously in the ranks of the 31st Massachusetts on the fourteenth was Charles Knackfuss, a "poor little German" who had enlisted at New Orleans. Doubly a foreigner, he was probably known to few others in the regiment. One who was acquainted with him was George Young of Company K, who related that Knackfuss "used to make us laugh at his broken English, and often when in conversation with him he used to tell me about his folks and what a good time he intended to have when he got back to Yarminy." On June 14, when the regiment was pinned down by incessant fire, soldiers were periodically designated to make a dash for water. Eventually, Knackfuss's name was called. As Young recalled, "We cautioned him not to jump up until he was ready to run and then to run as fast as he could (some of the fellows who always wanted to be funny said run as fast as the Devil will let you)." No sooner had Knackfuss put his head up over his cotton bag to see if the way was clear than Young "heard the yip of a bullet and at the same moment I saw poor Knackfuss put his hand up to his head. He held it there for a minute and then fell down alongside of me,—a most horrible sight." Horrified, he saw that "the ball had struck him in the forehead and knocked the top of his head off, or nearly so, for he put both his hands up again and seemed to make a grab for the wounded place, and when he took them away they were filled with flesh—blood, and I believe a part of his brains that came from the gaping hole that the bullet had made." Young and the soldiers around him "did what we could to soothe his agony. We plucked up handsful of stunted grass and having made it wet with water that at that time was worth more than its weight in gold, we put it on his head, then having cut off the tail of a blouse we threw that over him and had to lie there and hear him groan and see him die." Adding to this misery, "the sun was pouring down on our own heads most terrible."[45]

Despite two costly defeats, Banks still hoped to crack the Confederate defenses by assault. He now conceived the idea of a "Forlorn Hope," in which a thousand volunteers would storm one part of the enemy line. He had used similar tactics at Cedar Mountain, Virginia, in August 1862, resulting in unnecessary losses. Why he expected this would succeed when attacks by much larger numbers against most of the perimeter had failed is a mystery. By then his troops had learned from hard experience even if he had not, and nowhere near a thousand men raised their hands to volunteer. Among them, however, were Capt. Edward Hollister, Capt. Samuel D. Hovey, Lieutenant Howell, and Lt. James M. Stewart of the 31st Massachusetts.[46] This assault never took place in the form Banks had envisioned, but several other attacks were launched, all futile.

James Tupper by then was stationed at the quartermaster depot at Springfield Landing. He retained his contacts in the 31st Massachusetts, though, and reported that a superstitious dread had overtaken the army: "Many expressed fears yesterday that General Banks would take another Sunday to attack Port Hudson, but the Sabbath has passed by & no more fighting has been going on than the usual skirmishing & firing of sharpshooters & pickets." There was, according to Tupper, "a general feeling in the Army among officers & men against an attack on Sunday. The disastrous results which have followed engagements on that day have had the effect of creating a sort of superstition that that is an unlucky day among those who are not governed by motives of religion." He observed "an instinctive dread, distinct from any moral or religious view of the question," that if an attack was made on another Sunday, it would be defeated. Fortunately, "our general, governed by motives of prudence if no loftier principal, has wisely deferred the next great assault which we all feel confident is imminent."[47]

Independence Day 1863 arrived, and the Port Hudson stalemate continued. In a reminiscent mood, Fairbank reflected on the holiday: "How different it has been spent from what those at home have probably done. There the old iron cannon called them, and fire crackers and picnics were the order of the day. Here we have had cannon roaring enough, but no boy's play or blank cartridges fired."[48] It was hard to see what would bring the ordeal to an end. The Confederates were nearing their last extremity, with men and supplies approaching the final stages of exhaustion. Although they were better fed, the Union forces were in only slightly better condition, and their morale appeared to be collapsing. Most of them had little confidence in Banks, and some of the nine-month regiments had mutinied. Part of the 31st Massachusetts was even detailed to guard the 4th Massachusetts, whose men "had laid down their arms and refused to do duty because their time was up." Fairbank, though increasingly disenchanted, retained enough patriotism to declare, "They have always been a disgrace to Mass., and Mass. soldiers were always ashamed of them."[49]

Adversity revived the politically based discord that had always afflicted the Army of the Gulf. One historian of Port Hudson observed:

> There apparently were two political cliques in the Federal army, the first being the old Butler group, consisting of the officers who had come to Louisiana with Butler and were closely associated with him. Weitzel was the most prominent example. The second clique consisted of Banks's men—those who had come to Louisiana with the general in December, 1862, and who were considered loyal to him. The Banks clique was split by a division between the volunteer and regular officers.[50]

In the end, outside events determined the fate of Port Hudson. On July 8 news arrived that Vicksburg had surrendered on July 4. After a truce, during which General Gardner confirmed this unwelcome information, the Confederate commander began negotiations to surrender. Port Hudson might have held out a few days longer, but with the fall of the upriver stronghold, further resistance seemed pointless. In any case, the soldiers determined the issue by ceasing hostilities and mingling on the battlefield. With this placid anticlimax, the longest siege of the Civil War crept to a close. Official casualty figures for the 31st Massachusetts in the period May 23–July 8, 1863, were thirteen enlisted men killed and two officers and forty-seven men wounded.[51] The combatants soon learned that on the day Vicksburg fell, Gen. Robert E. Lee had begun his retreat from Gettysburg. While these simultaneous defeats seemed to spell the downfall of the Confederacy, the war would grind on for nearly two more years, characterized by increasing ferocity and ruthlessness.

A week or so after Port Hudson surrendered, Tupper visited the site. Men from both armies were still mingling freely, and a great deal of coarse joshing took place. One Confederate officer told him that "mule steak was good &

palatable food, but rat meat was far superior." Tupper, however, was dismayed to see that "the rebel officers are treated with great attention by our officers. They ride around on fine horses which they are allowed to retain, are seen eating & drinking with our officers, & spending with apparent liberality green-backs which no doubt were plundered from the bodies of our dead & wounded heroes of the battles of May 27th & June 14th." Another Southerner told him that "one man got $600 from one of our colonels left on the field & another got $60 from the body of the captain of a negro company. After the hardships endured & the loss of life sustained in taking this place, it makes our soldiers indignant at attention shown the rebel officers. One would think they were our guests."[52] This display must have reinforced the widespread feeling that the West Pointers felt more affinity toward one another than toward which-ever side they were fighting for. Around this time Tupper received notification that he had been discharged from the army and given a position as civilian clerk in the Navy Department, probably through the intervention of Navy Sec-retary Welles. The subsequent history of the 31st Massachusetts was thereby deprived of his informative and thoughtful commentary.

8

MOUNTED WARRIORS

JULY 1863–FEBRUARY 1864

At Port Hudson, suddenly quiet, the 31st Massachusetts had been chosen to participate in the surrender ceremony but, before that occurred, it was called away to face a new threat. While Banks's army was engaged along the Mississippi, various Confederate forces under the overall supervision of General Taylor took advantage of its absence to administer some stinging defeats on Union outposts. They returned to the country Banks had supposedly subdued before he turned his attention to Port Hudson, retaking Brashear City, capturing many Union prisoners, returning blacks who had worked for the Union to slavery, and resupplying their army at the expense of the U.S. government. For a time, the Confederates also seemed to threaten New Orleans, then held by only a few hundred Union troops, but instead turned their attention to the strategic river port of Donaldsonville. Union forces there were able to hold them off, however, gaining Banks time to send a large part of his army to defend the town. At first, the victors from Port Hudson, under the command of Brigadier Generals Weitzel and Grover, were mauled by a much smaller rebel force, but eventually the Confederates had to withdraw in the face of superior numbers.

Soon afterward, Banks was compelled to perform a major reorganization and restructuring of his command, not due to strategic considerations but because of the departure of the nine-month regiments. These units had given the general an impressive numerical advantage, at least on paper. In the field much of this advantage was negated by their lackluster performance. With their short and finite term of service, these soldiers were often more interested in marking days off the calendar than in conducting military operations.

George Young later recalled that the men of one of these regiments (undoubt-edly a reference to the 4th Massachusetts) refused to do duty after reaching what they believed was the end of their enlistment. Arrested, they were sent to prison in Baton Rouge, where Young "saw them looking out of the Prison windows. They were laughing and joking and having a good time generally, and we believed . . . that they were making fun of our tired and shabby appear-ance as we marched past them." It must have seemed politically unaccept-able to court-martial most of a regiment, so the men were discharged. Young wrote, with understandable bitterness, that "when they arrived in Boston they were received with unbounded demonstrations of enthusiasm, and each man being counted a hero in himself was presented with a miniature American flag—quite different . . . was that given to our Regiment when they returned after serving faithfully for three years and four months."[1] Thomas Norris, not yet eighteen years old, voiced similar sentiments: "You tell me all about the reception of the *nine months* men at home. I wonder if they will receive the *soldiers* in the same manner. The folks at home seem to think more of the big *Bounty Men* than anybody else."[2]

Banks had no hesitation in blaming the repulse of his assaults at Port Hud-son on the convenient target of the nine-month troops. "The reduction of Port Hudson has required a longer time than at first supposed," he reported, "First, because it is a stronger position. Secondly, because a large part of my force consists of nine-months' men, who openly say they do not consider them-selves bound to any perilous service. It is this wholly unexpected defection that has prevented our success."[3]

Lt. L. Frederick Rice was almost irrationally hostile toward the unsatisfac-tory soldiers. He singled out two units as the "meanest, and most despicable," and "the only regiments that to my knowledge have ever disgraced the old Bay State." These were the 4th and 48th, "the last of which has on three oc-casions ignominiously and disgracefully lost its colors, and had them retaken and saved for them by other regiments, and the first, which enjoys the proud celebrity of laying down their arms and refusing to do duty in the very midst of the Siege of Port Hudson, when the order for storming was daily expected, because forsooth, 'their time had expired.'" That time, he concluded with ex-treme disgust, was the "paltry nine months for which the people of Massachu-setts were so foolish as to give them from 150 to 250 dollars bounty."[4]

There is no record that any former members of the 31st served in the ranks of the 48th Massachusetts, but the 49th Massachusetts, drawn from Berkshire County, included four men who had originally enlisted in the 31st. Contrary to some of Rice's suppositions, this unit suffered sizable casualties, losing 56 percent as many men during its nine months as the 31st eventually did during thirty-four months of service.

Perhaps as a result of reading too much literature in college (although he was an engineering student), Rice remained imbued with the romantic idea of war as a proving ground—an attitude that led to the premature death of many a young lieutenant. Earlier he had written that he would not consider a furlough "till the 31st Reg. of Mass. Volunteers, is heard of beyond the narrow circle of those who have friends in it. When we have a few honorable holes in our flag and perhaps in our bodies, then I could, without feeling ashamed, try to get a chance to see you all for a little while."[5]

With the nine-month regiments, the Lincoln administration bridged a period of scarce manpower but at the price of reviving the problems associated with the short-term militia call ups of the War for Independence and the War of 1812. Banks lost twenty-one regiments when the nine-month men returned home, but, with Vicksburg subdued, Grant replaced them with the Thirteenth Corps, numbering 14,712 officers and men.[6] Banks gave command of his Nineteenth Corps to Maj. Gen. William B. Franklin (1823–1903), who had never quite fulfilled the brilliant promise of his cadet days at West Point. Within this organization, Weitzel commanded the First Division, Brigadier General Emory the Third, and Grover the Fourth (there was no second). Soon after, Brigadier General Dwight was given command of the Third Division. (Although Dwight was from Springfield and should have had some kinship with the Massachusetts soldiers, his pomposity made him unpopular. Fairbank wrote of the general, "None of us like him.")[7] The 31st Massachusetts became part of the Third Brigade (commanded by Colonel Gooding) of Weitzel's division. Under a reorganization of the Department of the Gulf, effective August 31, 1863, the 31st Massachusetts was listed as part of the Second Brigade, First Division; commanders seemed to enjoy the game of frequent reorganization.[8]

Texas continued to fascinate the Union leadership, and General in Chief Halleck ordered Banks to establish a base in that state. The initial efforts were unrewarding but form a backdrop to the more famous 1864 Red River Campaign. After an amphibious operation against Sabine City was humiliatingly repulsed, Franklin was sent back into the Teche country. Retracing much of

Banks's earlier campaign, his forces penetrated as far as Opelousas before he decided that low water and the oncoming winter rendered an invasion by that route unpromising. Franklin began a slow retreat, with Confederates following closely on his trail, and reached New Iberia in mid-November. Meanwhile, the Thirteenth Corps had finally grasped a weak hold on Brownsville, Texas.

Thus we have a tableau of almost continuous operations after the capture of Port Hudson, even though no major battles occurred (even if the entire available Confederate force was engaged, their numbers were so small that it is questionable if any contest could be termed a major battle). Other than placing troops within the boundary of Texas, Banks seemed to lack any unifying strategic concept, though his practice of dividing his forces kept the much weaker enemy on the defensive. While portions of the Army of the Gulf were spread over several hundred miles, the 31st Massachusetts remained relatively inactive, not participating in any of these far-flung movements. After the armies' attention shifted away from Donaldsonville, which Fairbank referred to as "the region of chimney stacks" due to the destruction inflicted by the Union navy, the regiment returned to Camp Magnolia at Baton Rouge in early August.[9]

While the seven active companies of the 31st Massachusetts plodded hundreds of weary miles, absorbing the dust of central Louisiana and finally engaging in the grinding, squalid siege of Port Hudson, the three companies detached at Fort Pike continued their uneventful service there. Organizationally, they were separate from the rest of the regiment, being part of the Defenses of New Orleans. Their duties followed a repetitive cycle of raids, patrols, and drills. In case there was any doubt that this too was part of the routine, mosquitoes returned in full ferocity in March. William Rich reported an unpleasant incident on January 31, when some members of Company I refused to do guard duty. One man was struck with a sword by Sgt. Henry S. Stearns of Company G, while others were thrown in jail.[10] This potentially serious confrontation was smoothed over somehow, and Rich does not mention it again. (Lieutenant Rice, who was also at Fort Pike, does not mention the incident in his letters, though it is the sort of thing he might have been reluctant to discuss.)

Complex interaction with the wide spectrum of residents inserted some spice into the monotonous routine. At least one boat came up from New Orleans every day, and the post sutler had his own vessel make deliveries most days. As a result, men in the Fort Pike garrison had closer relations with locals than with men in their seven fellow companies. There was little opportunity for physical interaction between the two parts of the regiment, and mail passed through a circuitous process. Moreover, since most of the companies had each been recruited in specific areas, the men would always have had stronger connections with comrades in their own unit. Occasional accounts of visits between the detached portions of the regiment bear a curious resemblance to reports of calls by relatives that filled the local columns of newspapers back home. While hospitalized at Saint James, Asa Wheeler received a pass on February 20 to visit friends in the 31st at Carrollton, among them Sgt. Francis Clary.[11] Richard Underwood obtained a pass and, with his friend William Stockwell, looked up acquaintances in the 26th Massachusetts and the 53rd Massachusetts (a nine-month regiment). He visited his own regiment's camp at Carrollton but found that most of the men had gone off on the Plaquemine expedition, leaving only a few sick behind. Capt. William Rockwell of Company I came down to Algiers to visit friends in the 31st after they returned from the first expedition against Port Hudson.[12] War reports reached Fort Pike from New Orleans quickly, but 90 percent of them were wrong or exaggerated. Meanwhile, news from the rest of the regiment arrived slowly and irregularly. Men at Fort Pike learned of the capture of Vicksburg on July 8, the same day as those at Port Hudson, but word of the fall of Port Hudson itself did not arrive until July 10, two days after the event.[13]

The Fort Pike garrison not only welcomed but also sought out diversions that would crack the prevailing monotony. Underwood described forays into the countryside to shoot semiwild hogs and occasional brushes with supposed guerillas. On the theory that "we would occasionally volunteer to endure the torment of the mosquitoes, rather than stay at the fort all the time," he joined a picket guard at Pleasanton Island Light House, even though the mosquitoes were more avid there. The guards took five days' rations and went on board the *Firmeza*, better known as the "Green Sloop," for a pleasant sail of seven miles to the post.[14] On a later occasion he was detailed to accompany the paymaster to Ship Island. After a stormy and dangerous voyage, he passed a night there. The visit became an exercise in premature nostalgia, as Underwood found the island greatly changed. It now was garrisoned by only seven companies of a black regiment, and there were a number of prisoners who had been sentenced to hard labor working on a new fort there. By then, the masonry work was nearly finished, but no guns were mounted inside. Underwood found that in the year since he had last seen Ship Island, "the city of tents was gone. The village on the lower end had increased wonderfully. And several batteries had been built on the sand hills around the lower end, and the barren sand, where our camps were formerly situated, was covered with a thin but tall growth of coarse grass." It was probably disheartening that he had "some difficulty in finding our former camping ground, which I had the curiosity to visit. I went to the grave yard where a few of the 31st boys lie sleeping. Sad feelings took possession of my fancy. I picked up a few simple shells to keep as a memorial of the place."[15]

Ordinarily, the post sutler would provide a welcome link to the outside world and its delights, but many in the Fort Pike garrison had hard feelings toward the merchant, a man named Fabacher, voicing the common complaint that he charged exorbitant prices. One day in April the 128th New York appeared, giving men in the 31st Massachusetts an opportunity to vent their animosity toward Fabacher by goading the newcomers to raid his establishment, "frightening him considerably and taking some of his goods, a dozen or two hats, some tobacco and other things." A short time after the New York regiment departed, some members of the 31st conducted their own raid, "battering in his door and window with the boom of an old schooner, bricks, etc. The next day, the Sutler moved his goods into one of the casemates, and that night the boys took a boat and went around into the moat, up the port hole, where they climbed in and stole two hundred dollars worth of Sutler's goods, which they hid in the marsh, and wherever they could find a good place."[16] Rich voiced no sympathy for Fabacher: "Wish they had tore all [of it] down."[17] This was not the regiment's first pillage of the sutler, as a few months earlier some members of Company I had stolen nine barrels of ale that he had stored in the sally port of the fort. In consequence of the latest attack, the 31st was assigned to guard the sutler's shanty, an unwelcome extra duty that forestalled further brigandage. It does not appear that any soldiers were punished for these raids, and there is no mention of reimbursing Fabacher for his losses (nor of agents knocking on the sutler's door to offer inventory insurance).

The craving for novelty may be partly responsible for another unfortunate episode that marred the 31st Massachusetts record at Fort Pike. This time, the sutler came in from the city, bringing four or five ladies in his sloop. "They stayed in the Citadel all night and Capt. Rockwell used our flag for a mosquito bar, so the Serg't of the guard could not get it to raise over the fort until nine o'clock, and then it hung lifeless a half day as though aware of the disgraceful use that it had been put to." In the morning Capt. Eliot Bridgman, commander of the fort, "had dress parade for the gratification of the women, as it was the only time we ever had dress parade in the morning. In the forenoon, the officers took the ladies out to ride in the *Polly,* giving the men that manned the boat a ration of whiskey for their services. The ladies went back to New Orleans in the afternoon in the *Lelia,* or Sutler's boat."[18]

A similar troubling incident occurred a few weeks later involving a class of inhabitants styled "registered enemies" because they refused to take the oath of allegiance. Underwood claimed that they numbered ten thousand, adding that General Banks had decreed that all such persons should leave Union lines and go over to the enemy. Free transportation was furnished, and Underwood observed that "about twenty loads of them passed Fort Pike on their way to Biloxi and Mississippi City. . . . As soon as landed, the able bodied men were conscripted by confederate officers waiting for the purpose, so in fact, we helped to fill their ranks." Two or three additional loads of registered enemies were taken out on the steamer *J. M. Brown.* One afternoon Captain Bridgman allowed a dozen or more of the passengers to land at the wharf, "showing them about the outer works, and allowed some of the ladies to go inside to dress parade, setting chairs for them upon the barbettes, and we could see as we went through the ceremony of dress parade, their scornful looks at us Yankees, and more than one had a book, taking notes of the guns, etc.; and as we marched out by the rebel gentlemen, they looked with scorn on us as we passed."[19]

One who was especially disturbed by these proceedings was Cpl. Marcus M. Thompson, a farmer from Dana. Thirty-six when he enlisted, he was older than most privates and retained a strict New England righteousness. Thus he reported these incidents to higher authority, and in due course "an officer belonging to the General's Staff came to the Fort to examine the facts of the case." This development must have been worrisome and irritating to Captain Bridgman, as it would have brought back memories of an unpleasant inspection in January in which Brig. Gen. Thomas Sherman berated the officers "pretty severely" after observing their bumbling handling of the troops.[20]

As it emerged, Bridgman's fears were unfounded. The investigating officer heard the corporal's testimony but was evidently in cover-up mode and did not attempt to collect additional evidence. Thompson damaged his case by failing to bring witnesses to corroborate his statements. As Underwood concluded, "it was fixed up some way." The rewards of a whistleblower are ever uncertain. Soon after the staff officer departed, Bridgman reduced the corporal to the ranks. "This ending of the case worried Thompson considerably, and with some other causes, it turned him crazy." He was kept at the fort a few days "until he had become a raving maniac, tearing his clothes, shrieking, gibbering, and acting in a horrible manner, until we could do nothing with him. He was then taken to New Orleans by his cousins, Chas. and Harry Horr, and admitted to the Charity Hospital at that city, where he remained for a few days, until he got so bad they could not manage him. He was then taken to the Parish prison, where he was chained up in one of the cells and died in that place a few weeks after."[21]

After nearly a year at Fort Pike, the garrison made a valiant effort to overcome the loneliness with festivities on Independence Day 1863. This turned out to be the day on which Vicksburg fell, which would have inspired a real celebration had the troops known of it. As it was, Lieutenant Rice noted that the men could not obtain fireworks, and since there was little point in creating a disturbance that no one would witness, they invented their own amusement. Money for the celebration had been saved from the "company fund," contributions to which were deducted from rations.[22] The resulting holiday had a more military tone than the celebrations back home in New England:

9 ½ A.M. Non-commissioned officers drill. 3 prizes, copy of tactics, Corp. [Patrick J.] Dinan of Comp. I win the first. Corporals [Frederick] Blauss and [Chauncey W.] Smith of Comp. I the second and third. 10 ½ Privates drill, 3 prizes. Copy of Tactics. [Henry] Hanchet[t] Comp. G win the first, [Benjamin] Taylor and [Charles F.] Clark Comp. I the second and third. 11 ½ A.M. Lemonade with a stick in it. 12 Dinner. After target shooting, Sergt. [Charles L.] Moody Comp. G win the prize, a silver goblet, also hunting the gold. Contrabands, wheel-barrow race, sack race, climbing the greesed [sic] poles and other amusements winding up with a tatoo [sic] and three cheers for the officers and three more for the Union.[23]

One of these improvised activities, "Hunting the Gold," exploited the civilian blacks in camp, although the victims seemed to participate willingly. Lieutenant Rice explained the set up: "about half a bushel of flour was put in a small tub and a silver quarter dollar put down at the bottom of the Flour." After this preparation, he then "arranged all my male darkies (nearly thirty) in a line, and drawing lots for the turn set them at work with their hands tied behind them, diving for the quarter. The one who found it and picked it out with his teeth was to have it and a three dollar greenback." Describing the results once the game began, he continued: "You can imagine the effect of a darky of such intense blackness as is never seen at the North, covered with perspiration, going to the bottom of eight or nine inches of flour and rooting about there as long as his breath lasts, and you can perhaps form some estimate of the appearance created by twenty seven of these interesting creatures." Having been unsuccessful in extracting the money from the flour, the participants were, "without allowing their faces to be washed, put down on their hands and feet, and then, on all fours, required to run about 250 feet and back again, the money being given to the winner in the race. If you don't think this makes fun try it sometime."[24] Many of the contests in which the white soldiers engaged were physically embarrassing, but they lacked the demeaning racial aspect.

The companies at Fort Pike contained a few men of German origin who had been recruited at New Orleans, with whom Rice had an unusual relationship: "Something in my appearance gave them the idea that I was German, either by birth or parentage. So strong was this belief that, though they never heard me speak the language, or give any evidence of understanding it when I heard it, they were always very guarded in their conversation when they saw me about." The lieutenant enjoyed playing along with this: "Of course I did not seek to dispel the illusion, but used occasionally to look wise, and smile slightly when I heard a remark that made the others laugh."[25]

Rice had hauled up an old barge or launch that had sunk in the fort's moat and had it reconditioned. He did not report this endeavor in his letters home since it reflected poorly on his engineering abilities, according to Underwood's account: "It was hauled up and the barnacles scraped from its bottom, the seams calked with oakum, and the whole of it painted. Then the Lieut. had some paddle wheels made and fitted to the boat and turned by long levers fixed to the crank of each." Unfortunately, this system required "thirty-two men to man the boat, & as many more could ride in the boat. Lieut. Rice then had a carriage built and one of our two small mountain howitzers (12 pounders) mounted in the bow. It was very hard work to propel this boat, and it was of no great use, so the men here gave it two names: one, The Mankiller, the other, Rice's Folly."[26]

The split of the regiment, a relic of the controversy surrounding its formative period, finally came to an end on September 5, when Companies F, G, and I departed Fort Pike on the steamer *Savory*. They spent the night in New Orleans, where even sleeping in a cotton press, a warehouse-like building, "seemed to the men a paradise, because they didn't have to put up mosquitoes bars."[27] In a telling comment Fairbank observed of the three, "They number more men than the other six companies."[28] Rice used similar terminology: "Our three companies came with[in] a dozen of numbering as many men as the other six [apparently not counting Company H, then serving with the provost guard in New Orleans]." Underwood simply stated that the three Fort Pike companies had as many men as the other seven.[29]

It remains debatable why the regiment had not been reunited earlier. One could speculate that Banks was suspicious of the 31st, which he might have regarded as one of Butler's pets, but it would seem that Gooding could have exerted influence to bring the awkward schism to an end. Regardless, on September 9 the reunited regiment headed off to Baton Rouge under command of Major Bache. Five enlisted men of Company F, accompanied by Captain Bridgman, remained behind at Fort Pike to take commissions in the Corps d'Afrique, the body of troops that was being formed from the local black population.[30] Bridgman was commissioned a colonel and commanded the Corps d'Afrique regiment that replaced the 31st Massachusetts. Since many white officers considered it degrading or detrimental to their careers to command black soldiers, this created opportunities for those who felt otherwise to make a rapid jump from enlisted to officer status. General Weitzel had sent Butler an agonized request not to be placed in command of black regiments, but although he was a Butler favorite, the commanding general offered little sympathy.[31] Judging by the results, the subject must have been analyzed intensively within the Fort Pike companies. An astonishing total of twenty-four men of all enlisted ranks took commissions in the "colored" regiments: nine from Company F, six from G, seven from I, and two from the regimental staff.

A revealing example of the perceived difference in status of such officers occurred in the 31st Massachusetts. On an occasion in early 1864, Fairbank reported that "Lt. E. Sagendorph made us a visit and was merry as could be. Milt told him to leave the tent. Ed says Milt turned him a shoul colder [sic] because he is in a negro regiment."[32] Here the issue came as close to home as could be, for "Milt" was undoubtedly Lt. Milton Sagendorph, and Edwin Sagendorph, previously a private, had been discharged on September 2, 1863, to become an officer in a black regiment. The two were almost certainly brothers, as both were painters from Ware and mustered on the same day; their surname was not a common one. Edwin was actually older than Milton by two years.

Rice had reported earlier that "Mr. Hepworth has resigned his position as Chaplain in the 47th . . . and taken a lieutenancy in a darky regiment. I think he might have done better, though I am not one of those who think the darks won't fight."[33] If a report by James Tupper is correct (and it seems to be supported by orders issued at the time), the quality of recruiting for the later black regiments had declined dramatically: "Hodge['s] Negro regiment is full. There was no volunteering about it, but they forced every nigger they got hold of right into it."[34]

The Union commander at Baton Rouge, Brig. Gen. Philip St. George Cooke (1809–95), professed to believe that the city was threatened by Confederate attack in the late autumn of 1863. He placed a line of artillery in front of his camp and set soldiers and black laborers to work strengthening breastworks and clearing fields of view.[35] Whether he genuinely feared an attack or was primarily concerned with keeping his men busy and disciplined is a matter of conjecture. In any event, he made sure that, during a generally quiet period, the men of the 31st and his other units were not allowed to forget that they were still in the army.

Lt. J. L. Hallett, formerly of Company F, had transferred to the Signal Corps, which gave him a much different experience than the rest of the 31st Massachusetts.[36] He and two others from Company F and a man from a Maine regiment were captured by a party of Confederates at their isolated and unprotected post six miles from Vermilionville (present Lafayette) on the night of October 20. Col. W. G. Vincent, commanding the 2nd Louisiana Cavalry, allowed the prisoners to ride at the head of the column with his staff. Later, the colonel invited them to join in a gratifyingly substantial dinner. On the following day, however, the prisoners "were corralled and taken in charge by as rough looking fellow as we had ever seen. His attire was a red flannel shirt, leather trousers, slouched hat, top boots and physique of the roughest sort, and wore a leather belt filled with cartridges, two pistols and a bowie knife." His principal assignment was "to hunt refugees for the Confederate service and had shot and killed fifteen men in one week because they refused to join the Rebel army. His men were well mounted and kept a keen eye on us while we walked." This was a case study of the kind of psychopath who was able to flourish when war shattered the customary restraints of civilization. As they marched, Hallett and his men were examined intently by people who had never seen a Yankee. Eventually, they reached the Confederate prison at Tyler, Texas, but were exchanged on December 25 after negotiations revealed that each side had accumulated a similar number of prisoners.[37]

Hallett was severely emaciated when he returned to Union lines and was granted leave to visit home, which he had not seen in more than two years. He recovered considerably on the sea voyage so that, by the time his ship landed, "there was not much evidence of hospital and prison life." His friends, who had been prepared to treat him as an invalid, "on observing my robust condition, the diet was changed and there was a continual round of feasting; beef, pies, cake, floating island, with wine jellies, fruit and confectionery for dessert. . . . Just how I survived the surfeit of cake and pie, and again reported for duty at the expiration of my furlough, is a problem that has never been solved." Later, Hallett enjoyed the surprise of seeing many of the 2nd Louisiana Cavalry officers who had captured him themselves held as prisoners (though more comfortable than he had been) in New Orleans houses.[38]

Also missing from the main body of the 31st Massachusetts were the men who were hospitalized. Even in March 1863, after almost a year in Louisiana, Corporal Hawkes reported that half the regiment had diarrhea.[39] While commonplace to acknowledge that more Civil War soldiers died of disease than from battle injuries, the actual experience of hospitalized men was utterly unromantic and is seldom described in detail. In the nature of things, hospitalizations were generally short periods of absence, but the service history of the 31st Massachusetts provides two accounts of long-term convalescence; there may have been others who did not leave a written record.

Except insofar as rest allowed the body to recuperate on its own, extended hospitalization did not contribute to a cure since the medical profession was unaware of the cause of most diseases or the importance of sanitation. It would have made sense to discharge the most chronically ill men at the earliest opportunity, but there was tremendous pressure to keep them on the rolls in the faint hope that they might return to active service. Hawkes sometimes feared that Capt. John Lee was too lenient, but that apparently did not extend to ill soldiers. The corporal informed his mother that "it is against Capt. Lee's principles to *discharge* any of his men. Had rather they would *die* here, as in the case of Hathaway."[40] Fairbank made a similarly bitter remark in early January, noting that "John Parker died today. He was not excused from duty until unable to stand."[41] Parker, a farmer from Hardwick, was nineteen or twenty when he died at Fort Jackson; Tupper, from the same hometown, eulogized him as "a quiet fellow, but kind & the boys all liked him." When John Woodis died of consumption on July 14, 1862, Fairbank noted that he had been sick most of the time since leaving Massachusetts and classed him as "another victim to the red-tape policy of military law."[42] A shoemaker from Ware, Woodis was forty-five at the time of his death, one of the oldest men in the regiment. He had been discharged for disability a month earlier and thus might not have been counted as a war death.

Captain Lee himself took ill with typhoid fever and found himself in the hospital.[43] Although already on furlough, Lee was still in New Orleans awaiting transport as of July 23. This prompted Hawkes to remark maliciously, "It seems to me were I an officer I could afford to pay my passage on a Mail Steamer rather than lay around in this enervating climate."[44] Perhaps to take his mind off the heat and humidity, the corporal occupied himself reading Dr. Elisha Kane's account of his Arctic explorations.[45] Around this time, Charlie Wright of Conway was discharged and sent home, probably none too soon. Hawkes wrote that "he has got the consumption, and I am afraid would not live many months in this climate. He is a good hearted fellow, always cheerful with a joke ready, so that as regards my selfish enjoyment I am rather sorry to have him go."[46]

Hawkes acknowledged that he had a melancholy disposition, often unable to see a bright side to things. His own recovery was not advanced by the experience of seeing the wounded brought down to Saint James Hospital after the May 27 assault on Port Hudson. Many had arms or legs already amputated or displayed other dreadful injuries, and the sensitive Hawkes could not help thinking that "only a few days ago these men were in their full vigor, now—many, such is the heat of the climate, will soon die, while others after long days of pain will recover, but not to mingle in the busy scenes of life, as once."[47] He later reported that the army took over the former Hotel Saint Louis to use as a hospital for the wounded. His condition fluctuated, sometimes seeming to have recovered, but his last preserved letter reports a relapse of both diarrhea and heart palpitations.[48] Probably to his surprise, Hawkes was discharged the following day.

Wheeler was in Saint James during much of the same period. When his condition permitted, he tried to relieve the monotony of the convalescent routine. He visited friends in his regiment at Carrollton and found friends in the 53rd Massachusetts. On one of his walks around New Orleans, he observed (in third person): "Flowers of every hue will greet him at every turn—those with which he has ever been accustomed to see in his distant Northern Home, others which he is not acquainted with, or that are not found on New England's hilly sides." He marveled that the magnolia, "with its verdure of living green, interspersed with large single flowers here and there over all its outer surface, is the most beautiful, the most fragrant—nothing so much so as this beautiful tree just after a shower, when the air has been cleansed and so is free from dirt and dust." His customary religious outlook may have been rendered more morbid by illness: "But I will no more attempt to paint the beauties that will ever attract one who has cultivated his taste for this great, this wonderful blessing, bestowed upon us worms of the dust by our kind and very indulgent Heavenly Father, but will leave it to those who are better able to express their minds and in more expressive language, and return to the Hospital, to think and reflect on what was seen in a few hours of recreation, spent on the Banks of the Old Mississippi."[49]

Wheeler's religious feelings did not find a satisfactory outlet in whatever services were provided in the hospital or in his regiment, and he began the practice of attending Sunday services at a "colored" church, Saint Paul's. It is interesting that he felt more congenial in this setting than in any of the white churches he might have attended. Still, although he enjoyed the experience and at times found it moving, he remained a detached observer. "Much pleasure was derived by attending this place of worship," he wrote. "To those who had ever in the past attended quietly, from Sabbath to Sabbath, those quiet God-like places of worship and noted the heaving bosom or starting tear spring from eyes that had from early infancy watched over us, such would criticize the proceedings, even condemn their form, and call it all excitement. But charity must be allowed even to them." He believed that the black congregants were "different by Nature, different in practice, their surroundings have been altogether different. And so sincerity must be allowed in all their acts. If they go to extremes, we must allow that ignorance has been their Master." Wheeler then continued, "But politeness is a virtue, so far as strangers are concerned, who care to visit at their Church. One does not have to stand at the Door stone or at the entrance, waiting for the Sexton to show him a seat, till patience becomes a virtue, but are politely shown a seat up in front of the desk reserved for their especial use while staying with them." He noted that their style of singing had gone out of fashion in New England—"the Pastor reading 2 lines, and then old and young joined in singing the song of praise, with a zest almost unimaginable, or impossible to be conceived."[50] Wheeler remained essentially an outsider, regarding the church and its black congregation as something of a stage set. He did not report any conversations with his fellow worshippers, nor did he seem aware of the effect his mere presence might have had on them. For the congregants, the sight of a white soldier on the benches was surely a jolting reminder of the immense upheaval that had disrupted the seemingly eternal prewar social structure and was sweeping them into an era of vast uncertainty.

Underwood similarly reported attending a "negro dance and meeting" one evening, but it seems to have been an isolated venture.[51] When they were not actively campaigning, Northern soldiers always exhibited an element of tourism in their daily existence while stationed in the Deep South. They were endlessly intrigued, puzzled, and amazed by the alien culture and climate they encountered, and the black inhabitants were an unavoidable feature that lent the region its exotic quality. Most of the Northerners instinctively modeled themselves on the white explorers who were probing the steadily shrinking unknown areas of the globe, and their letters home resemble the dispatches sent back by such intrepid pioneers. Conditioned to look at the black residents as "natives," most soldiers lacked Wheeler's relative ability to recognize them as fellow humans, shaped by their history and environment. In a letter to his four-year-old daughter, Lieutenant Colonel Hopkins observed that "black women with . . . pails and bundles on their heads" were not a familiar sight on the streets of Northampton.[52] Curiosity led young Norris to attend a black church service, and his reaction was probably typical of the blue-coated interlopers: "One of the most comicle [sic] sights I ever saw is a nigger *meeting*. Such *hollering* you never heard. It beats the Methodist prayer meeting. When the minister is praying the rest of them set up to yelling and groaning. When we first heard them we burst out laughing."[53]

On duty at the Signal Corps relay station in Carrollton, Lieutenant Hallett had an observer's experience similar to many recorded by Northern soldiers. Large numbers of former slaves had gathered there from outlying plantations, bringing with them the custom of treating Sunday as a festive occasion: "A fiddle and a pair of bones made up the orchestra; the playing was lively and set the dancers a merry round, their broad feet came down with a ring like an ax on an empty barrel head, and the faster and louder the music the more they enjoyed it and danced for half an hour, then rested only long enough to wipe the perspiration from their faces."[54]

Wheeler visited Saint Paul's on other occasions—and there is no telling where this experiment might have led—but his stay in New Orleans came to a sudden end when a physician finally discharged him on disability and sent him home. After about seven months in the hospital, he boarded a steamer for New York on June 18. As he perceived all too clearly, "they have kept me till life has about ebbed in these old bones," and the sea journey itself extended his ordeal. Still, Wheeler retained the ability to marvel at phenomena like the visible boundary between fresh and salt water in the Gulf and to describe some of the hard characters who were deposited at Key West, Florida, to be imprisoned at the isolated outpost of Dry Tortugas. He kept a death watch for one profane man and observed storms and sunrises at sea. On June 26, as they were approaching New York, Wheeler reported that of the seventy-five soldiers who had been discharged from Saint James, six had died in the previous eight days. There is little doubt that he was correct when he observed, "Had I remained much longer, such would have been my condition."[55]

The Reverend Chubbuck was traveling to New York on the same ship and had asked Wheeler to watch over the dying man. Wheeler had little respect for the regimental chaplain, regarding him basically as a Southern sympathizer. That accusation may be unfair, but it appears that most of the soldiers had a poor opinion of Chubbuck, yet another source of dissension in the troubled 31st. In addition to earlier disparaging comments, Hawkes commented that "Chaplain Chubbuck is married and gone North. 'Twill make very little difference here I am thinking if he should not come back."[56] One who had a different opinion was Dr. Bidwell, who was not concerned with Chubbuck's ministerial abilities but was impressed with his handsome appearance, his handling of fast horses, and his general charm. Bidwell knew that before the war the chaplain "had been a teacher in the Maplewood Institute, a high-toned seminary for young ladies at Pittsfield." Chubbuck was obviously more at ease in the company of women than the typical hill-town soldier in the 31st, which may explain the possibly envious complaint about his "running around with the women." As recounted by Dr. Bidwell, the chaplain made the acquaintance of two women, originally from the North, who ran a female seminary in Baton Rouge and through them met and fell in love with a pupil-assistant.[57] The doctor gave her name as Emma Wrotnoska (more likely Wrotnowska), the Polish origin of which was confirmed when they named their first son Stanislaus. Contrary to some expectations, Chubbuck did return to Louisiana. No longer confined to the 31st Massachusetts, he conducted general services as late as October 1864.[58] He was mustered out on November 26 of that year and later became a minister in southern New Jersey, where he died prematurely on January 2, 1872, at the age of thirty-five.

Even death sometimes only prolonged the anguish for some New England soldiers. Tupper and Frank Knight had been friends in Hardwick, and most of Tupper's letters home contain some mention of Knight, who was about three years older. Knight came up from Fort Jackson to spend a night with his friend in early December 1862. When he left Tupper reported, "He is running down under the influence of the Malaria of these swamps & couldn't walk around much."[59] Knight returned directly to the hospital and died there January 10, 1863. Because it was readily accessible and his family had sufficient means, Knight's body was shipped home for burial. In a letter of January 27, Tupper wrote: "I suppose poor Frank's body has reached home & been buried before this. We all miss him & mourn for him." By the time it reached home, the body was not in condition to be viewed: "I was sorry but not much disappointed to learn that the remains of Frank Knight were not in a condition to be exposed." In sorrow Tupper added: "I was in hopes his friends & relatives would have the privilege of seeing the features of the boy before consigning it forever to the gloomy home of the dead, but still knowing the difficulty of preserving a body stricken down by the disease he died of, I thought it only a chance if it remained fresh for so long a time as it would take to get it home."[60] Tupper's father conducted Knight's funeral service.

A similarly melancholy scene played out with the remains of Sgt. Henry S. Church of Company F, who died at Fort Pike on May 31, 1863. According to Underwood, Church died of typhus after an illness of only two days. "The next day," as described by Underwood, "Serg't [Charles H.] Horr was sent to New Orleans to procure a metallic coffin, for we decided to send the remains home to his wife in Deerfield. The remains were placed in one of the casemates and a watch kept over them, in which I took my share." But the coffin did not arrive until sunset on the second day, "when it was found that the body had bloated so that it was impossible to get it into the coffin. So, at nine o'clock at night, he was placed in a wooden coffin, silently and without a funeral procession was taken to the lone graveyard in the marsh, and there buried in sorrow." He was the third man who had died in Company F, and Underwood added resignedly: "He will rest as well there as in his native place in Mass. There he lies in the swamps of Louisiana, one of the many sacrifices offered on the altar of his country. Peace be to his remains."[61]

From its base in Baton Rouge, the reunited 31st Massachusetts fell into a relatively calm routine of drilling, camp duties, and occasional forays into the surrounding country to seize contraband. Casualties from these activities were minimal, but losses continued from disease and disability. During the second half of 1863, the 31st Massachusetts suffered no combat casualties (two men deserted). In this generally quiet time, twenty-nine members of the regiment died of disease, including a couple who died of wounds received at Port Hudson. Another forty-eight men were discharged, almost all for health reasons. (This figure does not include those who transferred to other military organizations.) Although these totals include a few men who enlisted locally, the great majority were part of the original, but shrinking, Massachusetts contingent. Many who were discharged on disability died on their way home or soon after and thus were not tallied as war casualties. Others survived a few years but died prematurely as a result of war-related wounds or chronic illness. A facile argument is sometimes made that a certain number of these deaths would have occurred at home in the normal course of events, but there can be little doubt that the mortality rate of men in the prime of life was much higher among those who had served in the war than it would have been otherwise.

This may be one of the few aspects of the Civil War that has not received as much study as it should. In a recent effort to rectify that deficiency, Brian M. Jordan has observed: "In 1892, John Shaw Billings, who served as an army medical inspector, concluded 'the exertions, privations, and anxieties of military service . . . must necessarily have lowered the vitality and diminished the power of resistance to subsequent exposure and causes of disease.' After years of hoarding extant vital statistics, Billings demonstrated what he knew intrinsically—that veterans were significantly more likely than non-veterans to suffer from chronic illnesses and disease."[62]

The losses to disease were not always permanent. After a period of recuperation, many who had been discharged found that whatever factors had motivated them to volunteer still applied, and they enlisted in different regiments. One man, Amos Davis of Pownal, Vermont, discharged for disability on November 13, 1863, actually reenlisted in the 31st Massachusetts on August 30, 1864, and served until the regiment was mustered out a year later. In addition to the eight men who joined nine-month regiments, at least twenty-four reentered Union service. Six of these signed up in the 60th Massachusetts, a regiment organized in August 1864 to serve only one hundred days during another manpower crisis. This special regiment did not see action but even so lost eleven men to disease during its brief existence. Six former members of the 31st who enlisted in the 57th Massachusetts had quite a different experience. This regiment was organized in Worcester, thus covering some of the same recruiting region as the original 31st. It was sent to Virginia to participate in the bloody fighting that closed out the war and suffered considerably more losses in its fifteen months of service than the 31st Massachusetts did in a period more than twice as long. Another forty-four men who had been discharged from the 31st were transferred to the Veterans Reserve Corps, comprising men who were no longer considered fit for combat but who could perform guard, hospital, and administrative duties. In sum, assuming no duplication, seventy-six former members of the 31st continued to serve in some form during the war.[63]

Two respected officers died during this period: 1st Lt. F. A. Cook (Company K) of Springfield on August 6, 1863, and Captain Rockwell of Pittsfield of typhoid fever on December 3. The melancholy assignment of writing to "the girl [Cook] left behind him" fell to Lieutenant Rice.[64] Cook's passing created an opening for 2nd Lt. Milton Sagendorph to be named first lieutenant of Company K. Fairbank, with his usual bluntness, observed, "We are not sorry to get rid of him."[65] He was one of the escorts at Rockwell's funeral on December 5: "He was conveyd to the Church on a caisson covered with the stars and stripes,—and, after the funeral services were over, we escorted him to the boat. Somewhat different from a Private's burial, where they nail them in a box and dump him into the first grave they come to,—but he is Judge Rockwell's son."[66]

Several officers, among them Capt. Edward Hollister and Lts. Luther Howell and Horace F. Morse, were dispatched to Massachusetts on recruiting duty to restore the depleted ranks. They returned on October 20; Howell was promoted to captain on January 27, 1864.[67] In early November the regiment was cheered by the return of Lt. Nelson Bond, who had improbably survived his terrible wound and gone home for a brief furlough. Fairbank was pleased to observe that "he looks tough and hardy."[68] He was pretty well recovered before leaving on his furlough, though Rice noted that "it makes him squirm a little to laugh heartily," an early appearance of the timeworn comic line "it only hurts when I laugh." Bond was assigned as an aide to Colonel Gooding, who, Fairbank said approvingly, "knows a good officer."[69]

The other officer wounded at Port Hudson, Capt. W. I. Allen, had also largely recovered, though with some medically interesting effects: "The shell came from one of our guns, and struck with sufficient force to tear through his coat, vest, and shirt, but didn't break the skin." Nevertheless, "the blow was sufficient to kill the flesh beneath, so that it rotted out, leaving him with a hole in his back nearly four inches in diameter and over half an inch deep, which although not now painful, must fill up before he can return to active duty."[70]

For the soldiers, the last months of 1863 in Baton Rouge proved a relaxing, almost pleasant, interlude. While on picket duty, Fairbank reported, "The yellow and mulatto girls made good company most of the night."[71] On another occasion he and a comrade visited a cemetery "and fell in with some handsome girls, and they invited us home,—but we waited until after Dress Parade, then went over and made an evening visit."[72] The young man from Ware seemed to be bumping against the color barrier that ran like a fault line through the South, yet even he was not ready to push it very far. Earlier in the year he had written, "The first wench I ever saw hugged by a white man was today after coming from work, and oh! She was black as coal,—lips like a horse, and feet that cover a square foot each."[73] He thus expressed much the same racial attitude as the cavaliers who filled the officer corps in the enemy army.

One can speculate that this sort of interaction was common but that most of the men were not as willing as Fairbank to acknowledge it openly. Even he was forced to add the codicil, "What would the Queen at home say?"[74] This is puzzling because he had recorded sending his 1862 diary home; if he did the same for 1863, the "Queen at home" (his mother) would presumably read it.[75] Furthermore, Fairbank, despite his efforts to encase himself in a shell of worldly nonchalance, was subject to the same ripe sentimentality that pervaded the blue-coated ranks. One day the mail brought a letter from home that contained a picture of his mother, "the best treat I could have," he exclaimed. "A mother's picture to look at! What pleasant thoughts it does bring to my mind of bygone days! Alas! How I miss a mother's care!"[76] No mulatto girl could compete with this burst of primal emotion. From Virginia to Texas, this was the unfiltered cry of the heart of thousands of young men in the Federal army.

Fairbank was lucky or shrewd enough to avoid the fate of two men of Company I at Fort Pike who "went across the Rigolets [the strait between Lake Pontchartrain and the Gulf] on a pass, and, following the example of certain Brigadier Generals and others, their superior in rank, allowed themselves to be decoyed three or four miles back into the country to visit certain she seceshers." These luckless men were duped into emptying their revolvers in a marksmanship dare, after which "up jump two scalawags from behind a bush, who presenting double barreled shot guns and other convincing arguments, persuade them to accompany them a little further back into the country." Captain Rockwell led a party in pursuit the following morning, but by then the captives were part of an involuntary tour group well upcountry.[77] Sergeant Rich, who was in the same company, identified the men as "Cook" and "Bradburn," presumably Albert Cook, a laborer from Lenox, age about twenty-seven, and Charles E. Bradburn, a farmer from Great Barrington (both towns in Berkshire County) who was then about twenty. Rich surmised that guerillas had taken them to Confederate Camp Moore. Underwood noted the event as taking place in June, adding, "In a few weeks however, they returned and reported that they . . . had good treatment and were then paroled."[78]

A partial exception to the theme of tranquility in late 1863 was a report of a huge brawl on Thanksgiving between Wisconsin and Massachusetts soldiers. Norris is the only source for this event, and according to his account, it stemmed from an earlier incident in which the 38th Massachusetts had supposedly fired on Wisconsin men. Underwood believed that the quarrel with the 4th Wisconsin originated over "the possession of a boarding house for frail fair ones."[79] The battle resumed at night: "Our company, which is composed for the most part of *Irishmen,* a great many of whom were drunk, fell out at night with their *guns* and said they were going to clean out the whole of the Wisconsin regt. They went out and fired two or three guns and then were driven back to camp by the Provost Guard."[80] Underwood attributed the original clash to "roughs" from Company K, another way of saying the same thing as Norris.

A massive shift in the career of the 31st Massachusetts was the announcement in December 1863 that it would be converted to cavalry. There is no doubt that cavalry units were sorely needed in Banks's army, given the large distances involved and the proliferation of mounted irregulars and bandits, in addition to the regular cavalry, mostly Texans, in the Confederate forces. Butler had perceived this early in his regime and requested a colonel in Baton Rouge to "capture horses enough to enable me to mount another Cavalry Co."[81] During the Teche operation, only three months into his administration, Banks had already recognized the need for cavalry: "The want of cavalry, which I so frequently and so strongly represented, is felt almost hourly in every movement. . . . I cannot but regret that any consideration of economy should have prevented the Government from sending to this department all the cavalry which it could control."[82] Looking ahead to the Red River Campaign, Banks again pleaded with Halleck: "The want of cavalry is the greatest deficiency we suffer. It is indispensable in any movement in Texas that we should be strong in that arm. All the Texan troops are mounted men; their movements are rapid and their concentration effective and powerful. We must meet them in the same way. I earnestly urge upon the government the necessity of strengthening us in that arm."[83]

Halleck rejected this plea as he had similar ones from Banks and other commanders. In a brusque reply to the department commander, Halleck wrote: "I have already stated to you that it would be impossible to send you any cavalry very soon from the north. The great losses in that arm in recent battles, and by the discharge of two-years' and nine-months' men and the great difficulty in procuring cavalry recruits places this matter beyond question or discussion."

He added that he had "urgent" requests from various quarters for 20,000 or 30,000 additional cavalrymen.[84] Despite the undeniable need, the Union high command remained reluctant to create more mounted units. Beyond sheer irascibility, there were valid reasons for this attitude. It was difficult enough to provide food, shelter, and medical care to men; adding horses only compounded the problem. In addition, cavalrymen required an expanded inventory of weapons and equipment, increasing demands on the supply departments.

It was mainly due to Banks's persistence that his cavalry arm was strengthened, mostly achieved by converting infantrymen to cavalry or "mounted infantry." Banks cannot be credited entirely for devising this imaginative solution. He was likely aware of intriguing experiments conducted earlier in 1863 in Maj. Gen. William S. Rosecrans's army in Tennessee. Rosecrans, writing from Nashville in November 1862, was enthusiastic: "I want to mount some infantry regiments, arm them with revolving rifles, and make sharpshooters of them. I cannot elaborate all the consequences that will flow from this, but they will be immense."[85] As would be expected, Halleck dismissed the idea, but Rosecrans authorized one of his brigade commanders, Col. John T. Wilder, to form such a unit. As a volunteer officer, Wilder was less encumbered by military tradition. His Indiana and Illinois infantrymen were so ardent that they advanced personal funds to acquire Spencer repeating carbines, reimbursing Wilder, who had purchased them in his own name. Before long these men had earned the title "Wilder's Lightning Brigade."[86] Halleck finally agreed to allow Rosecrans to form mounted infantry units but warned against creating too many. Characteristically, he declared that "mounted infantry are neither good infantry nor good cavalry."[87] Beyond the fact that many of the existing infantry and cavalry were not as good as the general in chief wished, he was missing the point that mounted infantry was a different kind of unit with a different purpose. He was correct in one assertion, however, that whether designated cavalry or mounted infantry, horses were required in abundance, and they were in increasingly short supply. It was easier and less costly for the Union to produce boots than mounts.

It is questionable to what extent the cavalry expansion in the Gulf was accomplished with Washington's support or primarily on Banks's initiative. Whatever the source, Banks was able to inform Halleck at the end of 1863 that, as the 31st Massachusetts knew from personal experience, "from the nature of the country in which we operate, a strong cavalry force is indispensable, and I am endeavoring to convert infantry regiments into cavalry as rapidly as possible."[88] Some staff officer must have recommended which regiments would be converted, which Banks presumably approved, but the reasons for selecting the 31st were not recorded. The small size of the unit may have been a factor.

As a mounted unit, the 31st Massachusetts Infantry was sometimes referred to as the 6th Massachusetts Cavalry, but this was an unofficial designation. Horses merely provided the mobility needed for the campaigning the soldiers engaged in, much as motor vehicles were employed in twentieth-century wars. Organizationally, the regiment was reassigned to the cavalry division's Fourth Brigade, commanded by Col. Nathan Dudley of the 30th Massachusetts; Brig. Gen. Albert Lindley Lee (1834–1907) was in overall command of the cavalry. Captain Howell described Lee as "a western man but much esteemed by his command."[89] The general was actually born in Fulton, New York, and had moved to Kansas only in 1858. At the start of the war, he was serving as a justice on the Kansas Supreme Court.

On December 9, 1863, the regiment returned to its old campground at Carrollton to begin the transformation from infantry to mounted troops, though the order converting them to cavalry was not issued until the nineteenth.[90] The men camped in "A" tents, so named because of their shape, which they soon improved by building floors and bunks with lumber salvaged from a nearby ruined plantation.[91] Over the next several weeks, deliveries of horses gradually arrived, and sabers and Remington revolvers were issued to the newly minted riders. The mounts were acquired from a large territory and varied greatly in appearance and temperament. Some of them, said Sergeant Rich, were "inclined to be a little ugly, and some three or four men have been kicked pretty badly but no limbs broken yet."[92] In early January 1864 he described another shipment as "very small and poor."[93]

Early winter proved to be harsh, with exceptional cold and much rain. Locals blamed it on the Yankee influence.[94] A dispirited Underwood wrote: "This old year went out dreary enough to us. The mud in our camp was six inches deep, and looked like a hog pen, and we had no boots, so our shoes were full of mud and our feet wet and cold all the time, and the year ended in a cold storm." On New Year's Day 1864, Fairbank complained: "It has been the coldest day I have seen south. It is impossible to keep warm unless one was over the fire." Next day, he reported, "I did manage to sleep warm last night by using every rag of clothing and using horse blankets."[95] The foul weather persisted well into the month. On January 5 Fairbank wrote, "I can hardly stir out without getting all covered with mud from head to foot and wet through"; he reported that trees were covered with ice on the eighth. With good reason, he said, "I pity the horses."[96] Rich confirmed these observations, noting that "the going is worse than I ever saw."[97] Lacking shelter for the newly arrived horses, the men had to slog through mud and chilled water to care for the animals. It was said that many soldiers became chronically ill as a result, adding to the list of those discharged for health reasons. Under these conditions, it was fortunate that the full complement of mounts had not yet arrived.

Fairbank's misery was intensified by his resentment of privilege: "Col. Hopkins can go to Orleans and ride up here in a hack. What does he care about how we are situated[?] He has good dry quarters."[98] On another occasion, when detailed to help clean out a brickyard for quarters, his feelings might have been expressed by GI Joe eighty years later: "We got wet through going down, but we went to work with a will and had the sheds nearly cleaned when one of Gen. Lee's staff came and told us we were in the wrong place, so we started for camp mad as wild cats because we had worked all day for nothing. Just the style of the 31st, always ass end to."[99] On the other hand, Fairbank had access to sources of warmth and comfort of which his mates seemed unable to avail themselves. On several occasions he spoke of an unidentified "Leana," and on January 18, by which time the weather was easing, he entered into his record, "We had a bully time all last evening, and it is useless to tell where I slept, suffice to say I slept well."[100]

After almost two years in Louisiana, the men of the 31st remained baffled and conflicted in their attitude toward the climate, partly because they could not help comparing it to what they were familiar with in New England. There were probably very few days in which Louisiana was actually colder than Massachusetts, but the men were ambushed by their preconceptions. One February day Captain Howell put down his thoughts about spring in a letter to his sister: "We have none of it here. May and June are only names for horrid heat and smothering dust. We have regular May weather here now so far as temperature is concerned but it lacks all the freshness which we love so. Give me a northern spring once more and I'll give you warm winters and hot summers if you like them."[101] At one point Lieutenant Rice, trying to persuade female members of his family to visit, lauded the abundant fruit of Louisiana, including fresh figs and berries available earlier than in New England. From

Fort Jackson and for fifty miles above, he said that the river was lined with orange trees. The fruit cost $1.00 or $1.50 a barrel, and the men ate them in such quantities that they grew tired of them. Still, Rice declared that he missed and preferred the North.[102]

Several troublesome incidents, humorous in retrospect, took place as the men adjusted to being mounted warriors. Most of those from the farms and villages of western Massachusetts had some acquaintance with handling horses, but this by no means made them cavalrymen. Still, their situation was enormously better than their colleagues in Company K, workingmen recruited mostly in Boston and surrounding urban areas who had minimal experience with horses. George Young, a member of this company, remembered: "Many of their fellows had never been on a horses back in their lives, that is not since when they were little boys when they rode on wooden rocking-horses in their own happy homes." That experience was poor preparation for cavalry service, "and they were just as much out of place on the back of a horse as the horse would have been if he could have been put on their backs. Especially was this true for the first few days, and when we had to take our horses down to the river to water." At these times, he added, "we were only allowed a halter, and when we were made to trot our horses, as was the case quite often, it was quite funny to see what tricks the fellows would resort to to keep from falling off. Many was the good tumble we had, and how sore we did get to be sure."[103]

Adelbert Bailey described another unforgettable scene. "The first lot of horses we drew did not supply all of the men," he recalled. "What few men in C Co. that got them were ordered to saddle up and go to New Orleans for more. Some of those horses were green, some of the men more so." One such was Pvt. Marcus E. Austin, who had a colt that had never seen service. "Austin saddled him and mounted with all of the equipments. The horse stood like a statue. One of the boys asked him if his horse would stand the spur. 'Of course he will, if he won't he has got to' and suiting the action to the word he gave both spurs to his horse." The consequences were not long delayed. "The boys will remember how we had those A tents set up on boxes, about ten feet from him was one with four boys sitting on the floor playing cards. The first thing they knew there was a game of pitch and Austin was trump. His horse didn't stir his fore feet at all, but his hind ones, what a circle they described, and Austin had gone over his horse's head with sabre, revolver and everything else he could take with him, and landed on top of the tent where the card players were." The tent went down, "and wasn't there music in the air for a minute as they came crawling out from under that tent and Austin. It was some time after that before that horse had any spurs in him."[104] Captain Howell reported a memorable incident of this sort. Although it did not take place in the 31st Massachusetts, it is worth relating. "A few days ago a trooper in the 1st New Hampshire Regt had an unmanageable horse & getting into trouble with him he started to curse & swear fearfully. When the chaplain of his Regt, being anxious to discharge his duty & reprove such wickedness, stepped up & said 'Sir—can you tell me who died to save sinners?' Go away with your d——d *conundrums,* I've got all I can tend to here, said the trooper."[105]

A few weeks into 1864, the third year of intensive fighting, the 31st Massachusetts moved down to New Orleans, where it was quartered in the Levee Steam Cotton Press. Howell termed it "a vast improvement on the mud of our former camp."[106] No one doubted that a serious campaign lay ahead. With nearly a full complement of horses and better ground conditions, the regiment spent its days in arduous training. The veteran soldiers must have recalled their early days of military service, but even if they felt like academy students taking elementary 'rithmetic, they understood the need to master their new role. They had been in uniform long enough to know that war had very little resemblance to a game and had learned that complaining served no useful purpose except to purge their systems. By January 17, a Sunday, the men were considered proficient enough to be paraded through the streets of the city.[107] In February their training was intensified, and the soldiers began to practice firing their revolvers from horseback and jumping a three-foot barrier.[108] General Cooke, the commander at Baton Rouge, may have had some influence on the training, as he was an old cavalryman and had written a manual on the subject. His own military performance during the war was undistinguished, and he is probably best remembered as the father-in-law of the illustrious Confederate cavalry leader Jeb Stuart.

Despite everything they had experienced, most of the men remained devoted to the cause, or at least to their comrades and regiment. Evidence of this is that a substantial majority accepted Banks's offer to enlist for three more years in return for a bounty and a home furlough of thirty days. Rich summarized: "The Government offers $462 bounty to every man who reenlists. Term of service three years, or during the war unless honorably discharged."[109] As he understood it, if a majority of the regiment reenlisted, it would be mounted.

179

(This too may help explain how the 31st was selected to become cavalry.) How-ell calculated that about a third of the men did not reenlist, confirming Rich, who estimated that two-thirds did extend their service.[110] Rice characteris-tically vowed, "I intend to see it through if it takes ten years." He took the occasion to fire another blast at the nine-month troops. Those who accepted the current offer "will be Veterans rather more worthy of the name than those weak kneed, white hearted, homesick, two-hundred-dollar-bounty-bought nine-month babies."[111] Seeming to display some inconsistency, Fairbank reen-listed on February 13, even though the day before he had been forced to wear a "wooden overcoat" (barrel) for the petty infraction of missing a formation.[112] An important consideration for him was that his brother George, exactly two years older and also a carpenter, was serving in the 1st New Hampshire Light Battery and seemed determined to see the war through to the end.[113] The men may have felt an infusion of patriotism when a group of Massachusetts ladies living in New Orleans presented a battle flag to the 31st on February 5. Gen-eral Banks's daughter Binney made the presentation on that occasion.[114]

For Norris, the decision as to reenlisting was so agonizing that he can be taken to personify the entire debate. He carried out his duties with generally good spirit, supported the purposes of the war, and was not especially given to questioning how it was conducted, yet he was by no means enthralled by mili-tary life. In no uncertain terms he advised his mother not to allow his younger brother to enlist: "Don't you give your consent to Willie's *enlisting* in the *army*. It is enough to have me here. Mother, I have *learned* more & seen more during the two years of my service than I would in ten years if I had stayed at home, but if you wish to give Willie up to all the *evils* & *vices* of the world let him go into the army."[115] He admitted to being "in a 'pickle'" over reenlisting, but his initial inclination was to resist: "One thing I know they will never get me, that is if I don't change my mind greatly."[116] What finally did change his mind was money. Norris calculated that his combined federal, state, and local bounties would amount to approximately seven hundred dollars, considerably more than a skilled worker could expect to earn in a year. With something of an understatement, he informed his mother of his decision: "You will perhaps be quite surprised to hear that I have 're-enlisted' after all I have said against it."[117] He seemed to have forgotten the scorn he had directed at the nine-month vol-unteers as "$200 men," although it is true that he had enlisted for a term four times as long.

Norris's problem was compounded by an odd family situation. Because he was so young, his father must have been a comparatively young man. Several of his business ventures had failed while his son was away, and although he might have been exempt from conscription, the bounties being offered appeared enticing. This set up the unusual situation in which the father asked his son's advice about joining the army. Young Norris showed no hesitation in his response: "No, not by any means. That is if you can possibly help it." He then added: "Don't let the big bounties lure you into the trap, for such you will find it. Although Uncle Sam would do the fair thing by you, the 'hirelings' & Things under him would abuse you most shamefully." The latter was a reference to the former drummer boy's feeling that he had been betrayed by a captain who had reneged on his promise to make him an orderly if he enlisted as a soldier. Finally, he recommended to his father, "if you should enlist, I would advise you to go into the 'Artillery,' for I think that is the easiest arm of the service, and give up the idea of trying to get with me, for I shall be home before this year is out."[118] His feelings about the artillery may have been based on limited exposure, perhaps mainly at Port Hudson. While that arm might have a slightly better existence when not in combat, in battle guns and their crews were singled out to be destroyed by counterbattery fire or being overrun by infantry. But it is understandable that even that might seem preferable to being the one charging against the guns. There are apparent cases in which fathers and sons enlisted in the 31st Massachusetts, but individual genealogical research would be required to confirm that.

As if all the regular, predictable, hazards of military service were not sufficient, a singular accident occurred on February 2, when a sink house (privy) occupied by many men fell twenty feet into the Mississippi.[119] Recalling the rustic boyhood practice of tipping over outhouses, this incident might have seemed humorous at first but had serious consequences. Some of the victims suffered broken arms and other injuries. As might be expected, estimates of the number of men inside the flimsy structure ranged from twenty-five (Fairbank) to fifty (Rich). In addition to the more serious injuries, Fairbank reported that "most . . . took a cold bath."[120]

9

THE RED RIVER CAMPAIGN

FEBRUARY–JUNE 1864

Texas retained its almost magical allure in the high councils of the Union. The more unattainable it seemed, the more it came to resemble the sort of mythical lands Odysseus might have encountered. Yet the Lincoln administration's reasons for wanting to occupy part of that vast territory were utterly prosaic. Some hope may have lingered that, under the protection of the army, a flood of Northern settlers could convert Texas into a free state that would return to the old Union on those terms. Blocking transportation routes from the state could deprive a portion of the Confederacy of vital supplies of beef. More to the point, Texas and western Louisiana produced large quantities of cotton, the market value of which was greatly enhanced as supplies from the rest of the South were cut off. This prospect appealed to the avarice of David Dixon Porter, now an acting rear admiral, who might be able to seize the commodity as a prize of war, while Banks, though he might not profit personally, would be able to boast of a military campaign that would more than pay for itself. (Butler had enjoyed making this sort of claim when he was in charge at New Orleans).[1] Banks, of course, was keenly aware of the demand of Massachusetts textile manufacturers for cotton. These domestic considerations, however pressing, were perhaps outweighed by concerns about a French expedition that had installed the Hapsburg archduke Maximilian as emperor of Mexico and seized Mexico City on June 7, 1863. Since the Confederacy lived in hopes that Emperor Napoleon III would grant recognition, the presence of a French army across the border represented a grave threat in the minds of Lincoln's cabinet members, in particular Secretary of State Seward. With ample justification, they suspected that the French would never have embarked

The Red River Campaign

on such a bizarre adventure if the United States had not been preoccupied with civil war.

General in Chief Halleck was a persistent supporter of a drive on Texas, though as usual he avoided issuing definite instructions that would make him personally responsible. Banks supported the idea of invading Texas, but he had long argued against the Red River route as impractical. Probably the fact that 1864 was an election year figured selfishly in his calculations: while a military campaign might remove him from the political arena, a signal victory would boost his prospects. So, despite some reluctance, the general finally endorsed the Red River route in January 1864.[2] This acceptance was, however, conditional, predicated on having a corps transferred from Maj. Gen. William T. Sherman's army in northern Georgia as well as full cooperation from Maj. Gen. Frederick Steele's forces in Arkansas and Porter's river fleet.

With preparations complete, the campaign began on February 29, when the 31st Massachusetts (mounted, sometimes referred to as the 6th Massachusetts Cavalry) crossed the Mississippi by ferry to Algiers and set off for Berwick City via Donaldsonville, Bayou Lafourche, and Thibodaux. Organizationally, it remained part of the Fourth Brigade of the Cavalry Division, commanded by Brigadier General Lee, in the Nineteenth Corps, under Major General Franklin. Colonel Dudley commanded the brigade, which also included the 3rd Massachusetts Cavalry, the 2nd New Hampshire Cavalry (apparently an informal designation of the 8th New Hampshire Infantry), and seven companies of the 3rd Illinois Cavalry.[3] The 31st Massachusetts mustered a total of 340 men on February 23, presumably consisting of those who had reenlisted for three years.[4]

Since they were mounted, the men rode overland the entire distance, while the remaining infantry took a shorter route by rail. The last fifty miles were covered in a day, as Lee had ordered Dudley to have at least two regiments in Brashear City on March 8. The 31st was one of those chosen, and as Capt. L. Frederick Rice (promoted in October 1863) remarked wryly, it was "a compliment to our marching capabilities, but as it entailed on us a march of from 45 to 50 miles before sleeping, one hardly desirable."[5] They reached Brashear City about midnight and lay down in an open field without waiting to pitch tents or eat. In an understatement William Rich said that they arrived "pretty tired."[6] It commenced to rain, but men and horses were too exhausted to mind it. Rice, Lt. W. H. Pelton, and Lts. N. F. and S. B. Bond "stretched ourselves on the piazza of a negro cabin, with our saddles for pillows, and thus, partially protected from the rain, slept till morning." During the afternoon of March 9, the troops crossed the bay by ferry from Brashear to Berwick City, which Rice observed "has at present but three houses, and but few signs of there ever having been any more."[7]

Resting briefly afterward, the Massachusetts solders found a sutler with a New York regiment who offered "a barrel of very good claret," which Rice termed "very acceptable after our hot and dusty march." Somewhat wistfully, he added: "I wish it could be obtained nearly every day. It would invigorate the men without producing the disorder that whiskey brings with it."[8] The wisdom of this observation was confirmed a few days later during a halt beyond Franklin, where the column left "the Lt. Col. [Hopkins] & Adjt. [James M. Stewart] . . . drunk beside the road." By then, Rice had developed a loathing of Hopkins for his betrayal of the regiment, his duty, and the honor of the officers, and added the comment: "Pleasant thing to be noised abroad. Therefore I consistently proceed to noise it."[9]

Beyond Berwick the regiment generally retraced the route of the previous year's march, passing the Fort Bisland battlefield, where Rich observed, "Everything is in ruins and we could see the cannon balls lying around."[10] Near Franklin, the mounted troops joined up with the infantry of the Nineteenth Corps. Rice thought that this town was "the prettiest place, excepting Pass Christian, that I have seen in Louisiana. It is more like a New England village than any other that I have yet seen."[11]

On March 13, while halted at Centerville, a sad accident occurred when Cpl. Alfred Fisherdick of Company D, a resident of Ware, was shot by a comrade, Pvt. Eugene Fletcher, also of Ware, who was cleaning his carbine. Struck in the head, Fisherdick lingered several hours before expiring.[12] Ever onward despite the tragedy, the brigade reached New Iberia the next day. There, "Cabel, the Sutler, came on with his stores, and was warmly greeted." Probably also influenced by encountering the sutler with claret, Rice conceded, "I begin to look upon Sutlers with a much greater degree of toleration than heretofore."[13] Sutlers were an undervalued feature of the Civil War landscape. Copious references in soldier writings speak to resentment of the supposedly high prices these merchants charged, but this requires perspective. Since soldiers were paid so little (thirteen dollars a month for privates), any price would seem high. Unless they had been retailers, they had insufficient appreciation for the immense effort and risk required to succeed, particularly as a sutler in a war zone. Sutlers were essentially peddlers with a wagon, and they had to anticipate what soldiers would want, acquire it, and keep pace with the army, which entailed making sure their draft animals were properly fed and cared for. At all times they were subject to being looted by the men they were supposedly serving, not to mention by enemy raids. This must have been especially true during the Red River Campaign, with its exceptional reliance on mounted troops. One can marvel at how sutlers managed to keep up with a fast-moving army and also replenish their inventories. Soldiers could maintain themselves by foraging over the countryside, but sutlers did not have that option.

As the brigade passed beyond Saint Martinsville toward Opelousas, the dust became so bad that Rice "couldn't tell whether the men were white or black."[14] Advance parties now began to encounter rebel soldiers on horseback more frequently, provoking occasional skirmishes. Somewhere between Washington and the hamlet of Holmesville, Rice enjoyed a wistful interval of relaxation in which he "passed the time very pleasantly talking with a pretty widow who lived in a house near by."[15] Six miles below Alexandria, the regiment camped in the sprawling front yard of the plantation of former Louisiana governor Thomas Moore, who had fled to Texas a week earlier. Mrs. Moore was still present, and she invited Lieutenant Colonel Hopkins to spend the night in the house. One hopes he did nothing to disgrace the 31st Massachusetts. Thanks to the governor's unintended largesse, the troops "riddled the hen coops and bee hives and got just all we could eat."[16] Rice enjoyed "a good breakfast of fried liver, broiled chicken, griddle cakes and honey. The honey was the involuntary contribution of Mrs. Moore, having been borrowed, without leave from her hives, as was shown by several swelled faces in the Company."[17] This, the first combat of the campaign, reversed the overused metaphor of Minié balls buzzing like hornets.

After covering more than three hundred miles in three weeks, the men anticipated a well-deserved rest when they went into camp along Bayou Rapides, a few miles beyond Alexandria. Instead, they were roused early on the morning of March 21 and ordered to dash twenty miles through a severe storm to support the attack on an enemy detachment at Henderson's Hill. Led by Brig. Gen. Joseph A. Mower (1827–70), a native of Woodstock, Vermont, commanding the First Division, the Union troops achieved surprise and captured 250 members of the 2nd Louisiana Cavalry, the unit that had earlier seized Lt. Joseph Hallett. The 31st did not see combat here, but detachments were deployed to guard bridges so that Mower's force would not be cut off. At Alexandria, Maj. Gen. Andrew Jackson Smith's corps of some ten thousand hard-bitten westerners, on loan from Sherman's army, had already arrived. On their way up the Red River, they had taken the small Confederate post of Fort De Russy and its garrison. The Confederates may have intended to make De Russy a stronghold that would block the entire Red River valley, but as usual this effort remained incomplete. From the Confederate perspective, that was probably just as well, as a more developed defensive work would have become simply a larger trap, as had happened with Port Hudson. General Taylor was a staunch advocate of maneuver in the field and resisted being tied to fixed positions.[18]

Banks himself arrived at Alexandria by boat on March 24. Over the next two days, the infantry of the Thirteenth and Nineteenth Corps, led by Franklin, joined the cavalry that was already on the scene. Franklin was about a week behind the original schedule, due in part to muddy roads. Such a delay was well within the bounds of normalcy for large military operations (and only became controversial in retrospect, under a bombardment of recriminations of every caliber). Despite this, the aggregation of Banks's army, the capture of Fort De Russy, and the brilliant action against Henderson's Hill seemed to have set the campaign off to a promising, vigorous start. Porter's gunboat flotilla had also reached Alexandria, where low water made it impossible for the boats to pass the rapids. Banks was dismayed to find the admiral busy confiscating cotton as fast as his sailors could haul it in. Under naval regulations, which governed his riverine fleet, Porter and his officers believed that they were entitled to the proceeds as "prizes," much as on the high seas. Having the advantage of greater manpower, Banks hastened to send troops with wagons into the countryside to seize cotton, presumably for the general account, before the sailors could find it. In failing to release its normal spring flood, the river, it almost seemed, was punishing Banks for going against the general flow of the war. (Banks and Porter did not realize that the low water was not entirely a natural phenomenon—Confederate engineers had succeeded in diverting some of the flow below Shreveport.)[19]

As 1864 unfolded, it became clear that the war would be decided far to the east of the Mississippi. Lincoln's patience with Halleck had finally become exhausted, and he replaced him with Grant, now given the rank of lieutenant general, on March 12, 1864; Halleck assumed the role of U.S. Army chief of staff. This move might have benefited the overall war effort, but it introduced confusion in a campaign, like the Red River, that had already been launched. Now in charge of all Union armies, Grant moved to Virginia and adopted a strategy in which he, together with Sherman in Georgia, would hammer the depleted South relentlessly until the North's superior manpower reserves ground down the Confederacy. Under this policy, anything that happened in Louisiana and Texas was little more than a distraction.

From Alexandria, the true Red River Campaign commenced. After taking several days to rest and regroup, the Union column marched out on March

26, heading relentlessly northwest toward Shreveport, more than 125 miles upriver. Only eight companies of the 31st Massachusetts participated in the ranks, as Company D was detached for duty at brigade headquarters and Company I at division. With Smith's corps, Banks had a total strength of about 30,000 effectives, a large army by the standards of this theater, of which Lee's mounted troops comprised perhaps 4,000. Banks also anticipated being joined by General Steele's army from Arkansas, which might increase his overwhelming superiority by another 10,000 men. These figures did not include the sailors in Porter's warships, which would accompany the army and mounted 210 heavy guns in support.[20]

Taylor's opposing force now became more visible, and occasionally the Federals were startled to see a dead rebel, toes up, on the side of the road. When the Confederates showed signs of contesting the crossing of the Cane River on March 29, a detail of a hundred men under Capt. Elbert Fordham and Lts. N. Bond and Milton Sagendorph joined a detachment that attempted to cut off the enemy's retreat. A trying march of 120 miles in sixty hours produced no more results than to make these men even more exhausted than the general run of the expedition. Another sharp skirmish took place on the thirty-first, when it looked like the Confederates would contest a second crossing of the Cane River (a discontinued former channel of the Red) near Cloutierville. A cavalry brigade generally led the Union advance, sometimes pausing for the wagons and infantry to catch up, with enemy troopers almost always in sight and sometimes making contact. Despite the brief interlude of recovery at Alexandria, the stress of hard marching and the need to be constantly ready for combat was beginning to tell. Many of the horses, fresh and spirited when the expedition began, were becoming worn out and had to be replaced with mules or ponies seized in the vicinity. When a Texas trooper blundered into the 31st's lines, he was sent to the rear, according to Rice, "but his horse never got further than my Comp'y being a timely relief to one of my nearly worn out horses."[21]

On the road from Alexandria to the considerable town of Natchitoches, Banks's troops marched through a haze of infernal smoke caused by the Confederates burning cotton, almost their last source of wealth, to keep it from falling into Federal hands. One Union soldier wrote, "From the day we started on the Red River expedition, we were like the Israelites of old, accompanied by a cloud (of smoke) by day, and a pillar of fire by night."[22] The region's inhabitants, who had hoped to sell the cotton, were undoubtedly embittered. When assigned to guard a plantation, Luther Fairbank was unable to apply his usual charm: "Such crabbed secess I never saw. They even refused to let us take cups to drink coffee."[23]

On April 1 at Natchitoches, the detail that had been sent out on March 29 rejoined the regiment. For a few days thereafter, the pace slowed, allowing the men to rest and supplement their diet by active foraging. On the fourth Rice savored a "nice breakfast of steak and fine mutton," and the following day was made memorable by a "big turkey for breakfast and dinner."[24] Beyond Natchitoches, the column, following an interior road that took it away from the river, entered a dismal stretch of gloomy, almost uninhabited, pine barrens, where, as Rice lamented, the men "were unable to obtain fresh meat of any description."[25] Constant skirmishing and sending out pickets and scouts meant that any respite gained from the interlude of partial recuperation was soon dissipated. Weary cavalrymen were forced to dismount and lead their horses to keep from falling asleep in the saddle. When the Union vanguard reached the village of Pleasant Hill on April 7, the troops desperately needed rest but had barely settled in when the bugle called them out to march farther along in a cold rain. Finally halted at 9 P.M., the men collapsed on the ground, sleeping without food or shelter in the rain.

Captain Fordham recalled, "This 7th of April was a raw, chilly day—just one of the sort to make one long for 'a little something' to warm one's self up—and it most unfortunately happened that our Regimental Commander [Hopkins] was overcome." Rice provided a more detailed and unsparing description: "Lt. Col. Hopkins took this opportunity to indulge his appetite for whiskey to such an extent that he became very drunk, and arriving at camp gave several absurd orders in so maudlin a tone as to excite the mirth of most of the Reg. and did not cease his performances till after falling at full length upon the floor of Brigade H'd Q'rs, he was conveyed in a stupefied state to his own."[26]

On the morning of April 8, which proved to be the decisive day of the Red River Campaign, "several of the Officers, feeling that the Reg. had been sufficiently disgraced by the repeated acts of public intoxication of Lt. Col. Hopkins, and that he was not a safe man to have charge of us in the presence of an enemy, went to Col. Dudley, who, at our request, placed Col. Hopkins under arrest."[27] These officers apparently attributed the regiment's leadership problems entirely to Hopkins and were therefore willing to see Major Bache, who had been with the regiment since its earliest days and had commanded on occasion, though never in battle, assume command.

Week after week, the Confederates had fallen back before Banks's stronger force, maintaining contact but never risking a large battle. A daily trickle of deserters and stragglers came into the Union lines, raising hopes that the enemy would just melt away. Rich described these captives as "a rather hard looking set."[28] Men were killed and wounded in obscure clashes that were often not dignified by a name. The endless retreats must have preyed on morale, but perhaps the Confederates had confidence that Dick Taylor hated retreat as much as they did and would someday turn the tables. Time and distance were growing short, however: as they approached Mansfield the Federals were only about thirty-five miles from Shreveport, beyond which there was not much left of Louisiana. When not arguing with Lt. Gen. Edmund Kirby Smith, commander of the Trans-Mississippi Department, Taylor studied his scouting reports and waited for an opportunity to strike, skirmishing constantly to buy time.

Approaching Mansfield, Banks's army followed a narrow road through dense pine forests. Lee's cavalry spearheaded the advance, which made sense, but behind his horsemen stretched their wagon train for several miles. Col. Thomas J. Lucas's First Brigade was in the lead, followed by Dudley's Fourth Brigade. With the 3rd Massachusetts Cavalry, the 31st was placed in the woods guarding the vanguard's flanks.[29] Lee was disturbed by signs of stronger resistance by Confederate cavalry and had received some infantry support, but the army's main body was stuck miles behind his wagons. Taylor, reinforced by both cavalry and infantry, saw the moment he had waited for and positioned his forces on advantageous ground behind a large opening in the woods. The battle commenced in the late morning of April 8, 1864, but remained inconclusive for several hours as the two sides maneuvered. Late in the afternoon, Taylor, growing impatient, launched an all-out assault. Though outnumbered overall, the rebels enjoyed nearly a two-to-one advantage at the point of contact.

Few regiments have ever been placed in more dire circumstances than was the 31st Massachusetts on that disastrous day. At the critical time when the unfavorable military situation threatened its survival, its two highest-ranking officers behaved shamefully, leaving their men without effective leadership.

Though written for the twenty-fifth anniversary of the battle, the fullest account of these dramatic events remains the one presented by Captain Fordham. He described how the men, anticipating battle, spent the previous night preparing their weapons and equipment, while he gathered packages of lint and linen, as well as a flask of whiskey, in case it was needed to aid some fellow soldier. The captain also took the precaution of filling his saddlebags with handkerchiefs, extra socks, a toothbrush, and "a few other essentials" in case he was taken prisoner.[30]

As recalled by Fordham, the brigade marched out about 9 A.M. and took position in the rear of Lucas's brigade. They advanced slowly against increasing resistance until early afternoon, when they came to "an extensive clearing, surrounded on all four sides by thick woods." There they paused and formed a line of battle diagonally across the clearing. The 31st Massachusetts was on the extreme left, in the woods beyond the clearing, with the rest of the First Brigade to its right. In the rear of this line were several batteries of light artillery under Brig. Gen. Richard Arnold (1828–82), a native of Rhode Island, and in the woods behind the artillery was a portion of the Thirteenth Corps under command of Brig. Gen. Thomas E. G. Ransom; General Emory's Nineteenth Corps, however, remained several miles behind. Now in charge, Major Bache ordered the regiment to be dismounted and formed into two lines, with Capt. Edward Nettleton commanding the front and Fordham the rear. Looking out from their position, Bache, Nettleton, and Fordham could see the Confederates marching through the woods to come around the clearing, preparing to turn the left flank of the Union line.[31]

> The suspense, 'ere the battle opened was certainly appalling, and I regret to say that in the case of our Regimental Commander it made him seek courage in drink. And I very well remember how, as we field officers sat upon our horses awaiting the onslaught of the Enemy, Maj. Bache rode towards me, and tipping me a wink, invited me to join him in a tipple. And I very well remember how I said to him, "Maj. Bache, not a drop for me at such a time and place as this in the very face of the enemy, and I advise you not to let a drop pass your lips." In that old jolly, easy way of his, he answered, "Well! I'm going to take a little, all the same" and he did, with the result of his fleeing the field like a coward at the very first shot of the Enemy.[32]

Almost immediately after that, the battle began. Fordham described this opening action: "An entire Brigade of the Enemy, ample to annihilate us, came down in splendid form upon our little Regiment, and sent a volley into us which killed and wounded many in both Nettleton's line and my own, and so far shook and broke us up that it was impossible to maintain the two lines." At that moment a highly agitated Captain Nettleton rode up, shouting: "Capt. Fordham! Maj. Bache has fled the field like a coward. I assume command of this Regiment and wish you to assist me in the command." The two officers formed the remains of the regiment into a single line and continued a fighting retreat under heavy enemy pressure. The Federals had the advantage of being armed with breech-loading carbines, which could be loaded and fired much more rapidly than the muzzle-loading weapons carried by the rebels, thereby giving the enemy the impression that they faced a substantially larger force.[33]

With the benefit of their superior weapons, the 31st continued to pull back, contesting each piece of ground. Then an overwhelming Confederate onslaught drove back the troops on their right, forcing Nettleton and Fordham to fall back through the woods in order to maintain a solid line. An hour of this steady withdrawal brought the regiment back through the woods to the lower edge of the clearing, abreast the remnant of the Thirteenth Corps infantry. Here, Nettleton came upon a small body of the regiment who were holding some thirty or forty horses of those who had been fighting dismounted. He immediately ordered these horses remounted and, himself at the head, made a charge upon their pursuers, with Lts. N. F. Bond, Sagendorph, and Pelton at his side. This charge, as Fordham said, "I doubt not, was one of the most daring and brilliant ever attempted—a little troop of forty into the ranks of perhaps twenty times that number." This unexpected counterattack stunned the rebels for a moment, but quickly, "seeing the insignificance of Nettleton's little force, the Rebs gathered themselves and poured volley after volley into them, compelling their retreat."[34]

Captain Rice witnessed the desperate charge, a true "forlorn hope." Captains Nettleton and Horace F. Morse and Lts. Bond and Pelton went in, "and every one came out on foot, Bond, sabre still in hand, but his horse bleeding and tottering from his wounds." Earlier, Rice had encountered Sgt. Danforth Converse "lying on his face, or nearly so, looking very pale and speaking but faintly. I told him that we had to fall back then, but that if we regained the ground, I would come to him."[35] But there was little chance of returning; indeed, Banks's army never got closer to Mansfield than it was at that moment.

Until then the withdrawal, though steady, had been fairly orderly. Suddenly, as Fordham described, "one of those unaccountable things occurred as if by a common impulse—a possible fear or dread of being overwhelmed, took possession of our army, and in an instant Cavalry, Infantry, and Artillery were in a mad, wild race to the rear." Seeing that it was hopeless to resist this flood, Nettleton and Fordham ordered a retreat. At that instant Pete McCrory of Company G., who was mounted, was struck in the back by a bullet, "the thud of which I can hear even at this late day, as well as McCrory's cry of, 'My God! I'm shot.' A couple of our men lifted him from his horse and laid him down to die." Fordham also saw Lieutenant Sagendorph sitting under cover of a tree with a wound in the top of his head, "evidently stunned, and wholly indifferent to the fact of his probable capture by the Enemy." Fordham and others lifted him from the ground into his own or another's saddle and helped him on to the rear.[36]

The wild rout continued for about an hour, until about 7 P.M., with twilight settling in. Several miles back, the fleeing troops came upon Emory's Nineteenth Corps, formed in line to meet the enemy; the 31st passed through their lines and a short distance to the rear. As Fordham rode along, he saw General Banks riding up and down in front of the infantry, charging them to hold the line against the oncoming rebels, who soon "came in multitudes, screaming and yelling with such fiendish yells as fairly made the woods ring; on, on, exultant, sure of still larger victory." All at once some five thousand Federal soldiers, well rested and organized, supported by half a dozen cannon, "belched forth a volley of Union shot and shell which made the wood tremble and which sent such havoc into the Rebel ranks that, in the next instant of perfect stillness, one could almost have heard a pin drop."[37] Thus ended the Battle of Mansfield, also known as Sabine Cross Roads.

Directly after the first contact was made, the 31st's Dr. E. C. Bidwell hastily set up a field hospital in a rural church:

But my possession was very brief. Very soon shot and shell began to fall around us. Our wounded were replaced in the ambulance from which they had just been taken, and forthwith we found ourselves participants in a general movement to the rear. The road was narrow through heavy timber and soon became blocked so that it was impossible to get out the wagons or the artillery. One of my ambulances with a load of wounded, by the skill and pluck of the driver did get out, very much to my surprise. All the rest were lost.[38]

These men, if they survived at all, became prisoners of the Confederates.

Fairbank's company had been assigned to brigade headquarters. During the rout, taking care to protect the regiment's flag, "we kept up a steady fire, and falling back, the rebs on both flanks and rear."[39] Once they passed through the firm lines of the Nineteenth Corps, most of the scattered and panicky infantry and cavalry that had borne the shock of the initial Confederate attack managed to reassemble. The men of the 31st Massachusetts, who had become separated during the scramble, gradually found each other and regrouped. It is a testimony to their underlying dedication, a solid residue of the Puritan sense of duty, that they remained a cohesive fighting force after a stunning defeat, accompanied by the shameful behavior of their highest-ranking officers.

Howell and others back up the account of shocking dereliction of duty by the regiment's presumed leaders. It is safe to assume that soldiers in their letters suppressed reports of alcohol abuse so as not to disturb the home folks. Even in their diaries they might hesitate to record such incidents, fearing discovery. Therefore, the few mentions of excessive drinking that pass through this self-censorship can be accepted as illustrative of a larger problem. Military service unintentionally promoted a culture of alcohol abuse. Away from the constraints of home and confronted with the constant uncertainty of army life, with its convoluted personal and hierarchical relationships, the volunteers found it difficult to resist the social pressures to drink. The boundless boredom of camp life made alcohol a tempting refuge, and the much higher pay of officers made it easy for them to purchase liquor. A contributing factor may be that the beverages that were both preferred and easiest to obtain were those, like whiskey, with a high alcohol content.

Scattered references to excessive drinking began on the stressful voyage to Ship Island, where the resort to strong liquor would have been defensible, if it was ever going to be. In New Orleans Joshua Hawkes reported that a lieutenant who had departed because Governor Andrew did not confirm his commission was replaced by Lt. John W. Cushing, "who was a military man, and quite a man when free from the influence of liquor."[40] Little is known about Cushing, who resigned soon afterward, presumably because he too did not have a commission from the governor. With customary lack of awe for superiors, Fairbank on another occasion commented, "We drilled in the forenoon, but the officers have got out of whiskey or something else, for they undertook to have battalion drill."[41] Nelson Bond reported in March 1863 that Major Bache was court-martialed; although he did not provide the reason, one suspects it was related to alcohol.[42] None of this should be taken to indicate that the drinking problem in the 31st Massachusetts was more severe than in other regiments. Temperance advocates had been waging a vocal campaign in New England for thirty years, and it is likely that alcohol abuse was less common among soldiers from that region.

Coming closer to home and to the humiliation at Sabine Cross Roads, Fairbank had made no effort to conceal his disgust in describing an incident in September 1863 in which "the line officers had a regular drunken frolic, and made the night hideous. They have disgraced themselves in the eyes of the men, and who can respect them now? They even used up the hospital bread, and the sick came to the Companies for bread this A.M."[43] A couple of months later, he reported that Lieutenant Colonel Hopkins and Adjutant Stewart were under arrest for drunkenness, though the outcome remains unknown.[44] Then at the beginning of 1864, in a startling stroke of prescience, Fairbank described Hopkins as "a miserable commander, brave in camp, but a coward in the field."[45]

Since Hopkins had been inserted into the position for which Bache thought he was entitled, it is unlikely that the two officers were drinking companions. Each must have succumbed to the influence on his own account. Bache was apparently a jolly fellow, and alcohol may have fueled that image. The fact that Hopkins drank to stupefaction during the Red River expedition without caring that a major battle was at hand indicates that he was by then a chronic alcoholic, not one who took a drink to fortify one's courage. Bache might fit into the latter category, but if so, the prescription did not work.

Fraternal consumption of "ardent spirits" was pervasive in the regular army, but Hopkins followed a different path in his descent into alcoholism (one that resembles those who have become unintentional victims of the modern opioid epidemic). He took ill almost immediately after arriving at desolate Camp Seward in 1861 and was treated by Dr. Cady, the Pittsfield physician who hoped to become regimental surgeon. Cady medicated his patient with whiskey, a common practice. Indeed, whiskey was less harmful than many other prescriptions in the medical kit of the time, but it still could have devastating effects on vulnerable individuals.

With the perspective of modern psychology, one can make a case that Hopkins was particularly susceptible to alcoholism. His mother had died on the day after his second birthday, which must have brought a dreadful feeling of abandonment, all the worse because it was only dimly remembered. As siblings later died, he was left as the only son, the sole repository of hope for his father, a famous, opinionated, and eloquent man. Hopkins's controversial elevation to command of the 31st Massachusetts would have added further anxiety. Together, these factors may have contributed to self-doubt. Soon after arriving at cold and dreary Camp Seward, he had told his wife, "You cannot know how sad it makes me sometimes feel when I think that I am necessarily away from you in this time of trouble." This sinking feeling at being torn away from one's cozy, familiar fireside and thrust into uncertainty is perfectly natural, yet Hopkins went on to admit, "But I can't afford to be broken down now and have therefore had to make up my mind that *I won't break.*"[46] This seems an excessive reaction to one's first night in camp.

His wife, Lizzie, could see the rocks toward which her husband was steering more clearly than he. As if looking out from the crow's nest, she wrote: "Now my dearest husband do mind what I said as regards your drinking spirits. Your family are all very much troubled about your love for it and censure your Physician for ordering you to take it so much. Pittsfield people do not approve of Dr. Cady ordering the use of whiskey so much, I have it from good authority. I can't help feeling anxious about you dear."[47] Hopkins disapproved of dancing, which Lizzie loved almost "better than to eat." They made a pact that she would forego dancing if he gave up alcohol; although she had a couple of lapses, she kept her vow much better than he did.[48]

Earlier, in New Orleans, James Tupper reported that Hopkins's "health is not good," and in June 1862 the officer went home on a sixty-day furlough. In a significant comment the correspondent from the 31st Massachusetts reported to a Pittsfield newspaper that Hopkins was taking his furlough "to recuperate."[49] Tupper opined that "we never expect to see him here again & the company think he ought to resign."[50] This was scarcely a gleaming endorsement, but he is ambiguous as to whether his attitude was due to concern for Hopkins's health or a generalized feeling that the company would do better if he were replaced. Perhaps to Tupper's dismay, the captain returned in mid-August.[51] Stationed at Fort Jackson, surrounded by swamplands and considered unhealthy, Hopkins informed his wife, "By order of the Doctor the whole Command, officers included, take a dose of quinine in whiskey at reville [sic] every morning—this as a preventive."[52] Conveniently, this gave him cover for drinking whiskey.

Lieutenant Colonel Hopkins seemed to have commanded effectively at Fort Bisland in 1863 and produced a coherent account of his part in the battle. Later that year he reported that, in addition to the ordinary demands of managing and drilling a regiment, he was serving as president of a general court-martial and was on a board that examined officers for competency.[53] Of course, this does not guarantee that he did not resort to strong drink on occasion, as not every episode of overindulgence was reported. At the start of the siege of Port Hudson, Hopkins said that he had marched a hundred miles too much and was "played out." He was hospitalized at this time, and it is not clear when he resumed command of the regiment.[54] (Since Major Bache was presumably still at Fort Pike, Captain Hollister took command of the regiment in their absence.) It is likely that Hopkins's constitution was simply not rugged enough to endure the rigors of active campaigning in the Deep South. His father suffered from hypertension and died at age sixty-two, while William himself lived to only sixty-four. If he had resigned due to poor health after putting in some service, no one would have faulted him. The plot twist that turned the situation into a tragedy is that young Hopkins could not contemplate leaving because it would devastate his father, whose influence had placed him in command of the regiment. As in classical tragedy, the story had to play out to its ordained conclusion.

Captain Fordham described how the Confederate forces at Mansfield, thrilled at seeing the blue backs of their enemies for the first time in months, pressed onward after a brief delay to examine the wagons. As in many Civil War battles, the attackers, having smashed the enemy line, lost their own organization and rolled forward on momentum until they encountered the first opposing line that retained integrity. This was Emory's infantry, which remained firm and halted the wild Confederate advance late on April 8. Casualties had been heavy on both sides.[55] Nevertheless, this battle was a stunning victory for the South. They had captured many men and guns and had seized the cavalry wagon train, enabling Taylor's men to resupply at the expense of the U.S. government. More important, the contest completely reversed the course of the Red River Campaign, shattering the morale of the Union army while restoring that of the Confederates to unparalleled heights.

Sheltered behind Emory's unwavering line, the fragments of the 31st Massachusetts regrouped. Fordham found several occasions to relieve the suffering of wounded or exhausted men with the whiskey he had set aside for that purpose. Pulling back, the New Englanders reached Pleasant Hill about 3 A.M. on the ninth and were thrilled to find that Colonel Gooding "had ordered out all the cooks of his headquarters command to make coffee and cook rations for the famished officers and men of both our own Reg't and others, and as far as possible, provide us with blankets." Despite having only a log for a pillow, Fordham and other officers fell into a deep sleep, though one of short duration. At about 8 A.M. they were aroused by gunfire and saw Confederate skirmishers close at hand, engaged with Gooding's cavalry.[56]

Banks's shaken army was concentrated back at Pleasant Hill, which it had left the previous day secure in the belief that Shreveport was within reach. Flushed with his stunning victory at Mansfield, Taylor was eager to renew the contest. He may have had visions that one more battle could crush the invaders, overlooking the fact that his victory had been gained over only a portion of Banks's force. After considerable maneuvering and shifting of position by both sides, heavy fighting again commenced well into the afternoon of April 9. At first it looked like a repeat of the previous engagement, as the Confederates, though sustaining heavy losses, smashed the Union left, throwing it back in disorder. Though conducted on a smaller scale than the immortal battles in the East, Pleasant Hill was replete with the same confusion, poor communications, command errors, incidents of firing on one's own troops, and surprise when unsuspected regiments leaped out of concealment and delivered deadly barrages. As the day wore on, the Confederate attack broke down, and by the time it became too dark to continue, the Federals had pushed the enemy back beyond their original lines. Confederate losses were severe—greater in absolute numbers than the Federals, which meant even higher proportionally. The 31st Massachusetts had been assigned to guard the wagon train and thus did not participate in this costly engagement, during which Gooding had a rebel bullet pass through his hat.[57]

The reversal of fortunes on the battlefield, in addition to the severe losses sustained, must have damaged morale in Taylor's army. After Pleasant Hill, Banks could have pressed forward and perhaps taken Shreveport after all, and there are indications that he wished to do so. But, in council of war after the second battle, Generals Franklin, Emory, and Dwight all advised discontinuing the offensive. Only A. J. Smith argued to press ahead, although he was under a deadline since Sherman had requested that his troops be returned as soon as possible.[58] From a military standpoint, there were cogent reasons for abandoning the campaign. For one, water in the Red River was lower than normal for the time of year, resulting in Porter having trouble bringing his vessels even as far as Alexandria. It was questionable whether they could ascend to Shreveport, and more doubtful that they would be able to return. Without the gunboats' participation, Banks could not supply his army far in the interior. Then there was the question of what to do with Shreveport even if it were captured. Banks had already had to leave 3,600 men to guard Alexandria; Shreveport would require an even larger garrison. But setting aside a sufficient force to defend such a distant place might not leave Banks with enough troops to conduct meaningful operations thereafter. Many of these arguments were not specific to the circumstances of April 9 and had challenged the entire concept of an expedition up the Red River from the start. Pleasant Hill was a larger and more costly battle than Sabine Cross Roads, but the fight before Mansfield is now better remembered and more consequential: defeat on April 8 knocked Banks stumbling backward, while success on the ninth did not enable him to resume the advance.

A forced march brought the Union army to Grand Ecore, the landing for Natchitoches and a strong defensive position, on the night of April 10. The men were weary from days of incessant marching and fighting, made more acute by lack of water, and many could not keep up the pace. These unfortunates were scooped up by Confederate cavalry following close behind and reached Texas under different circumstances than they had anticipated. At Grand Ecore the army reunited with Porter's fleet, and both forces took time to recuperate. Fordham's dominant recollection of this hurried retreat was hunger: "For the first and only time in my life, I ate raw pork, being part of a bone which Lieut. Sagendorph had procured somewhere, and came to share it with one or two other officers and myself." He enhanced this by chewing on some leaf tobacco that some soldiers had "scooped from a deserted tobacco warehouse along our route." Despite his starving condition, upon arriving at Grand Ecore, Fordham immediately fell asleep, only to be joyfully aroused about 8 A.M. "by some of the soldiers of my own Co. B. shoving a frying pan of freshly cooked mutton under my nose. That I was immediately wide awake needs no saying." This hunger march inspired visions of food, and Fordham recalled "the greatest craving for some pork and beans and felt that if I might only have my fill of these, I would gladly part with all my earthly possessions." After being reenergized by breakfast, the captain ordered his servant to lay in a stock of pork and beans from the commissary and prepare a dinner for 2 P.M., to which he invited several other officers. "I don't know how it was with them, but for myself, suffice to say, I ate so hearty of the pork and beans it was two or three weeks before I could endure the taste of them."[59]

Various figures are given for the number of wagons lost when the cavalry train was overrun on April 8. Capt. Luther Howell, who was in a position to know best, put the figure at 176 wagons.[60] Many of these contained forage for the horses, but others held personal effects and spare clothing, particularly of the officers. Howell lost everything and had to plead with his family to replace his clothing. Fordham had a similar experience: "While en route to the Commissary's, I fell in with Capt. Peter French, A. I. G., on the Staff of General Emory, who was one of my own townsmen (from Sag Harbor, N. Y.), who knowing my destitute condition in the matter of clothing etc., because of the loss of all our effects in the capture of our wagon train . . . , kindly provided me with such as he could spare in the way of shirts, socks etc., for which I felt more than grateful to him."[61]

"Who is to blame for this disaster?" asked Captain Howell, anticipating the congressional inquiry that would begin later in the year. "I can't certainly say, but one would naturally say Franklin since he made out the order of march, & Banks, although he was on the ground, only arrived the same morning and had hardly assumed the direction of things."[62] The later investigation brought out information to support Howell's surmise. Analyses of the battle often stress that the cavalry train was placed directly behind the cavalry, with no infantry support for several miles, and the entire army was stretched over twenty miles.

An important factor is not simply the placement of the wagons but also the fact that they had been allowed to approach so close to the cavalry, and thus to the enemy, once the battle commenced. Apparently, the train had continued advancing for some time after the horsemen halted to skirmish and reconnoiter upon encountering the enemy. It is true that the narrowness of the road made it difficult for the advance force to retreat and for reinforcements to come forward, but having the wagons bunched so close contributed to the confusion.

Banks did not consider that he was entirely safe at Grand Ecore and began to construct defensive works as if threatened by a mighty host. Captain Rice reported building gun platforms and rifle pits, activities that must have had detrimental effects on both the morale and physical condition of the men. The commanding general also used this interlude to make personnel changes, replacing Colonel Dudley and General Lee, who he blamed, perhaps unfairly, for the debacle at Mansfield. Lee was replaced temporarily by General Arnold and Dudley by Col. Edmund J. Davis (1827–83), a Texas Unionist. Arnold had been in charge of the artillery and thus seems an odd choice to assume command of the cavalry; Davis, at least, had been in command of the 1st Texas Cavalry (U.S.). Fairbank reported being present, probably reluctantly, at Dudley's farewell speech.[63]

Banks took care to avoid discrediting General Lee completely by assigning him "to assume charge of the Cavalry Depot in N. O. for the purpose of reorganizing the Cavalry of the Dep't."[64] This fabricated assignment barely qualified as face-saving, but it had the effect of showing that Banks retained confidence in Lee and implied that it was the other generals, namely Dwight, Emory, and Franklin, who were clamoring to remove the cavalry commander. Lee left with a rather touching farewell message: "Common perils, shared alike by Officers and Men of the Cav'y Div'n, thro' a march of near 500 miles—a march brightened by victories and saddened by graves—have cemented attachments that I know must last life long." Before wishing the troops Godspeed, he concluded: "As while I have been with you, so when I am gone, I entreat you, by your bravery, your endurance, your self-denying devotion to the cause you have espoused, to make the full record of the Cav'y Div'n a continuance of that for which I have no cause to blush—one of brightness and glory."[65] Lee tried to defend his reputation, pleading with Banks to release his report on Mansfield "as the people and press of the country are doing me an injustice."[66] There is no evidence that Banks complied; scapegoats generally have to await vindication by historians.

A similar, though more localized, upheaval took place in the 31st Massachusetts. As soon as they regrouped after Mansfield, the officers resolved to draw up charges against both Hopkins and Bache; Captain Rice had the satisfaction of preparing this statement.[67] Under unforgiving pressure, Hopkins and Bache immediately tendered their resignations, which were accepted just as rapidly (effective April 14), thus avoiding the public embarrassment of a court-martial.[68] The disgraced officers, responsible for the performance of a regiment, received honorable discharges; an enlisted man guilty of similar behavior, though responsible only for himself, would likely have been court-martialed and punished. Surprisingly, since he had little regard for this prominent resident of Ware, Fairbank scarcely mentioned Hopkins nor gloated over his downfall. It made a difference in his duties, however, as his company (D) was relieved from headquarters duty.[69] Simultaneously, his company commander, Capt. W. I. Allen, was given a staff job with the brigade headquarters.

At the unanimous request of the other officers, the vacant positions were filled temporarily by Captains Nettleton (as lieutenant colonel commanding the 31st) and Fordham (as major), who had performed admirably under adverse circumstances. Colonel Gooding formally endorsed the recommendations only on May 2, and one wonders, if he had indeed been an advocate for Hopkins, what distress this may have caused him. Massachusetts commissions for the two officers were not issued until June 4, though made effective April 15.[70] Fordham was moved by the expression of confidence: "In all my army experience I recall nothing which touched me so profoundly as this assurance of the regard and confidence of my Command."[71] Any stain on the regiment's reputation thus faded rapidly, but the awkwardness lasted into the future, straining personal relations after the surviving veterans returned to civilian life. Hopkins and Bache's behavior in the days following their resignations has not been recorded. Having earned universal contempt, they could hardly remain with the army, yet traveling through a countryside infested with brigands and enemy cavalry would have been dangerous. If they could have reached Alexandria, there might have been enough shipping left on the Red River for them to make it back to New Orleans and at least temporary oblivion. Under the same order that accepted the resignations of Hopkins and Bache, Fordham was detailed with three officers and one hundred men to escort prisoners to New Orleans—it is possible that the former officers accompanied them.[72]

Although several of William S. B. Hopkins's letters have been preserved, none seem to survive from the period immediately after his resignation. Some hint of their content appears in a letter from his youngest surviving sister, Mary Annette, known as "Nettie": "We sorrow for you in your loneliness but rejoice deeply in the sweet news that you are seeking Christ. . . . Oh, my brother, I would that I could fly to you & comfort you one little bit, & perhaps help you a little in finding the way to Christ."[73] Unfortunately for the family, at the same time William was undergoing his ordeal, his middle sister, Caroline, died at the age of eighteen. Erastus Hopkins fathered nine children, of whom only three reached adulthood; as noted earlier, William was the only surviving son.

Meanwhile, Admiral Porter had professed to believe that the water in the Red River would soon rise to normal levels, but for several days he watched as it continued to drop. This and a growing conviction that General Steele would not join him from Arkansas in time to do any good reinforced Banks's desire to return downriver. On April 21 he began the withdrawal, which more resembled a panicky flight than an orderly movement. This presented the extraordinary, and essentially unnecessary, spectacle of a smaller and more poorly equipped army pursuing a stronger one, at times almost besieging it. Despite having been compelled by General Smith to transfer some of his units to other commands, Taylor apparently still hoped, aided by the increasing impassibility of the Red, to destroy Banks's army.[74] There was no objective reason for Banks to retreat in such a precipitous fashion, the result of which was a "march [that] was the severest of the campaign for his men."[75] With food and water becoming scarce, the troops were pushed to the limits of endurance, and their spirits sank lower.

One of Walt Whitman's wartime vignettes, "A March in the Ranks, Hard-Prest," though set in Virginia, captures some of the feeling of the hasty withdrawal from Grand Ecore on the night of April 21. Logically, one would have expected Banks to be pursing the Confederates, or at least setting a trap in which their audacity would cost them dearly. Taylor was like a terrier chasing a bear, except that in this case the terrier expected to kill the bear, or at least force it to yield. Part of the problem was that Banks, like many another Civil War commander, persistently overestimated enemy strength. Commanders who genuinely wanted to win—among them Robert E. Lee, Ulysses Grant, Stonewall Jackson, Nathan Bedford Forrest, and Richard Taylor—either were not afflicted with this mental condition or learned to overcome the symptoms. In Banks's defense one must remember that he was not a domineering commander and that any of his generals (other than A. J. Smith, who he regarded as belonging to another command) could have challenged his decisions and perhaps persuaded him to change his mind. A general like Franklin, however, pushed his men ruthlessly, as if he could not get away from Banks and the Red River fast enough.[76]

Henry Barber said that during the movement from Grand Ecore, the 31st Massachusetts had its horses unsaddled but one night.[77] During this punishing retreat, which would have been exhausting even if unopposed, the regiment was almost continually engaged, either in front or as the rear guard. As a unit of the cavalry division, it performed the typical functions of mounted troops. After inconsequential skirmishing around Cloutierville on April 22, Taylor hoped to head off the Union column at a place called Monett's Crossing and prevent its clearing the Cane River. One of his subordinates got there before the Federals and took up a strong position. The Union army spent all day on the twenty-third looking for a way around this obstacle and finally resorted to a frontal attack that dislodged the Confederates but with considerable loss. In this battle the 31st's soldiers participated mainly as scouts and skirmishers and had only one man killed.

Yet amid the general grimness and hardship of a forced retreat, a few bright rays penetrated. Who better to enjoy such blissful moments than Private Fairbank: "I am on guard to a plantation where there is a fine young lady and she invited me in and I had such a supper as soldiers seldom get." This time he even provided her name: "I sat up with Annie until the small hours of the night and for one to have seen us he would not have taken us for anything but friends." According to Fairbank, "she had a beau in the rebel army, a Lt.," but it is not clear whether he was using the present or past tense in referring to him.[78] An historical novelist could have made this encounter the foundation for an epic romance, a struggle toward fulfillment that mirrored the South's struggle for independence. In the cruel glare of reality, though, there is no evidence that Luther and Annie ever saw each other or had any contact after this one episode. Still, it presents a near-perfect illustration of how the fickle currents of war—or the whims of the gods, as the ancients would have said—

create unforeseen and unlikely encounters. No wonder that for those who were fortunate enough to survive in good health, the incidents and sensations of war proved unforgettable. They compare to the mundane existence of pre-war life as paintings stand out on the plain walls of a gallery.

The retreat continued, interrupted by repeated clashes, until Banks reached Alexandria on April 29. During the last miles, the 31st was pushed back by another Confederate attack until it gained the support of the Thirteenth Corps. That corps itself continued to fall back, leaving behind some of its camp equipage.[79] As the season advanced, weather became more of a factor; Rich, for example, began to use terms like "a dreadfully hot day" and "terrible dusty."[80] Instead of turning on his weaker foe, Banks continued to behave as if he was fleeing for his life. Once secure in Alexandria, the army settled in for an extended stay while it recuperated. There was really little choice in the matter since Porter's fleet was still trapped by low water above the falls. Some vessels had already been lost to enemy fire from the shore, and officers feared that the entire flotilla might have to be sacrificed. To save the gunboats, Lt. Col. Joseph Bailey, an engineer officer from Wisconsin, devised an ingenious scheme to block the river with a wing dam and float the vessels free. This required tremendous labor by the troops and conscripted blacks, who could hardly refuse.

Soon after arriving at Alexandria, the 31st Massachusetts formed part of a detachment sent on an arduous push to search for the enemy and destroy Bynum's Mill, which had been grinding meal for them. They started off on the wrong road—as Rice put it, they rode twenty-five miles to cover nineteen.[81] On the return leg on May 1, enemy cavalry attacked at Hudnot's Plantation but were repulsed. In the closing stage of the engagement, Captain Nettleton led a spirited charge, which captured eleven Confederate soldiers and drove the rest back a quarter of a mile. This engagement cost the regiment one killed and eight wounded, one of whom was Nettleton. Fordham found the captain "sitting straight upon his horse as he was, the fire of battle still in his eye, but pale as a ghost and all but ready to fall from his saddle from loss of blood." He exclaimed, "My God! Nettleton, what's the matter?" The captain answered, "I'm wounded, Fordham." Asking him where, he replied, "In the leg." Over Nettleton's protestations, Fordham sent for a surgeon and helped put the injured officer into a nearby ambulance.[82]

It is conceivable that Nettleton, who had been acting commanding officer

for only two weeks, was overcompensating for the performance of his predecessor. He was succeeded by Fordham, who thus advanced from commanding
a company to a regiment in that same stretch of time. Two days later Fordham
was in charge of a foraging expedition, which led to another brush with the
enemy; this time Fordham's horse was shot from under him. The 31st held off
a larger force, accompanied by artillery, at a cost of two men killed and four
wounded. General Mower, in command of the larger detachment, reported, "I
have seldom seen cavalry do as well—never better."[83] Fairbank reported that
his horse had a leg broken, probably during this engagement, writing with
some sorrow, "As poor old Ned has gone to rest I have no horse to feed."[84] Following that encounter, the regiment occupied a post on the Opelousas road
seven miles from Alexandria, performing picket duty and participating in several foraging expeditions until the general withdrawal resumed.

"Poor old Ned," one of the few horses whose name is recorded (another
was Captain Fordham's mount, Dolly, destroyed on the same day), can stand
as a symbol of a larger catastrophe. There are numerous accounts of officers
and men having horses shot out from under them. Many other horses died
of disease, poor treatment, or simple exhaustion. Injuries like a broken leg,
though treatable in a man, were fatal to a horse. George Goodwin, who had
been troubled by inferior mounts from the start of the expedition, reported,
"When we reached Alexandria, my horse with many other was condemned
and shot and for a while I was dismounted." In the fighting on May 14, the
regiment captured some mules, and Goodwin secured one: "The mule proved
very docile and gentle and, after my former tribulations, I appreciated him
and almost cherished a brotherly feeling for him."[85] The number of horses
that were destroyed during the Red River Campaign, as with the Civil War as
a whole, is incalculable. Even if it were possible to derive a figure for the number of horses purchased by the two governments, it would not tell the entire
story, as many were confiscated by one means or another along the route (and
Confederates generally provided their own horses from home). An aspect of
the war not sufficiently appreciated is how the country was able to supply the
quantity of horses employed and ultimately wasted during the conflict.

On May 6 all or part of the 31st Massachusetts, along with other mounted
troops, embarked on an unusual and rather doleful assignment. The previous
day the transport *John Warner* and its two "tinclad" escorts (so dubbed because
of their light armor) were attacked by Confederates at Dunn's Bayou, some

twenty miles below Alexandria. The *Warner* was carrying men of the 56th Ohio, heading home on their veterans' furlough. Artillery disabled the vessels so that they could not be maneuvered, then pounded them steadily into debris, inflicting heavy casualties. Eventually, the helpless ships were compelled to surrender, with many of the surviving crewmen and Ohio infantrymen taken prisoner. Now, this mounted detachment, including the 31st Massachusetts sought to locate and recover these men. Many in the 31st, looking forward to their own furloughs, would have felt sympathy for the Ohio regiment. Although they set out less than a day after the battle, the prisoners had already been taken out of reach. Most wound up in the Confederate prison camp at Tyler, Texas.[86]

About a week later, although having suffered some losses, the last of Porter's flotilla finally passed below the Red River falls. Banks had little reason to remain in Alexandria; on May 13 the Army of the Gulf evacuated the town. Rice and his company were ready to move in light order at 6:30 A.M. and moved out at 7:30; then they were sent back to pack in heavy order. Even the usually dedicated Captain Rice became annoyed: "Then we unsaddled. Then we saddled up again. Then we unsaddled once more."[87] According to his later testimony, Banks had tried to protect the city during this evacuation, not least because fires would reveal to the enemy that his army was moving out; but ultimately much of Alexandria burned. Indeed, the entire route of the Union army, from Mansfield back to the Mississippi, was marked by devastation. Governor Moore's fine plantation, which figured significantly in accounts of the campaign, was burning as Lieutenant Barber rode past.[88] Soldiers broke into homes, wantonly vandalizing private property and leaving little of value standing. Thousands of blacks followed in the wake of the army, plundering and destroying anything the soldiers had missed. Most of the damage was attributed to A. J. Smith's troops, who tolerated, if not cultivated, a reputation for wildness. New England soldiers were appalled by this behavior, and General Franklin described it as "disgraceful to the army of a civilized nation."[89] The corps commander offered a five-hundred-dollar reward for conviction of "Incendiaries," but it seemed to have little effect. Weary, bitter, and resentful of both Banks and the Confederates, Smith's men relieved their frustrations on the defenseless population, foreshadowing if not inspiring Sherman's march through Georgia and the Carolinas (in which these same units participated). Historian John D. Winters estimates that more than half the wealth of Louisiana was destroyed in the war.[90] Yankee soldiers, with good reason, frequently referred to being in "the Land of Sugar," but the state's sugar production plummeted from 459,410 hogsheads in the good year of 1861–62 to around 10,000 in 1864–65. The value of the sugar industry was calculated at $194 million in 1861 but in 1865 had dropped to no more than $30 million. Sugar production did not regain its 1862 levels for thirty years, and was then produced by a much smaller number of plantations.[91]

It became impossible to maintain the pretense that the army could be supplied from its base. To a large extent, it sustained itself only by active foraging, in which cavalrymen enjoyed an advantage. Goodwin provided a realistic summary of the retreat from Alexandria: "As rear guard and flankers we found out what cross-country riding was. Most of the sleep we got, we took in the saddle. The Enemy seldom allowed us fifteen minutes for refreshments." During brief halts, "the pigs suffered when we could find them, each man skinning out what he could use and laying it on the fat pine fire, before it had done quivering, to cook a little and smoke a good deal." One day he acquired a ham from a good-sized pig, but "the Enemy seemed determined that we should eat our meat rare that day, and although I improved every halt to toast it, and between halts I would gnaw it till it bled, still I had enough left for supper. . . . I imagined I knew something how it would seem to be a Cannibal." He did not go hungry much on the retreat, "but I did often get terribly thirsty, sleepy and tired."[92]

Taylor's hopes of trapping Banks at Alexandria, perhaps unrealistic from the outset, had slipped away, but he continued his pursuit of the retreating army. There was almost continuous contact and several small engagements along the route, some named but most little more than background noise— except to those who became casualties. The 31st Massachusetts participated in most of these actions, and in one of them Asst. Surg. Elisha P. Clarke was taken prisoner while attending to the wounded. May 14 proved to be an active day for the regiment, as the rebels swarmed around the rear of the army like hornets. The cavalry formed a rear guard while the infantry straightened itself out along the river road. Rice's experience was typical. Halted at a bridge, his men were attacked about noon and stood off this force for an hour. After retreating to a slightly different position, the rebels resumed the attack, and "we had a smart fight lasting until 3 o'clock. My horse was shot, under me; [George H.] Munsell was wounded. We then fell back through the 3rd. Mass, to the river road." After that they marched all night, with two or three halts.[93] Nelson F. Bond added: "Our Regt. was ordered, after reaching the woods, to dismount and try 'bush-whacking' which we did successfully. Lost 2 men killed and 1 wounded."[94]

This kind of continuous skirmishing and hard marching continued through the next two days and nights as the regiment passed over the prairie through Marksville to Moreauville, moving overland rather than following a northward sweep of the Red River. The army marched through the nights of May 14 and 15, with only a couple of hours rest each night.[95] On the sixteenth Taylor drew up his forces at the village of Mansura. According to contemporary accounts, the two massed armies presented an impressive spectacle as they confronted each other on an open, elevated plateau. Whatever spurious grandeur warfare possessed was on display that day, with flags fluttering and horsemen galloping purposefully. Even more gratifying to the artist, there were few casualties, as the battle developed into mainly a long-range artillery duel. Taylor saw that his numbers would not allow him to challenge on the open field a Union force three times his size and withdrew behind the shield of his guns.

Because of the named battles of Mansura on May 16 and Yellow Bayou on the eighteenth, the sharp fighting that took place on the seventeenth has generally been neglected. Lieutenant Barber, who had been an officer for only about a month (previously he had been sergeant major, the highest enlisted rank), was in the thick of this daylong rearguard action. In the morning the 31st Massachusetts, together with the 2nd Illinois Cavalry, was sharply attacked while still on the bluff near Mansura. They retreated and formed a new line halfway between the bluff and the bayou, only to find that the enemy was already in force on the opposite side of the bayou. The two regiments then attacked to clear the way, in which they were successful. Assuming they were being followed by the rest of the brigade, the regiments continued to advance until they had moved half a mile up a causeway. At that point they were ordered back, having learned that the following regiment had been heavily attacked. Barber wrote that "Col. Davis, not understanding the ground, allowed himself to be pushed back into the bend of the Bayou." Here, they were in a rather dangerous position, cut off from the rest of the army until reinforcements of artillery and Colonel Gooding's cavalry appeared. The 31st Massachusetts had been detached from its brigade to reinforce Gooding, but at dusk, with the march having ended, the regiment rejoined its brigade at

Yellow Bayou.[96] "Unsaddling our horses and cooking a square meal for the first time since leaving Alexandria last Saturday A.M. [May 14]," the men enjoyed a well-deserved respite.[97] The bigger picture, as presented in the official reports, indicates that Taylor, unable to take on the entire Union force, sent some of his cavalry to ambush and attempt to cut off the Union rear guard, in which they nearly succeeded.

By the morning of May 18, the Union army was collected at the ruins of Simmesport, ready to cross the steep-banked channel of the Atchafalaya. Taylor by then held little hope of destroying Banks, but, determined to inflict punishment to the last moment, continued to press the rear guard with his hard-fighting cavalry. At length Banks ordered A. J. Smith to push back the troublesome Confederates, and Smith dispatched General Mower with three infantry brigades. This brought about the last major clash of the campaign, the Battle of Yellow Bayou. In its conduct, the fighting resembled an accordion as the two sides alternately pushed forward and fell back. As part of Mower's force, the 31st Massachusetts was heavily engaged. Lieutenant Barber described the beginning of the action as Mower advanced early on the morning of the eighteenth:

> Quite early in the day [we] recrossed the Bayou and, proceeding about half of a mile to the rear, formed line behind a large hedge. While this was transpiring, however, the enemy [was] beginning to show considerable strength along the picket line. Capt. Fordham had asked for his regiment, which had accordingly been ordered to the support of the picket line. The regiment was divided, a portion under, I think, Capt. Rice, being stationed on the road at the right, the balance was stationed across a wood road leading up to the left centre of the picket line.

About 9 A.M. the pickets, mostly off their horses and asleep, were surprised by a sudden advance of the enemy, who developed three quite-strong columns. Almost to a man the pickets leaped to horse and galloped to the rear, leaving Fordham, who was reported asleep under a tree, to gallop after them. The New Englanders rallied, however, before reaching the main line and, assisted by the fire of the infantry, turned on the attackers to drive them back to the woods.[98] Having succeeded in pushing back the Confederates, Mower advanced some distance but, fearing he was entering a trap, retired to his original lines.

Barber's unit, stationed on the left flank of the forces in the woods, was surprised to see the adjacent infantry line begin moving to the rear edge of the woods. The lieutenant was unable to tell "whether this was intentional on the part of Mower to draw on the enemy or was a mistake of a staff officer." In either case "the regiment suffered severely, for on the advance of the enemy we received the brunt of their blow."[99]

As Barber indicates, the Confederates responded with a fierce attack. Captain Fordham's report describes the intense action that began when his regiment was posted on the extreme left and rear to prevent a flank attack. He threw out a line of skirmishers from Companies H and D, under Lieutenants N. F. Bond and Pelton, connecting on the right with the infantry's skirmishers. The rebels soon advanced in large force, and almost instantly the infantrymen on the right began falling back, soon followed by their entire regiment, without firing a shot. With the Confederates now able to get behind his own skirmishers on the right, Fordham wheeled the 31st to the left and commenced firing. "The enemy outnumbering us at least five to one, I was compelled to fall back, which I did slowly, in good order, and firing constantly until I reached the opening behind the woods, where I formed on the left of a battery, which was supported by a regiment of infantry." These stronger units halted the enemy advance, upon which Fordham "improved the opportunity to draw sabers and ordered a charge. I completely routed the enemy, killing and wounding many, and capturing 28 prisoners, among them two captains and one lieutenant. The prisoners represented six different regiments of mounted infantry."[100] Fordham's phrase "improved the opportunity" is characteristic of New England and expresses the Puritan attitude that it is sinful to waste time in idleness.

During this phase, the regiment was divided nearly in half and served on both flanks of the Union line. Captain Rice's Company F was stationed on the far right. Falling back, the company "retired only to the bounds of the enclosure around the buildings, where it made a stand, which it maintained until the arrival of infantry re-enforcements." At this point what Rice called "some of the briskest fighting of the campaign" occurred.[101] The Confederates employed a portion of Nims's Battery, which they had captured at Sabine Cross Roads. After this attack was repulsed, Company F rejoined the regiment, which was not relieved until 8:30 P.M. Later, the brigade returned across Yellow Bayou to the Atchafalaya position. Not surprisingly, casualties were significant, with the 31st Massachusetts suffering eight killed and twenty-four wounded, a substantial toll considering the small remaining strength of the regiment. (Fordham's report indicates that the seven companies he commanded on the left presented a strength of only 125 officers and men.) In Company B Sgt. Henry Talmadge was killed and John W. Babcock was "shot through the mouth, severing his tongue, and he had to starve to death."[102] Another loss that day was John Broze, one of the Louisiana recruits in Company D. As a French speaker, he had often been mentioned by Fairbank as invaluable in negotiating for food with the inhabitants.

Writing more than forty years later, Sgt. Marshall Clothier recounted an example of conspicuous bravery by a soldier he identified as "Hilman," actually Pvt. Fordyce L. Hillman of Charlemont. Clothier noted May 17 as the date of this clash, but his description more closely resembled the course of the May 18 fighting. Hillman was angry because his horse had been shot earlier in the day. When someone shouted "My God, the boys are giving ground," Hillman rose up and roared, "D—d if they are." Described by Clothier as "a fine specimen of physical manhood," he shouted to the man on his left "Good by, Jake," turned and did the same to the man on his right, then "fell forward Dead. A bullet had pierced his heart."[103]

Accounts of the battle from other sources note that "much of the fighting took place in a thicket of undergrowth and dead trees, which eventually caught fire and sent up sheets of flame and clouds of smoke, adding to the already scorching heat of the sun."[104] Overall, the 31st Massachusetts, engaged in the heat of combat throughout a long day, had performed effectively, highlighted by Fordham's unexpected and impetuous charge. Barber gave credit to the captain for this bold action but in other instances slipped in snide remarks about his performance, noting, for example, that he had been asleep when the enemy attacked.[105]

Yellow Bayou, also known as Norwood's Plantation, was one of the major battles of the campaign, producing significant losses, yet it has received little attention, mainly because it appeared to have no great strategic effect. In reality, it was consequential, for if the Confederates had broken through the Union lines, they could have disrupted the crossing of the Atchafalaya and caused heavy damage while Banks's army was vulnerable. Instead, Taylor was punished severely for this final desperate thrust to destroy the Federals. The Confederate commander later expressed pride in the fact that his army held the field after the fighting, but that was a meaningless claim, as Banks's objective was not to hold territory but simply to cover his own retreat.[106]

In a puzzling aspect of the day's events, General Arnold proposed to send the cavalry division to "cut off" the enemy, but "General [A. J.] Smith refused to permit the brigade to move to this side of Yellow Bayou through his lines." It is difficult to understand what Arnold expected to accomplish since the enemy, though repulsed, was by no means fleeing and had a strong artillery complement. Furthermore, he forwarded a request from Colonel Davis of the Fourth Brigade that his "command be relieved from duty and allowed to return to camp for the following reason: For five days and nights my men have been almost constantly in the saddle, and during that time the horses have had but one ration of forage. Since daylight this morning we have been in the saddle and engaging enemy, and both men and horses are exhausted and actually suffering."[107] Fordham's account confirmed that the 31st Massachusetts, with the rest of the Fourth Brigade, had been intensely engaged on May 18, in addition to the many weeks before, and was in poor condition to endure further heavy action. There may have been some misunderstanding between Arnold and Davis or between Arnold and his superiors, which may account for the fact that the general resigned his command on June 24, replaced by Brig. Gen. J. W. Davidson.[108]

According to a field order issued on May 18, the Fourth Brigade was supposed to remain on the west bank of the Atchafalaya until the rest of the army had crossed.[109] This directive must have been countermanded, however, as several diaries of men in the 31st Massachusetts indicate that they crossed on the nineteenth.[110] The troops were ferried over the river, while wagons and artillery crossed on a pontoon bridge of boats, another ingenious contrivance of Lieutenant Colonel Bailey. Apparently due to the improvised change of orders, the 31st was shifted from the rear guard to the vanguard and so may have crossed ahead of the infantry and artillery. Soon after this crossing, A. J. Smith's command, having been detained longer than Grant and Sherman had intended, departed the army. Grant also pulled two divisions of the Nineteenth Corps away from the Gulf to replace the Army of the Potomac's enormous losses in the Wilderness of Virginia (though these men ended up fighting in the last Shenandoah Valley campaign).

On May 22 the 31st Massachusetts arrived at Morganza (which most of the soldiers wrote as "Morganzia"). The regiment continued to be assigned to the Fourth Brigade, commanded by Colonel Davis, rather than to Gooding's Fifth Brigade. Even there, the cavalry was sent out as scouts almost daily and remained in contact with the enemy, sometimes bringing in a few prisoners, though there was no serious fighting. This pattern continued into early June. During this period, the activities of the men were sometimes confusing and uncertain because they moved frequently through unfamiliar territory in the low country between the Atchafalaya and the Mississippi. On one occasion a "scout" penetrated as far south as West Baton Rouge.[111] Probably during this venture, the party was bushwhacked near Rosedale. When this party finally returned on June 5, Barber quipped, "I doubt if there was a *dry thread* in the command."[112]

Captain Rice related a mildly amusing incident on June 1, in which he was part of a considerable detachment consisting of a cavalry regiment, an infantry brigade, and an artillery battery. The artillery came in handy, firing at a mill across the Atchafalaya and causing a "grand skedaddle" of rebels who had taken cover in it, much as hens scattered during raids by soldiers of both armies. While this was going on, the rest of the men were busy picking and eating blackberries.[113] He was not specific as to the location of this encounter but elsewhere noted that his company was camped along Bayou Fordoche (which he writes "Fordoce"), placing them several miles south of Morganza.[114] The cavalry division finally collected on the bank of the Mississippi at Lobdell's Landing on June 3. With scouting reports in, Colonel Davis concluded: "I do not believe there is now a force exceeding 300 or 400 on this side of the Atchafalaya. These are lying around in small parties."[115] As Taylor's army had not crossed the Atchafalaya in force, the Red River Campaign faded into oblivion. If it had been a symphony, there was no grand finale.

Still, the cavalry remained active through incessant patrols and expeditions. On the eighth, the 3rd Maryland Cavalry, an outfit many in the 31st Massachusetts held in low regard, reported that it was in trouble. A hundred men under Captain Howell, with Lts. N. F. and S. B. Bond, were detailed to go to its assistance. "No enemy or trouble was discovered," but the detachment was ordered to remain overnight "to picket strongly a certain road to prevent a flank movement upon Gen. Nickerson, who was on a Scout towards Simmesport."[116] From June 18 to 21, some or all of the regiment set off on an expedition under General Grover, landing at Tunica Bend on the Mississippi and from there penetrating about fifteen miles north toward Woodville and old Fort Adams,

Mississippi.[117] For Barber, a highlight of this venture came when Captain Fordham chased his own advance guard three or four miles, thinking they were an enemy patrol.[118] Something larger may originally have been contemplated for this operation, for on June 18 Col. M. H. Chrysler, now commanding the Fourth Brigade, had ordered the 31st to "be at once put in readiness to move on board the transports, carrying 10 days rations, 2 of which shall be cooked when transports are nearly ready." This order further specified that no wagons were to be taken, that "horses will receive especial care while in camp," and that the regiment was to be relieved from picket duty. The following day word came to cook rations immediately.[119] All this urgent preparation seems out of proportion to the expedition that eventually took place.

All the Union troops who could be gathered—infantry, cavalry, and artillery—were assembled on June 14 to be reviewed by Maj. Gen. Dan Sickles, late of the Army of the Potomac. Luckily for the men, it was the first sunny day after a spell of rainy weather. Sickles, usually described as "colorful," was a Tammany politician who had raised a brigade and later commanded a corps at Gettysburg. Historians still debate whether his actions on the second day in moving his corps forward from its assigned position strengthened the Federal army or exposed it to destruction. Late in the day he was struck in the leg by a cannon ball, and the mangled limb was amputated in a field hospital. This dreadful injury may have saved him from being court-martialed. By mid-1864, he had largely recovered and was looking for a new assignment. To Grant, Sickles probably epitomized all that was wrong with the practice of political generals, but Lincoln, who was well acquainted with the now one-legged general, sent him off on an extended inspection of conquered portions of the South. This mission shows that the president considered the war to be already won. He may have genuinely needed information to plan for reconstruction and may have given Sickles confidential assignments, but Lincoln also wanted to remove the general from the capital without giving him another command and without humiliating him. As with Butler, the president dared not lose the support of an influential Democrat, who in this case was also a friend.[120]

The soldiers who passed in review before Sickles saw a handsome general with the evidence of heroism plainly visible and may have had little awareness of the disputes that swirled around his actions at Gettysburg, or that he was engaged in a tawdry campaign to discredit George Meade, commander of the Army of the Potomac. The war was conducted on multiple levels, and for the common soldier to be motivated to fight it through to a conclusion, it was often better not to know too much. Rich described Sickles as "a fine and smart looking man and he knows what fighting is."[121] Hallett observed that the general "was visibly affected as he sat on his horse with bared head, while the regiments passed and saluted with torn and threaded flags bearing but a semblance of what they were before the battles."[122] Captain Rice, who did not want to take furlough until the regiment's flags (and bodies) could show some bullet holes, had achieved his wish. Rich repeated a rumor that Sickles would be given command of the department, an idea that may have been considered. Grant would hardly have concurred, though he supported Sickles as military governor in the Carolinas after the war; and the New Yorker alienated fellow Democrats by backing Lincoln for president in 1864 and Grant in 1868.

As the incessant scouts by Union cavalry had confirmed, Taylor did not attempt pursuit across the Atchafalaya with the remnant of his army. As the Confederate general summarized of his small command, "The limits of human and equine endurance have been reached."[123] He had suffered over six hundred casualties at Yellow Bayou, a larger absolute number than the Union losses, which meant even higher proportionally. Almost until the end Taylor had genuinely believed that he could eliminate Banks's army, afterward blaming department commander Smith for the failure.[124] Relations between the two generals were strained already at the start of the campaign, and by the end they had broken down entirely. Nevertheless, Lieutenant General Smith and others had defeated General Steele in Arkansas and pushed him back to Little Rock, though they failed to destroy his army or retake the state capital, a disappointment as great as Taylor's over the escape of Banks. Elsewhere earlier in the year, a Federal incursion into Florida had been repelled at the Battle of Olustee (February 20), and on June 10 Maj. Gen. Nathan Bedford Forrest won his greatest victory at Brice's Cross Roads, Mississippi, a battle that in broad outline resembled Sabine Cross Roads. Taken together, it looked as though the Confederacy might be able to defend its interior even after losing its major cities. Added to these setbacks, tying up A. J. Smith's corps in the Red River adventure had delayed the projected attack on Mobile. All of these developments sustained the spirit of resistance in the increasingly exhausted South; whether it would win recognition from Britain or France or convince the North to accept Southern independence remained doubtful.

For the North, there were no redeeming features of the Red River Campaign, which had absorbed a considerable levy in lives and resources. More of Louisiana was under Confederate control at the end of the expedition than at the beginning, and Union vandalism had hardened the attitude of the remaining population. For Banks personally, the outcome was more catastrophic. Upon returning to Simmesport on June 18, he learned that a new commander, Maj. Gen. E. R. S. Canby (1817–73), had been appointed over him.[125] (Canby's message notifying Banks was dated May 14 but took time to reach him.) Though Banks remained in nominal charge of the Department of the Gulf, it was clear that he would no longer exercise military command. Once again, Captain Howell had anticipated this outcome, writing in late April, "Banks is used up in my opinion & I think we shall have a new Department commander before long."[126]

10

THE RED RIVER BLAME GAME

DECEMBER 1864–MARCH 1865

Everything was aligned to portray Banks as responsible for the disastrous outcome of the Red River Campaign. The wily Halleck, whose most prominent military attribute was the resolute defense of his reputation, twisted the record to make it appear that Banks had been an active proponent of the Red River strategy. Regular-army officers, however much they had concurred in Banks's decisions, had no interest in defending a prominent example of the despised category of political generals. Banks had undoubtedly made grievous mistakes at many points of the campaign but, seemingly aware of his deficiencies in handling troops, had left many of the details to his subordinates. A notable example was the order of march on the road to Mansfield.

After the campaign, a preexisting congressional committee, the Joint Committee on the Conduct of the War, conducted a lengthy, politically motivated investigation. This gave officers an irresistible opportunity to defend their performance and whatever their other personal differences, to keep Banks in the role of scapegoat. Despite the self-serving nature of the testimony before the committee, it retains value to historians and contributes greatly to our understanding of the expedition. Moreover, the formal nature of the proceedings cannot entirely suppress the personalities of the leading figures. Virtually all of them assigned blame somewhere else, beginning with Banks, who attributed the fiasco to Halleck's persistent advocacy of an expedition up the Red River. Halleck, for his part, made his customary argument that the distance of the field armies in Louisiana from Washington rendered it impractical to issue unequivocal orders and that he had allowed the general broad discretion in directing the campaign. Banks presented copious documentation showing that, being familiar with the territory from the 1863 Teche campaign, he had always opposed repeating the march up the Red River. He was fully supportive of invading Texas, but he favored doing so from the coast.

The testimony makes officer alignments clear. Banks and Major General Franklin were mutually critical, while Brigadier General Dwight defended Franklin. Dwight, by then serving in Virginia with the Nineteenth Corps, in effect accused Maj. Gen. A. J. Smith of insubordination, describing him as "a man who would take as much licence as he could get" and concluding that "General Banks did not exercise that authority and control over him which a superior officer should exercise over an inferior."[1] Banks confirmed that he did not consider himself to be in command of Smith.[2] Admiral Porter, meanwhile, regarded Smith as the only competent army commander on the expedition. The sharp criticism of the various officers for one another, in which Dwight was a leading participant, confirms Dwight's own summary: "The infantry force was a peculiar one. It was composed of three different bodies of troops, having great jealousy of each other, the commanders not being thoroughly in harmony."[3] According to Dwight, Banks was also not on good terms with his own chief of staff, Brig. Gen. Charles Pomeroy Stone (1824–87). Again defending Franklin, Dwight claimed that Stone was the most conspicuous exponent of the belief that the Confederates would not stand until Shreveport.[4] Ill feeling between Banks and Stone is somewhat unexpected since they shared certain similarities, leaving aside the fact that Stone was a career officer. Stone was also from Massachusetts (Greenfield) and earlier had been caught up in a nasty dispute with Governor Andrew, who felt that Stone, a Democrat, was insufficiently abolitionist. He had also run afoul of the joint committee, which may explain why he was not asked to testify for the Red River investigation.

The level of discord alone created a poor outlook for the expedition, but even more critical was the one area in which Banks, Dwight, Franklin, and cavalry commander Brigadier General Lee were in accord—that the whole concept was unwise. While busy criticizing one another, none of them rose to defend the strategy or purpose of the Red River Campaign. Even Halleck's support was no more than tepid (although his style was not to issue decisive statements or orders on any subject in which he might be held responsible for the outcome). Typical is Dwight's view that the expedition "should never have been undertaken at all. There was nothing to be gained by operations on the west bank of the Mississippi as soon as the river was held by us."[5] Banks, as noted, made a persuasive case that he had always opposed going up the Red

River. Moreover, he believed that, even if he was able to seize Shreveport, he could not have held it a month.[6] During his testimony, Lee went further and asserted, "I never supposed we could get to Shreveport."[7]

The troops, though tired from hard marching and worried about uncertain rations, seem to have maintained reasonably good spirits. But a general defeatism seeped down through the officer corps, as evidenced by a letter Capt. Luther Howell sent to his brother as the campaign neared its end: "Let me say that I deem this expedition a most foolish one ever undertaken . . . , for had we succeeded in getting to Shreveport we should have been out of supplies, & the Red River is so low that it is with difficulty we could get transports back from Grand Ecore, & some of the gunboats have been dismantled and blown up."[8] History and personal experience teach that any demanding, risky endeavor like the Red River Campaign is unlikely to succeed unless its leaders believe in it wholeheartedly. To a large extent, the disappointing outcome was a self-fulfilling prophecy.

General Franklin's testimony before the committee on January 6, 1865, was significant and sometimes startling. His personality broke through the curtain of formality, coming across as unpleasant and arrogant, with an unjustifiably high regard for his own abilities. In giving his opinion of Banks, Franklin unintentionally confirmed the discord that crippled the high command: "From what I had seen of General Banks's ability to command in the field, I was certain that an operation dependent upon plenty of troops, rather than upon skill in handling them, was the only one which would have [a] probability of success in his hands." When asked whether the disposition of his force at the start of the Sabine Cross Roads battle was a good one, he answered simply, "Not at all." The follow-up question, naturally, inquired as to who was responsible. "I suppose to a certain extent I am responsible," Franklin replied. This was virtually the only example of an officer being willing to accept some degree of blame, but he quickly shifted the cause of the failure to Lee: "The cavalry general had always been asking me to put his train behind the infantry troops, and let it march in front of the infantry train. I had always refused to do that."[9]

Succeeding remarks by and about Franklin reveal that he had a strange perspective on his cavalry, seeming to regard it as an alien body rather than a vital component of his forces with important functions to perform. He admitted telling Lee that "it was his business to take care of his own train."[10] Lee affirmed that "General Franklin used to send me word that the cavalry was in the way."[11] Col. John S. Clark, an aide to Banks, testified that Franklin had refused to send reinforcements to Lee, saying that "he must fight them alone—that was what he was there for."[12] After the Battle of Pleasant Hill, General Emory suggested sending in the cavalry: "I think it was General Franklin who told me that the cavalry were gone, and anticipated that we could get nothing out of them."[13] One of the fundamental tragedies of the Civil War is that it inflated multitudes of officers rapidly to high rank, where they held life-and-death authority over thousands of men, but seldom did their competence or personal attributes expand to fill such new responsibilities.[14]

Franklin's animosity toward his cavalry commander may have deeper roots. As Banks and others noted, Franklin, with his usual smug certainty, regularly assured everyone that the Confederates would not make a stand until Shreveport.[15] Lee, who was in daily contact with the enemy, reached a different conclusion, insisting that the Federals would have to fight prior to reaching Shreveport and warning persistently that the order of march was not suited for an engagement that could occur at any time. As he told the committee, "I am very certain that the parties to whom my remonstrances were made . . . began to think I was getting panicky, as they say, and I had to stop it."[16] Given the prevailing culture of the officer corps, one can sympathize with Lee's predicament. His repeated warnings could have been taken to indicate not only that he was worried but also fearful—"old-womanish" in the stock phrase—a reputation that would be a death sentence to any military career.

General Dwight, who at the time was Franklin's subordinate and later his strong defender, voiced a far more sweeping condemnation of Banks's mounted arm: "For the work of cavalry proper it was utterly unfit. The men were not good riders, and did not understand how to take care of their horses properly. They were infantry soldiers who had been put on horseback; they were not properly cavalry." He went on to say that the disposition of this force was "perfectly proper," as the enemy was "similarly situated, only in greater numbers." Dwight elaborated: "Their Texan troops were almost wholly mounted, and armed with Enfield rifles. It was a mounted infantry force, to which it was eminently proper we should oppose a mounted infantry force." The trouble, in his opinion, was that "our force of cavalry, mounted infantry, etc., was badly commanded; that the officer commanding it did not well understand the manner of leading an advance, of obtaining proper information concerning the enemy, or of penetrating any little curtain that the enemy might throw in front of him." In summary, the general declared: "The cavalry force of that army was a very bad one; ill drilled, ill instructed, and very badly organized. But it was quite well mounted for the objects it had in view, and it was thoroughly equipped."[17]

Dwight's savage criticism of the Cavalry Division is important in the history of the 31st Massachusetts, which was part of the body he found so deficient. He regarded the cavalry as a mass and made no effort to distinguish individual regiments (in fact, particular regiments are rarely cited anywhere in the hearings). Nevertheless, it is reasonable to accept that his assertions contained some validity. It was only in December 1863 and early January 1864 that horses were issued, and the quality of the mounts was wildly inconsistent. The weather in much of January was atrocious, which rendered it difficult to care for the horses, much less train on them. Luther Fairbank wrote at the time, "My horse knew more than I did about the drill."[18] Yet as the writings of many men in the 31st reveal, there was intensive training for at least a month and a half, culminating in saber exercises, jumping, and firing pistols from horseback. Colonel Dudley, wearing white gloves, liked to parade the men through the streets of New Orleans on Sundays, but their training went deeper than that. During the campaign itself, the cavalry carried out the duties assigned to it with little or no difficulty, and the men almost invariably held their own or better in their frequent clashes with the enemy. The one conspicuous exception, of course, was Sabine Cross Roads, where the Union force was overwhelmed by sheer numbers and the horsemen swept back with the rout of the small infantry support.

Banks by nature shied away from confrontation. When pressured by some of his generals—Franklin and Dwight prominent among them—he dumped Lee. Later he came to regret this hasty action:

General Lee was relieved from the command of the cavalry subsequent to this affair at Sabine Crossroads, but it was not on account of this action. It was because the general officers expressed to me so positively their want of confidence in the organization and condition of the cavalry, and advised so earnestly a change. That was an act which I afterwards regretted. It was done because of the demoralized condition in which the cavalry found itself after this affair, and the very important part it must have in our subsequent movements. I have no complaint to make of General Lee's general conduct. He was active, willing, and brave, and suffered, more or less unjustly, as all of us did, for being connected with that affair.[19]

By December 14, 1864, when he voiced these telling remarks, Banks had endured the consequences of being made the goat for the failure of the expedition, a realization that made him more sympathetic toward Lee's plight. Lee remained a general and stationed in the Department of the Gulf, but his reputation was permanently damaged. Not being a military careerist, he resigned at the end of the war and returned to civilian life, though apparently not to Kansas, where he had been living when the conflict began.

In criticizing the performance of the mounted infantry, Dwight was also taking a swipe at Banks, who had created it, avoiding the question of how else cavalry could have been obtained in the department. One can also question if the condition of the cavalry was as desperate as depicted by Banks, Dwight, and Franklin. The various accounts by members of the 31st Massachusetts do not indicate catastrophic disintegration or irretrievable damage to morale; in fact, there are many examples of the cavalry being sent out on sensitive and dangerous missions. Once they regrouped after Sabine Cross Roads, the New Englanders' spirit seemed good and they performed effectively. General Mower's praise of the 31st carried considerable weight, as he seems to have been an officer who was devoted to performing his duties and less concerned with career infighting and political maneuvering. Dwight also ignored the fact that the cavalry fought many of its battles dismounted, in which they functioned basically as infantry skirmishers, regardless of how they got to the field.

One officer who was deeply offended by the shabby treatment of Lee was Captain Howell. Just a few days before the encounter at Sabine Cross Roads, Howell had written this assessment to his brother: "Gen. Lee is my *beaux* [sic] ideal of a soldier, calm under all circumstances & a fine looking fellow as one would see in a thousand miles travel. I don't know how he will fight the division but I think he must do it well. No Red Tape arrangements about the man."[20] Given that sterling endorsement, what Howell wrote three weeks later is not surprising: "Banks is trying to make a scapegoat of General Lee and has relieved him of his command much to the disgust of the whole cavalry Division, but I fear it will not work. *We know* that no blame can justly be attached to Gen. Lee's management of the cavalry, & so we blame Banks all the more for this unjustifiable step." The victimization of Lee, not the course of the action, was what threatened Howell's morale: "Now I feel like leaving the army and country to work out its own salvation & go home to see a little comfort. It may be that my patriotism will again rise but I must say it is now at a low stage."[21]

The appearance of Admiral Porter, representing the navy perspective on the contentious campaign, was eagerly awaited. When he testified on March 7, 1865, the hearings had been in session periodically for almost three months, giving him ample time to study evidence and prepare his position. The admiral accompanied his presentation with several documents, notably his correspondence with Navy Secretary Welles. These letters establish that Porter was preparing a case to blame Banks in the event it became necessary to abandon his flotilla due to low water at the falls at Alexandria. In a letter of April 28, 1864, Porter told the secretary, "I still have confidence . . . that the nation will not permit this fleet to be sacrificed when it has so well performed its part in what should have been a complete success." In a separate confidential message of the same date, he was more explicit: "Unless instructed by the government, I do not think that General Banks will make the least effort to save the navy blockaded here [Alexandria]."[22]

As portrayed by Banks and other officers, Porter showed a strange indifference toward the fate of his fleet at the time. He either believed or hoped the river would rise (against the advice of many who were more familiar with it), but beyond that he had no plan to rescue his vessels. When first presented with the idea of building a dam to float the boats free, he replied with scorn. Banks, Dwight, and Franklin might not have agreed on much else before the joint committee, but they were in accord on this; Franklin said that Porter viewed the dam plan "with derision."[23] Nearly all the labor of constructing the dam was performed by army personnel, often standing waist deep in the current while doing this dangerous work. At the start of the expedition, Porter had boasted "that wherever the sand was damp he could run his boats."[24] Obviously that was hyperbole, but it was a sign of his overconfidence and an indication that he never expected to depend on the army to rescue him.

Once most of his fleet had been freed, Porter, in a rare unselfish gesture, publicly praised Banks: "To General Banks personally I am much indebted for the happy manner in which he has forwarded this enterprise, giving it his whole attention night and day, scarcely sleeping while the work was going on, attending personally to see that all the requirements of Colonel Bailey were complied with on the instant."[25] This limited endorsement probably had no bearing on Porter's appraisal of Banks's overall ability, as stated in a postscript to Welles: "The only man here who possesses the entire confidence of the troops is General A. J. Smith, and if he were placed in command of this army he would, I am convinced, retrieve all its disasters."[26] Smith and Porter had worked together in a previous campaign, and he must have been one of the few army officers with whom Porter got along and respected.

At the start of his testimony, Porter referred to the Red River expedition as a "cotton speculation" or a "cotton raid."[27] This, as he well knew from following the course of the investigation, was like throwing meat to lions. The committee members had doggedly pressed the inquiry about cotton and the campaign, trying to show that seizing it had taken precedence over military concerns or that officers and politically connected individuals had profited illegally from cotton transactions. A large body of testimony affirmed that Porter, and perhaps other naval officers, had confiscated cotton on their own account and sent parties ranging several miles from the river to seize it before the army arrived on the scene.[28] With astonishing boldness, Porter simply denied or dismissed these accusations. In doing so, he denied the corollary, which is that the Confederates, who had hoped to sell their cotton, commenced destroying it only after the Union navy began to seize it without payment.[29]

Banks was generally restrained and mild mannered in his official conduct. It is therefore extraordinary that he was so angered by Porter's testimony that he felt compelled to insert into the record a formal rebuttal, a rebuke in which he flatly accused the admiral of lying:

Any statement, from whatever source, that the army contemplated moving from Grand Ecore towards Alexandria against the advice, or without the approval of, the naval officers in command, or until after the departure of every vessel on the river, is without the slightest color of truth. . . .

In view of the published despatches of Admiral Porter, it is proper for me to say, that every position of difficulty in which the army was placed in this campaign was the immediate and direct consequence of delay in the operations of the navy. . . . I feel it to be a solemn duty to say, in this official and formal manner, that Admiral Porter's published

official statements relating to the Red River campaign are at variance
with the truth, of which there are many thousand living witnesses, and
do foul injustice to the officers and soldiers of the army, living and
dead, to whom the Navy Department owes exclusively the preservation
and honor of its fleet.[30]

Banks also was firm in asserting that "the construction of the dam was exclusively the work of the army." With only one exception, "but little aid or encour-
agement was rendered by the officers of the navy."[31]

The committee members asked nearly every officer who appeared what
they knew about cotton transactions, but they were never able to amass evidence that Banks had given any speculators preferential treatment. Most of
the officers were wise enough to avoid becoming entangled in the fibers of
corrupt cotton, but even if they knew something, it was in their career interest
to maintain that they had devoted attention exclusively to their military duties. In a similar vein, many congressmen inquired whether Banks's progress
had been delayed because the general was busy fostering a Unionist government in the state. By this, the radicals were attempting to show that Banks was
carrying out Lincoln's plans for reconstruction at the expense of the army and
to the detriment of their own harsher schemes.

Almost exactly a year before the Battle of Sabine Cross Roads, while engaged in the Teche campaign, Lieutenant Howell made the prescient assessment: "I dont think much of Banks, he dont seem to have any pluck or dash
about him."[32] Personally brave, Banks managed his army cautiously and me-
thodically. It is easy to attribute this behavior to self-doubt when surrounded
by cocky professional officers who made little effort to conceal their contempt
for him as a political general. Despite the often unwarranted self-assurance
they displayed, generals such as Franklin, Emory, and Dwight revealed no
more imagination than Banks, creating a climate in which initiative quickly
withered. Banks was almost certainly truthful when he said that he wanted to
advance after the fight at Pleasant Hill and gave orders to that effect; unsur-
prisingly, his three subordinates talked him out of it. Afterward they could fall
back on the excuse of having given this advice because they lacked confidence
in Banks.

The one general who strongly favored resuming the advance was crusty A. J.
Smith, but his own corps was not sufficient to defeat the Confederates, and the

other corps commanders would hardly submit to his authority. In this instance Porter's lavish praise of Smith may be justified, and in command he might have destroyed Taylor's army. Banks did not recognize the importance of the steady stream of Confederate deserters taken during the Union army's advance. They indicated a waning commitment to the Southern cause, and some of them said that "there are a great many more who are only waiting for a chance to get away."[33] After the reverse at Pleasant Hill, a strong Union counterthrust might well have shattered Confederate resistance. It is true, as the three cautious generals counseled, that the navy would not have been able to support a further advance and that there was no ready source of supply on the line of march; yet if the rebel army was demolished, much of the incentive for continuing to Shreveport would have been removed.

After Sabine Cross Roads, the rapid retreat of the Union army made desertion a less tempting prospect for the Confederates, one that would have been difficult to accomplish. Meanwhile, Banks continued to overestimate the strength and condition of his foe, and the steady retreat made it difficult for his cavalry to gather accurate intelligence. If he had placed more importance on obtaining and exploiting such information, he might have developed a different idea of the forces opposing him. In summarizing the Red River Campaign, it may well be that Banks is most culpable not for his conduct of the battle at Sabine Cross Roads, but for his failure to turn on the Confederates at some opportune time in the succeeding weeks. Except for that engagement, Union forces had prevailed in almost every encounter with the enemy, but that exception was so conspicuous that the campaign (and Banks's reputation) could never be redeemed.

Grant, recalling his difficulty in coordinating with Banks during the Vicksburg and Port Hudson Campaigns, maintained an almost obsessive desire to rid himself of the general; the futile Red River venture now handed him the opportunity. Writing from Culpeper Court House, Virginia, where one might think he would have been fully absorbed in fighting Robert E. Lee, Grant found time to inform Chief of Staff Halleck of his analysis: "I have just received two private letters, one from New Orleans and one anonymous, from the 13th corps, giving deplorable accounts of General Banks's mismanagement. His own report and these letters clearly show all his disasters to be attributable to his incompetency."[34] It is hard to know whether to be more amazed that Grant relied on sources of that sort to form his opinion at a distance or that he freely acknowledged such reliance. In writing to Halleck, however, he was addressing someone who shared his feelings.

Grant's dominant trait was persistence, and he applied it to Banks as he did against Lee. Three days later, overlooking his own approval (though conditional) of the expedition, Grant told Halleck, "General Banks, by his failure, has absorbed ten thousand veteran troops that should now be with General Sherman, and thirty thousand of his own, that would have been moving toward Mobile, and this without accomplishing any good result."[35] As if frustrated by the lack of immediate action, he followed up a few days later with a more severe condemnation: "I do think it is a waste of strength to trust General Banks with a large command or an important expedition."[36] Although Halleck was now subordinate to Grant, he was physically in Washington, and the general in chief may have believed that his former boss still possessed political influence. Finally, if there was any remaining doubt of his intentions, Grant reiterated them: "Private letters and official statements from the department of the Gulf show such a state of affairs there as to demand, in my opinion, the immediate removal of General Banks. The army has undoubtedly lost confidence in him." This was written from "near Spotsylvania Court House," where Grant was engaged in desperate combat with Lee's army.[37]

On the same day of this last communication, Grant had the satisfaction of learning from Halleck, "Nearly all your wishes in this matter have been anticipated."[38] In typical style the administration had not actually relieved Banks but had rendered him militarily powerless by inserting another layer of command (Canby) above him. This was the same slick tactic that was employed in dealing with General Meade, who was left in command of the Army of the Potomac while Grant, in control of all the Union armies, accompanied him. As Halleck informed the general in chief, "Canby has full authority to make any changes in commanders he may desire." The congressional testimony that might have exonerated Banks to some degree would not be assembled until many months later and almost certainly would not have altered Grant's resolute determination to remove him. Nor would Canby's surprised report on taking command that "this army is in better condition than I had supposed from the accounts that had reached me, and will soon be ready for offensive operations," alter the unswerving judgment.[39] (Canby had used the same language in his report to Halleck on May 18.)[40] In another letter to Halleck a few days later, Canby was more restrained, writing that the troops, "although in better state than I had supposed, are not in a condition to take the field."[41] Somewhat ironically, Grant was then dealing with a similar problem in the person of none other than Benjamin F. Butler and had to repeat much the same procedure. It is curious that Banks's military failure largely demolished his political aspirations, whereas a politician like John A. Andrew, who had not chosen the military route to inflate his prospects, remained politically viable (though ultimately impeded by his character flaws). Banks's career, and later Butler's, seemed to illustrate in a perverse way the adage that he who lives by the sword perishes by the sword.

Banks had been thoroughly discredited by the congressional testimony and by his removal from active command, but his humiliation was not yet complete. In late November he had been authorized "to communicate to the President any matters relating to the civil administration of your department which you may deem it important to the public service for him to be appraised of by direct communication with him." Banks apparently wrote or approved an article in a Washington paper that the administration found embarrassing, which brought down a stinging reprimand from Secretary Stanton: "you have henceforth no leave or permission from this Department to correspond or communicate with any authority, civil or military, except in accordance with the rules and regulations of the military service."[42] Here was a major general, who had commanded up to 50,000 heavily armed men accompanied by the full panoply of prancing horses and rumbling caissons, being dressed down like a junior lieutenant, which Banks had never been.

After the Battle of Sabine Cross Roads, more than fifteen hundred Federal soldiers were listed as missing. Some found their way back to their units in succeeding days, but most were hauled away as prisoners of war. During the rest of the campaign, each side brought in a steady flow of captives, perhaps roughly equal in numbers. The Confederates held some advantage in this since they were able to pick up Union soldiers who could not keep pace with the hasty retreat of their army. The experience of these men contrasted radically with that of their free-ranging comrades.

Banks's decision to withdraw after the repulse of the Confederates at Pleasant Hill meant that the wounded had to be left on the battlefield. A. J. Smith protested passionately against this, pleading for a delay until the wounded could be recovered and the dead buried. In this instance Banks was adamant, showing a firmness and willingness to command the loaned general that had not been displayed on other occasions. In defending his stance he argued that wagons were no longer available and that the enemy held the only source of water in the vicinity.[43] Abandoning the wounded created a scandal that provided ammunition to Banks's critics during the congressional investigation. One surgeon, asked how it happened that the wounded were left in the hands of the enemy, replied, "This is a great mystery to me."[44] Most of the wounded men became prisoners, though many died along the way to captivity due to inferior medical care and the hardships of being moved to prison houses and camps.

One of the most harrowing such experiences was recounted by Sgt. Danforth Converse. As noted previously, Captain Rice had found Converse wounded on the battlefield and reluctantly left him: "I did not then feel that I had a right to take two or three well men from the Co. to take care of this one, and therefore decided to abandon him, as I hoped, temporarily." Rice removed the sergeant's carbine "as I was determined that the Rebs shouldn't have that, anyhow."[45] Converse held a different perspective of this. Severely wounded by a bullet in the thigh, he had fainted from loss of blood.

> I soon recovered consciousness, however, and was fully aware of everything around me, but unable to move a muscle or even open my eyes. While in this condition, our Army was obliged to fall back before the superior and overwhelming numbers of the Enemies' forces, and I remember distinctly how Capt. Rice and Orderly Sergt. Chas. H. Horr came to my side, and hearing them both pronounce me dead. Oh God! How I struggled to open my eyes to speak; to make even a sign of life. But there was no time to loiter by the side of the dead, and they passed on, leaving me there to be buried by stranger hands.[46]

Converse lay helpless on the battlefield for four days, during the nights listening to wild hogs devouring the dead and perhaps some who were not quite dead. Finally, on April 12, Confederates found him and brought him to Mansfield. During all that time, he had had nothing to eat or drink except a sip of brandy that one of his captors gave him. At first local women visited the prisoners and brought them food, but later that was prohibited; an old black

woman who disobeyed was "stripped of her clothing, tied to a tree, and severely whipped." Converse learned that Sgt. George B. Canterbury of Company
D and Cpl. Edward Regan of Company F were being held in the local jail and
visited them. He took credit for keeping Canterbury alive by giving him wine
that he had managed to obtain through one of the guards. Converse was probably moved to Texas eventually, though is memoir makes no mention of this.

John W. Gibbs was one who became well acquainted with the prison camp
in Texas. Captured at Bynum's Mills, he was interrogated intensively by General Taylor and, assembled with other prisoners, sent on the arduous march
west. When they passed through Shreveport, the goal that Banks never obtained, Gibbs observed: "That town was not such a place as I expected to see
at the head of the Red River. It was in a dilapitated [sic] condition. One of the
prisoners expressed the idea of the company when he said, 'What Banks will
want of this God forsaken place I don't see.'" Gibbs's description of the prison
camp at Tyler, Texas, makes it resemble on a smaller scale the infamous Andersonville in Georgia (since he was writing many years later, he might have
been influenced by accounts of the Georgia facility): "The stockade was built
in the side of the forest and the trees inside and around it were used in its construction. About 12 or 14 ft. high on the inside, logs split in two and set close
together with the split side in and the bark on the outside, high enough for the
guards to be head and shoulders above it. The 'Dead Line' was an imaginary
line said to be 15 ft. from it but it was not safe to go as near as that to it."[47]

Gibbs claimed there were 4,500 men in that confined space of four acres.
After being marched inside, the prisoners were divided into detachments of
60 men and given a number. Each detachment received an iron kettle that
would hold six quarts, a skillet with a cover ("or what we would call a Dutch
oven"), and a wooden bucket. Many of the prisoners were "without a single
rag of clothing upon them and others with the remains of a pair of pants, or a
shirt or a few rags." Men who already had been there two years had had most
of what they started with taken from them and were left with nothing in the
way of clothing. Gibbs was fortunate in linking up with thirty-eight members
of his regiment: "We had a little spot that we claimed as our own and had to
watch it that others did not crowd us out."[48]

During strenuous action on May 3, Sgt. Charles B. Jackson of Company F,
a Belchertown resident, seized a moment to sleep beside the road, where he
was left when the Federals moved on. When he woke up, as Captain Rice put

it succinctly, "the Johnnies had him."[49] Later in the month, during the clash at Marksville on May 17, the regiment's assistant surgeon, Dr. Elisha P. Clarke of Milford, found himself surrounded by enemy cavalry and was compelled to surrender. According to Rice, he had joined the regiment only on April 5 and may not have known his way around well. Clarke's account suggests that the rebels who captured him were irregulars: "When we came opposite the house from which the shots had been fired, upon the piazza were two men clothed in grey homespun, and two bare-footed women with uncombed hair, and dressed in what I judged to be white sheeting which had been colored with some kind of bark. They were altogether a bad-looking mess."[50] After that, being a physician, he was well treated and met General Taylor and Brig. Gen. Camille Armand de Polignac, a French prince who had volunteered for the Confederacy. Clarke was allowed to treat Union prisoners before being paroled to rejoin his unit, which he reached on June 17. The prisoner interlude had deleted only a month from his regular routine and may have compensated with novel sensations.

Sergeant Converse was also paroled on June 17, though not before another trying experience. On the previous night "one of the surgeons, Dr. Hess, . . . came quietly through on his round, and informed each of us that a squad of rebel thieves would make a raid on us before morning, and if we had any money, watches or jewelry, if we would give it to him he would preserve it for us." The sergeant marveled at "how the man ever managed to walk off under his weight of watches, jewelry and money, I don't understand, for we had to march about eight miles before reaching the boat." When the searchers went through that night, they found "naught but empty pockets." The next day, true to his word, Dr. Hess returned every man his property after they were aboard the boat.[51]

Gibbs was finally exchanged too, though he relates it as a near thing. The guards found during a roll call that they lacked thirty-nine men, and "Capt. Hall suggested that there was just that number inside, all of one Reg't (which was ours). Well, as we are ready to start, we will take them if they have just the number."[52] The figure for 31st Massachusetts captives given by Gibbs seems large but lies within the bounds of credibility, based on the official roster; if accurate, it represents substantially more than 10 percent of the regiment's strength at that time. The parolees set off on a difficult march to Shreveport, followed by a long boat trip down the Red River, during which they had little to eat. William H. Rich, then at Baton Rouge, confirmed that a boat came down on June 17, carrying four hundred paroled prisoners. He listed several of the other sergeants he recognized: George B. Canterbury (Company D), Converse (Company F), Elliot Durkee (Company G), and William Kayhoo (Company K). The first three had been left for dead on the Pleasant Hill battlefield but made unexpected recoveries.[53]

11

GUERILLA WARFARE

JUNE 1864–FEBRUARY 1865

A period of quiet, undoubtedly welcome, descended after the Red River Campaign concluded. Both sides were exhausted and nursed their injuries, while the destitute countryside could not support being further devoured by ravenous armies. Major General Taylor was preoccupied with his feud with Lieutenant General Smith and after a time found himself relieved of command. Banks seemed to be stunned by the disastrous outcome of his expedition, while Canby, cautious by nature, was finding his way around his new assignment. General Sherman, then heavily engaged in the Atlanta Campaign, agreed with Canby that Union forces should "attempt nothing offensive in West Louisiana this year."[1] Banks, in addition to his military responsibilities, had worked to set up a Unionist government in Louisiana. Lincoln and other Republican strategists supported this, fearing that they might need these electoral votes, however tainted, in the 1864 presidential election. The loyal government flourished in a sheltered environment like a hothouse plant. When it sent representatives to Congress, however, that body refused to seat them, an ominous portent of the trouble over Reconstruction that would arise while Lincoln was still in office.

The 31st Massachusetts passed a few quiet days at Morganza until June 29, when the men turned in their horses and cavalry equipment and prepared to head off on their promised furlough.[2] They probably were fortunate to leave when they did, as conditions in the Morganza camp deteriorated, bringing an alarming increase in illness. "Epidemics of scurvy, chronic diarrhea, swamp fever, and smallpox began to take an appalling toll."[3] The troops reoccupied their old campground at Algiers until they finally departed for Massachusetts on July 21.

Soon after returning to New Orleans on July 2, Luther Fairbank had gone up to Carrollton and renewed acquaintance with Leana. During these easy-going days, memories of the recent campaign and its hardships melted away. As if to highlight the contrast, Fairbank reported that "some of the boys, just for amusement, go over to the city and play checkers with their nose all night and in the morning take a ride in the Star line coach."[4] It is difficult to know whether he meant this literally or whether these were ephemeral slang expressions. Fairbank, who had been ill at intervals (perhaps due to malaria) since returning from the Red River, seemingly found energy when it was needed. Boldly, he entered in his diary one day: "The girls, thinking we were to leave soon, have been over to see their fellows and we have had some fun criticizing their beauty. One was what I should call a mulatto, but her fellow calls her a creole, but the one that takes the shine off of all is a Spanish girl." He then added, "Madam Wallace is all the go now"—leaving us to speculate on the kind of establishment she operated.[5]

Fittingly, the men headed home by journeying up the Mississippi River, which they had helped reopen, rather than returning by sea as they had come. A special order had directed that the veterans would travel by way of Cairo, Illinois, "if it is impracticable to furnish [transportation] by way of the Ocean."[6] One can hardly begin to unravel the emotions they must have felt as their boat, the *Pauline Carroll*, steamed upriver. There would have been pride and relief simply at having survived when so many others from the original contingent had fallen away. This might have been accompanied by annoyance that the war was not over, perhaps amplified with anger at the poor leadership they had witnessed. Above all, like a bright banner in the breeze, floated the sweet vision of home that had been their guiding star through the fearful service in the alien Deep South. Some may have wondered if they or their homes had changed so much that they would no longer blend in effortlessly, but Civil War soldiers rarely recorded that kind of introspection.

On the second day out, July 22, Colonel Gooding came on board for the trip north. Two days later the characteristic luck of the 31st Massachusetts reasserted itself when *Pauline* struck a snag about thirty miles below Vicksburg. The port wheel was disabled, making progress against the current still slower, and the vessel labored into Vicksburg on July 24. As some of the men had supplied themselves with whiskey, the cruise upriver could have had a holiday aspect, but still the war intruded. At a temporary landing on the twenty-fifth, they met a portion of the 6th Michigan, a regiment they had encountered two years earlier on Ship Island, whose boats had grounded on the west bank of the river and were then burnt by Confederates.[7] At several points during the journey, their transport was fired on from the shore. Although the troops had turned in their weapons in New Orleans, there were several cases of muskets on board, though no ammunition. Nevertheless, in each instance the boat landed and the soldiers formed up on shore. Although unable to fire, their numbers frightened off the rebels. The steamer *Leviathan* helped the *Pauline* pass some rebel field batteries below Memphis, but even with this kind of assistance, the steamboat did not reach Cairo until July 30.[8] There, they transferred to a slow Illinois Central train for the trip to Chicago.

Along the route they encountered a heartwarming sight that confirmed they were in friendly territory at last: "As we passed one of the little stations we saw standing in front of a small but neat farm house a sight that called forth innumerable cheers from our men. A little girl some five or six years old waving a large American flag, on one side of her was her mother dressed in mourning (the significance of which we knew pretty well) and waving her white pocket handkerchief." On the other side of the little girl "was a boy looking two or three years older, dressed in soldier's clothes having a wooden gun which he was holding as well as he could in the position of Present Arms. Behind them all and sitting on a tree that looked as if it had just been hauled up from the timber was a grey haired old sire waving his straw hat with both hands, and we could very well imagine him to be saying—God bless all of you." After passing them, George Young recalled, "a lot of the fellows voted to drink their health, which I believe they did in corn whiskey." After performing that duty, "I presume a good many of the men never thought of it after, but it is a picture that often comes up before my memory after all the years that have passed since that time."[9] Later in the journey, the train was moving so slowly on a long upgrade that the men were able to get off, collect apples, and reboard.

The regiment reached Chicago at last at 5 P.M. on August 1. The train through Illinois was made up of "emigrant" cars, with only long, hard benches for seating, but from Chicago to Boston the troops traveled first class.[10] They arrived in Boston on the evening of August 4, after brief stops at Pittsfield and Springfield, and were received by state and city authorities. Sgt. William Rich was pleased to report that "there were tables set with plenty of not 'hard tack' but biscuit, cake and cream." The mayor made a welcoming speech, to which Colonel Gooding responded; Lt. Col. Edward Nettleton and Maj. Elbert Fordham also spoke briefly.[11] In this way the atrocious failure of their predecessors was glossed over. For those who did not know better, the regiment presented an undisturbed countenance. Next morning the men started on their furlough, a solid stream gradually dispersing into rivulets until individuals trickled home to their families.

To their credit, the authorities gave the regiment a full month's furlough and did not count the time spent travelling. Fairbank reached his home in Ware on August 7 and, according to his summary, remained true to character for the duration of his leave: "We had a party at Enfield, a dance at Greenwich and two at Pierce's Hall and a shin dig somewhere every night. I got a certificate of marriage and left the folks in a stew. The last night the town of Ware got up a supper. We did not attend but broke in the door of John Grant's and then each one took to his hole to finish up our thirty days' furlough."[12]

At the end of the allotted time, most of the men assembled at Pittsfield on September 7 (some, such as Sergeant Rich and Fairbank, missed connections and had to catch up). From Pittsfield, the regiment travelled to New York City by the Housatonic Railroad rather than returning to Boston. They spent one night in barracks at The Battery, then boarded the steam transport *Victor*. Surely on this sea voyage, those who had been present from the beginning recalled their adventures two-and-a-half years earlier, when Butler was in command and every experience was novel and thrilling. As if some stage manager was heightening the contrast, this passage seemed to be uneventful except for the drowning of a man from Company G, John Burton (or Bunton) of North Adams, during a stop at Tortugas, Florida. After ten days at sea, the ship reached New Orleans on September 19. The 31st Massachusetts now entered the final phase of its odyssey.

The "veteran" contingent was approaching the end of its three-year enlistment, beyond which the men had signed up for three more years of service; but no one could guess how much longer the war would last. The Confederacy, though severely depleted—certainly more than it dared acknowledge—was still full of fight. A U.S. presidential election was approaching, and in the absence of a decisive military event, it was possible that Lincoln would be defeated and the Democratic candidate, none other than Maj. Gen. George Mc-Clellan, would make a peace that recognized Southern independence. For the returned veterans of the 31st Massachusetts, the seeming interminability of the war must have added to the sinking gloom that settles in at the end of any vacation. Capt. Luther Howell was only being more open than most in conceding, "I feel more lonesome than I did before I had been home."[13] Unknown to one another, Sergeant Rich had expressed similar melancholy before departing New York: "I am lonesome as the d—l, wish I was back to old Pittsfield and a free man."[14] The authorities had taken a calculated risk in releasing these men to taste the simple pleasures of home and make the inevitable contrasts with military life.

Having missed the regiment at Pittsfield, Fairbank had to stay there overnight. After spending time at a horse show in Springfield, he again missed connections in New York City, thereby demonstrating why he never advanced in rank (or evinced any interest in doing so). In the city with Capt. Nelson Bond, who was in charge of the stragglers, he succumbed to the same sadness that weighed on his comrades: "It grows worse and worse. I feel as bad about leaving home this time as the first."[15] Preparing to ship out on the next steamer, the *Merrimac,* he wrote sardonically, "We are to leave this low, ill begotten hole tomorrow and start for the land of sugar, hurrah, boys hurrah."[16] After a relatively smooth journey of only eight days, Fairbank and the other latecomers disembarked at New Orleans on the twenty-second.

For a surprisingly large number in the 31st Massachusetts, the thought of returning to army life in the Deep South proved unbearable, and they responded by deserting. A justifiable war weariness had spread throughout the North, and thousands of Union soldiers had deserted and somehow hid themselves within the general population. Probably, this was less common among the older volunteer regiments than among the later draftees, who were not as committed to the cause nor as bound by ties of locality and acquaintance. In the 31st, however, something approaching mass desertion took place. At least twelve men were recorded as having deserted at Pittsfield, five from Company K and the remainder from four other companies. At least for the group from Company K, this had the appearance of being an organized plan. One might suspect that some of these men were merely delayed temporarily, but the records do not indicate that any of them ever returned to the colors.

Thomas Norris took sick while on leave and spent time at an army hospital in Readville, Massachusetts. He did not leave Boston until January 3, 1865, taking an Old Colony train to Newport, Rhode Island, and then the Long Island Sound steamer *Empire State* to New York. He departed from the city for the

South on the fifth, a voyage that took a full two weeks, due in part to making stops at Key West, Pensacola, and Fort Morgan (in Mobile Bay). This winter voyage on the transport *Empire City* was not only longer but also considerably more stressful than the one experienced by the bulk of the 31st Massachusetts. On the second day out, Norris felt slightly dizzy and went up on deck. There he encountered "a sight for an artist. Here were several of the boys arranged along the rail feeding the fishes with the food they had demolished the two or three previous days. I very soon joined them and oh heavens, if I ever felt seasick and homesick it was then." After a relatively pleasant afternoon watching porpoises, a violent gale set in off Cape Hatteras, which inevitably recalled the ordeal the *Mississippi* had passed through nearly three years earlier: "The sea ran terrible high all night. The waves broke over the deck of the old craft. The water rushed down the hatches into the hold where we were quartered, soaking every one of us to the skin and nearly drowning us all out." At the peak of the storm, "a very heavy wave struck the ship with an awful crash. It sounded just as if the old hulk had struck a rock and was coming to pieces. There was then a continued rush of water down on us. We all gave ourselves up as lost. Some were praying, others cursing, and all running about making all sorts of noises. As for myself I felt just as if I wanted to go down."[17] As with the *Mississippi,* the remainder of the voyage was relatively uneventful. Norris compensated for his lost meals along the way before the ship reached New Orleans on January 20.

While the veterans were enjoying their well-deserved furlough, men who were not eligible were assigned to guard Confederate prisoners in a cotton warehouse in New Orleans. After the regiment was reassembled, it was initially ordered to draw Springfield muskets and return to infantry duty in response to an order dated July 25, 1864, issued while most of the men were on furlough, which revoked the order that had converted the 31st to cavalry.[18] The record does not offer any clues as to the reasons behind this action. It was probably not so much a reflection on the performance of the regiment as a general desire to reduce the cost of maintaining mounted troops now that their primary advocate, Banks, was no longer in a position to support them. Moreover, although the congressional hearings on the Red River Campaign had not yet started, officers like General Dwight had assuredly expressed their opinions about the Gulf cavalry in general.

Canby soon thought better of this and, just as the furloughed men were returning, made them horsemen again, this time as mounted infantry rather than cavalry.[19] In his history of the Union cavalry, Stephen Starr expresses astonishment at the frequent changes of designation in the Department of the Gulf: "In no other theater was the conversion of infantry regiments to cavalry, of cavalry regiments to infantry, and of the same regiment from one arm to another more than once, practiced with the same abandon as in that department."[20] As Howell explained to his sister, "This is the next best thing to being made cavalry & the only real difference is that we shall carry long guns instead of short ones [carbines] as we did before."[21] The men were now expected to dismount and fight as infantry, which they had already done on several occasions as cavalry. This proved to be a wise decision in view of the type of action the regiment saw during its remaining months in Louisiana. The men who had returned from Massachusetts rejoined those who had stayed behind and together took up quarters in Fassman's Cotton Press, which Fairbank described as "bully quarters, everything handy."[22] Being Fairbank, the items he included under "handy" were probably not limited to military needs.

Alas, Fairbank's advances against the local females seem not to have resulted in many conquests. By February 1865, he was forced to concede mournfully, "After traveling Carrollton all over to find some woman who would share her bed with me, without success, I returned to the camp to sleep in wet blankets."[23] He compensated in part with frequent visits to the theater, indicating that New Orleans's lively cultural life had recovered. Christmas was a pleasant occasion, as Fairbank feasted on "a great dinner of pies, chicken, etc. brought in by our friends the citizens." He had ample reason to exclaim, "Hurrah for Christmas!"[24] On New Year's Day 1865, which fell on a Sunday, Fairbank enjoyed "a nice pair of ducks given by Mr. Seales, a planter living five miles below here."[25] The donors of these lavish repasts were probably Unionist planters who lived within the narrow zone of protection provided by Federal troops. Even when fully mobilized, the reach of Union arms was limited across the vast expanse of the South, and this foreshadowed the problems of Reconstruction.

In formation on September 28, 1864, Lieutenant Colonel Nettleton presented the regiment with two flags on behalf of the State of Massachusetts (though the account does not specify whether they were national, state, or regimental banners). Probably, these had been promised during the recent furlough with the intent to pull the men out of the inevitable doldrums occasioned by their return to oppressive military life. Nettleton was keen to establish his authority and, from his perspective, repair the damage done by the former senior officers; Sergeant Rich reported that "he is very particular" with the manual of arms.[26] After an inspection, Fairbank observed drily that "everything passed off well as could be expected considering the military man we have for a commander."[27] Nettleton's sternness on the drill field gave no clue as to other events in his life, but Captain Howell recorded: "Col. Nettleton and Miss Benjamin are in the last stages of a heavy fever. They only wait for the close of the war to claim the kettle according to agreement."[28] (Some of the officers must have had a wager as to who would get married first. Nettleton's obituary states, however, that he married Mary E. Tucker, not a Miss Benjamin.)[29]

To complete its reinstatement as mounted infantry, the 31st Massachusetts had to be issued horses and accoutrements, which took place in December. Capt. W. I. Allen informed Lieutenant Colonel Nettleton, who was detached on court-martial duty, that Brig. Gen. T. W. Sherman, commander of the Defenses of New Orleans, "urges us to improve every moment in camp for drill and instruction, but there is hardly a moment when the men and horses are not resting from labor or doing work."[30] Allen's remarks contrast noticeably with Fairbank's depiction of a rather leisurely existence, though each man was probably seeing what suited him. By the end of the month, the captain was able to report that "the horses are improving *rapidly*. We have got all our stables comfortably arranged now, and are fully settled and running. The men are behaving splendidly, and win already the good opinion of the people, who have been accustomed to the depredations of such men as the 14th N.Y. and Scott's 900."[31] Matching men and horses must have been an ongoing process, for two months later Fairbank reported that "after having some six or eight different ones, I have one that suits me."[32] This expression of satisfaction proved to be premature: "After getting the bloody horse clean, he will lay down and roll, making himself look as bad as ever, and you must go to work again, or get scolded for having him so dirty."[33]

Soldiers followed the critical 1864 election campaign with understandably intense interest. Just as there was no precedent for a conflict of the magnitude of the Civil War, there was no precedent for conducting a presidential election in the midst of one. On November 7 Fairbank reported: "Great discussions tonight. Some are for old Abe, others for little Mac, and each party is praising their candidate."[34] On election day the men used the occasion to indulge in the kind of military satire that might have delighted Ernie Pyle eighty years later: "Votes were cast for more rations and company cooks, 'more bread' and one was cast for Old Abe on conditions that he gave us more rations and better officers."[35] On that day Rich recorded a sham election in which a significant proportion of the regiment participated: of 252 votes cast, McClellan received 132, Lincoln 114, Ben Butler 3, and the remaining 3 scattered. This was a surprising outcome since the overall soldier vote was overwhelmingly Republican.[36] Butler's intention of forming a regiment of Democratic Unionists apparently had endured. The soldiers who cast votes for their former general may not have realized that Lincoln had toyed with the idea of making "the Beast" his running mate; Butler, after his military aspirations were humiliated, came to regret refusing the offer.[37] None of the soldier accounts speak of actually voting, although Massachusetts was one of the states that permitted soldier voting and, as a Republican stronghold, had an interest in encouraging such participation. By then, there were probably only a few hundred Massachusetts soldiers in Louisiana, so no one may have made the effort to set up voting facilities for them there.

When the 31st Massachusetts returned to duty in Louisiana, the time for grand movements had passed. Confederate forces still occupied Shreveport and the Teche country, while Federals controlled New Orleans, Baton Rouge, and the line of the Mississippi, with a number of free-labor plantations scattered throughout. Neither side had the strength to undertake a major campaign, besides which the depleted countryside could not have supported one. The only major plan afoot was to capture Mobile, Alabama, which had been high on the Union agenda since 1862 but repeatedly deferred. It might have been undertaken in September 1864 but for an outbreak of yellow fever at New Orleans.[38] Union victories, notably Sherman's taking of Atlanta, had persuaded the North to continue the war and ensured Lincoln's reelection. The importance of the president's experiment with the Unionist Louisiana government thus diminished.

The state afterward became the scene of small, though often vicious, clashes. In late October Companies F and H, under Captains Rice and Bond respectively, were issued the first horses that the regiment acquired and sent upriver on the steamer *St. Mary* to Plaquemine in Iberville Parish.[39] They landed near the town on the morning of October 30. Company F took up quarters in the courthouse and Company H in the jail, while officers were placed in nearby houses and the horses were settled in "very fair stables." Less than a week later they were dispatched downstream to Bayou Goula to destroy bridges, an expedition that covered some fifty miles. The numbers that went out may indicate the small size of the companies at this stage in the war: four sergeants, three corporals, and thirty-three privates from Company F and three sergeants, two corporals, and twenty-one privates from Company H, all led by a total of four officers. After that grueling action, it may not be surprising that a Sunday inspection found "room for great improvement in the appearance of both companies."[40] What is surprising is that these companies, which had been back in Louisiana for only about a month and barely had time to equip themselves in their new assignment, were being sent out on a demanding mission. It testifies to the strained manpower situation of Federal forces in the region.

It is possible that the remainder of the regiment was being kept fairly inactive while awaiting more extensive reorganization. During November and December, the three-year terms of the men who had not reenlisted expired, requiring a large discharge of members on November 20, 1864.[41] In sharp contrast to their attitude toward some of the nine-month troops, none of the "veterans" begrudged the well-earned departure of their former comrades. Fairbank, who had shared three years of adventures with them, extended a heartfelt farewell: "they have done their duty and may they arrive safe home."[42] The pending departure of these men had put him in a nostalgic mood, and he reflected on the third anniversary of his group's going off to camp in Pittsfield: "Of the six that bunked together, Lamberton, Warburton, Marsh, Bennett, Lashua and myself, two last are left. Bennett found a grave in southern soil."[43]

It was impossible not to notice the reduced numbers of the 31st Massachusetts, and department headquarters decided to consolidate the remaining troops into a battalion of five companies. Lieutenant Colonel Nettleton was put in charge of this reorganization as well as placing those who were returning to Massachusetts into a temporary detachment.[44] The companies went through several permutations, which made it seem that the men were constantly being shuffled around. In fact, the men stayed together, only their company designations were altered. The battalion only took on its final form in February 1865. At that time interim Company K, made up of original Companies A and B, became Company A; Company I, made up of original Companies I and K, became B; Company G, made up of original C and G, became C; Company H, made up of original F and H, became D; and Company E, made up of original D and E, continued as E. Through all of this scrambling, it appears that only Company E retained its original identity and membership. Available data on the strength of some of the companies reveals that sixty-three men remained in the original Company A, thirty-nine in B, forty-seven in C, and thirty-nine each in D and K.[45] Applying the average to the remaining companies indicates that the strength of the regiment after discharging those who did not reenlist was about 450 men. Since this figure includes all of those who joined in New Orleans or who were added from Massachusetts after the regiment returned from furlough, the number remaining from the 1861 contingent must have been much smaller.

The reduction of the battalion created a surplus of officers, of whom several were mustered out in November 1864. While Lieutenant Colonel Nettleton was given responsibility for distributing the enlisted men, the choice of which officers to dismiss was made at a higher level, perhaps with his input.[46] Among those discharged were 1st Lt. Fordyce A. Rust (original Company B), Capt. Horace F. Morse (original Company B), 1st Lt. Emory P. Andrews (original Company C), Capt. John W. Lee (original Company C), Capt. Lester M. Hayden (original Company E), and Capt. Orrin S. Hopkins (original Company H). Although Howell opined that "the officers to go are the poorer ones & most of them want to go," some of the choices seem surprising, with Colonel Gooding and Major Fordham among those discharged.[47] Both men had served effectively at critical moments, and it would seem that the army could have found other uses for their abilities. Fordham, promoted to major after having filled in admirably as commander while Nettleton recovered from his wounds, had been detailed to become inspector of cavalry for the division. Apparently, the policy was not to reduce active officers to lower ranks, so it became necessary to commission two noncommissioned officers as new second lieutenants: Patrick J. Dinan and Charles I. Wade, both of the original Company I. Dinan (it may be recalled) had won the prize for best drilling at the July 4 festivities at Fort Pike in 1863, so his promotion at least appears to be based on merit. The departing men, despite the privileges accorded to officers, must have concluded that they had had enough of military service or that there were better opportunities available to them as a civilian. Joshua Hawkes had opined that Captain Lee, having been seriously ill, would not return from the furlough he took in July 1863.[48] He was mistaken in that prediction, but during the shakeup in November 1864, Lee was either bumped aside or chose to leave the service.

During this period of turmoil, the chief of cavalry for the department, Brig. Gen. Benjamin Stone Roberts (1810–75), threw another element into the mix with orders he issued in mid-November. Some of the themes of this message occur regularly in such general orders, but Roberts's phrasing is striking. After affirming that Colonel Gooding was in command of the Fifth Brigade, consisting of the 18th New York Cavalry, 3rd Rhode Island Cavalry, 31st Massachusetts Mounted Infantry, and 16th Indiana Mounted Infantry, and instructing him to set up his headquarters at Thibodaux in the Lafourche District, the order made various demands of Gooding:

> Make such personal inspection of the troops of his Brigade as will make known to him their status in discipline and efficiency and their wants in arms, horses and equipment and general mount, that in any way impairs the most effective power of the Cav'y arm of service.
>
> He will make a special report to these Hd. Qrs. of the result of his inspection.
>
> In cavalry service officers must know and do their duties and Col. Gooding will at once establish such a system of inspection and recitation in all the Reg'ts as will attest the capacity of officers to fill their positions, and distinguish the willing from the unwilling, and the capable from the incapable, and the indolent and shirk from the energetic and zealous performers of duty. He will report the names of officers who by their vicious habits or want of capacity or moral character, may in his judgment be disqualified for their positions as commissioned officers.[49]

Some of this might be a typical assessment by a newly arrived commander, as Roberts had assumed this position only on October 26, after more than three months on sick leave of absence. While there is an implied criticism of Gooding, the document provides no indication that the colonel would soon be dismissed. Thus, while the order seems to revive the complaints made against the cavalry during the Red River Campaign, it also reveals deficiencies in communication and coordination within the command structure of the Department of the Gulf. In the event, little of the program contained in Roberts's order was carried out, as Gooding was discharged soon after and the general himself was transferred to the District of West Tennessee (effective January 24, 1865).[50] By then, the cavalry brigade, whether or not it needed extensive training and inspection, had been scattered over a multitude of small posts, where such attention would have been difficult to apply.

Before the war, the regular army, with its glacially slow advancement, was notorious for infighting and political rivalries. Bringing state authorities into the mix added another element to the intrigue. The maneuvers that led to the replacement of Civil War generals are often well documented, but the undercurrents that affected colonels and majors are obscure at this distance. On several occasions Gooding could have been given his brigadier's star, and there was some expectation among the officers that this would happen, but the fact that it never did is significant. (In a letter from February 1864, Howell observed, "Gooding is back—did not get his star.")[51] Upon resuming mounted duties, the 31st Massachusetts had been assigned to the Fifth Brigade, of which Colonel Gooding was in command. Gooding entertained hopes of recruiting the regiment to full strength locally so that he could remain as its colonel (and senior in the brigade); of this Howell accurately predicted, "I doubt it."[52]

Gooding's military career dribbled away to a rather anticlimactic conclusion. Having been deemed superfluous, the colonel was discharged from the volunteer service on November 26, 1864. He probably spent his final days in the service as inspecting officer at Kennerville.[53] Although Gooding was no longer in the volunteer service, there may have been consideration of reinstating him. In the early part of 1865, Captain Allen and Lieutenant Colonel Nettleton, who was still on court-martial duty in New Orleans, conducted a detailed and highly personal correspondence concerning officer placements in the 31st Massachusetts. In the course of this, Allen passed on a report that "there is some chance of Gooding's being retained as substitute for you. Do not, for Heaven's sake, allow it. Give us timely notice of any movement of the enemy in that direction, and we will try to counteract it."[54] Whether due to a stout defense put up by Allen and Nettleton or other causes, Gooding did not resume command of the 31st. After the regiment was reduced to battalion size, higher authorities probably considered it unjustifiable to assign a full colonel to command it.

Unlike many regular officers who reverted to their permanent rank and resumed their peacetime careers, Gooding resigned from the U.S. Army on March 20, 1865, when the war was not yet over. A week earlier he had been brevetted brigadier general and major general for "meritorious services" and "gallant conduct" in previous campaigns.[55] This was the military equivalent of giving a watch to a retiring employee, but it allowed Gooding to use the title "general" for the remainder of his life. Reviewing his career, it seems apparent that some superior did not want him to advance to that actual rank in the volunteer service and perhaps did not want him in the army at all.

The private correspondence between Allen and Nettleton in early 1865 represented the final phase of the effort to reassemble the pieces after the massive reorganization of December. The decision as to which officers to retain had been made at a higher level (though possibly with input from officers like Nettleton and Allen), but assignments within companies (officially they were squadrons within a battalion) were made at the regimental level. Nettleton and Allen attempted to assign lieutenants to captains who requested them, or to achieve, in their judgment, the most compatible combination of officers, but they also tried to make some adjustments in the list of officers to be retained. They succeeded, for example, in replacing William H. Pelton with Henry Barber as first lieutenant.[56]

By manipulating the number of men in companies, they made a concerted effort to push out Capt. George Darling.[57] Darling had been detached on provost duty since 1863 and thereafter had little contact with the rest of the regiment, not participating in either the Teche or Red River operations. Nevertheless, it appears that Allen and Nettleton still considered this posting a temporary assignment so that Darling might return at any time and displace another officer due to seniority. Within the diminished scope of the 31st Massachusetts, these were understandably sensitive topics. Allen feared that Lt. Milton Sagendorph might have to be made a "scapegoat" in the process of pushing out Darling. In addition, he felt that Howell held a grievance against him, probably relating to the assignment of subordinate officers.

In what appears to be merely a startling coincidence, Captain Darling was captured by the enemy soon afterward. According to recollections provided much later by his wife, Sarah, the couple were living on the Deslonde plantation in La Place, home of General Beauregard's father-in-law, André Deslonde, more than thirty miles from where the 31st Massachusetts was stationed. (Beauregard's wife, Caroline, had died in March 1864.) On March 25 a Confederate raiding party eluded the ineffectual picket guard and broke into the house; Sarah believed it was for the purpose of seizing papers that would show a list of men who were slated to be drafted, presumably into the Union army. At that moment the whistle of a boat bringing Captain Darling back from a trip to New Orleans sounded. The raiders waited and captured him when he came up to the house. He was carried off to a location deep in Mississippi but soon exchanged for a major held by Union forces. It might thus appear that the seizure of Captain Darling was a kidnapping for the purpose of exchange, but the leader of the raiders, Capt. Felix P. Poché (1836–95), probably just wanted to remove Darling as an obstacle to his guerilla operations.[58] Sarah was interviewed by L. Frederick Rice in 1905, but her memory of events forty years earlier was fuzzy (for example, she was no longer able to recall the precise date of the incident).[59]

The capture of Darling was not reported for four hours, and by then the raiders had a considerable start. Over the next two days, parties of Federal troops ranged into the countryside searching for him, but without success. It may be that Sarah gave them confusing information as to the direction the raiders had taken. The searches were under the control of Maj. Edward Byrne of the 18th New York Cavalry, but although it was a cavalry outfit, it appears that the parties traveled on foot or in small boats. On March 28 the last group returned and reported that "further pursuit is useless, as the rebels are too far away."[60]

The Darlings were well treated by the courtly Captain Poché. As depicted by Sarah, his behavior was the fading echo of the code of the planter aristocracy, now on the brink of catastrophic defeat. Poché had fought through the Red River Campaign, but at this point in 1865, amid the general disintegration of the Confederacy, he was reduced to commanding a small band of guerillas. Captain Darling was released on parole and allowed to go to New Orleans to arrange the release of the Confederate major held by the Federals. He succeeded in this but then, for reasons that remain unclear, was reportedly imprisoned by his own army. Finally, General Banks intervened: "There are no charges against Capt. Darling in this office and never have been. Release him immediately."[61] Nettleton's papers contain an order from headquarters, Department of Mississippi, at Vicksburg, stating that Darling had been released by the Confederate agent of exchange on May 2, 1865, and "will proceed to New Orleans and report to Capt. W. H. Sterling, Commissioner of Exchange." A report from the War Department in Washington included Darling's name on a list of officers who had been mustered out effective May 15 "on account of their service being no longer required, and physical disability."[62] By a convoluted and unpredictable sequence of events, Nettleton and Allen had succeeded in disposing of the unintentionally troublesome captain, albeit at the end of the war.

When Private Norris returned to New Orleans some four months after the rest of his regiment, he was dismayed by what he found. By then the consolidation had been completed, and his old Company K had been merged into B, commanded by an officer who, for unexplained reasons, he had always "despised." This was Captain Howell, of whom Norris said, "I hoped I should never have anything to do with, let alone being under him." Meanwhile, to make matters worse, the men were "quartered in a small cabin of their own construction and rather rough at that. It was *ventilated* first rate, for the roof *resembled* a sieve."[63] It is not surprising that he told his mother, "had I known the situation of our company while at home as I do now, I should never have shown my face in the Regt. again." In this letter Norris informed his mother that, in what he termed "a curious accident," one of his "chums," Cpl. Ken Sturtevant, after "a very few words" with a young lady, had gotten married while on furlough.[64]

On a couple of occasions the 31st received groups of recruits, though not enough to restore it to regimental strength. Being so far from home, it was more difficult for this unit to recruit in Massachusetts than for those in the eastern theater. Rich reported that sixty new men arrived in October 1864 (though Fairbank reported only seven), and Norris recorded that about thirty more arrived from Boston in March 1865 after a voyage of only nine days.[65] One of these late recruits must have possessed natural military aptitude: George Lingenfelter, a thirty-year-old blacksmith from Berkshire County, enlisted in August 1864 and was mustered out in July 1865, having attained the rank of first sergeant. After July 1864 the 31st had the unexpected distinction of being the last Massachusetts regiment still assigned to the Department of the Gulf. Its sister regiment, the 30th Massachusetts, had remained in the Gulf until that month, when it was shipped east to help defend Washington against a raid by Lt. Gen. Jubal Early. Later it was active in the final Shenandoah campaign.

The repeated passage of armies had thoroughly shattered the firm prewar social structure of Louisiana. In the resulting chaos, an element bubbled to the
surface that had previously been unable or unwilling to show itself. These
men, known variously as guerillas, jayhawkers, bushwhackers, and renegades,
were byproducts of social disintegration, emboldened by the breakdown of
order. Drawn mostly from the lowest strata of society, they were coarse, uned-
ucated, violent, and unprincipled. At first, many were guerillas authorized by
the Confederate government as auxiliaries to the regular army. Later, as Confederate draft enforcement tightened, many Louisianans took to the swamps
and canebrakes to escape. These men nursed a fierce hatred of the Confederate government and often aided Union forces as scouts and spies. As the
war and its resulting devastation continued, an increasing proportion of the
irregulars were simply bandits, preying on anyone weaker without regard to
their political sympathies. They had little concern with the causes or outcome
of the war that had opened the country to their brigandage. Contending with
the outlaws meant that the regular armies of both sides were each engaged in
two simultaneous wars; there were even examples where they cooperated to
allow for the suppression of brigands.

Accounts of this social breakdown are customarily told from the perspective of cultured planters, who lost their idyllic way of life as well as their property, but it may be blacks who suffered most. If Union forces appeared, slaves
were liberated but often mobilized for forced labor; then if Confederates regained control, captured blacks might be returned to their masters. Either
way, these African Americans were abused and plundered of what little they
had. Some, however, were able to attach themselves to the tail of a Union
army and participate in looting and destruction.

One important historical question, deserving further investigation, is if the
experience with irregulars in Louisiana influenced Confederate generals there
(and elsewhere) to reject President Davis's recommendation to adopt guerilla
warfare when the Confederacy was approaching collapse in April 1865. In fact,
the Confederacy already employed such irregulars throughout the South, so
the question really was whether to disband the organized field armies and, no
longer bound to defend territory, use guerilla tactics exclusively. Victory in
this case would not come on any battlefield but from wearing out the North so

that it no longer believed that conquering the South would be worth the effort (nor might there be much of value left to conquer). Beginning with Robert E. Lee, no general seemed willing to become a guerilla chieftain. Even men like Forrest and Richard Taylor, who had engaged in countless small actions that often resembled guerilla warfare, demurred.

Louisiana illustrates starkly the class aspect of the question. The South entered the war guided by an established code of honor, of which the highest personification was the Confederate officer in dress uniform. This code, practiced by the aristocracy and those who, if not born to the class, adopted its values, did not countenance intentionally making war on civilians. This is why William T. Sherman's tactics were so angrily deplored in Dixie—but that was only part of the story. A resort to guerilla warfare over an extended period, with no central authority or command structure, would cause massive social upheaval. As was seen in Louisiana, this turmoil could allow the dregs of society to flourish, with unpredictable results. For Southern aristocrats, such an outcome might be worse than honorably losing a war gallantly fought.

It was into this physical and human swamp that the men of the 31st Massachusetts, mostly the descendants of Puritans, were thrust. By now familiar with Louisiana and accustomed to the saddle, they performed effectively in an assignment that demanded constant vigilance. The tone and strategic rationale for this kind of warfare had been set forth by Thomas W. Sherman, in charge of the Defenses of New Orleans. Writing on November 1, 1864, before the 31st had been fully reequipped as mounted infantry, the general requested that

the Thirty-first Massachusetts, as soon as mounted, be placed at my disposal in the La Fourche District. It is my desire to more effectually close that country from raids. No fears are entertained of any regular attack upon any portion of the La Fourche line, but it is important to wholly prevent the enemy from indulging in the only thing they appear to be now capable of doing. They are intent upon getting possession of all the horses, mules, &c., in the hands of loyal citizens, and that country is so difficult and routes of travel so uncertain that they occasionally succeed in their purposes, and get away without molestation.[66]

On November 27 the 31st, under Captain Allen in the absence of Nettleton, was ordered to occupy the eastern shore of the Mississippi opposite Donaldsonville, a territory extending as far as the Amite River, some ten or fifteen miles distant, to conduct these minor but dangerous operations.[67] This order directed the regiment to protect plantations between Bayou Manchac and College Point. Later, Brigadier General Sherman issued further instructions to Allen: "keep your force . . . as much concentrated when in camp as possible. All that is necessary above the telegraph station on the levee plantations and roads are outposts furnishing the necessary pickets and vedettes." In a significant addition he ordered Allen to "keep an active system of instruction the whole time your men are in camp—that is, off the outside duties, so that they may become perfect in all duties connected with their arm."[68] The phrasing suggests that Sherman did not feel fully confident in entrusting a challenging command to a captain or in the level of competence the battalion had achieved. With two companies already stationed at Plaquemine, once Allen's force departed the 31st Massachusetts no longer had a presence in the familiar city of New Orleans.

The unit set up operations at the Hermitage (L'Hermitage) Plantation. Fairbank noted that they took up quarters "in a shed adjoining the sugar mill" on the plantation.[69] It is not clear whether any Union personnel occupied the mansion. This was very familiar territory for the men of the 31st, perhaps more so than they wished. Within it lay several government plantations, a freedmen's school, a telegraph station, and a settlement of loyal refugees. Once again the New Englanders entered the area of responsibility of Major General Taylor, assigned to the Department of Mississippi and East Louisiana after his dispute with Lieutenant General Smith; it seems that few regular troops remained under Taylor's command.

Previous Federal detachments in the area frequently had been surprised, absorbing embarrassing losses of men and equipment; initially, the 31st blundered into this pattern. A rebel attack on November 21 captured five men from the two Plaquemine companies, one of whom, Pvt. William C. Pomeroy of Agawam, was killed trying to escape; Pomeroy had earlier been captured at Sabine Cross Roads and apparently did not want to repeat the experience. Another member of this company who was taken prisoner that day, Truman Munsell of Belchertown, eventually was released on May 27, 1865, only to die of disability a week later. Although not listed as killed in action, and perhaps not classified as a military fatality at all, Munsell was surely a casualty of war. Cases like his illustrate why many believe that official figures on military losses are understated. In this same unit (the former Company F), 1st

Sgt. Charles H. Horr of Pelham was accidentally shot by one of his men on December 7, 1864. He was one who had not reenlisted and was scheduled to be discharged two weeks later, along with Cpl. Harrison Z. Horr, probably his brother. The remainder of the Plaquemine detachment pursued the attackers sixteen miles, though by then it was too late to overtake them. But the mishap proved instructive to the rest of the men, and thereafter their own raids regularly captured renegades, including some notorious individuals.

One or more companies routinely went out on "scouts" into the countryside, sometimes staying out overnight. Company I, for example, patrolled on December 1, 17, and 19, bringing in seven presumed enemies on the second venture.[70] A long report by Captain Allen covering the period December 14, 1864, to January 5, 1865, including the December 17 action, typifies the demanding, strenuous duty the 31st performed. Allen learned of an obscure settlement on Black Bayou, between the New and Amite Rivers, at which guerilla bands "had a rendezvous where they lay in safety while we were scouting the ordinary roads and whence they came at other times to make conscription and plunder about the lower end of New River." Allen had trouble finding a guide who knew this location because it was so remote and "no Federal scout had ever been there." Captain Howell's detachment of thirty men entered this "terra incognita" on December 17. They surrounded the village and went through it house by house, finding five Confederate soldiers. On the following day Allen designed a plan to capture a large body of renegades under Henry A. Doyal, but, apparently alerted to his presence, they avoided the trap. The continuous pressure on areas that had been considered safe seemed to discourage the guerillas, however, and Allen reported that eleven of them had come in to sign an oath of allegiance. During the period covered by his report, the 31st took twenty-one prisoners—an assortment of soldiers, deserters, renegades, and spies. This was war at the retail level, far from the mighty battles in which a hundred thousand men might be engaged. In contrast to the mass graves into which unknown dead were piled, each captive received individual processing and attention, probably more than they wished. At other times the soldiers of the 31st might have found this activity adventurous, but carried on through the winter in a region where the boundary between land and water constantly shifted, it was an exhausting business.[71]

In late December Captain Howell led a detachment that boarded the steamer *Thomas* to set up a post opposite Plaquemine. Their main purpose was to guard a nearby telegraph station.[72] Howell's force included twenty-five black soldiers, who Rich identified as members of the 11th Rhode Island Colored Artillery.[73] In his letter to Nettleton on personnel affairs, Captain Allen fretted that Howell's transfer "removes him from our command almost entirely, making him report to the C.O. at Plaquemine as much as Rice."[74]

As a result of these moves, the 31st was once again broken up, scattered over more than twelve miles on both sides of the big river. This was done before the reorganization of the regiment into a battalion was finalized, so the original company designations were still in effect. Companies F and H, under Captain Rice, remained at Plaquemine, on the west side of the Mississippi. The other companies were stationed on the east bank at several plantations in Ascension Parish. Company E, under Lieutenant Lee, occupied the Hermitage plantation, named for Andrew Jackson's home in Tennessee and which served as battalion headquarters, opposite Donaldsonville. Companies I and K, under Captain Howell and Lieutenant Bond respectively, were posted at Doyal's plantation opposite Plaquemine, about nine miles above the Hermitage. The owner of this plantation, Henry A. Doyal, was a Confederate officer, considered by many Union men to be a guerilla.[75] Company G, under Lieutenant Sagendorph, was posted at John L. Manning's plantation, a few miles below the Hermitage. Subsequently, the post at Doyal's was considered too exposed, and the men were moved to the Le Blanc plantation, closer to the Hermitage and a telegraph station.[76]

From these outposts, refugees guided the troops on surprise raids, frequently at night, against renegade camps. These attacks brought in a motley haul of irregulars, but a party under Lieutenant Bond killed one McRory, leader of a band that had long been a terror to Unionists in the area. It was arduous, often dangerous work and scarcely mentioned in the history books. A hasty note from Bond confirmed that the duty was wearing on men and horses alike: "I would resp'y [respectfully] represent to the Capt'n Command'g that the horses of my Company have had nothing to eat since Friday morn'g, except two small feeds of hay,—and today nothing whatever,—and ask for permission either to borrow at Donaldsonville, or to seize corn near here."[77]

A larger push across the Amite on January 30, 1865, captured seventeen prisoners, with the loss of one man drowned. Noteworthy among those taken was the notorious guerilla leader Samuel King, who had tormented Union forces for more than two years. Captain Allen recounted this triumph with great delight: "Bond had the distinguished honor of charging into that settlement [the so-called French Settlement] and capturing the most prisoners, while Sagendorph immortalized himself by running old King down and capturing him with his own hand." He added: "Sag emptied his revolver at the old scoundrel, and deserves to be scolded, as we all told him, for not killing him then. But when we took him out in the woods, and stood around him, 12 men with loaded muskets and 5 officers, and listened to his appeal for life, we were not bloodthirsty enough to kill him *outright*." Allen was apparently surprised to find that King's "first appeal was by a Masonic sign. I did not acknowledge it then, but afterwards tried him and found him quite bright, says he is a Royal Arch." Coming late in the war, this action, though of only local importance, was perhaps the most satisfying and unalloyed success the 31st Massachusetts had achieved. No wonder that Allen crowed, "we have been treading on air ever since."[78]

While being transported to prison in New Orleans, King tried to escape and was shot by a guard, Pvt. John White of Company E, one of the men recruited locally after the occupation of New Orleans. The steamer *Ohio Belle* had landed at the Hermitage plantation, where it had picked up the batch of prisoners and their 31st Massachusetts guards. "The corporal in command of the Guards had particular orders to watch closely the motions of King, as he was known to be a desperate character." Due to fog, the ship had to lay over that night, and shortly after midnight King "attempted to wrest the gun from the hands of a sentinel." White's shot killed him almost instantly. The *Ohio Belle* proceeded to sink during the night, but the corporal, William H. Exford of Pownal, Vermont, kept the prisoners under control and loaded them on the next boat. King was buried at a place called Twelve Mile Point (probably long since effaced by changes in the river's course). Private White was temporarily arrested by the captain of the ship but quickly released and commended by the officer who reported the incident.[79] These successes were much appreciated by Brigadier General Sherman, who issued a testimonial:

> The general commanding tenders his thanks to Captain W. I. Allen, 31st Massachusetts Volunteers, and the battalion of mounted infantry under his command, for their uniform good conduct since occupying their present position, and particularly for the unusual success which has thus far attended their operations in capturing the noted guerilla leader and desperado, King, and at various times large numbers of gue-

rilla bands infesting that region, thus promoting security and good order upon that frontier, with the exercise of a good judgment that led to no unnecessary bloodshed.[80]

Meanwhile, the two companies (later combined into one, Company D) stationed at Plaquemine, under the command of Captain Rice, functioned as mounted pickets. At first, relatively small parties went out, and then only infrequently and not usually for long distances. On the last day of 1864, one of these forays, led by the provost marshal, Lt. Jules Masicot, "returned, minus three of their number, and the Provost Marshall," according to Rice. "Verdict: whiskey did it." At Indian Village the men ran into a larger party of rebels, numbering thirty or forty. Rice continued: "The P. M. walked directly into the hands of the rebs. and two of the men were probably taken while trying to gratify an illegitimate appetite for poultry. How the third man was taken we don't know." The three captured were Cpl. John L. Hall of Great Barrington and two privates, all from Company H.[81] As a result of having his men "gobbled" in this way, Rice decided "never to willingly send out any more of my men under charge of any officers than those of our own Reg't."[82]

In the latter part of January, the commander at Plaquemine, Maj. R. G. Shaw of the 11th U.S. Colored Artillery, picked up the pace of activity so that the two companies of the 31st there were out almost constantly. The weather resembled what the men had experienced during the previous January, with frequent cold snaps punctuated by rain and resultant mud. On the twenty-sixth Lieutenant Barber took seventy men to Indian Village "to remain in that vicinity, guarding the roads leading to or from Bayou Goula."[83] Their purpose was to cut off a party of rebels commanded by a Captain Williams. Even Rice had to admit that this foe was "very enterprising, and has thus far been a very successful leader." His forte, Rice explained, "has been to intercept and capture the couriers running between Donaldsonville and Plaquemine." After losing nearly twenty men in this way, and "the patience of our military authorities being somewhat tired by such unwarrantable proceedings on his part, an expedition was sent from the vicinity of Donaldsonville to clear him out." The plan was to have Barber's force, which mustered perhaps half of the available manpower of the two Plaquemine companies, intercept Williams if the main body drove him in their direction. Williams, however, was able to slip away, and Barber's men caught only a brief glimpse of three members of his advance guard.[84]

Frequent contact allowed the guerillas to form an idea of Union troop dispositions and led to a plan that, by massing their strength, might allow them to bag entire small garrisons. Late at night on February 3, Rice was "awakened by one of the men rapping on the door and calling out 'Captain, the rebs. are charging in upon us.'" As the captain said, "This was rather a startling announcement with which to disturb ones peaceful slumbers, but there was no time to stretch or rub my eyes." Hurriedly, he formed up his men outside, where they could "plainly hear the rebs. coming thro' the water, (for the roads and fields below us are all over-flowed at intervals for miles) and yelling like fiends. From the splashing they made, we thought they were on horseback, and the shouting convinced us that we were outnumbered." Rice was determined not to have his detachment "gobbled" without a fight, and as soon as the enemy drew close enough to be seen in the darkness, his men commenced firing. "It was so dark that a man could not be distinguished at more than four or five rods distance."[85]

A rebel who approached too close was wounded and captured. He informed Rice that the attackers numbered 160 men. Against this the captain had only thirty-one men plus himself, but the enemy might not have been fully aware of this advantage. Moreover, Rice's men by then were veteran soldiers, accustomed to working together. Many of the guerillas were experienced fighters, though not in organized combat; in order to have amassed so large a force, they must have included many inexperienced "citizens of a jayhawking turn of mind," as Rice phrased it. Still, the odds were daunting, so the captain sent for Lieutenants Bond and Barber, who had the rest of the company at Indian Village.

At a critical moment, when the rebels could be heard shifting men to Rice's rear, "the welcome sound of galloping broke upon our ears." The volume of hoof beats and cheering made it seem that the entire relief force had arrived, but in reality it was only Bond's squad of eight men. Five or ten minutes later, Barber came up with thirteen or fourteen additional reinforcements. Immediately after, the attackers blew a horn signaling retreat and melted back into the swamp. Barber recalled that his men spent the rest of the night in water nearly waist deep, firing in the direction of any noises they detected.[86] It proved to be a highly satisfactory encounter for the Plaquemine detachment, as they had beaten off an enemy force of up to 160 irregulars. Rice believed that the attackers were commanded by King, not knowing that that notorious renegade was already dead. On the following day the 31st Massachusetts brought in two mortally wounded rebels, while five others came out of the swamp and gave themselves up. Only one man of Rice's force was killed, Michael Haggerty of Adams, "who had the top of his head blown off, killing him instantly. He was one of the recruits that have joined since our return from furlough, and this was his first experience under fire, and, poor fellow, his last, too."[87] This constituted the battalion's last major clash in Louisiana before heading off on its final adventure.

Initial reports of Rice's engagement indicated that he had faced a force of 500 rebels. When Brigadier General Sherman was informed, he wrote: "If the enemy is as numerous as represented, Captain Rice should have fallen back. But it is presumed that the number is much exaggerated."[88] The general's surmise was correct, and subsequent reports amended the number to about 150. Sherman's frustration with this kind of fighting, what the French call *petite guerre*, was amply displayed when he wrote, "Let all these scoundrels be either captured or driven well back into rebeldom."[89]

Captain Rice's personal adventures were not at an end, however. This time, as he readily admitted, "my tongue had got me into a scrape." Three days after the nighttime battle, he went up to Plaquemine and called on Major Shaw: "I tried to get the Company ordered back to town, as I could see no use in keeping us there any longer and the men were getting used up. I told him that the men had been ten days constantly on duty (wet through on six of them) without a chance to change their clothes and without a whole night's sleep." To Rice's chagrin, Shaw replied "that if I had used my men so, I had not managed my Company properly. I didn't enjoy having such a remark as that made in the hearing of half a dozen officers and citizens, and consequently rejoined in my peculiarly mild and polite way, 'If you think so, you ought to Court Martial me, and put some one in command of the Company who can properly manage it.'" The upshot of the matter was that Rice was arrested.[90] This outcome is recorded laconically in the diary of the Plaquemine detachment, almost certainly written by Rice himself: "Capt. Rice having returned to Plaquemine to endeavor to get his company relieved from such incessant duty, succeeded only so far as he was personally concerned. He was placed in close arrest by order of Maj. Shaw."[91]

When the 31st moved out, Rice remained under arrest. He was released early in March on orders of Brigadier General Sherman, who ordered "that no further proceedings be had in the case." The captain was pleased by this outcome: "In view of the whole matter, I cannot help thinking that my way of mismanaging my Comp'y was not displeasing to Gen. Sherman, who is an old regular officer, whose Battery gained distinction in the Mexican War, and who lost a leg at Port Hudson." He concluded: "I may without egotism, claim as fair a record as Maj. Shaw, concerning whom I heard the Colonel of his own Reg't say not three days since, 'Whiskey commands the Post of Plaquemine.' Still the three weeks in durance vile have been tedious ones, and I'm glad they're over."[92]

Rice's pen—in addition to his tongue—was capable of getting him in trouble. A few weeks earlier Lt. James M. Stewart, the regimental adjutant, wrote asking for a list of men being mustered out. Rice responded that he had not received the request and then gratuitously added "that a less overbearing tone in your communications would be quite as likely to ensure prompt and satisfactory replies to them."[93] Writing on order of Captain Allen, Stewart replied, "The language used in the foregoing instrument is considered disrespectful to Regimental Headqrs."[94] In his response a few days later, Rice concluded, "I stand ready at all times to defend myself against charges of conduct discreditable or unbecoming to me either as a soldier, officer, or gentleman."[95] Rice seems to have possessed the overly developed sense of honor that was prevalent in that age; on the other hand, he might have been reacting to some personal stress.

Former Major Fordham decided to set up a store inside the Union lines across from Plaquemine, and men of the 31st helped him build it.[96] Allen told Nettleton that "Hopkins" had obtained a permit for a store in the vicinity of the Hermitage plantation, where the main part of the regiment was stationed. This reference is almost certainly not to former Lieutenant Colonel Hopkins but to another former officer, Capt. Orrin S. Hopkins, who like Fordham had been mustered out in November 1864. Allen admitted that he had approved the application grudgingly "because there was no decent ground for refusal, but hadn't the least idea he could get it through." Conversely, he expressed the wish that Fordham could have gotten his permit to locate "here" instead of upriver near Plaquemine.[97] Even if these officers had no prospect of remaining in the service, it seems puzzling that they chose the uncertain future of keeping store for soldiers whose location was subject to the whims of higher command.

Hopkins and Fordham's timing proved unfortunate, as they evidently did not suspect that the stay of the 31st Massachusetts in Louisiana was coming to a close. If officers with presumably good connections were unaware that a move was coming, there was even less likelihood that this knowledge would have filtered down to lower levels. Almost as soon as the detachment arrived at the telegraph station opposite Plaquemine, the men began building quarters and shelters for horses. Since it was midwinter, this was understandable, but they included touches, such as fireplaces at each end of the barracks, that would not have been necessary if they thought their tenure would be brief.[98]

Only days after the former officers were granted permission to set up their stores, the 31st Massachusetts received orders to "immediately concentrate at Carrollton."[99] Although these instructions were in hand by February 11 and most of the regiment had departed for Carrollton soon after, a shortage of boats delayed the assembly. After an officer and twelve men from the 3rd Rhode Island Cavalry came over from Plaquemine to relieve the force at the telegraph station, Company E (and perhaps others) departed downriver on the steamer *Iberville*. Sergeant Rich, highly unimpressed, described the Rhode Islanders as "a pretty rough and dirty looking lot of soldiers," whose appearance was not enhanced by their "very poor horses."[100] Their shabby condition was probably due to the fact that they had been out almost constantly pursuing guerillas in the semiliquefied landscape. Other elements of the 3rd Rhode Island Cavalry later relieved the remaining detachments of the 31st Massachusetts, whose long wait ended on February 23, when the steamer *Henry Chouteau* docked to load Company H. A further delay ensued as the boat had to tie up overnight because of fog. At last, on the afternoon of the twenty-fourth, the last contingent reached Carrollton, rejoining the rest of the 31st "encamped in a perfect mudhole."[101] After enduring this for about ten days, the entire brigade was collected at the old campground above Carrollton. While there, another thirty-three recruits arrived from Massachusetts to join in this last adventure.[102] Ten members who had been missing and were listed as deserters also rejoined the 31st during this period and were reinstated without punishment except for loss of pay while absent.[103]

12

MOBILE AND HOME

MARCH–OCTOBER 1865

At last Union forces were ready to complete the conquest of Mobile, Alabama. In August 1864 Admiral Farragut had led a naval attack on Mobile Bay and the city in cooperation with the army. During the course of the fight, the admiral reportedly coined another of the U.S. Navy's unforgettable battle slogans when he exclaimed, "Damn the torpedoes [mines], full speed ahead!" Whether he really uttered something resembling those words cannot be confirmed, but the widespread belief that he had did wonders to expand his reputation. In the battle Farragut again passed two formidable coastal-defense forts protecting the outer harbor and destroyed the small Confederate naval force defending the city; the army subsequently captured the forts. At this time part of the 31st Massachusetts was performing provost-marshal duties in New Orleans, eventually taking charge of enemy soldiers captured at the Mobile forts and processing three hundred of them for transport to the sprawling prison facility at Elmira, New York.[1] These actions accomplished the main strategic purpose of the campaign, which was to close off Mobile as a haven for blockade runners. The Confederacy now had no open ports in the Gulf of Mexico east of Texas, but Union planners still deemed it important to seize the city itself.

The 31st Massachusetts had a presence at Farragut's assault in the person of Lt. Joseph Hallett. Long periods of gazing through field glasses and telescopes had damaged that officer's eyesight, forcing him to resign from the Signal Corps. Still eager to serve, he took on the duties of a quartermaster and ordnance officer and was on board one of the ships in the Union fleet during the battle. After running past the guns of Fort Morgan, Farragut confronted the defensive fleet, headed by the armored ram CSS *Tennessee*, considered one of the most formidable warships afloat. As Hallett observed, "opening of their stern ports to fire their guns was their fatal mistake" as it allowed Union gunners to fire through the open ports and eventually disable their foe. The captured *Tennessee* was repaired and turned against its former owners, its invulnerability confirmed when copious shot from Fort Morgan bounced off the ironclad without causing damage. This was a disheartening experience for the Confederates, who soon surrendered the fort. Hallett was able to enter the post "and viewed the destruction on all sides, dismounted cannon, broken stone and bricks everywhere, battered walls, confusion all around."[2]

The 1865 operation against Mobile itself remains little known, being completely overshadowed by the climax of the grand campaign around Richmond and Petersburg, Virginia. In preparation for the task, the army conducted the usual reorganization, in this instance combining the 1st Louisiana (U.S.), 2nd Illinois, and 2nd New York Cavalry Regiments with the mounted infantry of the 31st Massachusetts into the "Separate Cavalry Brigade" to be commanded by Brig. Gen. Thomas J. Lucas of Indiana.[3] Lucas, a volunteer officer, had performed well during the Red River Campaign. Lieutenant Colonel Nettleton's request to be relieved of his general-court-martial duty so that he could resume command of his battalion was granted.[4] In early March Lucas's brigade assembled at Carrollton. Orders specified that the troops would be armed with Sharps carbines and sabers but that only noncommissioned officers would be permitted to carry revolvers. This armament more closely resembled that of a cavalry unit than mounted infantry, which is unsurprising considering that three of the four component units of the brigade were designated cavalry.

Army strategists had determined that this operation would be conducted from Pensacola, Florida, rather than by marching overland from Louisiana. While Pensacola was closer to Mobile, it turned out that the country between the port cities was rather barren and unable to provide support for men and horses. Nevertheless, the plan was for Major General Steele to lead a force consisting of two infantry divisions (one colored), three artillery batteries, and the cavalry to attack Mobile's defenses from the rear while General Canby, also the department commander, approached from the front. (One of the batteries with Steele was Nims's, which had been reconstituted with new guns after being overrun at Sabine Cross Roads.) There was potential for discord, as Canby had been responsible for having Steele removed from command of the Department of Arkansas the previous November. In contrast to General in Chief Grant's relentless vendettas against generals such as Banks, Butler, and

Rosecrans, he supported Steele and had worked to secure another field command for him.

In this campaign Canby commanded 45,200 troops, including A. J. Smith's Sixteenth Corps. Steele's force totaled 13,200 of this, of which Lucas's cavalry comprised 2,500 men.[5] In addition, he was supported by the navy in the abundant navigable waterways around Mobile. This powerful aggregation far outweighed anything the Confederates could bring to bear. Canby had spent the preceding months accumulating information about his objective from prisoners, deserters, and scouts. One such report, by Elliot Bridgman, a former officer in the 31st Massachusetts, addressed "the geographical, military, political, and social conditions of the country lying on the coast between the Mississippi and Apalachiola [sic] Rivers." In addition to presenting a wealth of other data, Bridgman observed: "The political status of this section of country is favorable to the Union. The people generally are tired of the war, and, in fact, many of them were never in favor of it."[6]

On March 6 two sections of the battalion, among them Luther Fairbank's company, with their horses embarked on the *Warrior* for Fort Barrancas at Pensacola, arriving on the tenth and eleventh.[7] Some men managed to get drunk on these journeys.[8] Other vessels, such as the *Clyde, Alice Vivian,* and *Corinthian,* also carried troops, with the final company of the 31st Massachusetts transported on the steamer *General Banks* on March 9. In addition to the reminiscent name of that ship, these men passed Fort Pike and stopped at Ship Island, symbolically unwinding their careers in the Gulf.[9]

Already reduced in numbers, the 31st lost three more members to desertion at Fort Barrancas. These fellows had joined only two months earlier. Two gave their residence as Philadelphia and the other New Haven, so that although they listed the Massachusetts towns of Dudley (Worcester County) and Monson (Hampden County) as temporary locations, they may have had only a limited commitment to the state. They may have had only a limited commitment to serving at all once each had collected his $325 bounty. There is no way to determine whether the three belonged to the despised category of bounty jumpers, men who enlisted and deserted repeatedly to grab the generous bounties offered to volunteers. Desertion at Barrancas offered poor prospects for continuing that pursuit, though, as they were hundreds of miles from any point where they could enlist in a Northern unit with any credibility. The only realistic mode of traveling to the North was by ship, which would have raised unwelcome questions as to why men of military age were on the loose. Bounty jumping in the late months of the war could be a rewarding criminal activity but was also risky, as the usual penalty for those captured was death, and such men were granted little sympathy. Perhaps the approaching smell of gunpowder was more of a factor in the desertion of these men than any visions of further gain from criminal enterprise.

During several days encamped at Fort Barrancas while making final preparations for the march, Fairbank, who seems to have been skilled as a tailor as well as a carpenter, was kept busy repairing and altering clothing: "All government clothing needs to be sewed over again before wearing."[10] He did not bother to observe that contractors were becoming wealthy supplying this defective clothing to the army. Steele's column started off late in the afternoon of March 19 and crossed a bay to Pensacola by fording. The mounted soldiers had been ordered to be ready at 8 A.M., but in typical army "hurry up and wait" fashion, the order to move did not come until 5 P.M. Capt. L. Frederick Rice reported that "in the forenoon when the darky troops crossed, the water was hardly knee deep, but where our time came, the tide was in, and the darkness preventing the men from seeing precisely where they ought to go, some of them had to swim for it, and two lost their horses and nearly drowned themselves."[11]

Plans for the campaign called for Steele's force to move almost due north, generally following the Escambia River, into Alabama before turning west toward Mobile, rather than taking the shortest route. This would allow them to protect Canby's flank and to disrupt the vital rail line from Montgomery to Mobile. Roads in the region, poor under the best of circumstances, had been made worse by persistent rains. Canby informed Chief of Staff Halleck: "For the last forty days we have had but seven of favorable weather. During all the rest of this time heavy easterly and southeasterly gales and dense fog have prevailed, rendering the transportation of troops and supplies both tedious and dangerous."[12] Once the column got underway, almost one whole day was spent waiting for roads to be corduroyed (a process in which a layer of rough logs are laid at right angles to the course of the road to provide a more solid surface).

Contact with the enemy began on March 23, and a more substantial encounter took place a few miles inside the Florida border on the twenty-fifth. This battle, commonly identified as Bluff Springs but sometimes as Canoe Creek, is now almost unknown, yet it was the largest clash on the march to Mobile and had a decisive effect on the campaign. It appears that the engagement was fought entirely by cavalry without any infantry involvement. If Lucas had faced a more formidable enemy force, he might have been in trouble, but he was opposed by only two Alabama cavalry regiments, which, judging by the course of the action, were well past their fighting prime. One powerful charge by the Union horsemen smashed the Confederates and scattered them in all directions. Probably while trying to rally his fleeing men, Brig. Gen. James Holt Clanton was severely wounded and fell into Union hands. At the time it was thought that his wounds were mortal, but Clanton survived (only to be murdered in Tennessee in 1871).

The 31st Massachusetts was not heavily engaged in this fight, which was mainly borne by the 1st Louisiana Cavalry (U.S.). In a later stage, when some of the Confederates attempted to form a new line on the Escambia River, they were driven out by Lucas's artillery. At that point the 31st Massachusetts charged across the river, seized the enemy positions, and held them until infantry support arrived. It was a satisfying little action for the 31st, cited in Lucas's report, and better yet cost no casualties. Clanton's cavalry had been unable to make a successful defense of their home state. Lucas reported: "The enemy was demoralized to such a degree by the resistless force with which I pressed them, that arms, clothing, and everything that impeded their flight was thrown away and scattered along the road and through the woods."[13] He later noted capturing eighteen officers and 111 enlisted men out of a force estimated at 600 men and boasted that his foes were "completely disorganized and scattered." Steele's forces destroyed part of the railroad to Montgomery and captured two trains and their crews, a ruinous blow to the flimsy Confederate supply system. On March 28 the expedition continued its march toward Blakely, Alabama, over "roads worse than any we have yet travelled," and made about twelve miles.[14]

Farther on, the main problem became finding food for the men and forage for the horses. This was not a surprise, as at the outset of the campaign Steele had informed Canby, "From all the information I can obtain, it is probable that we shall find neither forage nor provisions between here and Pollard, except that the cavalry may find some on by-roads."[15] Lt. Milton Sagendorph's company was sent off on a scout and brought back news that supply ships from Pensacola were unable to ascend the Escambia River. As a result, the troops were immediately put on half rations. Capt. Luther Howell described the consequences: "We were two weeks in the most barren pine forest you ever saw—

not a house for many miles. We only took forage for two days for the horses and rations for 5 days for the men, so that we came very near starving." Cutting back allowed their hardtack to hold out ten days, but "after that we had only fresh meat and that of the poorest quality. The men were so hungry that they would beg for an ear of corn and would knock down a pig, cut out a portion and eat it raw and warm; and the horses became almost shadows by their total abstinence from all food for so long a time."[16] Thomas Norris added that the column traveled for five days "before we came to a single habitation."[17] Fairbank had the same impression: "Since leaving Pensacola we have been in the woods (pine) and have seen nothing but log cabins."[18] New England soldiers, unaccustomed to encountering such extensive desolate territory except in northern Maine, were appalled by this gloomy, primitive country.

In his message reporting the victory of March 25, Lucas also observed: "Our forage is entirely exhausted, and the country affords but an insufficient supply. Our rations also are nearly consumed."[19] No rations were issued on March 30, and "the men shared with their horses the few ears of corn dealt out."[20] Nevertheless, morale remained good, and the expedition covered ten miles. Scouts were sent out to look for corn in this dismal region. Finally, on March 31 a party under Captain Rice came upon a gristmill at Stockton on the Tensas River and ground enough corn to keep them going. Temporary relief for some of the men arrived from an unexpected source when they drove away two regiments of rebels who had been cooking supper. "They left it and our boys eat [sic] it for them," William Rich wrote with apparent glee.[21] It was testimony to how hungry they must have been if even meager Confederate provisions seemed appetizing. For the remainder of the men, their famine ended on April 3 when regular rations were delivered. Fairbank rejoiced with customary sarcasm: "Hurrah, our rations came today and once more I can taste good salt pork and hard tack and coffee for supper."[22]

There was almost constant skirmishing as the army approached Mobile, with Rich reporting that one man was killed and six or seven wounded on April 1.[23] Still, the inescapable impression was that the Confederates' fighting spirit, which had sustained the South against great odds for four years, was fading. In individual clashes the Southerners were often not greatly outnumbered, if at all—in one encounter Rich thought that the rebels were a thousand strong against five hundred, maintained an adequate complement of artillery, and knew that they could always fall back into strong fortifications.[24] Yet their resistance seemed perfunctory, carried out for appearance's sake rather than in any hope of success. By then, the quality of Southern soldiery had undoubtedly declined. The most dedicated and high-spirited fighting men lay dead at Malvern Hill, Gettysburg, Shiloh, Perryville, and countless other battlefields. Probably the same could be said of the Union, but the North had much larger reserves to draw from and could compensate with the weight of numbers.

On the approach to Mobile, Union forces encountered another distressing obstacle—"torpedoes," as they called them, but now known as landmines. Rich described them as shells four to sixteen inches long filled with powder and bullets or anything else that could be used as shrapnel.[25] An indignant Norris referred to them as "barbarous and murderous actions."[26] (Their advent and use was one more way in which the American Civil War anticipated the twentieth-century conflicts in Europe.) Considering the declining state of the Confederate military machine, these devilish devices worked surprisingly well, killing or wounding men and destroying horses. Norris reported that "a man had his head blown off by one," and Nettleton's report of April 2 confirmed that a man was killed by a torpedo. In addition to exercising still greater caution, the Yankees responded by setting enemy prisoners to remove the torpedoes—a clever tactic, though perhaps of questionable moral authority.[27]

Despite these impediments, Lucas's cavalry had succeeded in driving the Confederates into their extensive works at Blakely, on the eastern shore of Mobile Bay.[28] The job of the cavalry was done, and it was up to the infantry and artillery to dislodge the enemy. In an unusual case of excellent timing, Steele and his infantry caught up with Lucas and his horsemen only a day later, on April 2.

That same evening, in faraway Virginia, the Confederates began the evacuation of Richmond, though no one in Alabama would have been aware of that. Even lacking that knowledge, the Confederacy seemed to be crumbling, fighting fitfully but without its former zeal. The first Union forces to enter Richmond were commanded by Brigadier General Weitzel, well known to the 31st Massachusetts. Weitzel, who had once agonizingly pleaded not to be placed in command of black troops, now marched into the abandoned capital at the head of the all-black units (commanded by all-white officers) of the Twenty-Fifth Corps.

Soon after arriving near Blakely, Lucas advised Canby of the poor condition of his forces: "Our horses have suffered very severely from overwork and a lack of forage, the country through which we have been operating having furnished an insufficient supply." He recommended that "about 300 horses will be required to fully supply the deficiency existing and remount my command."[29] Perhaps before receiving this report, Canby ordered Lucas's weary horsemen to the northeast to guard "all the main avenues by land and river to Blakely." Those, he wrote, "must be permanently and strongly guarded, and zealous and effective parties must scour the country along the front of the guard."[30]

The Confederates were now bottled up in their strongholds of Blakely and Spanish Fort. Howell believed that there were four thousand men in the Blakely garrison, though probably an exaggeration. Remembering former encounters, he feared that the Federals "shall doubtless take it in due time, but when I remember how long we were taking Port Hudson I cannot be so sanguine about our immediate success."[31] General Canby, a methodical officer, shared this attitude and spent days collecting heavy guns in preparation for a long siege. Contributing to this caution was a report from the doomed city of Richmond, passed on to Secretary of War Stanton: "The preparations for the defense of Mobile are very complete. Provisions for a six-month's siege have been accumulated. General Taylor has done everything for the successful defense of the city."[32] Grant also subscribed to this line of reasoning, telling Stanton, "I have good reasons to believe orders have gone from Richmond to hold Mobile at all costs."[33] By this point, the most potent weapon in the Confederacy's arsenal was not its actual military capability but the embedded memory of its former strength. Military strategists are often accused of fighting the last war. In this case Union leaders were still influenced by an earlier stage of the current war. They did not yet grasp that the Confederate army of 1865 was a shadow of what it had been two years earlier.

The South had never had much success in holding fixed positions, and in the waning days of the Confederacy, there was much less chance of doing so. After putting up a show of resistance, Blakely and Spanish Fort surrendered on April 8 and 9. (The ninth was also the day Lee surrendered at Appomattox, but the two events were unrelated except as signs of general collapse.) Union troops assaulted two outlying posts, Batteries Tracy and Huger, on the night of the eleventh but found them unoccupied. Throughout the war, the Confederates had never been able to resolve the problem of holding besieged positions, though in this instance experience had taught them to let most of the garrison flee before the surrender. Norris, though only a young private, made a perceptive observation when he commented, "The whole Rebel army that occupied this place have skedaddled in dismay, leaving behind them one of the strongest fortified places in the whole Confederacy, not excepting Richmond."[34] Rich noted that the eighth was also the anniversary of "our skedaddle from Sabine." A tangible reminder of how much things had changed in that year was the discovery that one of the brass artillery pieces captured at Blakely had been taken from Nims's battery during the rout at Sabine Cross Roads.[35]

With its defenses vanquished, Mobile formally surrendered on April 12, thereby avoiding destruction. A week earlier General Canby had assigned the 31st Massachusetts to headquarters and provost-marshal duties, which gave it responsibility for handling prisoners, more of which were brought in each day. On April 10 the 31st took charge of 2,500 captives, and the eventual total may have reached 7,000 men.[36] In carrying out these duties, Fairbank witnessed an ugly but revealing incident. As black soldiers went to take control of some prisoners, "A nigger bayonetted one of them for saying they would come Fort Pillow on them again." As depicted by Fairbank, the response of the Northern soldiers was telling and foreshadowed the racial tensions of Reconstruction: "Our men were going to fire into the nigger troops to prevent them killing the rebs after surrendering in the Fort."[37]

The 31st Massachusetts moved into camp on Church Street in Mobile on April 14, the night on which Lincoln was shot in Washington. Sergeant Rich called the location "a beautiful pine grove" not far from the river.[38] When the battalion entered Mobile, the remaining veterans must have reflected on their arrival at New Orleans nearly three years before, even if they were unaware that Butler at that time had entertained hopes of adding the Alabama port to his conquests. This time there were no howling hostile mobs to greet the Northerners. Instead, Norris noted that "everyone seemed glad to see us, although they were a little frightened, but they soon got over that."[39] The spirit of defiance had faded, replaced by a dull resignation. Most Southerners still supported the dream of independence and hated those responsible for crushing it—perhaps more passionately than ever after the enormous sacrifices they had made—but the ability to achieve that goal had been drained by repeated defeat and hopeless impoverishment. Never had the feelings of the two sections, which were now about to be hammered back together by unforeseen methods, been farther apart. The North was riding a cresting wave of success that finally dashed against the horror of Lincoln's assassination, which brought about an emotional overload perhaps beyond comprehension at this great distance in time. The South, empty of much of its hope, manpower, and wealth, descended into a pervasive despondency. Flowers bloomed in that overwrought spring as they had in 1860, but both sides knew that they were entering an uncertain world.

News of Lincoln's death reached the troops at Mobile on April 20, which meant that they learned of his shooting and death simultaneously and did not experience the agonized waiting of people in and around Washington. Everywhere the tragic news brought a mixture of sorrow and anger. Conspiracy theories flourished—with good reason as it turned out, though not for those originally voiced that involved Jefferson Davis. Captain Howell said, "I hardly care whether the war stops now or not if its continuance could have the effect of bringing to *justice* those who are guilty of this terrible crime."[40] Later he added, "I have done nothing but think of it and talk of it for weeks, and I almost wish I could forget it."[41] Perhaps he succeeded in forgetting, as his surviving letters make no further mention of Lincoln. Whatever the men may have thought of him in the beginning, Lincoln had become a revered figure at the time of his death. Howell wrote, "Only one such a man lives in a century."[42] Most of the soldiers had come to see Lincoln as a comrade in arms, a fellow sufferer in the war. After the sacrifices they had made, both he and they were so deeply invested in pursuing the war to a finish that the men could not dare contemplate that it might have been avoidable.

Though surrounded by widespread misery, the remaining members of the 31st Massachusetts entered a halcyon period. As recently as their last campaign, the dismal march from Pensacola, they had undergone serious deprivation and danger. Now, safely encamped in Mobile, they could at last enjoy the pleasures of being soldiers. Duties were light and inconsequential, at times even pleasant, though the officers, concerned with maintaining military order, continued to hold daily drills. In contrast to their impressions of other places in the South, the Northern soldiers had a positive opinion of Mobile. Rich described it as "a very pretty city" and added that the inhabitants, seemingly relieved that the war and its privations were coming to an end, "appear to like the change very well." Norris agreed with this assessment, writing that Mobile was "very nicely laid out, [and] has very pretty buildings and parks," adding that he had met several Unionist families.[43] At one point he fancied that he might be courting a young woman in one of these homes: "She is in the room at the present time, which will account for the looks of this as my mind is anywhere but to writing."[44] This fleeting romance apparently took an unexpected turn when the young lady "won the good graces of one of our boys"—Jim Galletty—who, according to Norris, was going to take her home with him.[45] On his first night in town, Fairbank reported, "I am all right, for I am in with a yaller girl, so have plenty of grub."[46] The unpleasant racial incident of a couple of days previous had not left any lasting scars on this buoyant person; after recording many visits to the theater, he went so far as to assert, "I would live south if all was like this gay city."[47]

Yet the war sputtered along on its own energy like an abandoned campfire. Rich reported a skirmish as late as April 15, in which the rebels came out badly.[48] Only a day later news arrived that Lee had surrendered the remnants of the once seemingly invincible Army of Northern Virginia. "The blows fall thick and fast upon the sinking Confederate army," summarized Fairbank.[49] Combined with the taking of Mobile, these stunning triumphs had predictable effects on morale, and Norris confided that "most of the boys here are beginning to be taken down with the home fever."[50] Even after that, a few spasmodic twitches remained in the war. Rich estimated that Maj. Gen. Dabney Herndon Maury, Confederate commander of the District of the Gulf, still had five thousand troops under his control. Whether accurate or not, the number of men available to Maury was shrinking steadily: "The Rebs are deserting by companies every day."[51]

At that time there were still thousands of active Confederate soldiers, militiamen, and guerillas scattered throughout the South. If they had been assembled in one place, they might have composed a formidable force, though their support services would have been rickety, but there was no longer a central command structure to direct such a concentration. More to the point, the fight had gone out of most of these men, and their main desire was to go home. They had evidently concluded that if the revered Lee could not keep up the fight, nothing that transpired in the backwaters of Alabama could make much difference. The final proof of how far the tattered Confederacy had sunk came on April 20, when the two sides attempted a prisoner exchange. Out of the men held by Union forces, two hundred could not be found who wanted to return to the Confederate army. As Rich summed up, "They are sick of fighting."[52] It was a long descent from the days in which the belles of New Orleans gathered in their finery and waved perfumed handkerchiefs as they sent off exchanged Southern prisoners. By 1865, the Confederacy had been hollowed out to a shell that did not take much effort to push over, a collapse that foreshadowed the fall of the empires in 1918.

Once cracks appeared in the Southern edifice, disintegration proceeded rapidly. Much of what is termed "war weariness" in the South may have been sheer physical debility. Civilians had made immense sacrifices to support the armies; by 1865, many in both segments of the populace lacked adequate food, clothing, and medical care. They had plunged with enthusiasm into a cavalier war, but the ceaseless demands of industrial warfare had ground them down. The visible decay of the Confederacy emboldened the Unionist element present in most of the states but that had been suppressed by Southern authorities. In the twilight of the Confederacy, they came forward to assist the Federal invaders. Where opportunities presented themselves, white Unionists had formed regiments in the Union armies. Many in the North (branded with the derogatory label "Copperhead") were sympathetic to the South, or at least opposed the war, but they did not form units for the Confederate army. There were no Pennsylvania or Indiana Confederate battalions or regiments, though before the war some secessionists had professed to believe that Northern states outside New England would support them or remain neutral. (Maryland, Kentucky, and Missouri were the only states not to secede that provided organized units for the rebel armies; all three were slave states.)

Thirteen recruits for the 31st belatedly arrived from Massachusetts on April 20, lucky fellows who stumbled into a blissfully atypical experience of military life. Still, simply being in the army was risky; a man from Ware, Philo Shumway, who enlisted in March 1865 died of disease on May 14. The small remaining strength of the 31st Massachusetts gave it little weight as a military force, but this reduced size, coupled with long and varied experience, made it attractive for use in special assignments. As noted previously, it had been detailed for duty at Canby's headquarters on April 4 and thus left behind when Lucas's horsemen were sent far upcountry to support Maj. Gen. A. J. Smith. A detail accompanied General Canby on May 4, when he negotiated a truce with General Taylor. Taylor had long recognized that the Southern cause was hopeless, and after Gen. Joseph Johnston surrendered to William T. Sherman in North Carolina, he agreed to surrender at Citronelle, Alabama, on the eighth.[53] He and Canby had established a trusting relationship and agreed to the same terms Grant had offered Lee at Appomattox. Numbers are uncertain, but Taylor must have had few troops under his command at the end. He had never again commanded as many men as he had at Pleasant Hill, though he was promoted to lieutenant general late in the war.

With Lincoln dead and fighting ended east of the Mississippi, the administration no longer had reason to worry about General Banks's sensibilities and subjected him to a final thrust of humiliation. On May 17 the War Department abolished the Military Division of West Mississippi, which had been formed to wedge in Canby above Banks. It was reconstituted as the Department of the Gulf once again, this time with Canby in charge. Banks was relieved of departmental command and offered nothing in return.[54] He thus suffered the same treatment Butler had received in late 1862, except this time there was no hope that an ongoing war would offer redemption.

By mid-May the streets of Mobile were full of former Confederate soldiers and officers, but as Rich noted, "they keep pretty straight."[55] It probably helped that occupation authorities had ordered citizens to turn in arms on April 17, and Rich observed that "some very nice double-barrel shot guns" were brought in. This confiscation of weapons was a wise precaution as racial friction continued. As late as September 3, in its last week in the city, the 31st had to break up a "row between colored soldiers and white citizens."[56] Well before the formal surrender, Fairbank observed: "Go where you will, you will see the Union and rebel soldiers locked in arms enjoying themselves. One would hardly believe that but a few days ago we were trying to kill each other."[57] Again, this anticipated the course of Reconstruction, in which the former enemies achieved a convenient reconciliation. In the pose of generous victor, the North inhaled the camellia-scented myth of the Lost Cause and abandoned the freedmen to a bleak future.

Canby moved his headquarters to New Orleans on May 29, but the 31st Massachusetts continued to perform headquarters duty in Mobile, only now for Maj. Gen. Gordon Granger, a career army officer from New York State commanding the Thirteenth Corps. It seems that there was confusion in the higher levels of authority as to how best to employ the 31st Massachusetts. An order issued by one element of the Thirteenth Corps in Galveston, Texas, in early June directed it to "proceed as soon as practicable by steamer to New Orleans" and report to the cavalry commander there, Brig. Gen. Benjamin Grierson.[58] Three days later another headquarters of the Thirteenth Corps, this one in Mobile, confirmed that the 31st would remain attached to the newly defined Post and District of Mobile, under command of Brig. Gen. T. Kilby Smith.[59] Still expecting the 31st to appear, Grierson in New Orleans wrote that the unit was "ordered to this point from Mobile on the 9th instant, and have not yet arrived, owing to the failure of the quartermaster at Mobile to furnish transportation. They were ordered here for the purpose of being dismounted that their horses might be used for the equipment of the troops for Texas."[60]

Federal commanders expected that a campaign in Texas would be necessary to subdue Confederate forces under Gen. E. Kirby Smith in the Trans-Mississippi. President Davis and other Southern diehards had hoped to prolong the struggle in Texas, but as elsewhere in the South, Confederate forces disintegrated there too. Though not appropriate to the climate of Mobile, which had turned sultry by June, the erosion of any remaining Southern military forces would have reminded the Massachusetts soldiers of snow melting in the spring sunshine. Soldiers in the 31st surely would not have complained about an arrangement in which their horses served in Texas while they remained in Mobile or New Orleans, but Smith's surrender of all Trans-Mississippi rebel forces made even that unnecessary. The New Englanders thus retained their mounts for a while longer.

Still in Mobile, members of the 31st Massachusetts witnessed a terrible catastrophe on May 25, when an ordnance depot containing about two hundred tons of ammunition exploded. It was as though some implacable demon, unsatisfied by the slaughter that had already occurred, demanded more sacrifice. If it had happened before the surrenders, it might have been attributed to sabotage, but given the timing, most people accepted it as a dreadful accident. The precise total of deaths will never be known, but contemporary estimates placed the loss at three hundred lives. After the initial blast, body parts rained down with other wreckage, but most of the victims were crushed in collapsing buildings. Fires broke out, committing many who were trapped in fallen buildings to a horrible death by roasting. Many of those lost were Union soldiers, though none came from the 31st Massachusetts, which was stationed in another part of the city. Some eight city blocks were destroyed, and the bombardment of debris even sank ships in the river. It was profoundly ironic since the city had been surrendered to avert just that kind of devastation.

Even though there was no prospect of further fighting, promotions in

June rewarded successful officers. Nettleton became a full colonel, Allen advanced to lieutenant colonel, and Rice was promoted to major. Nettleton was later appointed provost marshal general of the Department of Alabama, commanded by Brig. Gen. Charles R. Woods, leaving Lieutenant Colonel Allen in command of the 31st Massachusetts. The new department was added to the Military Division of West Tennessee, under command of Maj. Gen. George Thomas. Captain Howell was appointed commissary of musters for the District of Mobile. In addition, 1st Lts. James M. Stewart and Sylvester Bond were promoted to captain, replaced as first lieutenants by 2nd Lts. Patrick Dinan and George W. Sears. Two more sergeants, Master Sgt. Egbert I. Clapp and 1st Sgt. George B. Oaks, were accordingly commissioned second lieutenants.

Rice had been drafted to serve reluctantly on General Lucas's staff and, for better than two months, had accompanied the cavalry brigade on an expedition far upcountry into eastern Alabama, entering Montgomery, while the rest of the battalion continued to perform headquarters duty in the relaxed atmosphere of Mobile. On mounts that were weak to start with, Lucas's cavalry ranged more than two hundred miles in a straight line from Mobile but covering far more in the saddle. Beyond the military objectives, this thrust had an exploratory aspect that, as described by Rice, resembled the probes that ventured into unknown regions of Africa.[61] He was finally released from staff duty in Columbus, Mississippi, on May 26 and made his way by train to rejoin the 31st Massachusetts.

Shortly after returning, Rice applied for and, after several rejections, was granted leave to travel to New Orleans to settle personal and military business. Considering the powerful contempt he had felt toward his former commander, it seems astonishing that he located and spent a Sunday evening with Hopkins more than a year after Sabine Cross Roads, "and a very pleasant evening we had too," he reported, adding that "Mrs. Hopkins is a very pleasant lady." They spent most of the evening singing, as "both Mr. and Mrs. Hopkins have very good voices, his a tenor and hers soprano." Rice did not entirely forget the past troubles, but he was "glad to say that Mr. Hopkins appears to have changed greatly for the better since last winter, and I think he is now doing very well, both professionally and otherwise." The couple lived "in a small comfortable house, away up town, where they have a good library, a fine piano, plenty of music (more I believe than I ever saw together outside a music store) and everything as cosy [sic] as could be desired."[62]

Hopkins's whereabouts were well known to his old regiment, as he had reported earlier visits from Lieutenant Colonel Nettleton, Captain Howell, and even Colonel Gooding (supporting the idea that Gooding had some hand in his rapid promotion).[63] These officers must have forgiven Hopkins for his breakdown or at least showed understanding of the circumstances that caused it. In contrast to Hopkins's high profile, no one reported seeing the other highly visible failure at Sabine Cross Roads, the affable Major Bache. His destiny remains a mystery, which highlights the difference in the two situations: whereas Bache fled the field in the face of the enemy, Hopkins was confined somewhere else and not present on the battlefield.

Hopkins remained in New Orleans after the war and set up a law practice with another former officer of the 31st. He might have stayed longer, but he became frightened and disillusioned by a riot in which Unionist politicians were attacked and several killed. Predictably, the rioters also turned on any blacks they found, killing and wounding many.[64] By then, Mrs. Hopkins had returned to Massachusetts, indicating a possible strain in their marriage. About a week earlier, he had informed his wife that he would like to return north but lacked the money. Whether this was meant to be a visit or a permanent move is unclear, as he wrote that becoming dependent on his father was "not a grateful proposition." Supporting the idea that his marriage was strained, Hopkins made a cryptic remark that he would give a pledge that Lizzie wanted for a term of one year, "not because I want to or consider it *now* necessary to my health and prosperity, but because you demand it."[65] Presumably, this is another reference to giving up drinking.

Somewhat grudgingly, his father loaned Hopkins the money to come home and rejoin his family in September 1866. The legal practice in New Orleans had not fared well, and Hopkins harbored doubts that he could succeed in that profession. Yet from that unpromising beginning, aided and advised by influential friends, he built a career in law, first in Greenfield, then in Worcester, that earned him statewide respect. According to his obituary, Hopkins had been considered for a seat on the state supreme court, but the nomination was not put forward because of his declining health.[66] As might be expected, he was a stalwart of the Republican Party, but, more surprisingly, he had gained acceptance and honor within veterans' organizations. Hopkins was a long-time commander of the elite ceremonial organization of Worcester Continentals. In Greenfield he was a charter member of the Grand Army of the Republic

(G.A.R.) chapter and held the post of commander for a time. Hopkins served one term in a statewide G.A.R. office. Everyone addressed him as "Colonel," ignoring the conspicuous blemish on his record, though it could hardly be kept secret. By some miraculous alchemy, Hopkins managed to erase that disturbing inkblot and live an exemplary family and professional life. Any shadows that lingered in the recesses of his mind will never be known.

Another officer who chose to remain in the South was Capt. Luther Howell, who bought a plantation at Haynesville, Alabama. That town, located less than twenty miles southwest of Montgomery, was not one that the 31st Massachusetts ever encountered in its service. This could have been an influential experiment, but Howell died there of fever on October 14, 1866, at the age of only thirty-one. The highly promising young man was buried in the family plot in Elmira, New York, mourned by a woman to whom he was betrothed and siblings with whom he had unusually caring relationships.[67]

Meanwhile, enlistments of the men who had joined the regiment in New Orleans were expiring. Since this came at a time when the war was obviously winding down, there was no incentive to offer them bonuses or, indeed, to keep them in the service at all. They were discharged routinely at the expiration of their three-year terms, sometimes even earlier, and left to make their own way home. The last two in that category in Rich's company departed on August 4.[68] Muster records show that 147 Louisiana men served in the 31st Massachusetts, amounting to more than 15 percent of the number of Massachusetts men who joined when the regiment was formed. Of this total, 83 (56 percent) served out their term and were discharged. Seven others died of disease; 7 were killed in action or died of wounds; 1 died of an unspecified cause; 19 were discharged for disability; 20 deserted; 3 were released to accept commissions or join the regular army; and 7 were transferred to the Veteran Reserve Corps. These figures compare favorably with the record of Massachusetts men in the regiment, with perhaps a somewhat higher proportion of deserters and lower proportion of discharges for disability. This could be the result of local men being more acclimated to conditions in the Gulf region, though many of the Louisiana recruits may not have been long-term residents of that state. It appears that only four of the Louisianans advanced to the rank of corporal and four others to sergeant, while none rose to become commissioned officers in the 31st Massachusetts. One such example was Frederic Forester, a thirty-four-year-old confectioner, who enlisted in Company D on May 16, 1862, and was mustered out as a sergeant. That is the highest rank to which these men realistically could aspire, as it is highly unlikely that the Massachusetts governor would commission Louisiana men to be officers in a Massachusetts regiment.

The total of Louisiana members in the 31st includes twelve "colored cooks," but the record does not reveal whether these men had previously been free or enslaved. Seven of them served their full term and were mustered out, four deserted, and one died of disease. Where civilian occupations are listed, only four had prior experience as cooks, but mastery of *haute cuisine* was hardly necessary to boil copious kettles of victuals for hungry soldiers. Often the greatest challenge was getting the food to the men while it was still warm. This had been a risky operation at places like Port Hudson, where the troops were pinned down by enemy fire.

Many from the original contingent and later replacements who were in questionable health were discharged on disability at this time, as there was little reason to keep them even in the unlikely event that they recovered fully. By late June 1865, there were probably only 5,000 Federals in Mobile out of some 50,000 who had initially occupied the area. Many of the rest had gone off to Texas when that state was expected to be the final theater of the war. If Norris was correct, in late July the 31st Massachusetts was the last white regiment left in the city.[69]

Despite their extended experience in the Gulf, the Northerners continued to suffer from the enervating heat. Writing to his mother, Norris informed her that "the heat is so intense here that it breaks out on all parts of our body. It is called prickly heat. It feels just as if you had needles sticking into you all the time. It has broken out on me from the top of my head to the bottom of my feet."[70] Nevertheless, he concluded, "My health is exceedingly good." Weather may have been a contributing factor in the insanity of Pvt. John Brewster of Company E (originally D), who shot himself in the head.[71]

Considering that the North had won a great victory at immense cost, one might have expected that the Fourth of July would have been celebrated enthusiastically, but at least according to Rich this was not the case. In his rather sour and disturbing account, only African Americans conducted a display: "The niggers turn out rigged up in great shape. They had the public Square all to themselves. They have some speaking." Undoubtedly recalling previous festivities, he concluded, "I never want to see the Fourth celebrated in such a way again."[72] Rich seemed to be unaware that "a masquerade and fancy ball" was held that night, which Norris, who was on guard, took the liberty to invite himself into.[73] Major Rice's impressions were similar to Rich's: "The Fourth amounted to nothing; here the secesh seem to consider all the old national celebrations, etc. as Yankee and so will have nothing to do with them. So the only demonstration was by the darkies who went in on there [sic] own hook with all the more gusto as they never before had any hooks of their own." He then added a prescient observation: "As the rebs. no longer dare to do anything but quietly snarl at the Yanks, they vent their spite by abusing the darkies all they can without being detected. Murders of 'niggers' are quite common, and the country being so thinly settled quite difficult as yet to punish or prevent."[74] This anticipated postwar developments, in which federal authorities were unable or unwilling to suppress Ku Klux Klan outrages because to do so would have effectively entailed remobilization and a more extensive occupation of the South.

A reorganization that created the Department of Alabama did nothing to relieve the pressing question of when the 31st Massachusetts would be discharged. For a long time, the outlook seemed unpromising; in late July Howell expressed the fear that "the govt has come to the wise conclusion that the 31st Regt is so valuable that they cannot possibly be spared."[75] The terms of those who had reenlisted in late 1864 would not expire until 1867, and some recruits had signed up even later, making it possible that their service would extend to a more remote date. Some of the men considered sending a delegation to the colonel to ask about being mustered out but, probably wisely, thought better of it.[76] Norris noted a suspicion that must have been circulating among the troops that the delay was due to a self-serving intrigue: "It has been currently reported that our Col. [Nettleton] has been the cause of it, all backed up by several other little ambitious officers who know they could never earn so good a living at home as they do now."[77]

When it finally came, the end was sudden. Financial, as well as political, factors favored rapid demobilization. An assignment to headquarters placed the 31st Massachusetts in a position to detect the latest news and rumors of discharge. On August 23, only two days after some of the restless soldiers had dropped their plans to send a delegation to Nettleton, thrilling orders came down to have the battalion mustered out by October 1. The men began turning in their horses and equipment soon after, though formal mustering out did not take place until September 9. On that day Rich made no effort to suppress his joy: "I was a free man again. Do not catch me in the army very soon again if I can help it."[78] Despite long association, the men felt little sentiment toward their mounts, and Rich said bluntly that they were "glad to get rid of them."[79] The sergeant left Mobile on the steamer *Francis* on September 10, while most of the regiment departed on the transport *Warrior* the following day, arriving in New Orleans two days later. There was no time for exploring the city they had come to know so well, as they embarked almost immediately on the steamship *Concordia*. A seemingly uneventful journey brought them to Boston harbor on the twenty-fourth. Their last days in service were passed on Gallops Island awaiting final pay and mustering out, which occurred on September 30, 1865. Rich, as perhaps others did who had had their fill of military life, spent fifty dollars of his own money to book passage from New Orleans on the *Atlanta*, which arrived in New York at 5 P.M. on September 20. He completed his journey to Pittsfield by rail the next day, three days before the bulk of the regiment reached Boston. Others who had traveled separately or had been delayed did not arrive home until October 3 or 4.[80]

A subcategory of military historians has conducted a valiant campaign to calculate the total of Civil War casualties unit by unit. Although this effort has been exhaustive, it can never be exact, and ambiguities will remain in any compilation. Some proportion of men slipped through the net while others were never recorded properly—or even at all. Soldiers listed as wounded might have survived their wounds and even survived surgery only to die of sepsis three weeks later. Such cases should properly be counted as battle deaths but may not be. Similarly, many men discharged for disability may have died soon afterward but might not be listed as military fatalities.

A compilation offered by the Civil War Archive indicates that the 31st Massachusetts had 52 enlisted men killed or mortally wounded and 150 who died of disease, accidents, or other causes.[81] Three officers died of disease or accidents, and none were killed or mortally wounded. Although there were some close calls, it remains extraordinary that no officers were killed in a regiment with such a long period of service. A calculation by this author using data contained in the regimental roster shows 58 men killed in action and 88 who died of disease, while 50 others were listed as having died of other causes. In addition, the extraordinary total of 306 men were discharged for health reasons, some of whom may have been enumerated as having died of disease in other compilations. These discrepancies, based on variation in methodology and interpretation, seem to be unavoidable. It is also of interest that the roster lists 100 men who transferred to other units, including the Veteran Reserve Corps, and 104 who deserted. (These figures include not only the original Massachusetts contingent but also the Louisiana recruits and later arrivals from Massachusetts.)[82]

Comparisons with two other regiments recruited mainly in western Massachusetts in 1861 are instructive. The 10th Massachusetts Volunteers, which was organized at Springfield on June 21, 1861, and fought through the battles of the Army of the Potomac, lists ten officers and 124 enlisted men killed and mortally wounded, while 55 enlisted men died of disease, for a total of 190. These numbers seem to support the common assumption that service in the Gulf was unhealthier. The 27th Massachusetts, organized at Springfield three months later, endured casualty figures of nine officers and 128 enlisted men killed and mortally wounded, with three officers and 261 enlisted men dying of disease, for an appalling total of 401 deaths. Since this regiment served primarily in North Carolina and in the Army of the James, the numbers seem to contradict the belief that the Gulf was unhealthier. But a special consideration affects these figures, for almost all of the men remaining with that regiment were captured during action along the James River on May 16, 1864, with most of them sent to the dreadful prison camp at Andersonville, Georgia. Those who perished at Andersonville were probably counted as having died of disease, which may have been true regarding the immediate cause, but they may not have died at all if they had received humane treatment from their captors.[83]

In summarizing the history of the 31st Massachusetts Volunteer Regiment, it is apparent that its main claim to fame (fortunately) is not an extraordinary toll of casualties, but rather the exceptional variety of service it experienced. There must be very few regiments in the Union army that served at different times as infantry, mounted infantry, and cavalry. The troops performed stationary duty in an army of occupation and at other times were part of a field army, marching or riding great distances through unfamiliar territory. They engaged both in intense siege warfare and in small-scale but nasty guerilla fighting. For some months it functioned, in effect, as an element of the coastal-defense establishment, while at other times many of its personnel performed guard and provost duties.

A revealing statistic for the 31st Massachusetts is that, despite death, disease, desertion, and transfer, 378 of the men who sailed from Boston on the *Mississippi* in February 1862 (approximately 40 percent) served their full tours. About one-third of the regiment's remaining strength, 120 men, chose not to reenlist as veterans and were discharged between November 1864 and February 1865 as their enlistments expired. Some two-thirds, or 250 men, who reenlisted were discharged in September 1865, five months after Appomattox. (The two figures do not add up because 8 men were discharged between March and August 1865, making it difficult to know which category to place them in.) Despite having many reasons to become disillusioned, a high proportion of the men in the 31st Massachusetts remained devoted to their duty.

The prevailing impression that remained with these soldiers long after their discharge was the enervating heat and humidity they had encountered in the Gulf region, accompanied in season by relentless attacks of hordes of mosquitoes. Nothing in their experience in Massachusetts prepared them for these conditions, but at least they had an intellectual awareness that it was possible. What proved more surprising to them was the damp chill and occasional ice they encountered during Louisiana winters. Even after he was no longer in the army, Hopkins wrote: "We hear of nothing which makes me want to go North more than that very cold weather which people so much dread. I think I should get fat on a continuous cold snap, but this wishy-washy uncertain winter of this climate hasn't an atom of exiliration [sic] in it."[84]

With no other ceremonies or speeches, the soldiers who had been mustered out in Boston dispersed to the scattered towns and farms from which they had come. They reverted at the end to what they had been at the outset: the Western Bay State Regiment, volunteers from interior New England who had responded to their country's call. Their motives, though generally similar, varied in balance within each individual. Though some, such as Nettleton, had advanced through the officer ranks, most remained volunteers at heart. Howell, who had been successful as an officer, wrote, "The longer I stay in the service the more distasteful and offensive become the ceremonies and

Regulations and by contrast the more desirable and endearing the society of home friends."[85] In his last surviving letter home, Norris shunned lofty rhetoric about liberty and union: "Mother, it is true that the army has ruined a great many young fellows, and I was not in the army many years before I had foresight enough to see what a demoralized people must be thrown upon this once happy country. At the end of the rebellion, alas, it has proved to be too true."[86]

Even after steady recruiting, there were less than half as many present at the final muster as at the first in distant 1861, when recruits shuffled in awkward formation at Camp Seward. Many of them—the fortunate ones—were greeted by overwhelming effusions of relief and love when they crossed a familiar threshold. Yet, because of what they had experienced together, some of their closest bonds would be with their fellow veterans, bound by unbreakable chains of memory that would finally rust away to nothingness only as each man's Civil War marker was placed above his grave.

NOTES

ABBREVIATIONS

31st Mass. Coll.	31st Mass. Volunteer Infantry Regiment Collection
Andrew-Butler Correspondence	*Correspondence between Gov. Andrew and Major-General Butler* (Boston: John J. Dyer, 1862)
Correspondence of General Butler	Jessie Ames Marshall, ed., *Private and Official Correspondence of General Benjamin F. Butler during the Period of the Civil War,* 5 vols. (Privately printed, 1917)
MoSH	Wood Museum of Springfield History, Springfield, Mass.
OR	*The War of the Rebellion: A Compilation of the Official Records of the Union and Confederate Armies* (Washington: 1880–1901, USGPO); all citations from ser. 1
Supplement to the OR	Janet B. Hewett ed., *Supplement to the Official Records of the Union and Confederate Armies,* Part 2, Record of Events, vol. 29 (Wilmington, N.C.: Broadfoot, 1996)

PREFACE

1. See folder 1, box 1, 31st Mass. Coll., MoSH.

2. Minutes of the Veterans Association, 31st Mass. Coll., MoSH.

3. It must be noted that almost all of the contemporary writings that touch in any way on race would be considered unacceptably racist by our standards. Despite the risk of causing offense, it is important to preserve the original language, both for reasons of historical accuracy and for present-day educational value as a gateway to discussing the topic of race.

CHAPTER 1

1. For Butler's biography, see Benjamin F. Butler, *Butler's Book* (Boston: A. M. Thayer, 1892; Chester G. Hearn, *When the Devil Came Down to Dixie: Ben Butler in New Orleans* (Baton Rouge:

Louisiana State University Press, 1997); Dick Nolan, *Benjamin Franklin Butler, the Damndest Yankee* (Novato, Calif.: Presidio, 1991); and Richard S. West Jr., *Lincoln's Scapegoat General: A Life of Benjamin F. Butler* (Boston: Houghton Mifflin, 1965).

2. In his late-life autobiography, though, Butler provides a different explanation, saying that his mother was advised that West Point was irreligious. See Butler, *Butler's Book*, 57.

3. Butler, *Butler's Book*, 124.

4. Nolan, *Benjamin Franklin Butler*, 43; West, *Lincoln's Scapegoat General*, 41.

5. Butler, *Butler's Book*, 127.

6. West, *Lincoln's Scapegoat General*, 45. On many of these ballots, Butler's individualistic vote was the only one Davis, who had not declared himself a candidate, received. Butler professed to believe that Davis was not an "original disunionist," though the Mississippian was prepared to follow his state if it seceded. Butler, *Butler's Book*, 139.

7. Nolan, *Benjamin Franklin Butler*, 51.

8. West, *Lincoln's Scapegoat General*, 46.

9. Nolan, *Benjamin Franklin Butler*, 67.

10. Butler, *Butler's Book*, 257–58; West, *Lincoln's Scapegoat General*, 82.

11. West, *Lincoln's Scapegoat General*, 84.

12. Butler, *Butler's Book*, 298. Butler reported this to his wife on August 8, so it was probably granted a day or two previous. See *Correspondence of General Butler*, 1:199.

13. War Dept. General Order 2, *Correspondence of General Butler*, 1:239.

14. War Dept. General Order 2, *Correspondence of General Butler*, 1:239; *Andrew-Butler Correspondence*, 9. Lincoln ended his message to Andrew by asking him to "answer by telegram that you consent."

15. Butler, *Butler's Book*, chap. 7.

16. Andrew to Lincoln, Sept. 11, 1861, *Correspondence of General Butler*, 1:240. In addition to Burnside, Andrew stated that he had made a troop commitment to another Rhode Islander, Brig. Gen. Thomas W. Sherman. Andrew to Cameron, Sept. 28, 1861, *Andrew-Butler Correspondence*, 13.

17. General Order 86, Oct. 1, 1861, *Andrew-Butler Correspondence*, 18.

18. General Order 78, Sept. 16, 1861, *Andrew-Butler Correspondence*, 11.

19. State of Massachusetts, General Order 23, Sept. 23, 1861, *Correspondence of General Butler*, 1:243.

20. Cameron to Andrew, Sept. 27, 1861, *Andrew-Butler Correspondence*, 17 (original all italics).

21. Cameron to Paymaster General, Oct. 2, 1861, *Andrew-Butler Correspondence*, 18.

22. West, *Lincoln's Scapegoat General*, 5. Schouler later perpetuated his opinion in a history of Massachusetts in the Civil War.

23. Andrew to Brig. Gen. Thomas, Adjutant General, U.S. Army, Nov. 27, 1861, *Andrew-Butler Correspondence*, 45–46.

24. Andrew to Butler, Oct. 26, 1861, *Correspondence of General Butler*, 1:265.

25. Butler to Andrew, Dec. 29, 1861, *Correspondence of General Butler*, 1:307.

26. Schouler to Andrew, Jan. 24, 1862, *Correspondence of General Butler*, 1:324.

27. Butler to Daniel Richardson, Feb. 3, 1862, *Correspondence of General Butler*, 1:340.

28. John Ryan to Butler, Dec. 30, 1861, *Correspondence of General Butler*, 1:308.

29. Andrew to Sens. Charles Sumner and Henry Wilson, Dec. 21, 1861, *Andrew-Butler Correspondence,* 84–86.

30. Since the Andrew-Butler correspondence was published in 1862, they would have been able to find out. Although the soldiers were out of the state by then, their families remained in Massachusetts.

31. Whelden biography from Edward Boltwood, *The History of Pittsfield, Massachusetts, 1876–1916* (City of Pittsfield, 1916), 237; Hamilton Child, comp., *Gazetteer of Berkshire County, [Mass.], 1725–1885* (Syracuse, N.Y., 1885), 315.

32. Arthur Chase, *History of Ware, Massachusetts* (Cambridge, Mass.: Harvard University Press, 1911), 197–99.

33. Bruce Laurie, *Rebels in Paradise: Sketches of Northampton, [Mass.] Abolitionists* (Amherst: Univ. of Massachusetts Press, 2015), 117–21.

34. Laurie, *Rebels in Paradise,* 141.

35. "Edward P. Nettleton, Civil War Soldier," Chicopee Archives Online, http://www.chicopeepubliclibrary.org/rchives/items/show/2743.

36. Nettleton to Whelden, Oct. 22, 1861, Charles M. Whelden Papers, 31st Mass. Coll., MoSH.

37. One source gives the date as November 29, but this is probably a mistake for November 20. See *Supplement to the OR,* 20.

38. Butler to Col. Brown, Asst. Adjt. Gen. of Mass., Feb. 15, 1862, *Correspondence of General Butler,* 1:355.

39. From roster compiled by author, based on James L. Bowen, *Massachusetts in the War, 1861–1865* (Springfield, Mass.: Clark W. Bryan, 1889); Thomas Wentworth Higginson, *Massachusetts in the Army and Navy during the War of 1861–1865* (Boston: Commonwealth of Massachusetts, 1896); Massachusetts Adjutant General, comp., *Massachusetts Soldiers, Sailors, and Marines in the Civil War,* vol. 3 (Norwood: Massachusetts Adjutant General, 1932); and 31st Mass. Coll., MoSH.

40. Howell to brother, Apr. 21, 1861, Amherst, Mass., Luther C. Howell Letters, Amherst College, Frost Library, Special Collections.

41. Howell to sister, Oct. 17, 1861, Howell Letters.

42. James B. T. Tupper to sister Augusta, Feb. 2, 1862, Camp Seward, Pittsfield, from the *Ware (Mass.) Standard,* James B. T. Tupper Letters, Hardwick Historical Society. The list totals a few short of the full complement of a company.

43. Hopkins to wife, Nov. 10, 1861, William Swinton Bennett Hopkins Papers, David M. Rubenstein Rare Book and Manuscript Library, Duke University.

44. Fairbank to sister, n.d., Camp Seward, Pittsfield, Mass., Luther M. Fairbank Letters, 1861–63, Special Collections, Louisiana State University.

45. Whelden to Butler, Nov. 12, 1861, Whelden Papers. Note the reference to overcoats, which Butler held a contract to manufacture.

46. Asa P. Wheeler Diary, Nov. 9, 1861, 31st Mass. Coll., MoSH.

47. Tupper to parents and sister, Jan. 3, 1862, Tupper Letters.

48. Frank S. Knight Diary, Jan. 20, 1862, 31st Mass. Coll., MoSH.

49. Richard F. Underwood Diary, Dec. 11, 1861, 31st Mass. Coll., MoSH.

50. Thanks to genealogist Michele (Patterson) Valenzano for providing this information.

51. Joseph L. Hallett, "Reminiscences of the Civil War," 31st Mass. Coll., MoSH, 3. Hallett probably did not know the full name of Mount Washington, with which he had little previous contact.

52. Hallett, "Reminiscences," 3.

53. Tupper to sister Libby, Dec. 24, 1861, Tupper Letters; Tupper to parents and sister, Dec. 25, 1861, ibid.

54. Knight Diary, Jan. 12, 1862.

55. Tupper to parents and sister, Dec. 25, 1861, Camp Seward, Tupper Letters.

56. Hallett, "Reminiscences," 6.

57. *Pittsfield Sun*, Feb. 13, 1862.

58. Joshua W. Hawkes to mother, Dec. 1, 1861, Joshua W. Hawkes Letters, 31st Mass. Coll., MoSH (emphasis in original).

59. Joshua W. Hawkes to mother, Nov. 23, 1861, Hawkes Letters. This was Hawkes's first night in camp.

60. Howell to brother, Nov. 25, 1861, Camp Seward, Howell Letters.

61. Tupper to parents and sister, June 24, 1862, New Orleans, Tupper Letters. The identity of this man is uncertain. Hawkes refers to "Old Sullivan," and a Michael Sullivan, age thirty-five, is listed on the roster as discharged for disability on June 21, 1862. See note 39 above. This man gave his residence as Willimantic, Connecticut, though he enlisted in Springfield—only a day before the attack on Captain Lee. Whelden to Butler, Nov. 24, 1861, Whelden Papers.

62. Knight to friends, Nov. 14, 1861, Camp Seward, Frank S. Knight Letters, 31st Mass. Coll., MoSH.

63. Tupper to sister Libby, Dec. 24, 1861, Camp Seward, Tupper Letters.

64. Howell to brother, Nov. 25, 1861, Camp Seward, Howell Letters (emphasis in original).

65. Hawkes to mother, Dec. 1, 1861, Hawkes Letters.

66. Hawkes to mother, Jan. 12, 1862, Hawkes Letters (emphasis in original).

67. Butler to Whelden, Jan 7, 1862, *Correspondence of General Butler*, 1:314.

68. Gen. J. Bradler to Butler, Dec. 1, 1861, *Correspondence of General Butler*, 1:293.

69. Butler to Brig. Gen. Thomas, Adjutant General, U.S. Army, Nov. 27, 1861, *Andrew-Butler Correspondence*, 47.

70. Col. George F. Shepley to Butler, Jan. 8, 1862, *Correspondence of General Butler*, 1:315. Shepley was in command of the 12th Maine.

71. Butler, *Butler's Book,* 309.

72. Tupper to sister Augusta, Feb. 2, 1862, Camp Seward, Tupper Letters.

73. Hawkes to mother, Jan. 20, 1862, Hawkes Letters (emphasis in original).

74. Butler to Whelden, Jan. 7, 1862, *Correspondence of General Butler,* 1:314.

75. Butler, *Butler's Book,* 310.

76. Andrew to Brig.-Gen. Thomas, Adjutant-General, U.S. Army, Nov. 27, 1861, *Andrew-Butler Correspondence,* 47, 50. The Battle of Balls Bluff took place along the Potomac River in Loudoun County, Virginia, on October 21, 1861.

77. Hopkins to wife, Nov. 10, 1861, Hopkins Papers.

78. Lincoln to Andrew, Jan. 11, 1862, *Andrew-Butler Correspondence*, 81.

79. Butler never displayed any interest in the 28th Regiment, which Andrew had once offered.

80. Andrew to Brig.-Gen. Lorenzo Thomas, Adjutant-General, U.S. Army, n.d., *Andrew-Butler Correspondence*, 64.

81. Hawkes to mother, Jan. 26, 1862, Hawkes Letters; Knight Diary, Jan. 17, 1862.

82. *Pittsfield Sun*, Feb. 13, 1862.

83. Knight to mother, Feb. 13, 1862, Camp Chase, Lowell, Mass., Knight Letters.

84. Underwood Diary, Feb. 6, 8, 1862. Underwood observed that the smashing of bottles was such "as to give one the idea of a temperance reform."

85. Hawkes to mother, Feb. 15, 1862, Camp Chase, Hawkes Letters.

86. Wheeler Diary, Feb. 12, 1862; Underwood Diary, Feb. 12, 1862.

87. Wheeler Diary, Feb. 12, 1862; Underwood Diary, Feb. 12, 1862.

88. George U. Young Recollections, 31st Mass. Coll., MoSH, 7.

89. Young Recollections, 5–7.

90. Tupper to parents and sister, Feb. 16, 1862, Camp Chase, Tupper Letters. Sutlers were private merchants who, usually with permission, came into camps to offer food specialties and other handy items that the army did not provide. It is interesting that, even though the regiment was slated to remain at Camp Chase for only a short time, it was long enough to attract sutlers.

91. Tupper to parents and sister, Feb. 16, 1862. Southworth, twenty-one, was a carpenter from Hardwick.

92. Butler to Secretary of War, Feb. 12, 1862, *Correspondence of General Butler*, 1:350.

93. Hawkes to mother, Feb. 24, 1862, "on board steamer Mississippi," Hawkes Letters (emphasis in original).

94. Norris to mother, Feb. 24, 1862, Fortress Monroe, Va., Thomas Norris Letters, 31st Mass. Coll., MoSH.

95. Hawkes to mother, Dec. 22, 1861, Camp Seward, Hawkes Letters.

96. Elizabeth Hopkins to W. S. B. Hopkins, Feb. 23, 1862, Northampton, Mass., Hopkins Papers (emphasis in original; punctuation added).

CHAPTER 2

1. George U. Young Recollections, 31st Mass. Coll., MoSH, 8; Richard F. Underwood Diary, Feb. 21, 1862, ibid.; William Shaftoe Diary, Feb. 21, 1862, ibid.; Tupper to sister Libby, Dec. 24, 1861, Camp Seward, James B. T. Tupper Letters, Hardwick Historical Society; Tupper to sister Augusta, Feb. 2, 1862, Camp Seward, ibid.

2. Charles L Dufour, *The Night the War Was Lost* (Garden City, N.Y.: Doubleday, 1960), 135.

3. Nolan, *Benjamin Franklin Butler*, 113.

4. Butler to Andrew, Oct. 11, 1861, *Correspondence of General Butler*, 1:251.

5. Cameron to Butler, Sept. 12, 1861, *Andrew-Butler Correspondence*, 10.

6. McClellan to Butler, Jan. 1, 1862, *Correspondence of General Butler*, 1:310; McClellan to Butler, Jan. 9, 1862, ibid., 318.

7. Butler to Mrs. Butler, Jan. 26, 1862, *Correspondence of General Butler*, 1:330.

8. McClellan to Butler, Feb. 23, 1862, *Correspondence of General Butler*, 1:360–61 (emphasis in original).

9. Hearn, *When the Devil Came Down to Dixie*, 46.

10. Asa P. Wheeler Diary, Feb. 21, 1862, 31st Mass. Coll., MoSH.

11. Shaftoe Diary, Feb. 22, 1862.

12. Norris to mother, Feb. 24, 1862, Fortress Monroe, Thomas Norris Letters, 31st Mass. Coll., MoSH.

13. Joseph L. Hallett, "Reminiscences of the Civil War," 31st Mass. Coll., MoSH, 8.

14. Hawkes to mother, Feb. 24, 1862, "At anchor between Fortress Monroe and the Rip Rap," Joshua W. Hawkes Letters, 31st Mass. Coll., MoSH.

15. "Itinerary kept by Joe. M. Bell, Major and aide-de-camp at the order of Major-General Butler," *OR*, 6:699.

16. Frank S. Knight Diary, Feb. 25, 1862, 31st Mass. Coll., MoSH.

17. Shaftoe Diary, Feb. 26, 1862.

18. Mrs. Butler to Mrs. Heard, addition to letter begun Feb. 25, 1862, *Correspondence of General Butler*, 1:364. The churning sea obviously mixed her metaphors. Mrs. Harriet Heard was Sarah Butler's sister.

19. Underwood Diary, Feb. 27, 1862.

20. Hallett, "Reminiscences," 9. The song he names was written around the time many of the Civil War soldiers were born and could well have been used as a lullaby for them.

21. Mrs. Butler to Mrs. Heard, addition to letter begun Feb. 25, 1862, *Correspondence of General Butler*, 1:365.

22. *Correspondence of General Butler*, 1:367.

23. Report of Cmdr. O. S. Glisson, n.d., *Pittsfield Sun*, Mar. 13, 1862.

24. Letter from "C," *Pittsfield Sun*, May 29, 1862.

25. Hawkes to mother, Mar. 7, 1862, Hilton Head, S.C., Hawkes Letters.

26. Hawkes to mother, Mar. 7, 1862.

27. Mrs. Butler to Mrs. Heard, addition to letter begun Feb. 25, 1862, *Correspondence of General Butler*, 1:364.

28. Hawkes to mother, Mar. 7, 1862, Hawkes Letters.

29. Hallett, "Reminiscences," 9.

30. Hawkes, to mother, Mar. 7, 1862, Hawkes Letters.

31. Hallett, "Reminiscences," 12.

32. Butler, *Butler's Book*, 350–51.

33. Shaftoe Diary, Mar. 10, 1862.

34. Underwood Diary, Mar. 12, 1862.

35. Hallett, "Reminiscences," 14.

36. Butler to Fulton, Mar. 12, 1862, *Correspondence of General Butler*, 1:373.

37. Shaftoe Diary, Mar. 17, 1862.

38. Shaftoe Diary, Mar. 18, 1862.

39. Mrs. Butler to Mrs. Heard, Mar. 23, 1862, Ship Island, *Correspondence of General Butler,* 1:380.

40. Fairbank to sister, Mar. 24, 1862, Ship Island, Luther M. Fairbank Letters, Special Collections, Louisiana State University.

41. The man Fairbank witnessed buried at sea was most likely Willard Packard, a twenty-three-year-old farmer from Erving. His brother, Ansel Packard, was a farmer from Easthampton. Both served in Company B.

42. Mrs. Butler to Mrs. Heard, Mar. 23, 1862, Ship Island, *Correspondence of General Butler,* 1:383.

43. Knight Diary, Mar. 8, 1862.

44. Tupper to parents and sister, Mar. 26, 1862, Ship Island, Tupper Letters.

45. Hawkes to mother, Mar. 20 (addition to letter begun Mar. 14), 1862, Hawkes Letters.

46. Shaftoe Diary, Mar. 20, 1862.

47. Hallett, "Reminiscences," 15.

48. Mrs. Butler to Mrs. Heard, Mar. 23, 1862, Ship Island, *Correspondence of General Butler,* 1:382.

49. Tupper to parents and sister, Mar. 26, 1862, Ship Island, Tupper Letters.

50. Norris to mother and father, Mar. 24, 1862, Ship Island, Norris Letters.

51. Norris to mother and father, Mar. 24, 1862.

52. Young Recollections, 14.

53. Dufour, *Night the War Was Lost,* 53, 66.

54. Butler, *Butler's Book,* 324.

55. Underwood Diary, Apr. 3, 1862; Tupper to parents and sister, Apr. 1, 1862, Ship Island, Tupper Letters.

56. Tupper to parents and sister, Apr. 11 (addition to letter begun Apr. 9), 1862, Ship Island, Tupper Letters. Unless the Springfield guns were obsolete flintlocks, exchanging them for Austrian rifles would be a downgrade in firearms for the Michiganders.

57. Mrs. Butler to Mrs. Heard, Apr. 4, 1862, Ship Island, *Correspondence of General Butler,* 1:402.

58. Tupper to parents and sister, Apr. 1, 1862, Ship Island, Tupper Letters.

59. Tupper to parents and sister, Apr. 4 (addition to letter begun Apr. 1), 1862, Ship Island, Tupper Letters.

60. Knight Diary, Apr. 4, 1862; Mrs. Butler to Mrs. Heard, Apr. 4, 1862, Ship Island, *Correspondence of General Butler,* 1:402.

61. Wheeler Diary, Apr. 5, 1862. James Tupper reported that two of the drowned men were from the 26th Massachusetts, and the other three came from a Maine regiment. Tupper to parents and sister, Apr. 6 (addition to letter begun Apr. 1), 1862, Tupper Letters.

62. Hallett, "Reminiscences," 15–16.

63. Tupper to parents and sister, Apr. 6 (addition to letter begun Apr. 1), 1862, Tupper Letters.

64. Tupper to parents and sister, Apr. 4 (addition to letter begun Apr. 1), 1862, Tupper Letters.

65. Tupper to friends at home, Mar. 29, 1862, Ship Island, Tupper Letters.

66. In a later letter Tupper elaborated on his unorthodox attitude toward conventional medical treatment: "You speak about the good effects of quinine to take now & then. Quinine may be very good. I never tasted it to see & never want to. Now I don't believe in putting medicine into a man's system & doctoring for this & doctoring for that. . . . It may be a peculiar notion of mine, but I would rely more on some old woman remedy than all the Calomel, quinine & 'pizen' in the Union." After medicine did not cure a persistent cough, Tupper "got an old negroe woman, Julia, who hangs around the ships to do some act of kindness to the suffering sailors or soldiers, to give up some stuff, mutton tallow & molasses, & it cured me right up." Tupper to parents, July 5, 1862, Tupper Letters.

67. Wheeler Diary, Apr. 11, 1862.

68. Wheeler Diary, Apr. 11, 1862.

69. Young Recollections, 14–17.

70. Tupper to parents and sister, Apr. 9, 1862, Ship Island, Tupper Letters; Underwood Diary, Apr. 13, 1862.

71. Young Recollections, 20.

72. Young Recollections, 20.

73. Underwood Diary, Apr. 13, 1862.

74. Shaftoe Diary, Apr. 14, 1862.

CHAPTER 3

1. J. E. Kaufmann and H. W. Kaufmann, *Fortress America: The Forts That Defended America, 1600 to the Present* (Cambridge, Mass.: Da Capo, 2004), 225–26.

2. *OR,* 15:413–20.

3. A contemporary map, which appears to be reliable, gives a total of seventy-five guns at Fort Jackson and fifty-three at Fort St. Philip. The Fort Jackson armament is broken down into forty-three heavy guns *en barbette* (located on the parapet and intended to fire through embrasures), twenty heavy guns in casemates, two light pieces, three mortars, and seven guns in the water battery. There is no breakdown by category for Fort St. Philip. Robert Knox Sneden, *Map Showing the Defenses of the Mississippi below New Orleans and Farragut's attacks, 24 April 1862*, Library of Congress, Washington, D.C.

4. John D. Winters, *The Civil War in Louisiana* (Baton Rouge: Louisiana State University Press, 1963), 84, 86.

5. Winters, *Civil War in Louisiana*, 82, 89.

6. Dufour, *Night the War Was Lost*, 203.

7. William Shaftoe Diary, Apr. 17, 18, 1862, 31st Mass. Coll., MoSH; Asa P. Wheeler Diary, Apr. 17, 18, 1862, ibid.; Frank S. Knight Diary, Apr. 17, 1862, ibid.; Abram J. Nichols Diary, Apr. 18, 1862, ibid. Nichols and Shaftoe are clear in confirming that they did not move upriver until the eighteenth.

8. Butler to Stanton, Apr. 17, 1862, *Correspondence of General Butler*, 1:414.

9. Shaftoe Diary, Apr. 23, 1862.

10. Letter from Hollister, Apr. 24, 1862, *Pittsfield Sun,* May 22, 1862.

11. Shaftoe Diary, Apr. 21, 1862.

12. Richard F. Underwood Diary, Apr. 21, 1862, 31st Mass. Coll., MoSH.

13. Shaftoe Diary, Apr. 25, 27, 1862.

14. Butler to Farragut, Apr. 24, 1862, *Correspondence of General Butler,* 1:420.

15. Butler to General in Chief, Nov. 18, 1861, *Correspondence of General Butler,* 1:282. The USS *Miami* was probably the same ship the *Mississippi* had encountered in distress off Virginia and had towed into Fortress Monroe. Ibid., 348.

16. Butler to Secy. Stanton, Apr. 29, 1862, *Correspondence of General Butler,* 1:424.

17. Shaftoe Diary, Apr. 28, 1862.

18. Butler to Secy. Stanton, Apr. 29, 1862, *Correspondence of General Butler,* 1:424.

19. Butler, *Butler's Book,* 371.

20. Butler to Farragut, Apr. 24, 1862, *Correspondence of General Butler,* 1:420.

21. Butler to Mrs. Butler, Apr. 26, 1862, *Correspondence of General Butler,* 1:422. Andrew Hull Foote commanded Union naval forces far upriver near Memphis and took no part in the campaign against New Orleans.

22. Shaftoe Diary, Apr. 30, 1862.

23. Knight Diary, Apr. 30, 1862.

24. Tupper to father and mother, Mar. 7 (addition to letter begun Mar. 5), 1863, Carrollton, La., James B. T. Tupper Letters, Hardwick Historical Society.

25. Kaufmann and Kaufmann, *Fortress America,* 247.

26. Kaufmann and Kaufmann, *Fortress America,* 249.

27. Shaftoe Diary, May 1, 1862.

28. Underwood Diary, May 1, 1862.

29. Hawkes to mother, May 1, 1862, "on board Str. Mississippi, New Orleans," Joshua W. Hawkes Letters, 31st Mass. Coll., MoSH.

30. Fairbank to sister, May 1, 1862, "sailing up the Mississippi River," Luther M. Fairbank Letters, Special Collections, Louisiana State University.

31. L. Frederick Rice Diary, May 1, 1862, 31st Mass. Coll., MoSH.

32. Hawkes to mother, May 1, 1862, "on board Str. Mississippi, New Orleans," Hawkes Letters.

33. Nichols Diary, May 1, 1862.

CHAPTER 4

1. William Shaftoe Diary, May 1, 1862, 31st Mass. Coll., MoSH.

2. George U. Young Recollections, 31st Mass. Coll., MoSH, 25. One has to wonder why so many active and demonstrably partisan young men were not in uniform; a psychologist might theorize that they were overcompensating.

3. Hawkes to mother, May 4, 1862, Custom House, New Orleans, Joshua W. Hawkes Letters, 31st Mass. Coll., MoSH.

4. Butler, *Butler's Book*, 373–74.

5. Tupper to sister Louisa, June 16, 1862, New Orleans, James B. T. Tupper Letters, Hardwick Historical Society.

6. Fairbank to sister, June 10 (addition to letter begun June 9), 1862, New Orleans, Luther M. Fairbank Letters, Special Collections, Louisiana State University.

7. The May 1 report is the most recent in that issue of the *Boston Journal*.

8. Tupper to sister Louisa, June 16, 1862, New Orleans, Tupper Letters. A search of the *Boston Herald* for June and July 1862 did not locate a letter of this kind.

9. Fairbank to sister, May 3 (addition to letter begun May 1), 1862, Fairbank Letters.

10. Hawkes to mother, May 23, 1862, St. Charles Hotel, New Orleans, Hawkes Letters.

11. *Boston Herald*, July 31, 1862.

12. Butler, *Butler's Book*, 386.

13. Luther M. Fairbank Diary, May 8, 1862, 31st Mass. Coll., MoSH.

14. Letter from "C," May 17, 1862, *Pittsfield Sun*, June 5, 1862. The author surmises that "C" was Capt. Cardinal H. Conant, who was then on General Butler's staff and had been a clerk in civilian life.

15. General Order 25, May 9, 1862, *General Orders from Headquarters, Department of the Gulf, Issued by Major-General B. F. Butler, From May 1st, 1862, to the present time* (New Orleans: E. R. Wagener, printer, 1862), 8.

16. Letter from "C," May 17, 1862, *Pittsfield Sun*, June 5, 1862.

17. Knight to mother, May 9, 1862, New Orleans, Frank S. Knight Letters, 31st Mass. Coll., MoSH.

18. Hawkes to mother, May 23, 1862, St. Charles Hotel, New Orleans, Hawkes Letters.

19. Fairbank Diary, May 13, 1862. "C" reported that the troops distributed "several thousand barrels of beef and provisions." Letter from "C," May 17, 1862, *Pittsfield Sun*, June 5, 1862.

20. Butler, *Butler's Book*, 450–51.

21. Hawkes to mother, June 15, 1862, Camp Morewood, New Orleans, Hawkes Letters.

22. Fairbank to sister, June 15, 1862, Louisiana Press Yard No. 3, New Orleans, Fairbank Letters.

23. Fairbank to sister, July 1, 1862, New Orleans, Fairbank Letters.

24. Fairbank to sister, July 5, 1862, New Orleans, Fairbank Letters.

25. Fairbank to sister, June 9, 1862, New Orleans, Fairbank Letters.

26. Butler, *Butler's Book*, 412.

27. Young Recollections, 26.

28. Joseph L. Hallett, "Reminiscences of the Civil War," 31st Mass. Coll., MoSH, 29.

29. *Correspondence of General Butler*, 1:490.

30. Young Recollections, 28.

31. The soldiers may have believed this account, but it is not the most common or likely explanation of how the nickname "Spoons" originated. See, for example, Hearn, *When the Devil Came Down to Dixie*, 222–23.

32. Fairbank to sister, June 15, 1862, Louisiana Press Yard No. 3, New Orleans, Fairbank Letters. The incident took place on June 13. Joshua Hawkes and Richard Underwood also describe this drill. See Hawkes to mother, June 15, 1862, Hawkes Letters; and Richard F. Underwood Diary, June 14, 1862, 31st Mass. Coll., MoSH.

33. Letter from "C," New Orleans, July 18, 1862, *Pittsfield Sun*, July 31, 1862. Some money was also sent home by other means, so the proportion of the pay received going to the men's families would have been even higher.

34. Butler, *Butler's Book*, 515.

35. *Boston Herald*, July 21, 1862.

36. Underwood Diary, July 4, 1862; Fairbank to sister, July 5, 1862, New Orleans, Fairbank Letters.

37. Tupper to parents, July 5, 1862, New Orleans, Tupper Letters.

38. Butler to Stanton, May 8, 1862, *Correspondence of General Butler*, 1:428.

39. Winters, *Civil War in Louisiana*, 108–9.

40. Butler to Williams, June 6, 1862, *Correspondence of General Butler*, 1:563; *OR*, 15:25.

41. Butler to Stanton, June 10, 1862, *OR*, 15:465. See also *Correspondence of General Butler*, 1:568.

42. Tupper to parents and sisters, July 22, 1862, New Orleans, Tupper Letters.

43. Maurice Melton, *The Confederate Ironclads* (New York: Thomas Yoseloff, 1968), 138–41.

44. Asa P. Wheeler Diary, Aug. 7, 1862, 31st Mass. Coll., MoSH.

45. Hawkes to mother, Aug. 16, 1862, Camp Morewood, New Orleans, Hawkes Letters.

46. Hawkes to mother, Aug. 16, 1862.

47. Tupper to parents and sisters, Aug. 16, 1862, Reading Press, New Orleans, Tupper Letters.

48. William H. Rich Diary, May 15, 1862, 31st Mass. Coll., MoSH.

49. Rich Diary, May 16, 1862.

50. Mrs. Morewood donated flags to two other regiments with a large Berkshire component, the 37th and 49th Massachusetts. While performing these generous deeds, this ornament to the social and intellectual life of Berkshire suffered from consumption (tuberculosis), which claimed her life on October 16, 1863, at the age of thirty-nine. Obituary, *Pittsfield Sun*, Oct. 22, 1863. After the war soldiers decorated her grave the same as they did for their comrades. Joseph E. A. Smith, *The History of Pittsfield, Massachusetts, 1800–1876* (Springfield, Mass.: C. W. Bryan, 1876), 626.

51. Hallett, "Reminiscences," 27. Lieutenant General Polk, widely beloved by his troops despite his questionable military ability, was killed by a cannonball fired under the direction of Maj. Gen. William T. Sherman in northern Georgia on June 14, 1864.

52. Tupper to parents and sister, June 24, 1862, New Orleans, Tupper Letters.

53. Hawkes to mother, June 15, 1862, Camp Morewood, Hawkes Letters.

54. Hawkes to mother, June 15, 1862.

55. Fairbank to sister, July 1, 1862, New Orleans, Fairbank Letters.

56. Fairbank to sister, June 15, 1862, Fairbank Letters.

57. Timothy Z. Smith to Sam, July 8, 1862, Camp Morewood, Yale Collection of Western Americana, Beinecke Rare Book and Manuscript Library, Yale University (emphasis in original).

58. Fairbank Diary, July 21, 1862. James Tupper was employed at the Reading Cotton Press as clerk. See Tupper to parents and sister, May 29 (addition to letter begun May 26), 1862, New Orleans, Tupper Letters.

59. Fairbank Diary, June 30, 1862.

60. Fairbank to sister, July 1, 1862, New Orleans, Fairbank Letters.

61. Fairbank to sister, July 5, 1862, New Orleans, Fairbank Letters.

62. Winters, *Civil War in Louisiana*, 140; Butler, *Butler's Book*, 424. Fairbank reported that

Butler was occupying the mansion. Fairbank to sister, July 5, 1862, New Orleans, Fairbank Letters. Butler earlier had issued an order that sequestered all property of General Twiggs while awaiting action of the U.S. government. Department of the Gulf, General Order 16, June 26, 1862, *General Orders . . . Issued by Major-General B. F. Butler*, 16.

63. Tupper to parents and sister, May 26, 1862, New Orleans, Tupper Letters.

64. Underwood Diary, July 14, 1862.

65. Butler to Postmaster General Montgomery Blair, July 23, 1861, *Correspondence of General Butler*, 1:177.

66. Page to Butler, May 27, 1862; *Correspondence of General Butler*, 1:524.

67. Butler to Phelps (two letters), Aug. 2, 1862, *OR*, 15:536–37.

68. Phelps died in Vermont in 1885. Considering the aggravation he had caused, it may be surprising that Butler still praised him lavishly in his autobiography. See Butler, *Butler's Book*, 252.

69. Butler to Secy. Stanton, Sept. 1, 1862, *Correspondence of General Butler*, 2:244. On another occasion Butler observed that most of these men were lighter than Pierre Soule, the Louisiana Creole former senator and minister to Spain, with whom he had many unpleasant interchanges early in his military administration. West, *Lincoln's Scapegoat General*, 168.

70. Winters, *Civil War in Louisiana*, 145.

71. Butler, *Butler's Book*, 493.

72. Butler to Stanton, May 16, 1862, *Correspondence of General Butler*, 1:494 (emphasis in original).

73. Tupper to sister Libbie, Aug. 12, 1862, New Orleans, Tupper Letters.

74. Butler to Stanton, Aug. 14, 1862, *Correspondence of General Butler*, 2:191; Butler to Stanton, Sept. 1, 1862, ibid., 244.

75. Tupper to sister Libbie, Aug. 12, 1862, New Orleans, Tupper Letters.

76. West, *Lincoln's Scapegoat General*, 168.

77. Tupper to parents and sisters, June 24, 1862, New Orleans, Tupper Letters.

78. Letter from "C," July 18, 1862, *Pittsfield Sun*, July 31, 1862.

79. Rich Diary, June 11, 1862. See also Knight Diary, June 14, 1862; and Hawkes to mother, June 30, 1862, Camp Morewood, Hawkes Letters.

80. Butler to Stanton, May 25, 1862, *Correspondence of General Butler*, 1:520.

81. Letter to Rice, Aug. 11, 1862; *Springfield (Mass.) Republican*, Aug. 26, 1862, L. Frederick Rice Letters, 31st Mass. Coll., MoSH (emphasis in original). This letter is attributed to Captain Nettleton in Rice to unknown, Sept. 11, 1862, ibid.

82. Underwood Diary, June 20, 1862.

83. Rich Diary, July 20, 1862.

84. Shaftoe Diary, Apr. 1, 1862. As noted previously, Sullivan's identity is not entirely certain. A Michael Sullivan was reported as "discharged for disability" on June 21. The one-day difference could be a simple clerical error, but the differing reason for leaving the regiment cannot be explained as easily (unless he was discharged for mental instability, which he displayed in committing his offense).

85. Underwood Diary, July 3, 1862.

86. Fairbank to sister, June 9, 1862, New Orleans, Fairbank Letters. Fairbank was presumably not using the word "scaffold" to refer to the platform; perhaps he meant the gibbet.

87. Tupper to parents, sister, and brother, June 9, 1862, New Orleans, Tupper Letters.

88. Butler, *Butler's Book*, 443–46.

89. Rich Diary, Sept. 30, 1862; Norris to mother Aug. 16, 1862, Camp Weitzel, Kenner, La., Thomas Norris Letters, 31st Mass. Coll., MoSH; Rice to Gus, Mar. 15, 1863, Fort Pike, Rice Letters.

90. Norris to father, Feb. 24, 1863, Camp Kearney, Carrollton, La., Norris Letters.

91. Norris to mother Nov. 7, 1863, Camp Banks, Baton Rouge, Norris Letters (emphasis in original).

92. Tupper to parents, sister, and brother, June 9, 1862, New Orleans, Tupper Letters.

93. Tupper to parents and sisters Aug. 16, 1862, Reading Press, New Orleans, Tupper Letters.

94. Lucius R Paige, *History of Hardwick, Massachusetts* (Boston: Houghton Mifflin, 1883), 215, 218.

95. Norris to mother, Dec. 2, 1863, Camp Banks, Baton Rouge, Norris Letters (emphasis in original).

96. Tupper to sister Louisa, June 16, 1862, New Orleans, Tupper Letters.

97. Tupper to sister Louisa, July 2, 1862, New Orleans, Tupper Letters.

98. Tupper to parents, Oct. 8, 1862, New Orleans, Tupper Letters.

99. Letter from "C," New Orleans, July 18, 1862, *Pittsfield Sun*, July 31, 1862.

100. Letter from "C," *Pittsfield Sun*, July 3, 1862.

101. Rich Diary, May 27, 1862.

102. Hallett, "Reminiscences," 24.

103. Hallett, "Reminiscences," 24. Hallett added that after the war "Mrs. Richards was not a woman of wealth and it is gratifying to know that the Government, hearing of her work and usefulness, bestowed on her a pension, which was of great help in her declining years. She died at Malden, Massachusetts, November, 1888."

104. Hawkes to mother, July 18, 1862, Camp Morewood, Hawkes Letters (emphasis in original).

105. Hawkes to mother, June 30, 1862, Hawkes Letters.

106. Wheeler Diary, June 27, 1862; Hawkes to mother, Aug. 16, 1862, Camp Morewood, Hawkes Letters.

107. Tupper to parents, sister, and brother, June 9, 1862, New Orleans, Tupper Letters.

108. Fairbank to unknown, May 30, 1862, New Orleans, Fairbank Letters.

CHAPTER 5

1. L. Frederick Rice to Massachusetts governor Frederic T. Greenhalge, May 1, 1894, L. Frederick Rice Papers Submitted to Attorney General, 31st Mass. Coll., MoSH. Another source gives the date as November 20. See Capt. Cooley to Whelden, Nov. 20, 1861, Charles M. Whelden Papers, ibid.

2. Gooding to Andrew, Aug. 4, 1862, Rice Papers Submitted to Attorney General.

3. Gooding to Andrew, Aug. 4, 1862 (emphasis in original).

4. Petition, officers of the 31st Regiment to Gov. John A. Andrew, Sept. 24, 1862, Rice Papers Submitted to Attorney General (emphasis in original).

5. Statement by officers, Oct. 15, 1862, "Copies of Papers from Vol. 38 of the 'Shoestring Library,'" Rice Papers Submitted to Attorney General. L. Frederick Rice apparently found these in the Massachusetts archives, then located in the State House.

6. Compare with the case of Captain Nettleton, described in chapter 1.

7. Erastus Hopkins to Andrew, Nov. 12, 25, 1862, Northampton, Mass., "Shoestring Library," Rice Papers Submitted to Attorney General. In the second letter Hopkins included an excerpt from a letter to the *Amherst (Mass.) Express* from a soldier in the 31st Massachusetts who asserted that Whelden and the quartermaster "indulge so freely in confederate whiskey, that they don't know half of the time whether they are fighting for the preservation of the Union, or to prevent the confederate whiskey from killing Jeff Davis."

8. Erastus Hopkins to Andrew, Nov. 12, 1862.

9. Erastus Hopkins to Andrew, Nov. 12, 1862 (emphasis in original).

10. Andrew to Sens. Charles Sumner and Henry Wilson, Dec. 21, 1861, *Andrew-Butler Correspondence*, 86.

11. *Correspondence of General Butler*. This absence reinforces the impression that documents unfavorable to Butler were edited out of the published collection, leaving only material that portrayed him in a positive light. The selection was probably done during Butler's lifetime and perhaps by the general himself, for it is unlikely that the editor would have taken it upon herself to delete valuable documents for any reason.

12. *Springfield Union*, Sept. 30, 1895.

13. *Pittsfield Sun*, July 13, 1893.

14. *Washington Post*, Apr. 2, 1895.

15. *Springfield Union*, Sept. 30, 1895.

16. Hawkes to mother, Sept. 28, 1862, Fort Jackson, Joshua W. Hawkes Letters, 31st Mass. Coll., MoSH (emphasis in original).

17. Hawkes to mother, Dec. 20, 1862, Fort Jackson, Hawkes Letters.

18. Hawkes to mother, June 30, 1862, Camp Morewood, Hawkes Letters.

19. Hawkes to mother, Oct. 18, 1862, Fort Jackson, Hawkes Letters.

20. *Pittsfield Sun*, July 13, 1893.

21. Howell to sister Bell, Aug. 10, 1862, Camp Morewood, Luther C. Howell Letters, Amherst College, Frost Library, Special Collections.

22. Joseph Hallett to H. M. Hallett, Dec. 24, 1862, New Orleans, Joseph F. Hallett Letters, MoSH.

23. Rice to unknown, Sept. 11, 1862, "Brown's Mill, La. on Pearl River" (emphasis in original), L. Frederick Rice Letters, 31st Mass. Coll., MoSH. Rice refers to a petition to Butler in August, which has not been found, whereas the petition that survives in the state archives was sent to Andrew in September. If his dates are correct, then it indicates that the officers petitioned the governor only after failing to obtain satisfaction from Butler.

24. "Oliver P. Gooding," in "George W. Cullum's Biographical Register," http://penelope.uchicago. edu/Thayer/E/Gazetteer/Places/America/United_States/Army/USMA/Cullums_Register/1821*. html. The *Official Records* does not seem to contain orders relating to Gooding's assignments.

25. Howell to sister, Aug. 30, 1862, Fort Jackson, Howell Letters.

26. Butler to Secy. of War, Feb. 12, 1862, *Correspondence of General Butler*, 1:350.

27. Richard Fay to Butler, Apr. 28, 1862, *Correspondence of General Butler*, 1:391. There is an insider pun here, as the Massachusetts recruiting officer was Brig. Gen. W. W. Bullock.

28. Hawkes to mother, June 30, 1862, Camp Morewood, Hawkes Letters.

29. Hawkes to mother, Sept. 15, 1862, Fort Jackson, Hawkes Letters.

30. Hawkes to mother, July 19 (addition to letter begun July 18), 1862, Camp Morewood, Hawkes Letters.

31. Hawkes to mother, Oct. 18, 1862, Fort Jackson, Hawkes Letters (emphasis in original). Chubbuck had been given the post of chaplain before the regiment left Massachusetts. *Pittsfield Sun*, Feb. 13, 1862.

32. Howell to sister Bell, Aug. 10, 1862, Camp Morewood, Howell Letters.

33. See Edwin C. Bidwell, "Our Chaplain: His Work at New Orleans and His Little Romance," 31st Mass. Coll., MoSH; and Tupper to parents, Dec. 15, 1862, New Orleans, James B. T. Tupper Letters, Hardwick Historical Society.

34. Butler, *Butler's Book*, 462.

35. Hesseltine report, July 17, 1862, *OR*, 15:523.

36. American Tract Society, *The Color Bearer, Francis A. Clary* (New York, 1864), 55.

37. Asa P. Wheeler Diary, Aug. 31, Sept. 9, 1862, 31st Mass. Coll., MoSH.

38. Letter from "C," New Orleans, Sept. 14, 1862, *Pittsfield Sun*, Oct. 2, 1862.

39. Hopkins to wife, Aug. 27, 1862, Fort Jackson, William Swinton Bennett Hopkins Papers, David M. Rubenstein Rare Book and Manuscript Library, Duke University.

40. Fairbank to sister, Aug. 25, 1862, Fort Jackson, Luther M. Fairbank Letters, 1861–63, Special Collections, Louisiana State University.

41. Wheeler Diary, Aug. 31, Sept. 9, 1862. In his report Hesseltine counted a diverse assortment of seventy-five artillery pieces and noted that "most of the guns are of too short range to oppose modern artillery." Hesseltine report, July 17, 1862, *OR*, 15:524. It is possible that more guns were collected and brought to Fort Jackson before the 31st Massachusetts arrived.

42. Hawkes to mother, Sept. 1, 1862, Fort Jackson, MoSH.

43. Howell to sister, Aug. 30, 1862, Howell Letters (emphasis in original).

44. Fairbank to sister, Aug. 25, 1862, Fairbank Letters; William H. Rich Diary, Aug. 2, 3, 1862, 31st Mass. Coll., MoSH.

45. Hopkins to wife, Aug. 27, 1862, Fort Jackson, Hopkins Papers.

46. Fairbank to sister, Aug. 25, Sept. 19, 1862, Fairbank Letters.

47. Richard F. Underwood Diary, Aug. 21, 1862, 31st Mass. Coll., MoSH.

48. George Goodwin Recollections, 31st Mass. Coll., MoSH.

49. Hesseltine report, *OR*, 15:524.

50. Frank S. Knight Diary, Sept. 5, 1862, 31st Mass. Coll., MoSH; American Tract Society, *Color Bearer*, 55.

51. Hopkins to wife, Aug. 27, 1862, Fort Jackson, Hopkins Papers.

52. Knight Diary, Sept. 5, 20, 1862.

53. Luther M. Fairbank Diary, Sept. 19, 1862, 31st Mass. Coll., MoSH.

54. Hawkes to mother, Nov. 16, 1862, Fort Jackson, Hawkes Letters.

55. Rice to unknown, Oct. 12, 1862, Fort Pike, Rice Letters, MoSH.

56. Rich Diary, Aug. 20, 1862.

57. Underwood Diary, Sept.–Nov. 1862. Captain Darling submitted an account of a skirmish that occurred. See Darling to Whelden, Nov. 26, 1862, Rice Letters. For another account of these activities, see Rich Diary, Dec. 23, 1862.

58. Rice to Gus, Jan. 22, 1863, New Orleans, Rice Letters.

59. Rich Diary, Sept. 6, Oct. 7, 1862, John F. H. Claiborne Letters, 31st Mass. Coll., MoSH; Tupper to parents and sister, July 22, 1862, New Orleans, Tupper Letters.

60. George U. Young Recollections, 31st Mass. Coll., MoSH, 46–52. All quotes in the this and the following two paragraphs come from this source.

61. Fairbank Diary, Dec. 2, 1862.

62. See Nelson F. Bond, "Affair at Des Sair Station," 31st Mass. Coll., MoSH; John E. McCarthy, "Affair at Des Sair Station," ibid.; Jeremiah McGraith, "Affair at Des Sair Station," ibid.

63. Norris to brother, Dec. 17, 1862, Bonnet Carre Point, La., Thomas Norris Letters, 31st Mass. Coll., MoSH.

64. Tupper to parents, Sept. 27, 1862, New Orleans, Tupper Letters.

65. Underwood Diary, Dec. 20, 1862.

66. Butler, *Butler's Book,* 522, 530; Nolan, *Benjamin Franklin Butler,* 227–28.

67. General Order 106, Department of the Gulf, Dec. 15, 1862, in Butler, *Butler's Book,* 502.

68. Farewell message, Dec. 24, 1862, in Butler, *Butler's Book,* 538–41. Of the modern biographers, only Richard S. West Jr. seems to give sufficient weight to this proclamation. See West, *Lincoln's Scapegoat General,* 203.

69. Hawkes to mother, Dec. 16, 1862, Fort Jackson, Hawkes Letters.

70. Hawkes to mother, Jan. 1, 1863, Fort Jackson, Hawkes Letters.

71. Hallett to brother, Dec. 24, 1862, New Orleans, Hallett Letters.

72. Hawkes to mother, Jan. 1, 1863, Fort Jackson, Hawkes Letters.

73. Howell to sister Clara, Jan. 1, 1863, Fort Jackson, Howell Letters.

74. Rice to Gus, Mar. 15, 1863, Fort Pike, Rice Letters.

75. Hawkes to mother, Jan. 1, 1863, Fort Jackson, Hawkes Letters.

76. Hawkes to mother, Jan. 13, 1863, Hawkes Letters (emphasis in original).

77. Rice to unknown, Sept. 11, 1862, "Brown's Mill, La. on Pearl River," Rice Letters.

78. Tupper to parents, Dec. 23 (addition to letter begun Dec. 22), 1862, New Orleans, Tupper Letters.

79. Howell to sister, Jan. 1, 1863, Howell Letters.

CHAPTER 6

1. Hawkes to mother, Feb. 27, 1863, Camp Kearney, Joshua W. Hawkes Letters, 31st Mass. Coll., MoSH (emphasis in original).

2. Norris to father, Feb. 24, 1863, Camp Kearney, Thomas Norris Letters, 31st Mass. Coll., MoSH (emphasis in original).

3. Tupper to parents, Dec. 22, 1862, New Orleans, James B. T. Tupper Letters, Hardwick Historical Society.

4. Hallett to Cousin Judah, Dec. 18[?], 1862, Joseph L. Hallett Letters, MoSH.

5. Hallett to mother, Dec. 31, 1862, New Orleans, Hallett Letters.

6. Hallett to brother, Dec. 24, 1862, New Orleans, Hallett Letters.

7. Ludwell H Johnson, *Red River Campaign: Politics and Cotton in the Civil War* (Baltimore: Johns Hopkins University Press, 1958), 21–23.

8. Halleck to Gen. William T. Sherman, May 3, 1864, *OR*, 34(3):333.

9. Tupper to parents, Jan. 18, 1863, Carrollton, Tupper Letters.

10. Tupper to parents, Mar. 5, 1863, Tupper Letters.

11. According to James Tupper, the 116th New York was soon transferred to another brigade and replaced by the 175th New York. Tupper to parents, Jan. 27, 1863, Carrollton, Tupper Letters.

12. Tupper to parents, Feb. 5, 1863, Carrollton, Tupper Letters.

13. Hawkes to mother, Feb. 9, 1863, Camp Kearney, Hawkes Letters.

14. Luther M. Fairbank Diary, Aug. 23, 1862, 31st Mass. Coll., MoSH; Captain Hopkins quoted in Erastus Hopkins to Gov. Andrew, Nov. 12, 1862, "Copies of Papers from Vol. 38 of the 'Shoestring Library,'" L. Frederick Rice Papers Submitted to Attorney General, ibid.

15. Sarah Hopkins to Hopkins's wife Lizzie, Sept. 1, 1863, William Swinton Bennett Hopkins Papers, David M. Rubenstein Rare Book and Manuscript Library, Duke University.

16. Erastus Hopkins to Gov. Andrew, Jan. 21, 1863, "Shoestring Library," Rice Papers Submitted to Attorney General (emphasis in original).

17. Tupper to parents, Jan. 18, 1863, Carrollton, Tupper Letters.

18. Fairbank Diary, Jan. 24, 1863.

19. Fairbank Diary, July 28, 29, 1862.

20. Hawkes to mother, Jan. 26, 1863, "near Carrollton," Hawkes Letters.

21. Howell to sister, Aug. 30, 1862, Fort Jackson, Luther C. Howell Letters, Amherst College, Frost Library, Special Collections.

22. Howell to sister Bell, Aug. 10, 1862, Camp Morewood, Howell Letters.

23. Rice to Gus, Mar. 15, 1863, Fort Pike, L. Frederick Rice Letters, 31st Mass. Coll., MoSH.

24. Rice to unknown, Mar. 29, 1863, Rice Letters.

25. Tupper to parents, Nov. 13, 1862, New Orleans, Tupper Letters.

26. Tupper to brother and sisters, June 30, 1862, New Orleans, Tupper Letters.

27. Tupper to brother and sisters, Oct. 8, 1862, Tupper Letters.

28. Tupper to brother and sisters, Feb. 25, 1863, Carrollton, Tupper Letters.

29. Butler, *Butler's Book*, 484.

30. *Red River Expedition*, extracts from U.S. Congress, Joint Committee on the Conduct of the War, *Report of the Joint Committee on the Conduct of the War, 1863–1866* (Millwood, N.Y.: Kraus Reprint, 1977), 307.

31. Banks to Halleck, Feb. 12, 1863, *OR*, 15:240.

32. Fairbank Diary, Feb. 12, 1863.

33. Fairbank Diary, Feb. 12, 1863; Tupper to parents, Feb. 13, 1863, Carrollton, Tupper Letters.

34. Fairbank Diary, Feb. 14, 1863; Norris to mother, Feb. 19, 1863, "on board Steamer Kepper off Plaquemine," Norris Letters.

35. Howell to brother, Feb. 15, 1863, Plaquemine, Howell Letters.

36. Tupper to parents, Feb. 13, 1863, Carrollton, Tupper Letters.

37. Fairbank Diary, Feb. 17, 1863.

38. *Red River Expedition,* 307.

39. Fairbank Diary, Feb. 13, 1863; Hawkes to mother, Feb. 17, 1863, "on Board Steamer Kepper off the village of Plaquemine, Mississippi River," Hawkes Letters. The drunken man was the German, while the other was reportedly a member of Company K, though the roster (see chap. 1, note 39) does not show anyone from that company dying on that date.

40. Hawkes to mother, Mar. 12, 1863, "Camp Magnolia near Baton Rouge," Hawkes Letters.

41. Joseph Hallett, "Feint on Port Hudson," in "Reminiscences of the Civil War," 31st Mass. Coll., MoSH.

42. Fairbank Diary, Mar. 11, 1863.

43. Edward Cunningham, *The Port Hudson Campaign, 1862–1863* (Baton Rouge: Louisiana State University Press, 1963), 22.

44. Banks to Halleck, Mar. 21, 1863, *OR,* 15:253.

45. Hopkins to sister Sarah, Mar. 23, 1863, Camp Magnolia, Hopkins Papers.

46. Hopkins to sister Sarah, Mar. 23, 1863.

47. Quoted in Lawrence Lee Hewitt, *Port Hudson: Confederate Bastion on the Mississippi* (Baton Rouge: Louisiana State University Press, 1987), 101.

48. Banks to Halleck, Mar. 21, 1863, *OR,* 15:255.

49. Fairbank Diary, Mar. 20, 1863; Nelson F. Bond Diaries, Mar. 18, 1863, 31st Mass. Coll., MoSH.

50. Hopkins to sister Sarah, Mar. 23, 1863, Hopkins Papers.

51. Hawkes to mother, Mar. 25, 1863, Camp Magnolia, Hawkes Letters.

52. Hawkes to mother, Apr. 3, 1863, Algiers, La., Hawkes Letters (emphasis in original).

53. Fairbank Diary, Jan. 6, 1863 (while still at Fort Jackson).

54. Fairbank Diary, Dec. 2, 1862.

55. Tupper to parents, Jan. 18, 1863, Carrollton, Tupper Letters.

56. Tupper to parents, Feb. 25, 1863, Tupper Letters.

57. Hallett to brother, Dec. 14, 1862, New Orleans, Hallett Letters.

58. Andrew Hanselmann, "Adventures in North America According to My Own Experiences," *Swiss-American Historical Society Review* 47, no. 3 (Nov. 2011): 1–51.

59. Bond Diaries, Apr. 8, 1863.

60. Fairbank Diary, Apr. 9, 1863.

61. Tupper to parents, Apr. 26, 1863, Brashear City, Tupper Letters.

62. Fairbank Diary, Apr. 9, 1863. Ware Center was the original town plot, largely superseded when factories were built along the Ware River.

63. *OR,* 15:330–31, 346–50. For the Confederate perspective of the fighting at Fort Bisland, see Richard Taylor, *Destruction and Reconstruction: Personal Experiences in the Late War. 1877* (1877; repr., ed. Richard B. Harwell, New York: Longmans, Green, 1955), 154–56.

64. Hopkins report, *OR,* 15:348–50.

65. Fairbank Diary, Apr. 14, 1863.

66. Horace J. Beach, "The Last Moments of the Gunboat Diana, and Her Almost Final Resting Place," 2010, www.youngsanders.org/Thearticle.pdf.

67. Oliver J. Semmes Diary, 31st Mass. Coll., MoSH. Private Allen provides the only direct

connection between Semmes and the 31st Massachusetts., It is unclear why Allen was in New Orleans, unless he was assigned light duties while hospitalized there. A note accompanying the diary states that the captain was being exchanged upon his release. But John Winters writes that General Weitzel, "a former classmate and friend of Semmes at West Point, placed a nominal guard over his prisoner, so that Semmes managed to escape." Winters, *Civil War in Louisiana,* 229.

68. *OR,* 15:1093–96. The luckless Sibley's middle name was Hopkins, his grandmother's family name, and the family appears to have originated in Massachusetts, so he might have been distantly related to the commander of the 31st Massachusetts.

69. Bond Diaries, Apr. 14, 1863; Fairbank Diary, Apr. 15–18, 1863.

70. *Red River Expedition,* 309 (emphasis in original).

71. Fairbank Diary, Apr. 20, 22, 1863.

72. Fairbank Diary, Apr. 27, 1863. The regimental roster lists "colored cooks" but does not show anyone named Freeman, which may represent his status rather than his name. See chap. 1, note 39.

73. Fairbank Diary, May 1, 1863.

74. Howell to sister, Apr. 25, 1863, Opelousas, Howell Letters.

75. Howell to brother, May 1, 1863, Opelousas, Howell Letters.

76. Fairbank Diary, May 6, 1863.

77. Fairbank Diary, May 7, 1863.

78. Bond Diaries, May 7, 1863, MoSH.

79. Charles P. Roland, *Louisiana Sugar Plantations during the Civil War* (Baton Rouge: Louisiana State University Press, 1997), esp. chap. 8 (which discusses the effects of various Federal invasions on plantation labor in the state).

80. Weitzel to Butler, Oct. 29, 1862, in James Parton, *General Butler in New Orleans* (New York: Mason Brothers, 1864), 580. The letter is not included in *Correspondence of General Butler.*

81. Weitzel to Butler, Nov. 1, 1862, *OR,* 15:170.

82. James G. Hollandsworth Jr., *Pretense of Glory: The Life of General Nathaniel P. Banks* (Baton Rouge: Louisiana State University Press, 1998), 117.

83. Winters, *Civil War in Louisiana,* 235–40. Dwight had been severely wounded and captured at Williamsburg, Virginia, in 1862.

84. Bond Diaries, May 9, 1863.

85. Fairbank Diary, May 9, 1863.

86. Bond Diaries, May 17, 1863.

87. Bond Diaries, May 18, 1863.

88. Bond Diaries, May 19, 1863.

CHAPTER 7

1. Cunningham, *Port Hudson,* 40; Hewitt, *Port Hudson,* 127.

2. Winters, *Civil War in Louisiana,* 240.

3. Nelson F. Bond Diaries, June 2, 1863, 31st Mass. Coll., MoSH.

4. Norris to father, Feb. 24, 1863, Carrollton, La., Thomas Norris Letters, 31st Mass. Coll., MoSH.

5. Hawkes to mother, Apr. 26, 1863, Joshua W. Hawkes Letters, 31st Mass. Coll., MoSH (emphasis in original).

6. Prince report, May 30, 1863, OR, 26(1):159.

7. Luther M. Fairbank Diary, May 25, 1863, 31st Mass. Coll., MoSH.

8. Fairbank Diary, May 25, 1863.

9. Bond Diaries, May 25, 1863.

10. Cunningham, Port Hudson, 48.

11. Banks to Halleck, Feb. 12, 1863, OR, 15:240.

12. Cunningham, Port Hudson, 70. John Winters puts Banks's total strength in this period at 30,000–40,000 men, but that may include the detached garrisons. Winters, Civil War in Louisiana, 248.

13. Winters, Civil War in Louisiana, 248.

14. Bond Diaries, May 27, 1863.

15. Hewitt, Port Hudson, 152–55.

16. Fairbank Diary, May 28, 1863.

17. Fairbank Diary, June 10, 11, 1863.

18. Fairbank Diary, June 5, 1863.

19. "Port Hudson to Clinton," Adelbert Bailey Recollections, 31st Mass. Coll., MoSH.

20. Fairbank Diary, June 5, 1863; Bond Diaries, June 5, 1863. The official reports of General Paine and Maj. J. P. Richardson, commanding the 38th Massachusetts, agree. "The excessive heat prostrated a large number of officers and men, who were sent back to headquarters in the evening," as Paine reported, but neither officer mentioned intervention by the surgeon. Paine report, OR, 26(1):126–27; Richardson report, ibid., 128–29.

21. Banks to Paine, June 5, 1863, OR, 26(1):127.

22. Fairbank Diary, June 6, 1863.

23. Perhaps contrary to expectation, blackberry-based compounds were sometimes used to treat diarrhea. Generally, however, such medicines used the vine's root, not its fruit. Michael A. Flannery, Civil War Pharmacy: A History of Drugs, Drug Supply and Provision, and Therapeutics for the Union and Confederacy (Binghamton, N.Y.: Pharmaceutical Products Press, 2004), 127–29.

24. Bond Diaries, June 7, 1863.

25. Bond Diaries, June 9, 1863.

26. Cunningham, Port Hudson, 77.

27. Howell to brother, June 17, 1863, "Before Port Hudson," Luther C. Howell Letters, Amherst College, Frost Library, Special Collections.

28. George U. Young Recollections, 31st Mass. Coll., MoSH, 68.

29. Young Recollections, 63. Although Young, writing at a twenty-year remove, has a tendency to conflate events, the association with the cotton bags makes his account credible.

30. Fairbank Diary, June 15, 1863. The phrase "seeing the elephant" originated in the experience of boys who saw the footprints left by traveling circus elephants on country roads but refused to believe that such a creature existed until they saw it in person.

31. Fairbank Diary, June 14, 1863.

32. Cunningham, *Port Hudson*, 92. He misidentifies Woods as Pvt. J. B. Woods.

33. Joseph L. Hallett, "Reminiscences of the Civil War," 31st Mass. Coll., MoSH, 48.

34. Bond Diaries, Apr. 18, 1863; Edwin C. Bidwell, "Remarkable Case of Capt. N. F. Bond," 31st Mass. Coll., MoSH.

35. Bidwell, "Remarkable Case of Capt. N. F. Bond."

36. Bond Diaries, June 14–16, July 1, 1863.

37. Fairbank Diary, June 14, 1863.

38. Tupper to "My Dear Balam," Jan. 22, 1862, Camp Seward, James B. T. Tupper Letters, Hardwick Historical Society.

39. William H. Rich Diary, May 31, 1862, 31st Mass. Coll., MoSH.

40. See, for example, Hawkes to mother, June 26, 1863, St. James Hospital, New Orleans, Hawkes Letters.

41. American Tract Society, *Color Bearer*, 89, 96–97.

42. Fairbank Diary, June 15, 1863.

43. See American Tract Society, *Color Bearer*.

44. Fairbank Diary, June 17, 1863.

45. Young Recollections, 66–67.

46. Fairbank Diary, June 15, 1863. Eight enlisted men also volunteered: Pvts. Chester Bevens, Patrick Carnes, Frank Fitch, William Thorington, Peter Valun, Ethan H. Cowles, William J. Coleman, and Maurice Lee. Except for Cowles, all were members of Companies A and K. *OR*, 26(1):62. Banks issued his call for volunteers in General Orders 49, June 15, 1863.

47. Tupper to parents, June 28, 1863, Springfield Landing, La., Tupper Letters.

48. Fairbank Diary, July 4, 1863.

49. Fairbank Diary, June 30, 1863.

50. Cunningham, *Port Hudson*, 111.

51. *OR*, 26(1):69.

52. Tupper to parents, July 17, 1863, Port Hudson, Tupper Letters.

CHAPTER 8

1. George U. Young Recollections, 31st Mass. Coll., MoSH, 74–75.

2. Norris to brother, July 25, 1863, "Camp near Donaldsonville," Thomas Norris Letters, 31st Mass. Coll., MoSH (emphasis in original).

3. Banks to Halleck, June 18, 1863, *OR*, 26(1):565. Halleck's advice, easy to give from his big desk in Washington, was to place guns loaded with grapeshot behind the reluctant warriors if they required motivation to do their duty.

4. Rice to unknown, July 26, 1863, Fort Pike, L. Frederick Rice Letters, 31st Mass. Coll., MoSH.

5. Rice to unknown, Jan. 4, 1863, Rice Letters.

6. Winters, *Civil War in Louisiana*, 293.

7. Luther M. Fairbank Diary, July 25, 1863, 31st Mass. Coll., MoSH.

8. *OR*, 26(1):711.

9. Fairbank Diary, Aug. 1, 1863.

10. William H. Rich Diary, Jan. 31, 1863, 31st Mass. Coll., MoSH.

11. Asa P. Wheeler Diary, Feb. 20, 1863, 31st Mass. Coll., MoSH.

12. Nelson F. Bond Diaries, Apr. 3, 1863, 31st Mass. Coll., MoSH.

13. Rich Diary, July 8, 10, 1863.

14. Richard F. Underwood Diary, Feb. 22, 1863, 31st Mass. Coll., MoSH.

15. Underwood Diary, Apr. 23, 1863.

16. Underwood Diary, Apr. 18, 1863. The raid took place on April 14.

17. Rich Diary, Apr. 14, 1863.

18. Richard F. Underwood, "The Life of Richard F. Underwood, Jan. 1863–Dec. 1863," 31st Mass. Coll., MoSH, May 1863.

19. Underwood, "Life," June 1863.

20. Underwood Diary, Jan. 22, 1863.

21. Underwood, "Life," June, Aug. 1863. Official records show that Thompson died of disease at New Orleans on October 21, 1863. See Mass. Adj. Gen., *Massachusetts Soldiers, Sailors, and Marines in the Civil War,* vol. 3.

22. Rice to unknown, July 12, 1863, Fort Pike, Rice Letters; Underwood Diary, July 4, 1863.

23. Rich Diary, July 4, 1862. Richard Underwood reported that the greased-pole contest was won by a drummer from Company F. See Underwood Diary, July 4, 1863.

24. Rice to unknown, July 12, 1863, Fort Pike, Rice Letters.

25. Rice to unknown, July 8, 1863, Rice Letters.

26. Underwood, "Life," May 1863.

27. Rice to Gus, Sept. 27, 1863, Camp Banks, Baton Rouge, Rice Letters.

28. Fairbank Diary, Sept. 10, 1863.

29. Rice to Gus, Sept. 27, 1863; Underwood Diary, Sept. 5, 1863.

30. Rich Diary, Sept. 5, 1863; Underwood, "Life," Aug. 1863.

31. Butler, *Butler's Book,* 497.

32. Fairbank Diary, Jan. 3, 1864.

33. Rice to Gus, Mar. 15, 1863, Fort Pike, Rice Letters. The 47th was a nine-month regiment nearing the end of its service.

34. Tupper to parents, Apr. 19, 1863, New Orleans, James B. T. Tupper Letters, Hardwick Historical Society. The reference is probably to Col. Justin Hodge of Connecticut, who was authorized to recruit the 1st Regiment of Louisiana Engineers.

35. Underwood, "Life," Nov. 1863.

36. Hallett's transfer may have been a consequence of a general order, issued while Butler was still in command, that called for "any soldiers in this Department who are acquainted in any way with telegraphic operations" to report. General Order 34, Department of the Gulf, Nov. 3, 1862, *General Orders . . . Issued by Major-General B. F. Butler,* 34.

37. Joseph L. Hallett, "Incidents of Prison Life," in "Reminiscences of the Civil War," 31st Mass. Coll., MoSH.

38. Hallett, "Reminiscences," 62, 65. A floating island was a popular dessert of custard and meringue.

39. Hawkes to mother, Mar. 29, 1863, Baton Rouge, Joshua W. Hawkes Letters, 31st Mass. Coll., MoSH.

40. Hawkes to mother, Apr. 17, 1863, St. James Hospital, Hawkes Letters (emphasis in original). Chandler Hathaway, a farmer from Charlemont, was thirty-six when he enlisted in October 1861 and died March 12, 1863, at Baton Rouge.

41. Fairbank Diary, Jan. 8, 1863.

42. Tupper to parents, Jan. 18, 1863, Carrollton, Tupper Letters; Fairbank Diary, July 14, 1862.

43. Hawkes to mother, June 13, 1863, St. James Hospital, Hawkes Letters.

44. Hawkes to mother, July 23, 1863, Hawkes Letters.

45. Hawkes to mother, June 26, 1863, Hawkes Letters.

46. Hawkes to mother, July 18, 1863, Hawkes Letters.

47. Hawkes to mother, June 4, 1863, Hawkes Letters.

48. Hawkes to mother, June 23, July 23, 1863, Hawkes Letters.

49. Wheeler Diary, Feb. 20, 1863.

50. Wheeler Diary, Feb. 22, 1863.

51. Underwood Diary, Dec. 31, 1862.

52. Hopkins to daughter, June 30, 1864, William Swinton Bennett Hopkins Papers, David M. Rubenstein Rare Book and Manuscript Library, Duke University.

53. Norris to Willie, Oct. 18, 1862, "Kenna [Kenner] LA," Norris Letters (emphasis in original).

54. Hallett, "Reminiscences," 30–31.

55. Wheeler Diary, June 18, 26, 1863.

56. Hawkes to mother, July 3, 1863, St. James Hospital, Hawkes Letters.

57. Edwin C. Bidwell, "Our Chaplain: His Work at New Orleans and His Little Romance," 31st Mass. Coll., MoSH.

58. Rich Diary, Oct. 9, 1864.

59. Tupper to brother and sisters, Dec. 3, 1862, New Orleans, Tupper Letters.

60. Tupper to father and mother, Jan. 27, Mar. 2, 1863, Carrollton, Tupper Letters.

61. Underwood, "Life," Aug. 1863.

62. Brian M. Jordan, *Marching Home: Union Veterans and Their Unending Civil War* (New York: Liveright, 2014), 127.

63. Data from roster compiled by author. See chap. 1, note 39.

64. Rice to unknown, Aug. 21, 1863, Fort Pike, Rice Letters.

65. Fairbank Diary, Oct. 1, 1863.

66. Fairbank Diary, Dec. 5, 1863. Captain Rockwell was the son of Julius Rockwell (1805–88), a politician and banker prominent in Berkshire County and statewide. He served as a U.S. representative and briefly as a senator. A GAR post in Pittsfield was named in honor of Captain Rockwell. Boltwood, *History of Pittsfield*, 234–35. Fairbank, from a different county and different company, felt no particular attachment to him.

67. Fairbank Diary, Dec. 5, 1863.

68. Fairbank Diary, Nov. 3, 1863.

69. Rice to unknown, July 26, 1863, Fort Pike, Rice Letters; Fairbank Diary, Nov. 3, 1863.

70. Rice to unknown, July 26, 1863.

71. Fairbank Diary, Sept. 4, 1863.

72. Fairbank Diary, Nov. 8, 1863.

73. Fairbank Diary, Jan. 14, 1863.

74. Fairbank Diary, Nov. 8, 1863.

75. Fairbank Diary, Jan. 27, 1863.

76. Fairbank Diary, Apr. 30, 1863.

77. Rice to unknown, July 8, 1863, Fort Pike, Rice Letters.

78. Rich Diary, July 9, 1863; Underwood, "Life," June 1863. The roster for Company I does not show any men who were captured on that date, but those records are mainly concerned with dates of enlistment and discharge. See chap. 1, note 39.

79. Underwood Diary, Oct. 21, 1863.

80. Norris to mother, Dec. 2, 1863, Camp Banks, Norris Letters (emphasis in original).

81. Butler to Col. D. W. McMillan, July 26, 1862, *Correspondence of General Butler,* 2:111. It does not appear that this request was carried out.

82. Banks to Halleck, Mar. 27, 1863, *OR,* 15:259.

83. Banks to Halleck, Aug. 17, 1863, *Red River Expedition,* 106.

84. Halleck to Banks, Sept. 8, 1863, *OR,* 26(1):719–20. Halleck further confessed in this letter that "volunteering had virtually ceased" so that the army was "much weaker" than it had been a year ago at that time, while he assumed that "Lee's army is probably as strong as before the battle of Gettysburg."

85. Rosecrans to Halleck, Nov. 16, 1862, *OR,* 20(2):58.

86. Thomas B. Buell, *The Warrior Generals: Combat Leadership in the Civil War* (New York: Three River, 1997), 253–54.

87. Halleck to Rosecrans, at Murfreesboro, Tenn., Mar. 21, 1863, *OR,* 23(2):155.

88. Banks to Halleck, Dec. 30, 1863, *OR,* 23(2):132.

89. Howell to brother, Mar. 21, 1864, near Alexandria, Luther C. Howell Letters, Amherst College, Frost Library, Special Collections.

90. Special Order 317, Department of the Gulf, Dec. 19, 1863, in *Supplement to the OR,* 5.

91. Underwood, "Life," Nov. 1863.

92. Rich Diary, Dec. 17, 1863.

93. Rich Diary, Jan. 2, 1864.

94. Howell to Bell, Jan. 17, 1864, New Orleans, Howell Letters.

95. Underwood, "Life," Dec. 1863; Fairbank Diary, Jan. 1, 2, 1864.

96. Fairbank Diary, Jan. 5, 8, 1864.

97. Rich Diary, Jan. 11, 1864.

98. Fairbank Diary, Jan. 5, 1864.

99. Fairbank Diary, Jan. 4, 1864.

100. Fairbank Diary, Jan. 18, 1864.

101. Howell to sister, Feb. 9, 1864, New Orleans, Howell Letters.

102. Rice to unknown, Jan. 4, 1863, Fort Pike, Rice Letters.

103. Young Recollections, 83.

104. "December 1863, Organization as Cavalry," Adelbert Bailey Recollections, 31st Mass. Coll., MoSH.

105. Howell to brother, Feb. 24, 1864, New Orleans, Howell Letters (emphasis in original). There is confusion about the designation of this unit. The original 1st New Hampshire Cavalry was formed in 1861 but was later incorporated into the 1st Rhode Island Cavalry. It was detached in 1864, brought up to strength, and then sent to Washington, D.C., but it never served in the Gulf. Meanwhile, the 8th New Hampshire Infantry, which had been part of Butler's expedition, also was converted to cavalry in December 1863. Until the original 1st New Hampshire Cavalry was re-formed, this transformed unit may have been considered the 1st but later was regarded as the 2nd New Hampshire Cavalry. During this interval, members of the 31st Massachusetts, such as Howell and Rich, wrote of it as the 1st New Hampshire Cavalry. Although they had shared many experiences, the men of the two regiments may not have been closely acquainted. As if encountering them for the first time, Rich dismissed the 1st New Hampshire Cavalry as "a dirty looking set." Rich Diary, Jan. 13, 1864.

106. Howell to Bell, Jan. 17, 1864, Howell Letters.

107. Howell to Bell, Jan. 17, 1864.

108. Rich Diary, Feb. 23, 1863.

109. Rich Diary, Sept. 26, 1863.

110. Howell to brother, Feb. 24, 1864, New Orleans; Rich Diary, Feb. 16, 1864.

111. Rice to unknown, Aug. 21, 1863, Fort Pike, Rice Letters.

112. Fairbank Diary, Feb. 12, 13, 1864.

113. *Springfield (Mass.) Republican*, Oct. 9, 1930. Luther Fairbank died on December 29, 1930, and George on March 3, 1931. Both are buried in Aspen Grove Cemetery, Ware, Massachusetts.

114. Fairbank Diary, Feb. 5, 1864.

115. Norris to mother, Dec. 2, 1863, Camp Banks, Norris Letters (emphasis in original).

116. Norris to mother, Jan. 26; Feb. 4, 1864, New Orleans, Norris Letters.

117. Norris to mother, Feb. 19, 1864, Norris Letters.

118. Norris to mother, Jan. 26, 1864, Norris Letters.

119. Rich Diary, Feb. 2, 1864.

120. Fairbank Diary, Feb. 2, 1864. Incidentally, this event confirms how little concern military authorities had for sanitation and water pollution.

CHAPTER 9

1. Butler, *Butler's Book*, chaps. 9, 10, and 12 passim. In his farewell address to his troops, Butler included this boast: "Landing with a military chest containing but seventy-five dollars, from the hoards of a rebel government you have given to your country's treasury nearly a half million of dollars, and so supplied yourselves with the needs of your service that your expedition has cost your government *less by four/fifths* than any other." Ibid., 502 (emphasis in original). Butler also quoted Treasury Secretary Chase to having said, effectly, "You are the cheapest general we have employed." Ibid., 518.

2. Johnson, *Red River Campaign*, 45.

3. Troop order, Jan. 31, 1864, *OR*, 34(3):196.

4. The American Civil War Research Database (http://www.civilwardata.com) gives the number as 330.

5. L. Frederick Rice, "The Red River Campaign of 1864," Mar. 8, 1864, 31st Mass. Coll., MoSH.

6. William H. Rich Diary, Mar. 9, 1864, 31st Mass. Coll., MoSH.

7. Rice, "Red River Campaign," Mar. 9, 1864.

8. Rice, "Red River Campaign," Mar. 9, 1864.

9. Rice, "Red River Campaign," Mar. 13, 1864.

10. Rich Diary, Mar. 10, 1864. Fairbank noted that "the works have all been levelled down." Luther M. Fairbank Diary, Mar. 10, 1864, 31st Mass. Coll., MoSH.

11. Rice, "Red River Campaign," Mar. 12, 1864.

12. Fairbank Diary, Mar. 13, 1864.

13. Rice, "Red River Campaign," Mar. 14, 1864.

14. Rice, "Red River Campaign," Mar. 16, 1864.

15. Rice, "Red River Campaign," Mar. 18, 1864.

16. Fairbank Diary, Mar. 19, 1864.

17. Rice, "Red River Campaign," Mar. 20, 1864.

18. Taylor had opposed the strengthening of Fort De Russy. He later observed of the post's capture, with typical acerbity, "Thus much for our Red River Gibraltar." *Destruction and Reconstruction*, 183, 186. Taylor was one of those uncommon generals who possessed broad strategic vision. Perhaps because he had not attended West Point and thus had not been trained as an engineer, he did not overvalue fortifications. On the contrary, he believed that "the policy of shutting up large bodies of troops in fortifications without a relieving army near at hand, can not be too strongly reprobated." Ibid., 177. Reviewing the war, as Taylor was doing when he wrote these observations, it is difficult to dispute his conclusion that such a policy had "fatal consequences" for the Confederacy.

19. Gary D. Joiner, *One Damn Blunder from Beginning to End: The Red River Campaign of 1864* (Wilmington, Del.: Scholarly Resources, 2003), 67.

20. Joiner, *One Damn Blunder*, 63. Joiner gives a figure of 32,500 for Banks's total strength, stating that Lee commanded 4,653 officers and troopers at the outset of the campaign.

21. Rice, "Red River Campaign," Apr. 7, 1864.

22. Quoted in Winters, *Civil War in Louisiana*, 335.

23. Fairbank Diary, Apr. 4, 1864.

24. Rice, "Red River Campaign," Apr. 4, 5, 1864.

25. Rice, "Red River Campaign," Apr. 6, 1864.

26. Elbert H. Fordham, "The Red River Campaign," 31st Mass. Coll., MoSH; Rice, "Red River Campaign," Apr. 7, 1864.

27. Rice, "Red River Campaign," Apr. 8, 1864.

28. Rich Diary, Mar. 27, 1864.

29. Report of Gen. A. L. Lee, *OR*, 34(1):456.

30. Fordham, "Red River Campaign."

31. Fordham, "Red River Campaign."

32. Fordham, "Red River Campaign."

33. Fordham, "Red River Campaign." Fordham states that at this time the regiment had been reduced to 210 officers and men.

34. Fordham, "Red River Campaign."

35. Rice, "Red River Campaign," Apr. 8, 1864.

36. Fordham, "Red River Campaign."

37. Fordham, "Red River Campaign."

38. Edwin C. Bidwell, "The Battle of Sabine Cross Roads as I Saw It," 31st Mass. Coll., MoSH.

39. Fairbank Diary, Apr. 8, 1864.

40. Hawkes to mother, June 30, 1862, Camp Morewood, Joshua W. Hawkes Letters, 31st Mass. Coll., MoSH.

41. Fairbank Diary, Nov. 10, 1862.

42. Nelson F. Bond Diaries, Mar. 27, 1863, 31st Mass. Coll., MoSH.

43. Fairbank Diary, Sept. 3, 1863.

44. Fairbank Diary, Nov. 20, 1863.

45. Fairbank Diary, Jan. 5, 1864.

46. Hopkins to wife, Nov. 10, 1861, William Swinton Bennett Hopkins Papers, David M. Rubenstein Rare Book and Manuscript Library, Duke University (emphasis in original).

47. Elizabeth Hopkins to W. S. B. Hopkins, Mar. 2, 1862, Northampton, Hopkins Papers.

48. Elizabeth Hopkins to W. S. B. Hopkins, Feb. 27 (addition to letter of Feb. 23), 1862, Hopkins Papers.

49. Letter from "C," *Pittsfield Sun,* July 3, 1862.

50. Tupper to sister Louisa, June 16, 1862, New Orleans, James B. T. Tupper Letters, Hardwick Historical Society.

51. Fairbank Diary, Aug. 18, 1862.

52. Hopkins to wife, Aug. 27, 1862, Hopkins Papers.

53. Hopkins to sister Sarah, Nov. 30, 1863, Baton Rouge, Hopkins Papers.

54. Hopkins to sister Sarah, June 8, 1863, Port Hudson, Hopkins Papers.

55. In the confused aftermath of the battle, it is unlikely that anyone was able to prepare a report of casualties in the 31st Massachusetts. The American Civil War Research Database (http://www.civilwardata.com) gives figures of six killed, forty wounded, twenty-one prisoners, and eight missing from the regiment for this battle. The roster prepared by the author (see chap. 1, note 39) shows six men killed or who died as prisoners immediately after the battle. Others may be listed under the general categories of "died of wounds" or "discharged for disability" without being attributed to the fighting of April 8. Heavy Confederate losses in the initial assault, especially among officers, are described in "Record of the Eighteenth Louisiana Regiment," in Napier Bartlett, *Military Record of Louisiana: Including Biographical and Historical Papers Relating to the Military Organizations of the State* (1964; Baton Rouge: Louisiana State University Press, 1996), "The Trans Mississippi," 42.

56. Fordham, "Red River Campaign."

57. Fordham, "Red River Campaign."

58. *Red River Expedition,* 326; Hollandsworth, *Pretense of Glory,* 192; Johnson, *Red River Campaign,* 162.

59. Fordham, "Red River Campaign."

60. Howell to Bell, Apr. 11, 1864, Grand Ecore, Luther C. Howell Letters, Amherst College, Frost Library, Special Collections.

61. Fordham, "Red River Campaign."

62. Howell to Bell, Apr. 11, 1864, Grand Ecore, Howell Letters.

63. Field Order, Dept. of the Gulf, Grand Ecore, Apr. 18, 1864, *OR,* 34(3):211; Fairbank Diary, Apr. 18, 1864.

64. Field Order, Dept. of the Gulf, Grand Ecore, Apr. 18, 1864, *OR,* 34(3):211.

65. Lee farewell message, Apr. 18, 1864, Grand Ecore, La., Edward P. Nettleton Papers, vol. 2, 31st Mass. Coll., MoSH. In the collection this group of items is titled "Index to Vol. 2 Col. Nettleton's Papers," but it is not really an index as it contains full documents, mostly orders and such. Since it follows Nettleton Papers, volume 1, it seems reasonable to refer to it as Nettleton Papers, volume 2.

66. Lee to Banks, May 5, 1864, *OR,* 34(3):452.

67. Rice, "Red River Campaign," Apr. 11, 1864. No such document has been found, but since Rice both wrote it and was in charge of assembling the regimental history after the war, this absence is explainable.

68. Special Order 89, Apr. 14, 1864, Nettleton Papers, vol. 2.

69. Fairbank Diary, Apr. 15, 1864.

70. Special Order 625, June 4, 1864, Nettleton Papers, vol. 2.

71. Fordham, "Red River Campaign."

72. No one in the regiment reported seeing Major Bache again after he fled at Sabine Cross Roads, so any discussion of his fate must remain speculative.

73. "Nettie" to Hopkins, Aug. 24, 1864, "Home," Hopkins Papers.

74. In his memoir Taylor asserts that, after the return of two divisions to Smith, he commanded only 5,200 men. See *Destruction and Reconstruction,* 233. If one of the major Union armies had been under the command of someone like Dick Taylor at the start of 1862, the war might have ended that year.

75. Johnson, *Red River Campaign,* 222.

76. Winters, *Civil War in Louisiana,* 362.

77. Henry D. Barber Diary, Apr. 28, 1864, 31st Mass. Coll., MoSH.

78. Fairbank Diary, Apr. 25, 1864.

79. Nelson F. Bond, "Chronology of Red River Campaign," Apr. 28, 1864, Nettleton Papers, vol. 1, 31st Mass. Coll., MoSH.

80. Rich Diary, Apr. 28, 30, 1864.

81. Rice, "Red River Campaign," Apr. 30, 1864.

82. Fordham, "Red River Campaign."

83. "The 31st Regiment of Infantry," 31st Mass. Coll., MoSH, typescript; Bowen, *Massachusetts in the War,* 474. Nelson Bond also noted this praise: "Gen. Mower gave us as Cavalry a very

high compliment." Bond, "Chronology of Red River Campaign," May 3, 1864. No written record of this remark has been found in the *Official Records* or in the Nettleton Papers. It may have been delivered informally, perhaps only verbally.

84. Fairbank Diary, May 3, 4, 1864.

85. George Goodwin Recollections, 31st Mass. Coll., MoSH.

86. Rice, "Red River Campaign"; Johnson, *Red River Campaign*, 255–57; Joiner, *One Damn Blunder*, 161–62.

87. Rice, "Red River Campaign," May 13, 1864.

88. Barber, "Red River Campaign," May 14, 1864.

89. Winters, *Civil War in Louisiana*, 366; Johnson, *Red River Campaign*, 224.

90. Winters, *Civil War in Louisiana*, 429.

91. John David Smith, introduction to Roland, *Louisiana Sugar Plantations*, xiii.

92. Goodwin Recollections.

93. Rice, "Red River Campaign," May 14, 1864.

94. Bond, "Chronology of Red River Campaign," May 14, 1864.

95. Bond, "Chronology of Red River Campaign," May 14–15, 1864.

96. Barber, "Red River Campaign," May 17, 1864.

97. Rice, "Red River Campaign," May 17, 1864.

98. Barber, "Red River Campaign," May 18, 1864.

99. Barber, "Red River Campaign," May 18, 1864.

100. Fordham report, May 22, 1864, *OR*, 34(1):465–67.

101. Rice, "Red River Campaign," May 18, 1864.

102. Lewis O. Frary, "Reminiscences," 31st Mass. Coll., MoSH. Written many years after the event, this account confuses casualties from the Port Hudson and Red River Campaigns but is probably correct as to the details of Babcock's injury, as the roster shows that he was injured on May 18 and died of his wounds on May 31, 1864. See chap. 1, note 39.

103. Marshall Clothier, "An Incident of 17th of May, 1864," 31st Mass. Coll., MoSH. The roster states that Hillman died on May 14, so there is an error somewhere. See chap. 1, note 39.

104. Johnson, *Red River Campaign*, 275.

105. For example, see Barber, "Red River Campaign," June 19, 1864 (also mentioned below).

106. Taylor, *Destruction and Reconstruction*, 232. Taylor acknowledged suffering heavy losses at Yellow Bayou.

107. Arnold to Headquarters, May 18, 1865, *OR*, 34(3):647.

108. Special Order 47, Military Division of West Mississippi, *OR*, 34(3): 531, 545.

109. Field Order 45, Dept. of the Gulf, May 18, 1864, *OR*, 34(3):645.

110. See, for instance, Rice, "Red River Campaign"; Rust Diary; and N. F. Bond, "Chronology of Red River Campaign." Bond sent his chronology to Colonel Nettleton on January 1, 1865, but it is presumably based on notes he kept at the time.

111. Bond, "Chronology of Red River Campaign," May 30–June 5, 1864.

112. Barber, "Red River Campaign," June 5, 1864 (emphasis in original).

113. Rice, "Red River Campaign," June 1, 1864.

114. Rice, "Red River Campaign," May 31, June 1, 1864. The incident is apparently described in Davis report, June 5, 1864, *OR*, 34(1):963–64.

115. Davis report, June 5, 1864, *OR*, 34(1):963–64.

116. Bond, "Chronology of Red River Campaign," June 8, 1864.

117. Bond, "Chronology of Red River Campaign," June 18–21, 1864. It might have been ironic for the men in the 31st Massachusetts to discover that Fort Adams was named in honor of Pres. John Adams of their home state.

118. Barber, "Red River Campaign."

119. Order, 4th Cavalry Brigade Headquarters, June 19, 1864, Nettleton Papers, vol. 2.

120. Two popular biographies of Sickles discuss his mission to the South but do not mention his review of the Department of the Gulf: W. A. Swanberg, *Sickles the Incredible* (New York: Scribner's, 1956), and Thomas Keneally, *American Scoundrel: The Life of the Notorious Civil War General Dan Sickles* (New York: Doubleday, 2002).

121. Rich Diary, June 14, 1864.

122. Joseph L. Hallett, "Reminiscences of the Civil War," 31st Mass. Coll., MoSH, 74. Hallett gives the date of the review as June 15, but Rich and Fairbank record it as the fourteenth. Since Hallett was writing in 1911, the earlier date is likely correct.

123. Winters, *Civil War in Louisiana*, 377.

124. He later expanded on this to blame Smith for the loss of the entire war. See Taylor, *Destruction and Reconstruction*, 233.

125. *Canby to Banks, May 14, 1864, OR*, 34(3):583.

126. Howell to Sid, Apr. 26, 1864, Alexandria, Howell Letters.

CHAPTER 10

1. Dwight testimony, *Red River Expedition*, 190.

2. Banks testimony, *Red River Expedition*, 339.

3. Dwight testimony, *Red River Expedition*, 187.

4. Dwight testimony, *Red River Expedition*, 190.

5. Dwight testimony, *Red River Expedition*, 191.

6. Banks testimony, *Red River Expedition*, 20, 340.

7. Lee testimony, *Red River Expedition*, 63.

8. Howell to Sid, Apr. 26, 1864, Alexandria, Luther C. Howell Letters, Amherst College, Frost Library, Special Collections.

9. Franklin testimony, *Red River Expedition*, 35.

10. Franklin testimony, *Red River Expedition*, 32.

11. Lee testimony, *Red River Expedition*, 64.

12. Clark testimony, *Red River Expedition*, 194.

13. Emory testimony, *Red River Expedition*, 219.

14. Although it addresses later wars, instructive in this regard is Thomas E. Ricks, *The Generals: American Military Command from World War II to Today* (New York: Penguin, 2012).

15. Banks testimony, *Red River Expedition,* 11. During his appearance before the joint committee, Franklin said that he expected a fight between Mansfield and Shreveport but wanted it to happen the next day (April 9, the day after the actual battle at Sabine Cross Roads), which may be true but did not address the same question.

16. Lee testimony, *Red River Expedition,* 63.

17. Dwight testimony, *Red River Expedition,* 185–87.

18. Luther M. Fairbank Diary, Jan. 24, 1864, 31st Mass. Coll., MoSH.

19. Banks testimony, *Red River Expedition,* 17.

20. Howell to Sid, Apr. 5, 1864, Natchitoches, Howell Letters (emphasis in original).

21. Howell to Sid, Apr. 26, 1864, Alexandria, Howell Letters (emphasis in original).

22. Porter testimony and letters, *Red River Expedition,* 250–51.

23. Franklin testimony, *Red River Expedition,* 22, 34, 190.

24. Banks testimony, *Red River Expedition,* 13.

25. Porter testimony and letters, *Red River Expedition,* 266.

26. Porter testimony and letters, *Red River Expedition,* 253.

27. Porter testimony, *Red River Expedition,* 270, 272.

28. Banks testimony, *Red River Expedition,* 18.

29. Dwight testimony, *Red River Expedition,* 224.

30. Banks testimony, *Red River Expedition,* 330, 338.

31. Banks testimony, *Red River Expedition,* 333.

32. Howell to sister, Apr. 11, 1863, "Brashier City," Howell Letters.

33. William H. Rich Diary, Mar. 27, 1864, 31st Mass. Coll., MoSH.

34. Grant to Halleck, Apr. 25, 1864, *Red River Expedition,* 167.

35. Grant to Halleck, Apr. 28, 1864, *Red River Expedition,* 169.

36. Grant to Halleck, May 3, 1864, *Red River Expedition,* 171.

37. Grant to Halleck, May 17, 1864, *Red River Expedition,* 173.

38. Halleck to Grant, May 17, 1864, *Red River Expedition,* 174.

39. Canby to Halleck, May 18, 1864, "Mouth of the Red River," *Red River Expedition,* 174.

40. Canby to Halleck, May 18, 1864, *OR,* 34(3):644.

41. Canby to Halleck, May 24, 1864, *OR,* 34(4):16.

42. Stanton to Banks, Dec. 6, 1864, *OR,* 41(4): 779.

43. Hollandsworth, *Pretense of Glory,* 193–94.

44. Eugene F. Sanger Testimony, *Red River Expedition,* 175.

45. L. Frederick Rice, "The Red River Campaign," Apr. 8, 1864, 31st Mass. Coll., MoSH.

46. Danforth L. Converse, "Experience of a Wounded Prisoner," 31st Mass. Coll., MoSH.

47. John W. Gibbs, "My Visit to Camp Ford, Tyler, Tx," 31st Mass. Coll., MoSH.

48. Gibbs, "My Visit to Camp Ford."

49. Rice, "Red River Campaign," May 3, 1864.

50. Elisha P. Clarke, "My Capture," 31st Mass. Coll., MoSH.

51. Converse, "Experience of a Wounded Prisoner."

52. Gibbs, "My Visit to Camp Ford."

53. Rich Diary, June 18, 1864.

CHAPTER 11

1. Sherman to Canby, June 4, 1864, *OR*, 34(4):212.

2. This was directed by Special Order 168, Dept. of the Gulf, June 26, 1864, *OR*, 34(4):559.

3. Winters, *Civil War in Louisiana*, 391.

4. Luther M. Fairbank Diary, July 14, 1864, 31st Mass. Coll., MoSH.

5. Fairbank Diary, July 16, 1864.

6. Special Order 169, Defenses of New Orleans, July 16, 1864, Edward P. Nettleton Papers, vol. 2, 31st Mass. Coll., MoSH. A supplement five days later determined that the trip would be made by riverboat.

7. William H. Rich Diary, July 24, 1864, 31st Mass. Coll., MoSH; Henry D. Barber Diary, July 25, 1864, ibid.

8. Charles S. Rust Diary, July 26, 1864, 31st Mass. Coll., MoSH.

9. George U. Young Recollections, 31st Mass. Coll., MoSH, 79–80. As with much of Young's writing, it is difficult to determine whether he really witnessed such a scene or was personalizing popular literature of the time. Luther C. Howell wrote a letter around this time but did not mention these encounters, and while Rich seems to allude to some of these occurrences, he does not relate them with such color. See Howell to brother, July 20, 1864, Luther C. Howell Letters, Amherst College, Frost Library, Special Collections.

10. Young Recollections, 80–82.

11. Rich Diary, Aug. 6, 1864.

12. Fairbank Diary, Aug. 7, 1864.

13. Howell to brother, Oct. 6, 1864, New Orleans, Howell Letters.

14. Rich Diary, Sept. 10, 1864.

15. Fairbank Diary, Sept. 11, 1864.

16. Fairbank Diary, Sept. 13, 1864.

17. Norris to mother, Jan. 25, 1865, New Orleans, Thomas Norris Letters, 31st Mass. Coll., MoSH.

18. Special Order 197, Dept. of the Gulf, *OR*, 41(2):381.

19. Special Order 255, Dept. of the Gulf, Sept. 21, 1864, *OR*, 41(3):283. As department commander, Banks signed this order.

20. Stephen Z. Starr, *The Union Cavalry in the Civil War*, vol. 3, *The War in the West, 1861–1865* (Baton Rouge: Louisiana State University Press, 1985), 327. There does not appear to be a history devoted to the subject of mounted infantry. Starr's book addresses the topic at various points, but its usefulness is reduced by the lack of an index entry for that subject.

21. Howell to sister Clara, Sept. 26, 1864, New Orleans, Howell Letters.

22. Fairbank Diary, Sept. 28, 1864.

23. Fairbank Diary, Feb. 14, 1865.

24. Fairbank Diary, Dec. 25, 1864.

25. Fairbank Diary, Jan. 1, 1865.

26. Rich Diary, Oct. 10, 1864.

27. Fairbank Diary, Oct. 23, 1864.

28. Howell to sister Clara, Nov. 10, 1864, New Orleans, Howell Letters.

29. Nettleton obituary, *Boston Journal,* Apr. 18, 1889.

30. Allen to Nettleton, Dec. 28, 1864, Nettleton Papers, vol. 1.

31. Allen to Nettleton, Dec. 28, 1864 (emphasis in original). "Scott's 900" refers to the 11th New York Cavalry, which had a reputation for wildness.

32. Fairbank Diary, Feb. 26, 1865.

33. Fairbank Diary, Mar. 1, 1865.

34. Fairbank Diary, Nov. 7, 1864.

35. Fairbank Diary, Nov. 8, 1864.

36. James M. McPherson, *Battle Cry of Freedom: The Civil War Era* (New York: Oxford University Press, 1988), 804.

37. Butler, *Butler's Book,* 632, 634. According to him, Butler had first been approached to join Treasury Secretary Chase's ticket if he had decided to challenge Lincoln.

38. Winters, *Civil War in Louisiana,* 391.

39. Special Order 146, Chief of Cavalry, Dept. of the Gulf, Oct. 25, 1864, Nettleton Papers, vol. 2; Special Order 51, n.d., Regimental Headquarters, ibid.

40. "Plaquemine Detachment," Nov. 13, 1864, 31st Mass. Coll., MoSH.

41. Special Order 312, Dept. of the Gulf, Nov. 18, 1864, Nettleton Papers, vol. 2.

42. Fairbank Diary, Nov. 26, 1864.

43. Fairbank Diary, Nov. 9, 1864.

44. Special Order 283, Defenses of New Orleans, Nov. 19, 1864, Nettleton Papers, vol. 2.

45. *Supplement to the OR,* 39:6.

46. Special Order 312, Dept. of the Gulf, Nov. 18, 1864, Nettleton Papers, vol. 2.

47. Howell to brother, Nov. 24, 1864, New Orleans, Howell Letters.

48. Hawkes to mother, July 18, 1863, St. James Hospital, Joshua W. Hawkes Letters, 31st Mass. Coll., MoSH.

49. General Order 43, Nov. 15, 1864, Nettleton Papers, vol. 2.

50. "Benjamin S. Roberts," in "George W. Cullum's Biographical Register," updated Aug. 3, 2018, Bill Thayer's Web Site, http://penelope.uchicago.edu/Thayer/E/Gazetteer/Places/America/United_States/Army/USMA/Cullums_Register/838*.html. Roberts had an interesting and varied career and probably merits a fuller biography. Although he was not among the most notable officers of his generation, his career illustrates the full professional life of an army officer, from his graduation from West Point in 1835 to his retirement in 1870.

51. Howell to brother, Feb. 24, 1864, New Orleans, Howell Letters.

52. Howell to brother, Nov. 24, 1864, Howell Letters.

53. "Oliver P. Gooding," in "George W. Cullum's Biographical Register," http://penelope.uchicago.edu/Thayer/E/Gazetteer/Places/America/United_States/Army/USMA/Cullums_Register/1821*.html.

54. Allen to Nettleton, Feb. 6, 1865, Nettleton Papers, vol. 1.

55. "Oliver P. Gooding," in "Cullum's Biographical Register."

56. Special Order 330, Dept. of the Gulf, Dec. 6, 1864, Nettleton Papers, vol. 2.

57. Allen to Nettleton, Feb. 6, 1865, Nettleton Papers, vol. 1.

58. Poché kept a diary in which he described the incident. See Felix P. Poché, *A Louisiana Confederate: Diary of Felix Pierre Poché*, ed. Edwin C. Bearss (Natchitoches: Northwestern Louisiana State University, 1972), 230–32. He confirmed that the capture of Darling was intentional but did not provide a direct explanation.

59. Sarah Darling Recollections, 31st Mass. Coll., MoSH. It is possible that Mrs. Darling was a local resident if her husband was the "Capt. D." Rice mentions in one letter: "Mrs. P . . . is now Mrs. Capt. D, and left for the North the first of the month." Rice to unknown, Aug. 30, 1863, L. Frederick Rice Letters, 31st Mass. Coll., MoSH. Captain Darling died in 1878 and does not seem to have left memoirs.

60. Byrne reports, *OR*, 48(1):154–55, 1263, 1283.

61. Darling Recollections. No confirmation of this order has been found, but Banks was nominally in command of the Department of the Gulf at this time. As for Poché, after the war he was a leader in Democratic politics, eventually became a judge, and socialized amiably with the Darlings.

62. Special Order 47, Dept. of Mississippi, May 2, 1865, Nettleton Papers, vol. 2; Special Order 297, War Dept., Adj. Gen. Office, June 12, 1865, ibid.

63. Norris to mother, Feb. 21, 1865, Plaquemine, Norris Letters (emphasis in original).

64. The roster lists a Corporal Sturtevant in Company K with a first name given as either Alonzo or Lorenzo. See chap. 1, note 39.

65. Rich Diary, Oct. 1, 1864; Fairbank Diary, Oct. 1, 1864; Norris to Will, Mar. 7, 1865, Norris Letters.

66. T. W. Sherman to Asst. Adj. Gen., Dept. of the Gulf, *OR*, 41(4):624.

67. Special Order 290, Defenses of New Orleans, Nov. 27, 1864, Nettleton Papers, vol. 2. An order to the quartermaster to transfer these companies was issued on November 28. See *OR*, 41(4):703.

68. T. W. Sherman to Allen, Dec. 22, 1864, *OR*, 41(4):384.

69. Fairbank Diary, Nov. 29, 1864.

70. Rich Diary, Dec. 17, 1864.

71. Allen report, Jan. 7, 1865, *OR*, 41:991–93.

72. Rust Diary, Dec. 26, 1864. This movement was dictated by orders specifying that the number of men guarding the station would at no time be less than twenty-five. Special Order 313, Defenses of New Orleans, Dec. 22, 1864, Nettleton Papers, vol. 2.

73. Howell to Bell, Jan. 8, 1865, Plaquemine, Howell Letters; Rich Diary, Dec. 27, 29, 1864.

74. Allen to Nettleton, Feb. 6, 1865, Nettleton Papers, vol. 1.

75. Mary Ann Sternberg, *Along the River Road: Past and Present on Louisiana's Historic Byway* (Baton Rouge: Louisiana State University Press, 1996), 169–70.

76. Nettleton "Narrative," 31st Mass. Coll., MoSH, 21; *Supplement to the OR*, 3–43.

77. Bond to Allen, Jan. 29, 1865, Le Blanc Plantation, Nettleton Papers, vol. 1.

78. Allen to Nettleton, Feb. 6, 1865, Nettleton Papers, vol. 1 (emphasis in original). In his diary entry for February 20, 1865, Felix Poché gives the names of several of the men who were captured by Bond's party. See Poché, *Louisiana Confederate*, 219.

79. William Brough, Capt., Co. C, 1st Ind. Heavy Artillery, to Capt. F. Speed, A.I. General, New Orleans, Feb. 9, 1865, Nettleton Papers, vol. 1.

80. General Orders 6, Defenses of New Orleans, Feb. 16, 1865, *OR*, 48(1):802.

81. Rich Diary, Dec. 31, 1864.

82. Rice to Gus, Jan. 8, 1865, Plaquemine, Rice Letters. In May a man named Guedry, who was accused of facilitating the capture of Lieutenant Masicot, was himself captured, commencing a discussion of bringing him to trial for the incident. Report of Brig. Gen. Robert A. Cameron, commanding District of La Fourche, May 6, 1865, *OR*, 48(1):239.

83. "Plaquemine Detachment," Jan. 26, 1865.

84. Rice to Gus, Feb. 2, 1865, "The Park," Rice Letters.

85. Rice report, Feb. 5, 1865, *OR*, 48(1):67–68.

86. Henry D. Barber, "The Indian Village Fight," 31st Mass. Coll., MoSH.

87. Rice to Gus, Feb. 7 (addition to letter begun Feb. 2), 1865, Rice Letters. Rice wrote an official report of the encounter, which conveys much the same content but lacks some of the personal embellishments. See Rice report, Feb. 5, 1865, *OR*, 48(1):67–68.

88. T. W. Sherman to Commanding Officer Plaquemine, Feb. 4, 1865, *OR*, 48(1):740.

89. T. W. Sherman to Commanding Officer Plaquemine (second message), Feb. 4, 1865, *OR*, 48(1):740.

90. Rice to unknown, Mar. 4, 1865, Carrollton, Rice Letters.

91. "Plaquemine Detachment," Feb. 6, 1865.

92. Rice to unknown, Mar. 4, 1865, Carrollton, Rice Letters.

93. Rice to Stewart, Jan. 11, 1865, Plaquemine, Nettleton Papers, vol. 1.

94. Rice to Stewart, Jan. 18, 1865, Nettleton Papers, vol. 1.

95. Rice to Stewart, Jan. 24, 1865, Nettleton Papers, vol. 1.

96. Rich Diary, Feb. 9, 15, 1865.

97. Allen to Nettleton, Feb. 6, 1865, Nettleton Papers, vol. 1.

98. Rich Diary, Jan. 2, 6, 18, 1865.

99. Special Orders 42, Dept. of New Orleans, Feb. 10, 1865, *OR*, 48(1):804.

100. Rich Diary, Feb. 12, 13, 1865.

101. Rich Diary, Feb. 23, 24, 1865.

102. Rich Diary, Mar. 6, 1865.

103. Special Order 61, Military Dept. of West Mississippi, Mar. 2, 1865, Nettleton Papers, vol. 2.

CHAPTER 12

1. Howell to brother, Sept. 19, 1864, New Orleans, Luther C. Howell Letters, Amherst College, Frost Library, Special Collections.

2. Joseph L. Hallett, "Reminiscences of the Civil War," 31st Mass. Coll., MoSH, 75–80.

3. Special Orders 39, Military Division of West Mississippi, Feb. 8, 1865, *OR*, 48(1):772.

4. Nettleton was recovering in Alexandria, then at Saint James Hospital until June 7, 1864, from the wound he received May 1 during the Red River Campaign before returning home on leave to complete his recovery. He returned to command the regiment on September 9 but on October 24 was detached for court-martial duty. Thus, although officially in command of the

31st, he had actually occupied that post for about a month and a half out of the previous nine months. "Edward P. Nettleton, Civil War Soldier." Chicopee Archives Online http://www.chicopeepubliclibrary.org/archives/items/show/2743.

5. Canby report, June 1, 1865, *OR*, 49(1):92.

6. Bridgman report, Oct. 31, 1864, *OR*, 41(4):337–39. It is not clear in what capacity Bridgman prepared this item. He had been discharged from the 31st Massachusetts on October 9, 1863, to become an officer with the U.S. Colored Troops. Since he prepared his report at Canby's request, he was probably on the general's staff.

7. Luther M. Fairbank Diary, Mar. 8, 1865, 31st Mass. Coll., MoSH. "The commanding officer of the Thirty-first Massachusetts (mounted) Infantry will move with his command remaining at Carrollton (including recruits) from his present camp at 7 A.M. 8th instant, with all transportation, baggage, &c., pertaining to his regiment, as allowed by existing orders, and with three days' cooked rations and forage, to Hickok Landing, when he will proceed to embark for Pensacola on board steamers assigned to him upon reaching that point." Special Orders 18, Special Cavalry Brigade, Mar. 7, 1865, *OR*, 49(1):859. Fort Barrancas now lies within the grounds of the Pensacola Naval Air Station.

8. See William H. Rich Diary, Mar. 10, 1865, 31st Mass. Coll., MoSH.

9. Rich Diary, Mar. 10, 1865; "Record of Events for Thirty-First Massachusetts Infantry, November 1861–June 1865," *Supplement to the OR*, 1–43.

10. Fairbank Diary, Mar. 17, 1865.

11. Rice to unknown, Apr. 8, 1865, "near Blakely, Ala.," L. Frederick Rice Letters, 31st Mass. Coll., MoSH.

12. Canby to Halleck, Mar. 7, 1865, *OR*, 49(1):856.

13. Lucas to Canby, Mar. 27, 1865, "In the field near Escambia River," *OR*, 49(1):302.

14. Lucas to Canby, Mar. 28, 1865, "four miles west of head of Perdido River, Ala.," *OR*, 49(2):119–20; Edward P. Nettleton, "Narrative of the Regiment, 1864–65," 31st Mass. Coll., MoSH.

15. Steele to Canby, Mar. 20, 1865, "from Pensacola," *OR*, 49(2):41.

16. Howell to sister Clara, Apr. 4, 1865, "Sibleys Mill near Spanish Fort," Howell Letters.

17. Norris to mother, Apr. 3, 1865, "In the woods near Blakely, Ala.," Thomas Norris Letters, 31st Mass. Coll., MoSH.

18. Fairbank Diary, Mar. 28, 1865.

19. Lucas to Canby, Mar. 28, 1865, "four miles west of head of Perdido River, Ala.," *OR*, 49(2):119–20.

20. Nettleton, "Narrative."

21. Rich Diary, Apr. 1, 1865.

22. Fairbank Diary, Apr. 3, 1865.

23. Rich Diary, Apr. 2, 1865.

24. Rich Diary, Mar. 25, 1865.

25. Rich Diary, Apr. 2, 1865.

26. Norris to mother, Apr. 3, 1865, "In the woods near Blakely, Ala.," Norris Letters.

27. Norris to mother, Apr. 1, 1865, Norris Letters; Nettleton, "Narrative."

28. Once a thriving place, curiously enough established by New Englanders, Blakeley is now

a ghost town, the site administered as a state park. "Blakely" was the spelling used by Union forces during the war.

29. Lucas to Canby, Apr. 3, 1865, *OR*, 49(2):211.

30. Canby to Lucas, Apr. 3, 1865, *OR*, 49(2):212.

31. Howell to sister Clara, Apr. 4, 1865, "Sibleys Mill near Spanish Fort," Howell Letters.

32. "Report from a Richmond Newspaper, Transmitted to Sec. Stanton," Mar. 29, 1865, Augusta, Ga., *OR*, 49(2):120. This was a serious misunderstanding of Taylor's strategic philosophy. The rebel general had done what he could to strengthen the Mobile fortifications, but he had no intention of committing his small remaining force to a siege and eventual surrender. See Taylor, *Destruction and Reconstruction*, 246.

33. Grant to Stanton, Feb. 22, 1865, *OR*, 49(1):754.

34. Norris to mother, Apr. 17, 1865, Mobile, Norris Letters.

35. Rich Diary, Apr. 13, 1865.

36. Fairbank Diary, Apr. 10, 12, 1865. Canby's official report stated that 4,400 prisoners and 103 pieces of artillery were captured, but this figure applied only to the "east side" of Mobile Bay. *OR*, 49(2):334.

37. Fairbank Diary, Apr. 11, 1865. The reference is to the Battle of Fort Pillow, on the Mississippi River in Tennessee, which took place almost exactly a year earlier. Although the issue continues to be disputed among historians, many in the North believed that Federal troops who had surrendered were massacred by the Confederates, with black soldiers in particular being slaughtered, as supported by the disproportionate ratio of deaths between black and white troops. If some Confederate prisoner at Mobile made the statement attributed to him, it would be tantamount to admitting that the action had constituted a massacre. As it is, none of the other surviving writings of men in the 31st Massachusetts mention this incident, and it does not seem to be noted in the *Official Records*.

38. Rich Diary, Apr. 15, 1865.

39. Norris to mother, Apr. 17, 1865, Mobile, Norris Letters.

40. Howell to brother, May 1, 1865, Mobile, Howell Letters (emphasis in original).

41. Howell to sister, May 9, 1865, Mobile, Howell Letters.

42. Howell to sister, May 1, 1865, Howell Letters.

43. Rich Diary, Apr. 14, 1865; Norris to mother, Apr. 17, 1865, Mobile, Norris Letters.

44. Norris to mother, May 7, 1865, Norris Letters.

45. Norris to mother, Aug. 21, 1865, Norris Letters.

46. Fairbank Diary, Apr. 14, 1865.

47. Fairbank Diary, Apr. 24, 1865.

48. Rich Diary, Apr. 15, 1865.

49. Fairbank Diary, Apr. 16, 1865.

50. Norris to mother, Apr. 17, 1865, Mobile, Norris Letters.

51. Rich Diary, Apr. 19, 1865.

52. Rich Diary, Apr. 20, 1865.

53. Taylor, *Destruction and Reconstruction*, 274–76.

54. General Order 95, War Dept., *OR*, 49(2):825 (found also at 48[2]:475).

55. Rich Diary, May 13, 1865.

56. Rich Diary, May 13, 1865.

57. Fairbank Diary, Apr. 24, 1865.

58. Special Order 71, Thirteenth Corps, *June 9, 1865, OR,* 49:976.

59. General Order 12, June 12, 1865, *OR,* 49:987.

60. HQ, Cavalry Forces, Dept. of the Gulf to Asst. Adj. Gen., New Orleans, June 23, 1865, *OR,* 49:977.

61. For a detailed account of this little-known but saddle-weary expedition, see letters from Rice, Apr. 26, May 7, and May 30, 1865, L. Frederick Rice Letters, 31st Mass. Coll., MoSH.

62. Rice to Gus, June 27, 1865, Mobile, Rice Letters.

63. Hopkins to sister Sarah, Feb. 2, 1865, New Orleans, William Swinton Bennett Hopkins Papers, David M. Rubenstein Rare Book and Manuscript Library, Duke University.

64. Hopkins to wife, July 31, 1865, New Orleans, Hopkins Papers. The riot, later the subject of a congressional investigation, began on July 30, 1866.

65. Hopkins to wife, July 22, 1866, New Orleans, Hopkins Papers (emphasis in original).

66. *Boston Herald,* Jan. 15, 1900.

67. Biography in finding aid for Howell Papers, Amherst College.

68. Rich Diary, Aug. 4, 1865.

69. Norris to brother Will, July 26, 1865, Mobile, Norris Letters.

70. Norris to mother, July 28, 1865, Norris Letters.

71. Rich Diary, Aug. 22, 1865; Fairbank Diary, Aug. 23, 1865.

72. Rich Diary, July 4, 1865.

73. Norris to mother, July 28, 1865, Mobile, Norris Letters.

74. Rice to unknown, July 31, 1865, Mobile, Rice Letters.

75. Howell to sister Clara, July 20, 1865, Mobile, Howell Letters.

76. Rich Diary, Aug. 21, 1865.

77. Norris to mother, Aug. 21, 1865, Mobile, Norris Letters.

78. Rich Diary, Sept. 9, 1865.

79. Rich Diary, Aug. 28, 1865.

80. Rich Diary, Aug. 28, 1865.

81. "31st Regiment Infantry," Union Regimental Histories: Massachusetts, Civil War Archive, http://www.civilwararchive.com/Unreghst/unmainf3.htm#31st.

82. Data from roster compiled by author. See chap. 1, note 39.

83. "10th Regiment Infantry," Union Regimental Histories: Massachusetts, Civil War Archive, http://www.civilwararchive.com/Unreghst/unmainf2.htm#10th; "27th Regiment Infantry," ibid., http://www.civilwararchive.com/Unreghst/unmainf2.htm#27th.

84. Hopkins to sister Sarah, Feb. 2, 1865, New Orleans, Hopkins Papers.

85. Howell to Bell, Mar. 17, 1865, "from Barrancas, before the start of the Mobile expedition," Howell Letters.

86. Norris to mother, Aug. 21, 1865, Mobile, Norris Letters.

BIBLIOGRAPHY

Manuscript Collections

Amherst College, Frost Library, Special Collections and Archives, Amherst, Mass.
    Howell, Luther C. Letters

Duke University, David M. Rubenstein Rare Book and Manuscript Library,
Durham, N.C.
    Hopkins, William Swinton Bennett. Papers

Hardwick Historical Society, Hardwick, Mass.
    Tupper, James B. T. Letters, 1861–63

Louisiana State University, Special Collections, Baton Rouge
    Fairbank, Luther M. Letters, 1861–63

Lyman & Merrie Wood Museum of Springfield History, Springfield, Mass.
31st Mass. Volunteer Infantry Regiment Collection
    Bailey, Adelbert. Recollections
    Barber, Henry D. Diary, 1864–65
    ———. "The Indian Village Fight"
    Bidwell, Edwin C. "The Battle of Sabine Cross Roads as I Saw It"
    ———. "Our Chaplain: His Work at New Orleans and His Little Romance"
    ———. "Remarkable Case of Captain N. F. Bond"
    Bond, Nelson F. "Affair at Des Sair Station"
    ———. "Chronology of Red River Campaign." Edward P. Nettleton Papers, vol. 1
    ———. Diaries, 1863, 1864
    Claiborne, John F. H. Letters
    Clarke, Elisha P. "My Capture"
    Clothier, Marshall M. "Incident in the Action near Bynum's Mill"
    ———. "An Incident of 17th of May, 1864"

Converse, Danforth L. "Experience of a Wounded Prisoner"

Darling, Sarah. Recollections

Fairbank, Luther M. Diary, 1862–65

Fordham, Elbert H. "The Red River Campaign"

Frary, Lewis O. "Reminiscences"

Gibbs, John W. "My Visit to Camp Ford, Tyler, Tx"

Goodwin, George. Recollections

Hallett, Joseph F. Letters, 1862

———. "Reminiscences of the Civil War"

Hawkes, Joshua W. Letters, 1861–63

Knight, Frank S. Diary, 1861–62

———. Letters, 1861–62

McCarthy, John E. "Affair at Des Sair Station"

McGraith, Jeremiah. "Affair at Des Sair Station"

Nettleton, Edward P. Letters, 1864–65

———. "Narrative of the Regiment, 1864–65"

———. Papers (2 vols.)

Nichols, Abram J. Diary, 1862

Norris, Thomas. Letters, 1862–65 (typescript)

"Plaquemine Detachment," 1864–65

Rice, L. Frederick. Diary, 1862–65

———. Letters, 1862–65 (transcripts)

———. Papers Submitted to Attorney General, 1894–95

———. "The Red River Campaign of 1864"

Rich, William H. Diary, 1862–65

Rust, Charles S. Diary, 1864–65

Semmes, Oliver J. Diary, 1863

Shaftoe, William. Diary

"The 31st Regiment of Infantry" (typescript)

Underwood, Richard F. Diary, 1861–63

———. "The Life of Richard F. Underwood, Jan. 1863–Dec. 1863"

Wheeler, Asa P. Diary, 1861–63

Whelden, Charles M. Papers

Young, George U. Recollections

Yale Collection of Western Americana, Beinecke Rare Book and Manuscript Library, Yale University, New Haven, Conn.

Smith, Timothy Z. Letter

Published Primary Sources

Butler, Benjamin F. *Butler's Book.* Boston: A. M. Thayer, 1892.

Correspondence between Gov. Andrew and Major-General Butler. Boston: John J. Dyer, 1862.

General Orders from Headquarters, Department of the Gulf, Issued by Major-General B. F. Butler; From May 1st 1862, to the Present Time. New Orleans: E. R. Wagener, 1862.

Hewett, Janet B., ed. *Supplement to the Official Records of the Union and Confederate Armies.* Part 2, Record of Events, vol. 29. Wilmington, N.C.: Broadfoot, 1996.

Marshall, Jessie Ames, ed. *Private and Official Correspondence of General Benjamin F. Butler during the Period of the Civil War.* 5 vols. Privately printed, 1917.

Massachusetts Adjutant General, comp. *Massachusetts Soldiers, Sailors, and Marines in the Civil War.* Vol. 3. Norwood: Massachusetts Adjutant General, 1932.

Poché, Felix P. *A Louisiana Confederate: Diary of Felix Pierre Poché.* Edited by Edwin C. Bearss. Natchitoches: Northwestern Louisiana State University, 1972.

Red River Expedition. Extracts from U.S. Congress, Joint Committee on the Conduct of the War. *Report of the Joint Committee on the Conduct of the War, 1863–1866.* Millwood, N.Y.: Kraus Reprint, 1977.

Taylor, Richard. *Destruction and Reconstruction: Personal Experiences in the Late War.* 1877. Reprint, edited by Richard B. Harwell, New York: Longmans, Green, 1955.

U.S. War Department. *The War of the Rebellion: A Compilation of the Official Records of the Union and Confederate Armies.* 128 vols. Washington, D.C.: 1880–1901.

Newspapers

Boston Herald
Boston Journal
Pittsfield (Mass.) Sun
Springfield (Mass.) Republican

Secondary Sources

American Tract Society. *The Color Bearer, Francis A. Clary.* New York, 1864.

Boltwood, Edward. *The History of Pittsfield, Massachusetts, 1876–1916.* City of Pittsfield, 1916.

Bowen, James L. *Massachusetts in the War, 1861–1865.* Springfield, Mass.: Clark W. Bryan, 1889.

Buell, Thomas B. *The Warrior Generals: Combat Leadership in the Civil War.* New York: Three Rivers, 1997.

Chase, Arthur. *History of Ware, Massachusetts*. Cambridge, Mass.: Harvard University Press, 1911.

Child, Hamilton, comp. *Gazetteer of Berkshire County, [Mass.], 1725–1885*. Syracuse, N.Y., 1885.

Cunningham, Edward. *The Port Hudson Campaign, 1862–1863*. Baton Rouge: Louisiana State University Press, 1963.

Dufour, Charles L. *The Night the War Was Lost*. Garden City, N.Y.: Doubleday, 1960.

Hearn, Chester G. *When the Devil Came down to Dixie: Ben Butler in New Orleans*. Baton Rouge: Louisiana State University Press, 1997.

Hewitt, Lawrence Lee. *Port Hudson: Confederate Bastion on the Mississippi*. Baton Rouge: Louisiana State University Press, 1987.

Higginson, Thomas Wentworth. *Massachusetts in the Army and Navy during the War of 1861–1865*. Boston: Commonwealth of Massachusetts, 1896.

Hollandsworth, James G., Jr. *Pretense of Glory: The Life of General Nathaniel P. Banks*. Baton Rouge: Louisiana State University Press, 1998.

Johnson, Ludwell H. *Red River Campaign: Politics and Cotton in the Civil War*. Baltimore: Johns Hopkins University Press, 1958.

Joiner, Gary D. *One Damn Blunder from Beginning to End: The Red River Campaign of 1864*. Wilmington, Del.: Scholarly Resources, 2003.

Jordan, Brian M. *Marching Home: Union Veterans and Their Unending Civil War*. New York: Liveright, 2014.

Kaufmann, J. E., and H. W. Kaufmann. *Fortress America: The Forts That Defended America, 1600 to the Present*. Cambridge, Mass.: Da Capo, 2004.

Keneally, Thomas. *American Scoundrel: The Life of the Notorious Civil War General Dan Sickles*. New York: Doubleday, 2002.

Laurie, Bruce. *Rebels in Paradise: Sketches of Northampton, [Mass.], Abolitionists*. Amherst: University of Massachusetts Press, 2015.

McPherson, James M. *Battle Cry of Freedom: The Civil War Era*. New York: Oxford University Press, 1988.

Melton, Maurice. *The Confederate Ironclads*. New York: Thomas Yoseloff, 1968.

Nolan, Dick. *Benjamin Franklin Butler, the Damndest Yankee*. Novato, Calif.: Presidio, 1991.

Paige, Lucius R. *History of Hardwick, Massachusetts*. Boston: Houghton Mifflin, 1883.

Parton, James. *General Butler in New Orleans*. New York: Mason Brothers, 1864.

Roland, Charles P. *Louisiana Sugar Plantations during the Civil War*. Baton Rouge: Louisiana State University Press, 1997.

Smith, Joseph Edward A. *The History of Pittsfield, Massachusetts, 1800–1876*. Springfield, Mass.: C. W. Bryan, 1876.

Starr, Stephen Z. *The Union Cavalry in the Civil War.* Vol. 3, *The War in the West, 1861–1865.* Baton Rouge: Louisiana State University Press, 1985.

Sternberg, Mary Ann. *Along the River Road: Past and Present on Louisiana's Historic Byway.* Baton Rouge: Louisiana State University Press, 1996.

West, Richard S., Jr. *Lincoln's Scapegoat General: A Life of Benjamin F. Butler.* Boston: Houghton Mifflin, 1965.

Winters, John D. *The Civil War in Louisiana.* Baton Rouge: Louisiana State University Press, 1963.

INTERNET SOURCES

American Civil War Research Database. http://www.civilwardata.com (subscription service).

Beach, Horace J. "The Last Moments of the Gunboat Diana, and Her Almost Final Resting Place." 2010. http://www.youngsanders.org/Thearticle.pdf.

"George W. Cullum's *Biographical Register of the Officers and Graduates of the United State Military Academy. . . .*" Updated August 3, 2018. Bill Thayer's Web Site. http://penelope.uchicago.edu/Thayer/E/Gazetteer/Places/America/United_States/Army/USMA/Cullums_Register/home.html.

"Edward P. Nettleton, Civil War Soldier." Chicopee Archives Online. http://chicopee-publiclibrary.org/archives/items/show/2743.

INDEX

abolitionism, 5, 15, 62, 71, 84, 92, 103, 115

Adams Express, 65

Agawam, MA, 20

alcohol abuse, 22, 88–89, 174, 185, 189, 191, 194–196, 298n7

Alexandria, LA, 131–132, 133, 186, 187, 199, 205, 206–207, 224

Algiers, LA, 32, 60, 125, 157, 184, 234

Allen, James M., 128

Allen, Washington Irving, 100, 127, 148, 172, 202, 241, 246–247, 259, 275; guerilla warfare, 251–255

alligators, 93, 95, 124

Ames Sword Co., 21

Amherst College, 18

Andersonville, GA, 231, 281

Andrew, John A., 5–6, 31, 34, 58, 95, 112, 219, 229; conflict with Butler, 7, 10–13, 23–25, 81, 89, 90, 107, 136; and Gooding-Whelden dispute, 84–86

Andrews, Emory, 244

Arkansas (CSN), 67

Arnold, Richard, 191, 201, 213

Austin, Marcus E., 178–179

Babcock, John W., 212, 313n102

Bache, Robert, 21, 84, 90, 93, 112, 162, 276; Red River campaign, 190, 191–192, 195, 197, 202, 312n72

Bailey, Adelbert, 142, 178

Bailey, Joseph, 205, 213, 224

Balls Bluff, VA (battle), 25

Baltimore, MD, 6–7, 57, 58, 129

Banks, Nathaniel P., 66, 90, 125, 150, 156, 182, 262; administers Dept. of Gulf, 108, 115, 159, 226, 234; advocates cavalry, 174–176, 239; Butte La Rose (campaigns), 116–118; replaces Butler, 102, 103–104, 108; personality, 108, 110, 204, 222, 225; Port Hudson (campaigns), 116–120, 135–152; Red River (campaign), 183, 187, 190, 193, 200–201, 203–204, 207–208, 210, 212–213, 218, 227–230, 234; relieved of command, 217, 227–229, 273; Teche, 123–134; testimony on Red River campaign, 220–226

Barber, Henry, 204, 207, 209–212, 214, 215, 247, 256–257

Barnard, John G., 46

Baton Rouge, LA, 33, 65, 67, 116, 118, 154, 179, 214, 242; battle, 67, 68, 104; 31st Mass. at, 156, 162, 170, 172, 232

Beauregard, P. G. T., 56, 65, 248

Belchertown, MA, 16, 19, 231

Berkshire County, MA, 14, 16–17, 26, 155, 173

Berwick City, LA, 33, 125, 130, 132, 184–185

Bidwell, E. C., 43, 84, 91, 147–148, 169; Red River campaign, 193–194

Big Bethel, VA (battle), 7

Billings, John Shaw, 171

black soldiers, 71, 72–73, 74, 108, 113–114, 140, 158, 162–163, 264, 267, 269, 278, 321n37

Blakely, AL, 265, 267–268, 320n28

Blauss, Frederick, 160

Bluff Springs (battle), 264–265

Bond, Nelson F., 136, 172, 195, 214; at Desert Station, 99–100; Plaquemine, 242–243, 254–255, 257; Port Hudson campaigns, 120, 121, 140, 143, 147–148; Red River campaign, 184, 188, 192, 209, 211; Teche campaign, 126, 128, 131, 134

Bond, Sylvester, 134, 148, 184, 214

Boston, MA, 17, 27, 28, 59, 178, 280

Bradburn, Charles E., 173

Brashear City, LA, 124–125, 132, 153, 184

Breckinridge, John C., 4, 67

Brewster, John, 278

Brice's Cross Roads (battle), 216

Bridgman, Eliot, 17, 263; at Fort Pike, 159–160, 162, 320n6

Broze, John, 212

Buckland, MA, 91

Burnside, Ambrose, 11, 12, 110

Butler, Andrew J., 1, 64

Butler, Benjamin F., 23–24, 27, 33, 96, 116, 151, 162, 174, 182, 229, 242, 262, 273; administers New Orleans, 57–78, 109, 309n1; campaign against New Orleans, 31–33, 41, 48–53; conflict with Andrew, 11–13, 23–25, 81, 89, 90, 95, 107, 136; departure from Louisiana, 101–104, 107–109; early life, 1–2; enters New Orleans, 56–57; and Gooding-Whelden dispute, 81–82, 84–86, 88, 90, 92; journey to Ship Island, 33, 37, 38;

in Mass. militia, 3–4; military activity 1861, 6–9; personality, 2, 4–5, 12, 61, 76, 108, 111; recruitment, 9–14, 72–74; and slavery, 8, 37, 72, 103; "woman order," 63, 106

Butler, John, 1–2

Butler, Sarah Hildreth (wife of Benjamin F.), 2, 33, 39; at Hilton Head, 36; *Mississippi* runs aground, 35; on Ship Island, 40, 42; storm off Cape Hatteras, 34

Butte La Rose, LA, 116–118, 129

Bynum's Mill, LA, 205, 231

Byrne, Edward, 248

Cady, Frank A., 82, 196

Cameron, Simon, 6, 11, 32

Camp Chase, MA, 13, 26–28, 39

Camp Magnolia, LA, 118, 120, 156

Camp Morewood, LA, 68

Camp Seabrook, SC, 36

Camp Seward, MA, 13, 14, 18–27, 80, 196

Canby, E. R. S., 217, 228, 234, 239–240; Mobile campaign, 262–264, 267–269, 272, 273

Cane River (battles), 188, 204

Canterbury, George B., 231, 233

Cape Charles, VA, 31

Cape Hatteras, NC, 30, 34, 48, 239

Carrollton, LA, 71, 113, 117, 118, 157, 166, 168, 176, 235, 240, 260

cavalry, 129, 142, 174–179, 184, 187–190, 199–201, 204–209, 214, 220–223, 227, 239, 245–246, 262, 265, 267

Charlemont, MA, 28, 212

Charleston, SC, 4, 6, 36

Chase, Salmon, 13, 317n37

Chicopee, MA, 15, 16, 21, 147

Chrysler, M. H., 215

Chubbuck, Francis E. R., 91, 168–169

Church, Henry S., 170

Claiborne, John F. H., 97

Clanton, James Holt, 265

Clapp, Egbert I., 275

Clark, Charles F., 160

Clark, William Smith, 18

Clarke, Elisha P., 208, 232

Clary, Francis A., 92–93, 148–149, 157

Clothier, Marshall, 212

Cohen, Patrick, 147

Conant, Cardinal H., 17, 50, 83, 294n14

Confederate military organizations: 2nd
    Louisiana cavalry, 163–164, 186

conscription, 77, 103

"contrabands of war," 8–9, 72, 93, 113, 115,
    131, 160

Converse, Danforth, 192, 230–231, 233

Cook, Albert, 173

Cook, F. A., 171

Cooke, Philip St. George, 163, 179

cotton, 37, 54, 97, 131, 182, 187, 188, 225, 226

Cushing, John W., 21, 195

Darling, George S., 19, 97, 247, 318n59;
    captured, 247–249

Davis, Amos, 171

Davis, Edmund J., 201, 209, 213–214

Davis, Jefferson, 4, 13, 56, 69, 105, 126, 135,
    250, 270, 274, 286n6

Department of the Gulf, 25, 32, 90, 104,
    155, 217, 223, 228, 249, 273

Department of New England, 11, 25

desertion, 28, 128, 190, 227, 238, 260, 263,
    271, 277, 281

Desert Station (battle), 99–100, 107, 134

Diana (CSN), 127–128

Dinan, Patrick J., 160, 244, 275

disease, 21, 39, 62, 67, 74–75, 78, 80, 104,
    120–121, 164–165, 168, 169, 170–171,
    234, 278

Donaldsonville, LA, 153, 156, 184, 251–252,
    254, 256

Dow, Neal, 92

Doyal, Henry A., 253, 254

Drach, Emil, 100

Dudley, Nathan A. M., 90–91, 101, 176;
    Red River campaign, 184, 189, 190,
    201, 222

Duncan, Johnson K., 51

Dunn's Bayou, LA (battle), 206

Durkee, Elliot, 233

Dwight, William, 133, 155, 199, 201; testi-
    mony about Red River campaign, 219,
    221–222, 239

Eastern Bay State regiment, 24, 28, 90

Edwards, Elisha A., 16

election of 1864, 241

emancipation, 115

Emory, William H., 111, 116, 126, 131, 133,
    155, 191, 193, 198, 199, 201

Fairbank, Luther, 19, 39, 54, 93, 112, 113,
    117, 119, 120, 121, 155, 156, 162–163,
    165, 171–172, 176–177, 180, 181, 195,
    237, 238, 241, 243, 252, 271, 309n113;
    Mobile campaign, 263, 264, 266, 269;
    in New Orleans, 58–60, 61–62, 69–70,
    76, 80; Port Hudson campaign, 138,
    143, 147, 150, 151; Red River campaign,
    189, 194, 202, 206, 212, 222; Teche
    campaign, 123–125, 128–133; and
    women, 172–173, 177, 204, 235, 240,
    271

Farr, Alpha B., 88

Farragut, David Glasgow, 31, 37, 41, 65, 116, 117, 261; attack on Port Hudson, 118–119; campaign against New Orleans, 44, 47–48, 50, 52–53; attack on Vicksburg (1862), 66–67

Fisherdick, Alfred, 185

Fisherdick, James S., 80

Fiske, William, 17

Fletcher, Eugene, 185

food, soldiers', 23, 36, 40–41, 49, 62, 68, 128–129, 141, 151–152, 198, 200, 208, 266

foraging, 97, 98, 128–129, 131–132, 138, 143, 186, 189, 208

Fordham, Elbert, 84, 215, 237, 259; Red River campaign, 188, 189, 191–193, 197–198, 199–200, 202–203, 205–206, 210–212, 244

Forester, Frederick, 277

Forrest, Nathan Bedford, 204, 216, 251

Fort Adams, MS, 214, 314n117

Fort Bisland, LA (battle), 125–128, 185, 197

Fort De Russy, LA, 186–187

Fort Jackson, LA, 45–53, 73, 74, 89, 92, 95, 178; 31st Mass. at, 81, 86, 90, 93–95, 103, 105, 119, 169, 292n3, 299n41

Fort Parapet, LA, 71–72, 101

Fort Pike, LA, 263; 31st Mass. stationed at, 81, 86, 87, 95–96, 156–162, 170, 173

Fort Pillow, TN, 321n37

Fort St. Philip, LA, 45–46, 50–51, 53, 73, 82, 89, 92, 292n3

Fortress Monroe, 7, 8, 10, 32, 33, 71, 81

Fox, Gustavus V., 30, 31

Franklin, LA, 125, 128, 185

Franklin, William B., 155–156, 184, 187, 199, 200, 201, 204, 207; testimony

about Red River campaign, 219, 220–221, 224

Fredericksburg, VA (battle), 106, 139

"free labor" plantations, 37, 98, 108, 242

French, Jonas, 90–91

Frink family, 20

Fulton, A. H., 38

Gardner, Franklin, 135, 138–139, 145, 151

Germans, 118, 149, 161

Gibbs, John W., 231, 232

Glisson, Oliver S., 35

Gooding, Oliver P., 34, 69, 73–74, 86, 95, 148, 235, 237, 244–245–247, 276; assignments, 89–90, 93, 111, 118, 155, 246; controversy over command, 34, 81–89, 107, 111; Port Hudson campaign, 140, 145; Red River campaign, 198–199, 202, 209, 214; Teche campaign, 124, 126

Goodwin, George, 206, 208

Grand Ecore, LA, 199, 201, 203, 204, 220, 225

Granger, Gordon, 273

Grant, Ulysses S., 66, 109, 110, 117, 124, 130, 133, 135, 155, 187, 204, 213, 215–216, 227–229, 268, 273

Greenhalge, Frederic T., 87

Grierson, Benjamin, 138, 142, 143, 273

Grover, Cuvier, 125, 127, 128, 145, 153, 155, 214

guerilla warfare, 97, 248, 250–258, 260

Haggerty, Michael, 258

Hall, John L., 256

Halleck, Henry W., 110, 120, 123, 133, 135, 139, 155, 174–175, 183, 187, 218–219, 227–228, 264, 308n84

Hallett, Joseph, 21, 33, 34, 38, 79, 88, 105, 108–109, 119, 147, 168; capture, 163–164, 186; at Hilton Head, 37; at Mobile, 261–262; in New Orleans, 63, 68–69, 122; recruiting, 20–21; on Ship Island, 40, 42

Hanchett, Henry, 160

Hanselmann, Andrew, 123

Hardwick, MA, 16, 77–78, 125, 165, 169

Hawkes, J. W., 24, 33, 54, 91, 93, 95, 103–104, 105–106, 108, 112, 113, 120–121, 136, 165–166, 245; on Gooding-Whelden dispute, 87–88; at Hilton Head, 36, 37; in New Orleans, 61, 67–68, 69, 80, 194–195

Hayden, Lester M., 244

Henderson's Hill, LA (battle), 186, 187

Hermitage Plantation, LA, 252, 254

Hesseltine, Frank S., 92, 94

Hickey, William, 127

Hillman, Fordyce L., 212

Hilton Head, SC, 36, 37, 39

Hollister, Edward P., 16, 26, 84, 95, 150, 172, 197; attack on New Orleans forts, 49

Hopkins, Elizabeth Peck (wife of William S. B.), 28–29, 196, 276

Hopkins, Erastus, 15, 84–85, 112–113, 196, 197, 203, 276, 298n7

Hopkins, Orrin S., 244, 259

Hopkins, William S. B., 15, 18, 28–29, 84, 112, 167, 177, 197, 203, 275–277; alcohol abuse, 185, 189, 195–197; in command of 31st Mass., 111, 189, 202; at Fort Jackson, 93, 95, 197; Port Hudson campaigns, 120, 149, 197; Red River campaign, 185, 186, 189, 202; Teche campaign, 126–127, 197

Horr, Charles H., 160, 170, 230, 253

horses, 39–40, 127, 134, 175–176, 177–179, 188, 204, 206, 208, 213, 222, 241, 242, 254, 265, 267–268, 274, 280

Hovey, Samuel D., 150

Howell, Luther Clark, 18, 22, 88, 90, 91, 93, 105, 106, 113, 117, 130, 172, 176, 177, 179, 217, 238, 240, 241, 244, 246, 249, 253, 270, 275, 276, 277, 279, 282–283; Mobile campaign, 265–266, 268; Port Hudson campaign, 144, 148, 150; Red River campaign, 194, 200, 220, 223–224

Independence Day, 65, 78, 150, 160–161, 278–279

Indian Village, 117, 256

Irish, 3, 5, 22, 66, 73

Jackson, Charles B., 231–232

Kayhoo, William, 233

Kenner(ville), LA: 31st Mass. stationed at, 81, 87, 98, 113, 119, 246

King, Samuel, 254–255

Knight, Francis, 22, 53, 61, 95

Knackfuss, Charles, 149

Knight, Frank, 169

Knowlton, Charles, 19

Lafayette, LA, 129, 163

Lee, Albert Lindley, 176, 177, 184, 190, 201–202, 219; testimony on Red River campaign, 220–223

Lee, John W., 16, 91, 105, 136, 165, 244–245; stabbed, 22, 75, 91

Lee, Robert E., 110 151, 204, 227–228, 251, 268, 271, 273

Lincoln, Abraham, 4, 25, 30, 70, 106, 107,

Lincoln, Abraham *(continued)* 109, 187, 215, 234, 237, 241–242; assassination, 269–270

Lincoln administration, 6, 7, 8, 9–10, 71, 89, 102, 110, 155, 182, 228; and Butler recruitment authority, 9–11, 25

Lingenfelter, George, 249

Louisiana (CSN), 50

Louisiana: economy and society, 54, 69, 98, 106, 131, 167–168, 207–208, 250–251

Lovell, Mansfield, 67, 70

Lowell, MA, 2, 13, 14, 27, 28, 58

Lucas, Thomas J., 190, 191, 275; Mobile campaign, 262, 265–268

Mansfield, LA, 190, 193, 230. *See also* Sabine Cross Roads

Mansura, LA (battle), 209

Marsh, George, 148

Masicot, Jules, 256, 319n82

Maury, Dabney Herndon, 271

McCarthy, John E., 100

McClellan, George B., 31–32, 47, 66, 76, 237, 241–242; orders to Butler, 32–33, 60

McCrory, Pete, 193

McGraith, Jeremiah, 100

Miami (USN), 50, 293n15

Mississippi (steam ship), 28, 33–39, 40, 44, 81, 104; campaign against New Orleans, 48–49, 53–54, 58–59; runs aground, 35–36

Mississippi (USN), 119

Mobile, AL, 33, 41, 65, 67, 216, 228, 242, 261; campaign against (1865), 262–269

Moody, Charles L., 160

Moore, Thomas Overton, 46, 60, 73, 131, 186, 207

Morewood, Sarah, 26, 68, 295n50

Morganza, LA, 134, 213, 234

Morse, Horace F., 105, 112, 172, 192, 244

mosquitoes, 69, 93, 94, 125, 144, 156, 157, 162

Mount Vernon (USN), 35–36

Mount Washington, MA, 20, 288n51

mounted infantry, 175, 221, 240, 241, 245, 262, 316n20

Mower, Joseph A., 186, 206, 210–211, 223

Mumford, William B., 75–76

Munsell, George H., 208

Munsell, Truman, 252

Napoleon III, 182

Natchitoches, LA, 188–189, 199

Native Guards, 72–73, 113

Nettleton, Edward P., 15–16, 76, 84, 107, 237, 240–241, 243, 246–247, 262, 267, 275, 276, 279, 282, 319n4; Red River campaign, 191–193, 202, 205–206

New Orleans, 45, 59, 78, 121–122, 124, 179, 242, 280; campaign against, 30–32, 41, 47–55; Adams House Hotel, 63; Annunciation Square, 68–69, 87; Custom House, 56, 58 59, 60, 68, 105; Hotel St. Louis, 166; St. Charles Hotel, 56, 59, 60, 64, 79; St. James Hospital, 157, 165, 168; St. Paul's Church, 166–167, 168; U.S. Mint, 60;

newspapers: *Boston Herald*, 59; *Boston Journal*, 57, 64; *Pittsfield Sun*, 78; *Springfield Republican*, 74

Nickerson, Ira, 75

Nine-month troops, 76–77, 103–104, 109, 135–136, 141–142, 153–154, 174, 180

Norris, Thomas, 33, 76, 78, 108, 136, 154, 167–168, 173, 238–239, 249, 267,

268–269, 270–271, 278, 279, 283; on reenlistment, 180–181

Northampton, MA, 15, 167

Oaks, George B., 275

Olustee, FL (battle), 216

Opelousas, LA, 129, 130, 131, 156, 186

Packard, William, 291n41

Page, Edward, Jr., 17, 72

Paine, Halbert E., 101, 133–134, 137, 140, 141, 143, 145–146, 147

Parker, John, 165

Patch, William, 79

Pauline Carroll (ship), 235–236

pay, soldiers', 26, 27, 64–65

Pelton, W. H., 184, 192, 211, 247

Pensacola, FL, 33, 41, 262–264, 265

Phelps, John Wolcott, 31, 71–72, 132, 296n68

Pittsfield, MA, 13, 14, 18, 20–22, 26, 35, 49, 84, 86, 104, 169, 236, 237, 238, 280, 307n66

Plaquemine, LA, 117, 243, 252–253, 256–260

Pleasant Hill, LA, 189; battle, 198–199, 221, 226, 227, 229, 233, 273

Poché, Felix P., 248, 318n61

Polk, Leonidas, 68–69, 295n51

Pomeroy, William C., 252

Port Hudson, 109, 124; campaigns against, 116, 118–120, 133, 135–152, 156, 157, 165, 229, 278

Port Royal, SC, 30, 36, 48

Porter, David D., 30, 65, 133, 182; attack on Fort Jackson, 47–48, 50–52, 92; Red River Campaign, 184, 187, 199, 203, 205, 207, 219; testimony on Red River campaign, 224–227

Prince, Edward, 137

prisoners of war: Confederate, 68, 78, 93, 122, 128, 203, 211, 229, 239, 253, 261, 265, 269, 271; Union, 153, 163–164, 173, 194, 199, 207, 229–232, 252

race issues, 72, 161, 172, 269, 273, 278–279

railroads, 7, 15, 20, 26, 28, 98–99, 100–101, 124, 184, 236, 237, 238, 264, 265

recruitment, 13–17, 21–23, 73–76, 172, 249, 260, 272

Red River Campaign, 183–192, 197–214, 248

Regan, Edward, 231

religion, 22, 91, 105, 148, 166–167

Rice, L. Frederick, xi–xii, 106, 107, 114, 162, 163, 171, 177–178, 180, 248, 275, 279; enters New Orleans, 54; at Fort Pike, 97, 156, 160–162; on Gooding-Whelden dispute, 88–89; Mobile campaign, 264, 266; on nine-month troops, 77, 154; Plaquemine, 242–243, 256–258; Red River Campaign, 184, 186, 188, 189, 202, 207, 208, 210–211, 214, 230, 231–232; research into Gooding-Whelden dispute, 82–87

Rich, William, 76, 95, 216, 236, 237, 238, 241, 242, 260, 271, 273, 277, 278, 280; at Fort Pike, 156, 158, 173, 176–177, 179–180, 181; Mobile campaign 266–267, 269; Red River Campaign, 184, 190, 205, 232

Richards, Augusta and Carol, 79, 297n103

Roberts, Benjamin Stone, 245–246

Rockwell, William W., 17, 21, 87, 88, 157, 159, 171–172, 173, 307n66

Rosecrans, William S., 175, 263

Rust, Charles, 148

Rust, Fordyce A., 244

Sabine Cross Roads, LA (battle), 190–193, 197–199, 201, 211, 220, 222, 223, 227, 229, 252, 262, 269

Sagendorph, Edwin, 163

Sagendorph, Milton, 121, 163, 171–172, 247, 255, 265; Red River campaign, 188, 193, 200

Sanborn, Eben K., 42

Schill family, 73

Schouler, William, 12

Scott, Winfield, 3, 7, 9, 31

Seabrook, James, 36, 37

Sears, George W., 275

Semmes, Oliver J., 127–128, 302n67

Seward, William, 13, 102, 182

Shaftoe, William, 39, 49

Shaw, R. G., 256, 258

Sherman, Thomas W., 12, 159, 241, 251–252, 255, 258–259, 286n16

Sherman, William T., 184, 186, 187, 199, 207, 213, 234, 242, 273

Ship Island, 25, 30, 31–32, 39–44, 157–158, 236, 263

Shreveport, LA, 117, 133, 187, 188, 190, 199, 219, 220–221, 231, 232, 242

Shumway, Philo, 272

Sibley, Henry H., 127, 128

Sickles, Dan, 215–216

Simmesport, LA, 134, 210, 214, 217

slaves/slavery, 8, 36–37, 54, 59, 66, 71–72, 103, 115, 131–132

Smith, Andrew Jackson: Red River campaign, 186, 188, 199, 204, 207, 210, 213, 216, 219, 225, 226–227, 229–230, 263, 272

Smith, Chauncey W., 160

Smith, Edmund Kirby, 190, 203, 216, 234, 252, 274

Smith, Timothy Z., 69

Somerville, MA, 78

Southworth, Constant E., 27

Springfield, MA, 16–17, 26, 79, 236, 238

Stanton, Edwin, 32, 48, 65, 66, 73, 74, 123, 229, 268

Stearns, Henry F., 156

Steele, Frederick, 184, 188, 203, 216; Mobile campaign, 262–264

Stewart, James M., 150, 185, 195, 259, 275

Stockwell, William, 157

Stone, Charles Pomeroy, 219

Sullivan, Michael, 22, 75, 288n61, 296n84

Sumner, Charles, 13, 57

sutlers, 27, 77, 157, 158–159, 184, 185

Talmadge, Henry, 212

Taylor, Benjamin, 160

Taylor, Richard, 153, 216, 234, 251, 272–273, 321n32; character, 125–126, 310n18; Red River campaign, 188, 190, 198–199, 203–204, 208, 209–214, 232, 252, 268; Teche campaign, 125–130, 133

Teche campaign, 123–134, 135

Tennessee (CSN), 261–262

Texas, 33, 109, 116,155–156, 182–183, 199, 219, 231, 273, 278

31st Mass. Inf. Regt., xi, 111; attack on New Orleans, 49–53; attrition, 28, 39, 44, 75, 113, 118, 151, 170, 212, 244, 277, 311n55; at Baton Rouge, 118, 120–121, 156, 162, 170, 172; Butte La Rose campaign, 116–118; at Camp Chase, 26–28; at Camp Seward, 18–26, 196; as cavalry, 174, 176–180, 184–193, 199–200, 204–215, 222–223; Clinton expedition, 142–143; at Fort Jackson, 81, 86, 90, 93–94, 103, 113, 119, 169; at Fort Pike,

81, 86, 87, 94, 96, 113, 156–162, 170, 173; enters New Orleans, 54–57; furlough, 179, 234–238; in New Orleans, 56–71, 87, 90, 121, 162, 179, 237, 240, 252; journey to Ship Island, 33–39, 194; at Kennerville, 81, 87, 98, 113, 119; Mobile campaign, 262–269; occupies Mobile, 269–273; as mounted infantry, 240–241, 251–257, 262, 265; at Plaquemine, 243, 252, 254–260; Port Hudson campaigns, 118–120, 138–152, 197; recruitment, 14–19, 23, 73, 172, 249, 260, 272; Red River Campaign, 184–193, 197–214; reorganization, 243–247; on Ship Island, 39–44, 75; summary of service, 277–278, 280–283; Teche campaign, 123–134

Thompson, Marcus M., 159–160

Tupper, James B. T., 27, 30, 53, 58, 91, 97, 99, 106, 108, 111, 117, 150, 151, 163, 169, 196–197; at Camp Seward, 19, 22; on emancipation, 114–116; in New Orleans, 66–67, 68, 70–71, 73, 77, 78, 121–122; railroad conductor, 100–101; on Ship Island, 39–40, 41–42

Twiggs, David E., 70–71

Tyler, TX, 164, 207, 231

Underwood, Richard F.,162, 173, 174, 176; at Camp Seward, 19–20; at Fort Pike, 94, 158–159, 160, 161, 170; in New Orleans, 71, 75, 167

uniforms, equipment, 23, 41, 134, 192, 240, 241

Union military organizations other than 31st Mass.: Cavalry Division, 184; 13th Corps, 155, 156, 187, 191–192, 205, 273; 19th Corps, 111, 124, 155, 184–185, 187, 193, 194, 213; 9th Conn., 31, 49, 66, 76; 13th Conn. 66, 68; 2nd Ill, Cav., 209, 262; 3rd Ill. Cav., 184; 7th Ill. Cav., 138; 16th Indiana Mounted Inf., 245; 21st Indiana, 50; 26th Indiana, 40; 1st Louisiana Cav., 101, 262, 265; 1st Maine Battery, 66, 101; 12th Maine, 66; 13th Maine, 28, 92; 3rd Maryland Cav., 214; 3rd Mass. Cav., 184, 190, 208; 4th Mass., 145, 151, 154; 6th Mass., 6, 58; 6th Mass. Battery, 101; 8th Mass., 6, 14; 10th Mass., 281; 21st Mass., 18; 26th Mass., 12, 25, 31, 49, 50, 58, 66, 74, 88, 89, 93, 157; 27th Mass., 281; 28th Mass., 12, 25, 289n79; 30th Mass., 28, 49, 65, 67, 136, 176, 249; 38th Mass., 111, 118, 126, 142, 173; 46th Mass., 104; 48th Mass., 154–155; 49th Mass., 104, 155; 52nd Mass., 136, 142; 53rd Mass., 118, 142, 157, 166; 57th Mass., 171; 60th Mass., 171; 6th Mich., 40, 41, 101, 235–236; 1st New Hampshire, 179; 8th New Hampshire, 142, 184, 309n105; 2nd NY Cav., 262; 11th NY Cav., 317n31; 14th NY, 241; 18th NY Cav., 245, 248; 91st NY, 142; 116th NY, 111; 128th NY, 158; 131st NY, 147; 156th NY, 111, 118, 126; 175th NY, 118, 126; 56th Ohio, 207; 3rd RI Cav., 245, 260; 11th U.S. Colored Artillery, 256; 7th Vermont, 101; 4th Wisconsin, 50, 56, 146, 174

U.S. Military Academy, West Point, 2, 7, 62, 87, 152

Van Dorn, Earl, 65, 67

Veterans' Reserve Corps, 171

Vicksburg, 124, 130, 160, 235; attack on,

Vicksburg *(continued)*
in 1862, 65–67, 139; attack on, in 1863, 109, 151, 157, 229
Vincent, W. G., 163

Wade, Charles I., 244
Wade, Lewis T., 100
Ware, MA, 14–15, 18, 54, 111, 121, 125, 165, 185, 237
Washington, LA, 131, 186
Weeks, Horace, 44
Weitzel, Godfrey, 32, 50–51, 53, 116, 140, 153, 155, 162, 267, 302n67; Lafourche expedition, 104, 132; on freed slaves, 132
Western Bay State Regiment. *See* 31st Mass. Inf. Regt.
Wheeler, A. P., 43, 67, 157, 168; hospitalization, 166–167

Whelden, Charles M., 35, 36, 39, 90, 91; background, 14; at Camp Seward, 19, 21, 23, 24; controversy over command, 33, 81–89, 107; departure, 101; recruiting, 14, 16
White, John, 255
Wilder, John T., 175
Williams, John, 148, 149
Williams, Thomas, 65–67
Woodis, John, 165
Woods, Edward P., 147, 149
Wright, Charlie, 165

Yellow Bayou, LA (battle), 209–213, 216
Young, George, 43, 178, 236; encounter with squatter family, 98–99; at Port Hudson, 144, 145–146, 149, 154